Sexual Regulation and the Law

A Canadian Perspective

Edited by Richard Jochelson and James Gacek

Sexual Regulation and the Law
A Canadian Perspective
Edited by Richard Jochelson and James Gacek

Copyright © 2019 Demeter Press

Individual copyright to their work is retained by the authors. All rights reserved. No part of this book may be reproduced or transmitted in any form by any means without permission in writing from the publisher.

Demeter Press
2546 10th Line
Bradford, Ontario
L3Z 3L3
Tel: 289-383-0134
Email: info@demeterpress.org
Website: www.demeterpress.org

Demeter Press logo based on the sculpture "Demeter" by Maria-Luise Bodirsky www.keramik-atelier.bodirsky.de

Printed and Bound in Canada

Front cover artwork: Michelle Pirovich
Typesetting: Michelle Pirovich

Library and Archives Canada Cataloguing in Publication
Title: Sexual regulation and the law: a Canadian perspective
Edited by Richard Jochelson and James Gacek
Names: Jochelson, Richard, 1973- editor. | Gacek, James, editor.
Description: Includes bibliographical references.
Identifiers: Canadiana 20190144939 | ISBN 9781772582109 (softcover)
Subjects: LCSH: Sex and law—Canada.
Classification: LCC KE8928.S49 2019 | LCC KF9325.S49 2019 kfmod | DDC 345.71/0253—dc23

Acknowledgments

This collection brings together a wide range of scholars—from early career researchers to established professors—from the disciplines of law, criminology, and sociology, and we are grateful to these authors for their insightful contributions and their enthusiasm in the project. Indeed, their thought-provoking, eye-opening, and fascinating chapters reveal a social world that is continually challenging sexual governance within Canada, and we thank them for pushing the boundaries of sexual regulation and the law along with us. We would also like to extend our thanks to the external reviewers of the collection for their support in the project and their helpful feedback and to Andrea O'Reilly and the rest of the team at Demeter Press for their assistance in the publication of this book. Special thanks to the Legal Research Institute at the University of Manitoba Faculty of Law and the Office of Research Services at the University of Manitoba, which provided generous funding for hiring research assistants during the duration of this project.

Richard would like to thank his family—Anna, Leah, and Emily—who put up with his antics when writing is at the top of his mind. Richard is also grateful to his colleagues at the Faculty of Law at the University of Manitoba who have supported his research. Richard also thanks James for his diligence, collaboration, and thoughtfulness throughout the project; Alicia, for her excellent organizational work as well as their contributions; Brayden, for his depth of research; and Christine Williams for her insightful editorial support in the final phases.

Finally, James would like to thank his family—Robin, Lauren, and Carly—and his parents, Rick and Nancy, for their continued support in his academic career, no matter where it takes him. James would also like to especially thank Richard for initiating him into the complex world of sexual regulation and the law with generously provided discussions and coffee in equal measure. Richard's conscientious management of the project—coupled with his brilliance as a mentor, colleague, and friend—ensured that the project's intention of challenging the boundaries of sexual governance would be done wisely and effectively, and for that, James cannot thank Richard enough.

Contents

Introduction
Let's Talk about Sex—Time to Tap Taboo?
James Gacek and Richard Jochelson
7

Chapter One
Indecency and Obscenity Law: From *Hicklin* to the
Post-*Labaye* Era—A (Tall) Tale of Risk?
Richard Jochelson and James Gacek
19

Chapter Two
Sex Work in Canada: Beginnings, *Bedford*, and Beyond
James Gacek and Richard Jochelson
57

Chapter Three
Intimate Images and the Law
*Richard Jochelson, Alicia Dueck-Read, James Gacek,
and Brayden McDonald*
101

Chapter Four
Technologies of Regulating Sexual Offences against Youth
Lauren Menzie and Taryn Hepburn
173

Chapter Five
Rethinking Bestial Regulation
Richard Jochelson, Alicia Dueck-Read, and James Gacek
209

Chapter Six
Our Pronouns Are Protected But Not Our Bodies:
How Gender-Based Protections Fail Criminalized Trans People
Leon Laidlaw
261

Chapter Seven
Considering Judicial Behaviour and Language
in Sexual Assault Trials
David Ireland
299

Conclusion
Reflections on Making the "Strange" Familiar
and Future Directions
James Gacek and Richard Jochelson
333

Notes on Contributors
343

Introduction

Let's Talk about Sex— Time to Tap Taboo?

James Gacek and Richard Jochelson

Since the inception of the *Canadian Charter of Rights and Freedoms*, there have been many significant legal cases in which justices have questioned the law's understanding of Canada's regulation of sexual activity. Whether it be concerning the sexually active, sexually vulnerable, sexually criminalized, and/or sexualized populations, or concerning the expression, performance, conduct, work, or perpetration of illicit sexual activity, these cases attract scholarly and popular attention. Certain laws have been deemed unconstitutional in the face of divergent and diverse sexual identities and activities, including, most recently, the Supreme Court of Canada's finding that Canada's long-standing sex work laws were unconstitutional (*Bedford*). At the same time, little academic scholarship has advanced a theoretical understanding of how the judiciary reads issues of sex and sexuality in modern contexts, what social forces mobilize the judicial decision, and to what extent is the judiciary beholden to the historical roots of the law versus modern conceptions of the rights contained within the *Charter*. Although studies focusing upon judicial activism and legal reform are currently available, the work in this book remains grounded in an apolitical approach to understanding the judiciary.

We draw from our previous work that sees the judiciary in Canada as producing a type of legal media (Jochelson et al.). This is not to say that we do not recognize the traditional role of the judiciary according to legal scholarship. We certainly acknowledge that courts are affected by their legislated and constitutional roles and that they are bound by precedent and constitutionalism, which can be competing forces. We merely suggest that parallel to this traditional analytic, the study of judge-made law as a type of media can evoke novel and thought-provoking discussions about the nature of law. As much as judicial legal decisions direct legal interpretation and bind the actions of Canadians, the script they create is also an intriguing piece of prose that provides ample opportunity for analyses outside of doctrinal pursuits.

For example, judicial prose may have something profound to say about the social ordering of Canadian society. Like any media, one can query whether the law, and in particular whether judge-made law, reflects, refracts (recreates), or sublimates the social conditions of our times. Could the law sometimes seek to direct us towards new socialities? These questions are at the heart of our previous work (Jochelson et al.), and we seek to bring this same approach to this edited collection. The chapters contained in this book explore the socio-legal thoughts, processes, and interpretations that undergird judicial reasoning in a late-modern Canada; they seek to understand the legal regulation of sex and sexuality in Canada, and explicate the historical roots and latent hypocrisies that can inure within law.

Does Canada need any more collections about legal regulation of sex and sexuality? Volumes exist dealing with sex work and pornographies. Certainly, volumes abound dealing with emerging sexualities in Canada and new sexual freedoms. We seek to do more than tell a story of broad generalities about the law. First, we are interested in the links between the history of the law and modern iterations of judgments pertaining to that law. Hence, the uncomfortable line between Victorian morality and modern regulation is thematically explored across several of the chapters in this work. Second, we also wanted to explore modern iterations of sexual regulation in Canada and understand the interplay between emerging digital technologies and legal regulation. Historically, the link between sexual expression and violence has been, at best, studied as incipient. Newer laws in Canada have been drafted to recognize that types of sexual expression can be inherently violent, and, thus, an exploration of modern sexual digital expression and its emerging jurisprudence represents a new frontier in the regulation of sex and sexuality in Canada. In particular, the demarcation between harassment and intimate digital expression no longer exists now that handheld digital technology is akin to an appendage for the average

Canadian. People have integrated their phones into their personal lives, and so intrarelationship criminal transgressions enmeshed with digital harassment have seen a steady increase in Canada as the means of production have become commonly held. We explore how legal regulation has responded to these new crimes.

This collection is founded upon our joint experiences in teaching in law and society programs in Canada. We have witnessed (and been complicit in) cobbled together curriculums that rely upon a potpourri of sources from law, criminology, criminal justice, and law and society disciplines. In past years, we, too, have assembled books and other articles to make course readings work while a comprehensive reader aimed at the law school and liberal arts programs remained elusive. There exists a growing interest from university students and legal scholars alike for a reader that examines judicial legal decisions in the context of law reform and legal change in respect to sexual politics and movements in Canada, especially as it concerns modern iterations of crime and sexual politics. Furthermore, although this collection is educational, we also intend to use it to open up broader discussions concerning the legal regulation of sex and sexuality in Canadian jurisprudence. As we have indicated elsewhere:

> Like a spectre, moral politicization surrounding sex and sexuality still haunts the criminal law... Even by today's standards of widespread acceptance and tolerance of sexual orientations, talking about sex and sexuality remains a social taboo—a topic quickly avoided and silenced by hesitant naysayers in an attempt to restrict the potential of sex and sexuality from producing alternative understandings and governing interactions between individuals, groups, and communities. (Jochelson et al. 42)

The contribution of our book lies in its broadening of the idea of how the work of the judiciary is exercised within and through law's creative exposition of judicial rhetoric and reasoning, making diverse sexual identities and controversial sexual topics more visible and governable within society. This new visibility forms a regulatory cloud—a loosely affiliated assemblage of sexual regulation. Each chapter mines these complex relationships and their place in the sexual assemblage in its own way. The study of judicial and juridical rhetoric and reasoning in the field of diverse sexual identities and expression, as well as taboo topics, allows us to make visible the sexual ties that bind us. This visibility allows one to attempt to drive, resist, or otherwise relate to sexual governance. Making visible the sexual assemblage allows the active student to understand and engage with such governance.

The sexual assemblage is a complex one because it invokes morality drawing on, in most cases, Judeo-Christian ideals, which are often expressed in the common law roots of our Victorian legal histories, but we would be wrong to think of sexual expression as only relating to legal responses to transgression. Broader regulatory effects coalesce outside of this legal order and outside the realm of what we understand as criminal law—sexual regulation implicates diverse fields, such as civil liberties, privacy, animal rights, technology, language, identity politics, cultural norms including consent culture, political lobbying, and the development of other social movements, to name a few. In this light, the goal of this collection is, in part, to expose judicial pockets of reasoning that reveal a more capacious conception of how sex and sexuality are regulated through justification for state intervention within the Canadian legal system at large and into the sexual lives of Canadians. This, in turn, may reveal aspects of our sociality, some of which may be troubling for the reader. Those that seek amelioration from oppression, whether incremental or revolutionary, agree that "the very purpose of producing knowledge about the social world is to change it" (Garland and Young 32). The fomentation of knowledge is often tortured, difficult, and challenging because it invokes the need to address taboo; it requires that we address difficult and socially troubled knowledge. Unmasking the sexual assemblage and understanding it allows for its dissection, repackaging and repurposing. It allows us to drive a progressive set of sexual ethics and to bridge, for some, one's personal and political self. This latter project is for the reader to delineate. Our job in this collection is to unmask.

The Juridification of Legal Decisions: Strange Currencies and "Stranger" Things

Our collection endeavours to explore recent developments, including emerging ones, in Canadian jurisprudence that have interwoven some late-modern logics of governance: risk, precaution, security, and privacy, to name a few. By drawing upon governmentality studies, each chapter examines how sociality becomes structured, represented, or reconstituted through judicial decisions in a multitude of ways with, at times, worrisome effects. This is not to say that changes in Canadian jurisprudence over the years have not been necessary or even welcomed—for example, the recognition and inclusion of progressive ideals in the form of the judicial acceptance of sexual orientation as implicit in *Charter* jurisprudence (an analogous ground under section 15 of the *Charter*, for equality), expressed in the countenancing of same sex marriage (*M v H*; *Reference re Same Sex Marriage*).

However, the cautious politics of judicial reasoning in high profile sexual cases at the level of the Supreme Court have left lower courts the jurisprudential wiggle room to respond inconsistently and in opaque and flexible ways, resulting in unpredictable and specious sexual governance. For example, the community standards of tolerance of harm test, which determined whether sexual expression was obscene, was ruled unworkable by the Supreme Court of Canada and is no longer in effect, yet the test is often described as one example of judicial subjectivity that allowed, and allotted, governance to lower courts, customs officials, and police forces in delineating prohibited sexual expression (*R v Butler*; *R v Labaye*; Jochelson et al.).

Therefore, case law can be a plentiful source of information that animates a larger project of, and discussions surrounding, governance, insofar as the legal decision can represent how social processes beginning outside of the law then become "juridified" as well as "accounting for the ways law *structures* decisions that govern social outcomes" (Jochelson et al. 6). A greater focus on juridification reifies how decisions are structured and how one makes sense of outcomes of modern criminal and quasi-criminal law, especially since such law operates more and more through varied forms of power and the further regulation of persons around scientific norms (Dean; Foucault; Golder; Hunt and Wickham). In other words, law provides a medium in which the citizen is constructed in sociality and also how the subject is incentivized, punished, or left alone. Law adds to this construction by performing a symbolic function by identifying normative social values from which legal subjects are formed (Dean; Golder; Hunt and Wickham). This construction, though, is challenged continuously through incursions by governing structures and social pressures. Yet understanding this construction means there is profound value in examining legal texts closely not just for precedential effects but for social constructions. In the context of sexual regulation, legal prose is one important site of assemblage generation—new understandings incorporate, alter, or create new undergirding regulatory mores of the sexual being.

Although we remain mindful of the doctrinal effects of studying legal text for rhetoric and reasoning, for us, the construction of these legal texts is more than precedent; it is a consolidated history of the present, packaging history and socio-political context together and revealing "the judicial and social rationales of the cases and social phenomenon that preceded the case" (Jochelson et al. 7). In effect, by studying the logics underpinning these legal texts ripened with "judiciomentalities" (legal expressions that imbed social constructions informed of history, politics, precedential strictures, constitutionalism, and personal/political judgment), we recognize legal texts themselves "as a type of technology that delivers the governmental effects of law separate and apart from the law that is itself created" (Jochelson et al. 7).

Another task this introduction entails, in a Foucauldian sense, is revealing the strange (or what was once held to be strange) to be profoundly familiar. "Strange" topics such as child pornography and bestiality have certainly been demarcated by the Supreme Court as abhorrent and immoral crimes, and we recognize that such topics may be concerning, frustrating, saddening, maddening, and nauseating to learn and read about in the coming chapters. Yet we firmly believe that education has the potential to encourage society to ameliorate suffering. "Strange" education may shift the winds of political, socio-legal, and legislative affairs away from further ill-perceived or relentlessly unnecessary criminalization.

Persons should be accorded a window of opportunity to struggle with the complex trade-offs that animate decisions about how to regulate sexual(ized) aspects of the social world. As we have indicated elsewhere:

[an] abject and uninformed populist sentiment is a barrier to law's malleability.... An uniformed populace believes in ill-perceived danger ... even in the absence of empirical evidence. Indeed, the belief in this danger undermines civil liberties, as it quashes public scrutiny of state intervention and obviates the need for substantial and progressive changes in the law (Jochelson et al. 114).

Providing empirical evidence for education and advocacy highlights the social ties that both bind law to society and vice versa. Law is malleable and iterative; various actors in civil society can seek redress when it comes to unsettling issues. You may be so moved as you read the chapters in this volume.

That certain behaviour needs regulation or is capable of governance, in and of itself, reveals the conduct to be engageable. Such a prospect for engagement means that there is a commonness to such conduct. Even profoundly disturbing conduct in this context may be familiar, and one ought to try to understand the routine nature of the so-called strangeness. In some cases what was once considered strange becomes acceptable, and, in this spirit, the study of what one considers odd, different, and perhaps sick or perverted is worthy of engagement. Scholars and students can gain little by ignoring what is considered unsightly. Understanding, unpacking, and observing what is at first blush objectionable can be elucidating. One may develop enhanced sympathies for complex social situations, and through the exercise of study one may develop prescriptions for amelioration of social injustices. In some cases, one may discover that what was once deemed strange within society is common and even liberatory. To study sexual governance requires a willingness to absorb the oppressive, the oppressed, the absurd, the disgusting, the difficult, and the challenging. This absorption can then animate social action, if one is so inclined.

For us, such considerations seem obvious and self-evident—robust interrogation of social phenomena is messy and can be disturbing, but to unpack the physics of sociality, one must embrace the chaos of the objectionable. This is different than condoning the cruel, sadistic, or oppressive. The embrace we seek is necessary to lay bare the multivalent perspectives that inform the historical and ongoing practices of sexual regulation. Research-based empirical evidence for education and advocacy remains a gold standard.

The Chapters

The edited collection attends to the relationship between sexual regulation and the law. In a variety of ways, each chapter navigates concerns regarding sex and sexuality and the law, underscoring a central need for warranted reforms in the Canadian legal system—from progressive changes in legislative and sentencing patterns to judicial and civil liberty activism. In this era of constitutionalism, where human rights inform our legal interpretations, the sexual politics animating the legal regulation of conduct discussed in each chapter are no less cogent than the oppression of years past, yet moments of profound change have occurred.

Chapter 1 begins a discussion of sexual regulation and the law by reviewing the genealogy of indecency and obscenity jurisprudence in Canada. Richard Jochelson and James Gacek note the judicial shifts from moral corruptibility concerns, to community standards of tolerance and finally to a harm-based neoliberal approach. Certainly, one could never expect a court to fully recognize the identity politics of all affected groups. Yet equally as certain—social science evidence of harm is often refutable. Although the authors contend that the community standards of tolerance test of harm was rightly problematized, they query whether the new harms-based test adopted by the Supreme Court in its infamous *Labaye* decision has shifted indecency and obscenity jurisprudence to promote sexual agency. The new test of culpability attempts to move away from subjective approval and judicial tastes to instead be informed by objectively ascertainable harm. Yet as Jochelson and Gacek assert, at its worst, the *Labaye* test does more than merely repeat the mistakes of the moral corruptibility objections to sexual conduct and materials of the past; this most recent iteration of the harms-based test seems to expand criminalization on the basis of the judiciary's perception of risk of harm and imagined negative effects of sexual conduct and materials. Inconsistencies in the application of *Labaye*, they contend, must be ultimately remedied going forward.

Chapter 2 examines the jurisprudence of sex work in Canada. Beginning with the vagrancy and solicitation laws prior to, and during, Confederation, as well as before the *Canadian Charter of Rights and Freedoms*, James Gacek and Richard Jochelson trace the factual, historical, legislative, and socio-political shifts in sex work jurisprudence. The authors review and examine different models of sex work regulation, such as criminalization, legalization/decriminalization, and the Nordic model, a variant of which is currently implemented in Canadian sex work legislation. Following this, they examine the *Prostitution Reference,* the first time in Canadian history where the Supreme Court was asked to consider the constitutionality of the federal criminal regulation of sex work. The authors then trace the judicial rationale regarding the implementation of sex work jurisprudence until the ground-breaking *Bedford* case, in which the Supreme Court of Canada deemed unconstitutional several provisions in the *Criminal Code* dealing with sex work. The Harper government's legislative response to the striking out of these provisions is discussed, coupled with their assessment of the Trudeau government's actions within the new criminalization regime. Taken together, the authors assert that sex workers often remain victims of abuse and dangerous conditions created and sustained by the current legislative framework and that by decriminalizing sex work (or aspects of sex work), this work could be made safer for those who engage in it in their daily lives.

Cyber sexual crimes have attracted new found interest in Canada after some high profile suicides and tragedies related to online bullying. In Chapter 3, Richard Jochelson, Alicia Dueck-Read, James Gacek, and Brayden McDonald discuss the social problems underscoring the phenomenon of non-consensual distribution of intimate images (NCDII); they explore the new *Criminal Code* provisions as well as other efforts to combat the phenomenon, such as provincial civil liabilities and new common law torts developed by Canadian courts. The authors endeavour to discuss the ways in which the judicial rationales and the law are being used to regulate and punish sexual bullying, cyber harassment, and revenge porn in Canada. The authors then review the latest legal developments in the area and the newly developing trend for provinces to pass laws allowing lawsuits based in civil court to regulate the distribution of intimate images. By reconsidering the legislative responses and some of the harms caused by NCDII, the authors suggest that a more nuanced NCDII socio-legal analytic is needed to appreciate the gendered issues and violence inherent in the phenomenon.

Chapter 4 by Lauren Menzie and Taryn Hepburn adds to the discussion of cyber sexual crimes by engaging in an examination of child sexual abuse and the judicial and legislative responses to regulating sex offences against youth. In particular, the authors discuss child luring and child pornography legislation and jurisprudence, respectively, and draw upon the developments in legislation and case law to not only redress the reciprocating relationship between law and society but also question how developments in technology will continue to challenge "our conceptions of morality and harm, and expose anxieties underlying youth sexuality and vulnerability" (Menzie and Hepburn, this volume). The authors contend that as the law attempts to regulate online interactions and foresee future technological innovations, regulations of sexual offences against youth are becoming a greater concern that can no longer be evaded, ignored or sublimated, yet the authors warn of the widening, and perhaps overbroad, net of culpability that digital policing may seek to construct.

Chapter 5 explores bestial crimes and its correlations with sexual abuse in Canada, including the involvement of animals in the scope of the abusive actions of sexual offenders. A relatively recent Supreme Court case, *R v DLW* (2016), defined bestiality in Canada as only including penetrative coitus. In 2019, Parliament finally defined the crime more broadly. What are the socio-legal ramifications of this Court decision and how could this alter human-animal relations in Canada? Richard Jochelson, Alicia Dueck-Read, James Gacek, and Brayden McDonald discuss the harm- and risk-based judicial rationale which underpins this legal decision and the diminishment of animals in the eyes of the law in the process. The authors explore the ways in which animals are conceived in Canadian law and examine the role of sentience in regulating conduct with animals. Should animals be constructed as rights-bearing subjects or does Canada's rural history and the neoliberal judicial rationale mean animals should be treated as property under the law? The authors note that the originalist approach to bestiality law not only frames the animal as mere property but also fosters an adjunct technology that can be used in the service of the abuse of humans.

Sexual regulation also raises concerns for transgender communities, including transgender rights, activism, and resistance movements. In particular, high profile events at the University of Toronto have raised the spectre of pronoun use in advocacy towards inclusions of trans persons in Canada. In Chapter 6, Leon Laidlaw reviews the Jordan Peterson case and explores the nascent and developing law that seeks to shield transgender persons using Canada's hate speech laws.

Adamantly disagreeing with Peterson's arguments, Laidlaw also examines Bill C-16, *An Act to Amend the Canadian Human Rights Act* and the *Criminal Code*, and explores the governing judicial rationale and provincial and federal regulation of the protection of transgender persons in Canada. In effect, this chapter raises the issues of the limits of free speech and freedom of sexual identity in Canada. As Laidlaw contends, positioning transgender rights merely as an issue of "political correctness" denigrates "the lived experience of trans oppression and the necessity for gender-based protections in the law" (Laidlaw, this volume); Laidlaw examines these experiences in the context of sex work and the justice system. Efforts to orient collective attention on transgender rights must remain foregrounded, lest one forgoes the goal of ascertaining legal protections for gender-diverse Canadians and the development of inclusivity in Canadian society.

Finally, Chapter 7 by David Ireland reviews the fundamentals of sexual assault law in Canada, including foundational cases. The author then explores how judicial rationales have transgressed emerging moralities about sexual assault using case studies in which judges have engaged in victim blaming behaviour. Specifically, the author discusses the roles of Justices McClung, Dewar, and Camp in infamous sexual assault cases. The author also reviews the recommendation for the removal of Justice Camp (who subsequently resigned) by the Canadian Judicial Council for victim blaming behavior in conducting a trial. Can disciplining judges influence rape culture's extinction?

There is considerable social value in researching sex and sexuality. In part, the information gleaned from these excavations has the potential to ignite or reignite public conversations concerning the implementation of jurisprudence and legislation into the lives of already marginalized persons and groups in Canadian society; it might force us to contend with the ways we self-regulate our own sexual lives. Sexual regulation is an arena of discussion that has historically motivated the personal and the political, from ancient Pompeii, to Victorian England, and through to late-modern Canada.

Works Cited

Dean, Mitchell. *Governmentality: Power and Rule in Modern Society*. Sage, 2010.

Foucault, Michel. *Power/Knowledge: Selected Interviews and Other Writings 1972-1977*. Edited by C. Gordon. Pantheon, 1980.

Garland, David, and Peter Young. "Towards a Social Analysis of Penality." *The Power to Punish*. Edited by David Garland and Peter Young, Heinemann, 1983, pp. 1-36.

Golder, Ben. *Re-reading Foucault: On Law, Power and Rights*. Routledge, 2012.

Hunt, Alan, and Gary Wickham. *Foucault and Law: Towards a Sociology of Law as Governance*. Pluto Press, 1994.

Jochelson, Richard, et al. *Criminal Law and Precrime: Legal Studies in Canadian Punishment and Surveillance in Anticipation of Criminal Guilt*. Routledge, 2017.

Jurisprudence

Canada (Attorney General) v Bedford, 2013 SCC 72, [2013] 3 SCR 1101.

M v H, [1999] 2 SCR 3.

R v Butler, [1992] 1 SCR 452.

Reference re Same-Sex Marriage, [2004] 3 SCR 698, 2004 SCC 79.

Chapter One

Indecency and Obscenity Law: From *Hicklin* to the Post-*Labaye* Era—A (Tall) Tale of Risk?

Richard Jochelson and James Gacek

Introduction

Over time, Canadian courts have come to realize that morals and taste are subjective, arbitrary, and unworkable in the criminal context and that a diverse society "could function only with a generous measure of tolerance for minority mores and practices" (*R v Labaye* para 14). In Canada, this realization is evident within the development of indecency and obscenity jurisprudence—as applied to conduct in the former and publications and/or materials in the latter. Yet matters as controversial as indecency and obscenity are "potential minefield[s]" riddled with responses of consternation by some and holding contested meanings for others (Jochelson, "After" 743). Indeed, within Canadian approaches to indecency and obscenity law, it is clear that this jurisprudence still remains in "an interstitial period of flux" (743).

In an attempt to resolve such fluctuations, in 2005, the Supreme Court of Canada (SCC) revised the meanings of indecency and obscenity, finally retiring the community standards of tolerance test, which had been in place prior to *Labaye*. The shift countenanced by the *Labaye* court adopted a new test for culpability that would move away from subjective approval and be informed by a "legal norm of objectively ascertainable harm" (*R v Labaye* para 14). Some scholars, optimistic that the court's rationale could leave more space for sexual agency, suggested that this shift would allow greater opportunities "within legal reasoning for sexual narratives," perhaps even sex-positive narratives (Craig, "Re-Interpreting" 328). Has *Labaye* progressed indecency and obscenity jurisprudence along this trajectory? Or does the most recent iteration of the harms-based test merely expand criminalization on the basis of the judiciary's perception of imagined negative effects of sexual conduct and materials? Our chapter endeavours to examine these questions in greater detail.

Accordingly, we begin this chapter by reviewing the historical developments of indecency and obscenity Canadian criminal law in four distinct phases: (1) the *Hicklin* era (1868–1962); (2) the community standards era (1962–1992); (3) the community standards for tolerance of harm or *Butler* era (1992–2005); and (4) the political harm or *Labaye* era (2005–present).[1] We also draw upon our previous work to illustrate "how the state has become justified in intervening in situations of attributed or even improbable 'sexual danger'" (Jochelson et al. 47). By undertaking a jurisprudential review from *Hicklin* (1868) to *Labaye* (2005), we demonstrate how the harms-based *Labaye* test, in principle, provides courts with an array of justifications for criminalizing sexual expression, conduct, and materials. However, where this chapter diverges from our previous work (Jochelson et al.) is through focusing on significant applications of the harms-based test by Canadian courts since the *Labaye* decision.[2]

Following the historical developments of indecency and obscenity jurisprudence in Canada, our chapter considers applications of *Labaye* since the inception of the harms-based test in 2005. In particular, we discuss two thematic trends that have emerged: (1) the difficulty and impossibility of finding bawdy-house harms, initially because of difficulty in proving the term, and now in light of the repeal of "bawdy-house" in section 197 of the *Criminal Code* (i.e., a place kept for the practices of indecency; the word "prostitution" had previously been removed by Parliament in the penultimate *Code* definition of "bawdy-house", which had caused difficulties for some courts in finding bawdy-house harms after *Labaye* and prior to the 2019 repeal of the term); and (2) the use of *Labaye* as a means of determining impermissible societal and sexual risk, especially in terms of so-called risky secondary effects when *Labaye* is applied beyond cases concerning indecency and obscenity.

We conclude the chapter by noting some challenges for the *Labaye* harm test going forwards. Our respective and collective work continues to examine and interrogate how Canadian jurisprudence attempts to control sexual expression and conduct through justifying state intervention into the sexual lives of Canadian citizens. As we continue this endeavour, we remain cognizant that discursive constructions of indecency and obscenity have broader regulatory or disciplinary effects beyond those individuals targeted for prosecution (Jochelson and Kramar, "Sex" 28). At first blush, it may appear that applications of *Labaye* slowed down considerably within indecency and obscenity jurisprudence. Yet, in reality, we witnessed the harms-based test emerging beyond its intended use in other realms of Canadian criminal law. Put differently, there appear to be contexts in which the *Labaye* test is applied to justify interventions aiming to combat alleged risks to society's proper functioning (*R v Labaye* para 52). The court's perception of danger (sexual or otherwise) to society's proper functioning conflates "a juridical justification for government action (imputed danger) with the establishment of criminality" (Jochelson and Kramar, "Governing through Precaution" 307). The result is criminalization "on the basis of how one's actions *might* threaten the political values that a court guards in the *Constitution*, as opposed to criminalization because one has committed a tangible criminal offence" (308). Through the legal rationalities of indecency and obscenity laws in Canada, we see SCC decisions as a reflection of a particular judicio-mentality that is iterative, limiting, and malleable, yet, at the same time, it is one that asserts a particular socio-moral order, which is in line with the administrative ends of a late modern society. Furthermore, such an expansion and diffusion of the *Labaye* test beyond indecency and obscenity contexts merits further investigation—an effort we begin to discuss and query in this chapter. In effect, incremental developments have been made in obscenity and indecency jurisprudence since the *Labaye* decision, but it remains clear that *Labaye* still leaves behind an evidentiary vacuum that the judiciary intangibly fills with largely circumstantial evidence (arguably, even inferences) to ensure that the proper functioning of society is maintained (*R v Labaye* para 52). These post-*Labaye* applications have the potential to remain explicative of, and be informed by, judicial tastes rather than empirical harm—a concern we can no longer suppress or evade.

The *Hicklin* Era (1868–1962)

For nearly a century, the governing standard for indecency and obscenity in Canada was set by *R v Hicklin,* an English court case. The construction of the *Hicklin* decision, derived from Victorian and Judeo-Christian morality, reveals the Victorian sensibilities underpinning sexual regulation in the law. In *Hicklin,* Lord Cockburn proposed an obscenity test that would influence indecency and obscenity cases arising in England, Canada, and the United States. The *Hicklin* test was the earliest common law juridical test established and was primarily concerned with the corruption of morals, especially among the so-called weak minded within society. Far from a central focus of harm or risk of harm, the *Hicklin* court saw itself as the guardian of the social and economic sphere of society, as the original aim of the *Hicklin* decision was condemnation of the immoral.

The leading question the *Hicklin* test asked was "whether the tendency of the matter charged as obscenity is to deprave and corrupt those whose minds are open to such immoral influences, and into whose hands the publication of this sort may fall" (*R v Hicklin* para 371). If the answer was in the affirmative, then the impugned material was rendered obscene. However, the court's concern—and its subsequent harms-based test—was not for the members of the upper class who might take possession of obscene materials. Instead, the regulation of the dangerous working classes was the main concern—namely, the regulation of the young and uneducated, as well as women and those "who were 'irrational' and unable to resist the material's influences" (Jochelson, "After" 745, citing Cossman et al. 12). Indeed, as Deana Heath has shown through meticulous historical research, British obscenity law (out of which Canadian obscenity law was founded) developed throughout the nineteenth century in British society primarily "to manage [the] population through regulating the culture and bodies of the working classes" (59). Ultimately, criminal regulation through the *Hicklin* test was produced, sustained, and justified on the grounds of protection from moral harm and to secure those in society who were allegedly susceptible to moral vulnerability (regardless of whether attaining viable evidence would suggest otherwise).

Following the *Hicklin* precedent, only five Canadian cases were reported between 1900 and 1940 (Johnson; see also Jochelson et al.). Within this codification, protections from moral harm ranged from intoxicants, such as alcohol and drugs, to the strict regulation of pornography. Without these protections, it was believed that lax regulations of these alleged vices would lead to the consumption of these vices by the morally inferior lower classes, which would cause these groups to break down their social cohesion, risking the sanctity of the monogamous heterosexual family form and, consequently, endangering society's proper functioning. In effect, the *Hicklin* obscenity test had secured proper moral and social values within the nuclear family unit while concomitantly regulating the dangerous working classes in the process.

The Community Standards Era (1962–1992)

Shortly after the enactment of what is now section 163(8) of the *Criminal Code*,[3] the court had to decide how to apply *Hicklin* to *R v Brodie*, thereby ultimately redefining the *Hicklin* test to fit within the aims of this new legislation. The issue before the court in *Brodie* was the criminal prosecution of D.H. Lawrence's *Lady Chatterley's Lover*, a novel describing an affair between an aristocratic woman and a working-class man. As a technique for determining the tolerance of harm in the community, the court started to appeal to positivist research garnered from the social sciences (Jochelson et al. 49). Whereas *Hicklin* had authorized the upper classes to prohibit access to sexually explicit materials—on the basis of their moral judgement of others' corruptibility—the *Brodie* court imagined and interpreted the "community" in a different way. Through this reimagination, the *Brodie* court attempted to create an objective technique by authorizing the community as "the arbiter of sexual morality" (Jochelson and Kramar, "Governing through Precaution" 292), and the test for obscenity was now to ask whether "the undue exploitation of sex is a dominant characteristic" (*R v Brodie* para 702). The application of such a test required that the work under the consideration of the court be read in its entirety to determine its dominant purpose (para 702).

Judson J., writing for the majority of the *Brodie* court, noted that community standards were pertinent in deeming whether undue exploitation of sex had occurred, since only the community had tangible views of decency, cleanliness, and dirtiness (para 705). Should the dominant purpose of the speech in question be the undue exploitation of sex, per Judson J., then the material would contravene the new legislation in place. However, if the dominant purpose of the material under consideration was not the undue exploitation of sex, the material would be acceptable by the community standards test and deemed appropriate for the community's purview (para 702). To determine the dominant purpose of the material, Judson J. indicated that a court must consider the literary or artistic merit of the work and whether the author had a serious literary purpose in creating the work or the purpose was simply exploitation (paras 702-3).

The *Brodie* court saw the community functioning as one when participating in determinations of harm. In theory, this provided a space for the use of empirical research and evidence as to what the community would tolerate others being exposed to in relation to sexual danger (Jochelson et al. 49-50). Unfortunately, the ideal of the community was far from what the *Brodie* court spoke. In practice, such determinations of harm were accomplished by the courts and not the community. In effect, the technique in the community standards test to determine harm to society was hardly different from the rationale that had underpinned the *Hicklin* test before it. The reality of the situation was that the judiciary represented the view of the community, and this representation became an implicit notion in the community standards test. According to Brenda Cossman, the community standards of tolerance test later served to reinforce heteronormativity (135).

The community standards test was further developed in *R v Dominion News and Gifts Ltd*. In this case, the SCC supported the decision of Freedman J.A.'s dissent in the Manitoba Court of Appeal, which noted that the community standards should be an average member of the community's thinking (Jochelson, "After" 746).[4] The community standard was somewhere between the lowest, most base, and most puritan tastes (*Dominion News and Gifts* para 80). Furthermore, using this test, the views of the margins of Canadian society would be excised to produce a more acceptable, middle-of-the-road standard. According to

Freedman J.A., this approach would avoid a subjective approach, as the results would vary with or depend on "the personal tastes and predilections of the particular Judge who happens to be trying the case" (para 116). However, in reality, few (if any) obscenity trials were held before juries, yet according to Judson J., the best arbiter of the community was the jury, not the judiciary: "there does not exist in any community at all times—however the standard may vary from time to time—a general instructive sense of what is decent and what is indecent, of what is clean and what is dirty, and when the distinction has to be drawn, I do not know that there is any better tribunal than a jury to see it" (para 116).

Finally, efforts to cloak the community standards test in objectivity through community standards were further refined and reinforced by the court in *R v Towne Cinema Theatres Ltd*. In this case, the SCC underscored the importance of liberal tolerance towards others to avoid projecting "one's own ideas of what is tolerable" (para 33). This test of obscenity was to be about "a standard of tolerance, not taste" (para 34). It was also concerned not with what Canadians would tolerate being exposed to themselves but with what they would tolerate other Canadians seeing (para 34). We see in these passages one of the many efforts to cloak the community standards test in objectivity. In doing so, the judiciary could infer the community standards from their own knowledge of Canadian attitudes about sexuality, instead of using substantiated empirical evidence of Canadian attitudes (Jochelson, "After" 746; Jochelson et al. 50).

The *Butler* Era (1992–2005)

In *R v Butler*, the view of community standards was further advanced and reformulated. *Butler* was the first SCC case to apply the approach in an obscenity case since the inception of the *Canadian Charter of Rights and Freedoms*. The SCC was to adjudicate the constitutionality of the obscenity provisions in the *Criminal Code*. The *Butler* court concentrated on the antipornography campaign as set out by one intervener, the Women's Legal Education and Action Fund (LEAF). LEAF sought to have obscenity described as an exercise of sex discrimination that harms women's equality (Yan). However, disagreeing with LEAF was another intervener, the British Columbia Civil Liberties Association

(BCCLA), which sought to protect freedom of expression. The BCCLA was more concerned with the effects of criminal regulation on sexual freedom than hypothetical harms associated with ostensibly obscene materials (for example, see Jochelson and Kramar, *Sex*). Subsequently, the SCC's decision largely sided with the policies undergirding LEAF's arguments; the majority of *Butler* ruled that the obscenity provisions were a justifiable infringement on the freedom of expression for Mr. Butler.

Furthermore, the SCC also considerably clarified the common law definition of obscenity for the purposes of criminal liability in *Butler*. Writing for the *Butler* majority, Sopinka J., argued that there is sufficient evidence that certain depictions of degrading and dehumanizing sex harms society, and adversely affects attitudes towards women, and in some cases men (*R v Butler* para 122). However, the court acknowledged that there is no direct link between pornography and discrimination or violence against women (para 117).

Nevertheless, the mere belief that such a connection exists could justify the suppression of pornographic speech (*R v Butler* para 117). Reconfiguring the community standards test as a type of harm test, the *Butler* court set out a three-tiered test for determining which materials would fail the community standards of tolerance for harm (undue exploitation) test, which flowed from the court's interpretation of pre-*Charter* case law. These three tiers included the following: (1) explicit sex with violence; (2) explicit sex without violence but which subjected people to treatment that was degrading or dehumanizing; and (3) explicit sex without violence that was neither degrading nor dehumanizing and did not involve children (para 484). Only the first two tiers count as potentially obscene for legal purposes; the first category is always violative, and the second category is only violative in the case of substantial risk of harm.

According to the *Butler* decision, the community would not tolerate the undue exploitation of sex because such exploitation caused harm to not only the participants but to citizens more broadly, as they all comprise a society based within liberal democracy that ought to be protected from harm (Jochelson et al. 51–52). In this context, harm would run across a wide spectrum, ranging from the harms that degrade or dehumanize some as a result of the promulgation of pornography throughout society to the harms imposed on those who actively participate in creating pornography. In particular, the *Butler* court recognized that harm could include harm to equality, a right guaranteed within the *Charter* (*R v Butler* para 479). Post-*Charter*, we begin to see the balance shift towards (or begin to include) "a vision of securitization that marshals the notion of inoculating society against (risk of) harm to equality" (Jochelson and Kramar, "Governing through Precaution" 294). Therefore, criminalization was justified to prevent harm to political values—such as equality—and ensured society's proper functioning at large.

The SCC would return to the community standards of tolerance test in *Little Sisters Book and Art Emporium v Canada (Minister of Justice)*. In *Little Sisters,* the SCC examined the constitutionality of a customs regime and administrative practice to determine whether a queer[5] bookshop was being unfairly targeted and having its freedom of expression suppressed by customs' supposedly discriminatory practices. The *Little Sisters* court considered the actions of the customs' officials in allegedly suppressing a multitude of sexually expressive material. The material seized over the years "not only included queer erotica but also ranged from sex education materials for the community to anthologies and essay collections" (Jochelson, "After" 748). Binnie J., in writing for the *Little Sisters* majority, found that with the exception of the reverse onus provision in section 152(3) of the Customs Act,[6] the legislation constituted a reasonable limit on the freedom of expression of the *Charter*. Specifically, the *Little Sisters* majority noted that the appellants suffered differential treatment when compared to importers of heterosexual explicit material, let alone more general bookstores that carried at least some of the same titles as the appellant bookstore (*Little Sisters v Canada* para 116). Therefore, the SCC *Little Sisters* majority was able to conclude that the customs officials' discretion was not exercised in accordance with *Charter* values and that the administration of the scheme was violative of freedom of expression:

> The Customs treatment was high-handed and dismissive of the appellants' right to receive lawful expressive material which they had every right to import. When Customs officials prohibit and thereby censor lawful gay and lesbian erotica, they are making a statement about gay and lesbian culture, and the statement was reasonably interpreted by the appellants as demeaning gay and lesbian values. The message was that their concerns were less

worthy of attention and respect than those of their heterosexual counterparts.

While here it is the interests of the gay and lesbian community that were targeted, other vulnerable groups may similarly be at risk from overzealous censorship. Little Sisters was targeted because it was considered "different." On a more general level, it seems to me fundamentally unacceptable that expression which is free within the country can become stigmatized and harassed by government officials simply because it crosses an international boundary, and is thereby brought within the bailiwick of the Customs department. The appellants' constitutional right to receive perfectly lawful gay and lesbian erotica should not be diminished by the fact their suppliers are, for the most part, located in the United States. Their freedom of expression does not stop at the border. *(Little Sisters v Canada* paras 123-24)

Despite its analysis in the justification phase of constitutional analysis, the *Little Sisters* court engaged with the meaning of community standards for the purposes of determining obscenity (albeit a limited engagement), and the analysis did not bolster an actual finding, since no impugned expression was before this court per se (*Little Sisters* para 53). *Little Sisters* and the supporting interveners[7] argued that the community standards of tolerance test either needed to be applied so as to account for the unique needs of queer communities or was not the appropriate test to apply to queer communities generally. The *Little Sisters* court both considered and dismissed these arguments in respect of *Butler* and did so notwithstanding its acknowledgment that it could not engage in a wide-ranging consideration of *Butler*, as no party provided a constitutional notice before them of this issue (para 53). The court majority refused to accept that queer sexual expression created by and for the queer community was in any way distinct from heterosexual sexual expression or deserving of unique consideration (para 42); they noted that the critique of the community standards test as overtly majoritarian and unduly relying on a judge's personal taste was unfounded, as "[a] concern for minority expression is one of the principal factors that led to the adoption of a national community standards test" (para 56).

Moreover, the *Little Sisters* court argued that the test could not discriminate against homosexuals because the obscenity section of the *Criminal Code* would not be applied differently to gay and lesbian sexually explicit materials (Jochelson and Kramar, "Governing through Precaution" 297). In other words, the test for obscenity was aimed at criminalizing expression that was incompatible with Canadian society as informed by equality concerns (*Little Sisters v Canada* para 58). The court's view was that its aim in *Butler* was to prevent (risk of) harm and that the state "is indifferent to whether such harm arises in the context of heterosexuality or homosexuality" (para 44). From this perspective, the (risk of) harm test applied here did not work against the interests of homosexuals because they too were members of society who benefited from state intervention to protect society's proper functioning and from (risk of) harm (para 58). As a result, harm to society became "a more abstract value replacing majoritarian community standards of tolerance for harm because it no longer required even cursory judicial consideration of contextualized sexual identity or difference" (Jochelson and Kramar, "Governing through Precaution" 297).

The SCC was provided few opportunities to directly rule on the issue of criminal liability for harm within the indecency and obscenity jurisprudence in the thirteen years following *Butler*. Only five cases during this time period addressed the issue of criminal liability in the context of indecency: *R v Tremblay*; *R v Mara*; *R v Blais-Pelletier*; *R v Kouri*; and *R v Labaye*. These cases used the community standards for tolerance of harm test to rule whether bawdy-houses were operating for the alleged purposes of indecency, or venues where supposed indecent performances were said to have been held. In these cases, it becomes clear the relevance of privacy as an arbiter of harm, and the question of whether the particular acts that took place were criminal drew upon the court's assessments of privacy within their adjudication. The SCC understands privacy within its indecency jurisprudence as one end of a spectrum moving towards public action on the other end—in other words, the more public a display of sexuality, the more of an affront the sexual action will be to an unassuming audience. Therefore, the tacit harm assumed in such cases is that exposure to unexpected sexual performances creates a criminal risk worth considering and sanctioning (Jochelson et al. 45).

These observations were initially evident in the SCC cases of Tremblay and Mara. Both Tremblay and Mara demonstrated a concern for the issues surrounding the differences between locations "which can come within the definition of public places"; however, judicial interpretations of the law stopped short of critiquing the definition of privacy itself (*R v Tremblay* para 970). Tremblay involved erotic dancing in a private room at an erotic club called the *Pussy Cat* in Montreal, whereas Mara involved erotic dancing in the open access area of *Cheaters Tavern* in Toronto. In both cases, the SCC had to determine whether the conduct at issue was criminally indecent. Since the Tremblay case involved private dancing, it was not adjudicated under the indecent public performance provisions of the *Criminal Code* but rather under sections 163 and 210 of the *Code*.[8] As such, the degree of privacy was relevant to the analysis, since a public display would render the indecency more egregious for the purposes of the law. The Tremblay court conclusively found that, in terms of where the acts took place, "sexual activities were conducted behind closed doors out of the view of the general public." (*R v Tremblay* para 969) Furthermore, although "the acts took place in a public place, as those words are defined by the *Criminal Code*, they were not a blatantly public display. Rather the closed room was *relatively private* with only consenting adults present" (para 970; italics emphasized). Writing for the Mara court, Sopinka J. distinguished Mara from Tremblay, noting that "it is important to recall that Tremblay involved an analysis of whether acts performed in private room were indecent," whereas Mara involved "the analysis of whether a performance was indecent" (*R v Mara* para 648).

Specifically, Sopinka J. deemed the physical contact between patron and dancer as indecent—the fondling and sucking of dancers' breasts by the patrons as well as the contact between the dancer or patron and the other person's genitals—because the acts are harmful to society through the further degradation and dehumanization of women, and desensitizing those watching. Remarkably, the risk of harm from sexually transmitted infections and the activity's similarity to prostitution only were relevant insofar as these matters created risk of social harm—the social harm of acceptance or desensitization to such activities (para 631). Indecency, as Sopinka J. indicates, "depends on community standards, which in turn depend largely on an analysis of social harm"; social harm, then, "is not a fact susceptible of proof in the traditional way, but rather where the activities or material in question involve the degradation and objectification of women ... the law infers simply from that degradation and objectification" (paras 45, 44).

In turning to *R v Blais-Pelletier,* the appellant at trial was fined one hundred dollars for operating a bawdy-house in Quebec. However, the *Blais-Pelletier* court was to determine whether the lap dancing occurring within the strip club constituted an indecent act. Arbour J., writing for the majority, determined that the trial judge carefully considered "all relevant factors in analysing the standard of tolerance" in concert with the "nature and character of the touching that took place between the dancers and the police, and the circumstances prevailing in the cubicle" (*R v Blais-Pelletier* para 1). The dance took place in a private cubicle with the curtain partly opened, and the strip club allowed patrons to touch the dancers for ten dollars (para 1; see also CBC News). Although the trial judge did not appear to rely on either *Tremblay* or *Mara* in his verdict,[9] Arbour J. agreed with the trial judge, indicating that in *Blais-Pelletier,* "it does not appear that the judge committed an error of law in his assessment of the standard of tolerance" (para 2), nor does it cross the line on what the community would tolerate (para 2; see also CBC News). As a result, the *Blais-Pelletier* majority upheld the appeal and restored the trial judge's acquittal.

Finally, and most significantly, *R v Kouri* and *R v Labaye* concerned charges against the proprietors of establishments alleged to be bawdy-houses. As defined under the now repealed section 197 of the *Criminal Code,*[10] a common bawdy-house at the time of the case was a "place that is kept or occupied, or resorted to ... for the purpose of prostitution or for the practice of acts of indecency."[11] *Labaye* and *Kouri* were companion cases. Counsel for both Mr. Labaye and Mr. Kouri argued that acts occurring in these establishments were not indecent under the criminal law and that, in effect, both cases turned on the statutory interpretation of indecency. Although neither case involved a constitutional challenge of the then bawdy-house provisions of the *Criminal Code,* the cases differed mainly because of the extent to which their activities were publicly accessible. Specifically, the issue in *Labaye* was whether the activities of a private members' sex club were indecent under the *Criminal Code,* whereas the issue in *Kouri* was whether the acts, which occurred at a nonmembers' club named *Coeur à Corps,* constituted acts of criminal indecency (*Kouri* para 1; see also Craig, "Laws").

For *Kouri,* Otis J. quelled the trial court's bawdy-house conviction in her Court of Appeal of Quebec majority decision. This was done on the basis that "sexual morality must be considered first and foremost the result of the personal responsibility human beings have towards themselves" and that "Canadian society does not condemn sexual modes of expression that...[are not] a source of social harm and are not offensive" (*Kouri* para 51). This decision was then reaffirmed by the SCC in its majority decision, as it drew upon the *Labaye* harms-based test to determine that not only did the club take reasonable steps to secure the acts from public view (*Kouri* paras 15–20) but that there was "no evidence of inducing anti-social attitudes through demeaning, abusive or humiliating treatment of any individual or group" (para 22) and "no suggestion of physical or psychological harm to the participants" within *Coeur à Corps* (para 23).

Notwithstanding the five cases indicated in this section, *Labaye* holds the most importance in terms of harms-based tests. This is because the *Labaye* test ultimately abandons the community's ostensible tolerance for harm test and attempts to shift towards a more objective harm test, which we have argued elsewhere was no more than a shift "towards political abstraction" (Jochelson and Kramar "Governing through Precaution" 306). Although the proponents of the *Labaye* test argue that the *Labaye* decision is a move towards a nuanced and (arguably) just approach to sexual expression and materials, one must query this move in practice. As we discuss below, we view this abstraction of the *Labaye* decision as one which creates a peculiar evidentiary vacuum, which ultimately persists even today.

The *Labaye* Era (2005–present)

In *R v Labaye,* Mr. Labaye was charged under section 210(1) of the *Criminal Code* with keeping a common bawdy-house for the practice of acts of indecency. The accused operated the *l'Orage* swingers club, a club in Montreal that permitted couples and single people to meet each other for consensual group sex. McLachlin C.J.C. (as she then was) wrote the SCC majority decision and held that the community standards of tolerance test, which must be violated in order to establish a charge of indecency, was to be replaced with a reconfigured harms-based test. In fact, the SCC majority determined that the former community standards of tolerance test would be impossible to apply objectively. As the *Labaye* court (para 18) states:

> In a diverse, pluralistic society whose members hold divergent views, who is the "community"? And how can one objectively determine what the community, if one could define it, would tolerate, in the absence of evidence that community knew of and considered the conduct at issue? In practice, once again, the [community standards of tolerance] test tended to function as a proxy for the personal views of expert witnesses, judges and jurors. In the end, the question often came down to what they, as individual members of the community, would tolerate.

The intention of this approach would determine, as best the judiciary could, what the community would tolerate others being exposed to "on the basis of the degree of harm that may flow from such exposure" (*R v Labaye* para 21, citing *Butler* para 485). For a finding of indecency, the *Labaye* majority proposed analyzing the nature of the harm, of which three types had emerged from prior case law: (1) harm to those whose autonomy and liberty may be restricted by being confronted with inappropriate conduct; (2) harm to society by predisposing others to antisocial conduct; and (3) harm to individuals participating in the conduct (para 36). In effect, the *Labaye* court held that "the stronger the inference of *risk of harm* the lesser likelihood of tolerance" (para 21; our emphasis). Although these categories of harm were not closed, the majority noted that the past obscenity and indecency cases fell within them. Moreover, the second step of the test would determine if the quantum of harm was sufficient to interfere with the proper functioning of society; such a determination would have to keep in mind the values fundamental to society—values that were rooted in constitutional values or similar legislative and rights-based rationales, such as equality, autonomy, and liberty, to name a few (paras 56-57).[12] Therefore, one must consider whether "the harm or risk of harm is of a *degree* that is incompatible with the proper functioning of society" (para 61).[13]

Although noting that harm is more discernable than community standards, the majority reviewed the basic tenets of harm and discussed the need for a modified theory of harm to resolve the limitations of the community standards of tolerance test as developed from *Butler*. However, the majority merely encouraged an "incremental" reassessment of this test and indicated that such a development of a modified theory of harm is beyond the scope of the *Labaye* decision:

> Developing a workable theory of harm is *not a task for a single case*. In the tradition of the common law, its full articulation will only come as judges consider diverse situations and render decisions on them. Moreover, the difficulty of the task should not be underestimated. *We must proceed incrementally, step by cautious step.* (R v Labaye para 26; our emphasis)

In effect, although the case at bar merely required "the further exploration of what types of harm, viewed objectively, suffice to found a conviction for keeping a bawdy-house for the purposes of acts of indecency," an incremental reassessment rather than a complete rework of a theory of harm was necessary (*R v Labaye* para 27). It is noteworthy that since *Labaye* the term "bawdy-house" has come to include only acts of indecency and not acts of prostitution as a result of adjudication on the antiprostitution regime in the *Bedford* case and Parliament's subsequent response (of which we discuss in greater detail in the following chapter); as a result, this made the *Labaye* test the threshold determinant of whether a bawdy-house offence has occurred – a matter that is now irrelevant since the repeal of s.197 in 2019. The test is still the governing law in all other indecency and obscenity based offences.[14]

Per the *Labaye* court, the new objective harms-based test would also be grounded in values recognized by the *Charter* and other Canadian fundamental laws underpinning the need to protect society from harm (*R v Labaye* para 30). Although the SCC *Labaye* majority recognized that value judgments cannot be avoided in public decency standards, they felt that trial judges must take pains to ensure that when making decisions, their decisions are as objective as possible:

> Value judgements in this domain of the law, like many others, cannot be avoided. But this does not mean that the decision-making process is subjective and arbitrary. First, judges should approach the task of making value judgements with an awareness of the danger of deciding the case on the basis of unarticulated and unacknowledged values or prejudices. Second, they should make value judgements on the basis of the evidence and a full appreciation of the relevant factual and legal context, to ensure that it is informed not by the judge's subjective view, but by

relevant, objectively tested criteria. Third, they should carefully weigh and articulate the factors that produce the value judgements. By practices such as these, objectivity can be attained. (*R v Labaye* para 54)

In addition, to determine whether the alleged harm reached the threshold level of incompatibility with society's proper functioning, the *Labaye* court suggested that, in most cases, expert evidence would be needed to establish actual harm. Yet, if the Crown relies on establishing risk of harm rather than actual harm, then such evidence may be absent. The question of evidence was largely the focus of the second phase of the *Labaye* analysis, in which the court asked whether the quantum of harm rises to the level of incompatibility with society's fundamental values, as exemplified in constitutional or related documents (in other words, harm to political values) (paras 60–61; see also Yan).

Therefore, with this new harms-based test, the *Labaye* court determined that the liberty and autonomy of members of the public were not affected by the *l'Orage* swingers club. In their view, sex in secure locations was deemed compatible with the proper functioning of society. As the *Labaye* court indicated, "consensual conduct behind code locked doors can hardly be supposed to jeopardize a society as vigorous and tolerant as Canadian society" (para 71). Per the *Labaye* court, the autonomy and liberty of members of the public "was not affected by unwanted confrontation with the sexual conduct in question" (para 66); only those who were already disposed to swinging participated at *l'Orage*, which was a matter guaranteed by the club's membership fees, locked doors, and screening meetings with potential club members. As the *Labaye* court states, no one was goaded or coerced into sex, no one was paid for sex, and no one was treated as a "mere sexual object for the gratification of others."[15] *Labaye*'s sister case, *Kouri*, applied the test to a less secure night club setting in which less precaution was taken and still found no harm.

In short, protecting society from harm continues to be a central feature of law. Yet sustaining and guarding society's proper functioning presumes and imagines a moral order based on consensus, "which embraces law as a means of imposing and delineating limits on actions" through often unsubstantiated risks of harm (Jochelson et al. 47). Therefore, we must question whether this pattern continues within cases decided since *Labaye*, a focus to which we now turn.

Exploring *Labaye*'s Area of Expertise: Indecency and Obscenity Contexts

Upon further examination of post-*Labaye* applications, we find varied usages of *Labaye* within indecency and obscenity contexts. We are aware that this may appear as unsurprising for readers, given the amount of discretion the judiciary typically has in their respective adjudications of the law (criminal or otherwise). Yet the varied usage of *Labaye* cannot go unnoticed, given the fact that *Labaye* was a landmark case on the adjudication of indecency and obscenity law.

Specifically, the *Labaye* framework was drawn upon for those cases that involved an accused charged with keeping a bawdy-house (for acts of indecency or prostitution)—a charge that was amended to keeping a bawdy-house for the purposes of acts of indecency (for pre-amendment examples see *Kouri; R v Ponomarev*) and now has been repealed entirely. In *Ponomarev*, the location in question was a massage parlour. Drawing upon *Labaye,* Chisvin J. determined that Mr. Ponomarev was not guilty, as the payment of money for masturbating clients within the massage parlour was for a full body massage, and the act of masturbation was optional at no additional fee (*R v Ponomarev* para 29). Furthermore, given that these acts are "done in private, as part of a massage, participated in voluntarily by all individuals, and a fee was paid regardless of whether or not the act[s] took place," the justice was not satisfied that the Crown had met its onus that the conduct constituted prostitution (para 29; recall, at the time, a bawdy-house offence included practices of indecency and prostitution). A simple application of the *Labaye* harm types prevented the court from finding attitudinal harm, predisposition to antisocial attitudes, or participant-based harms.

Other significant examples include cases in which an accused was charged with being found in a bawdy-house without a lawful excuse (see *Marceau c R*; the case was prosecuted before the bawdy-house provision removed prostitution as a constituting circumstance). In *Marceau,* ten applicants (eight female dancers, the doorman, and a customer) were charged and convicted with unlawfully being present in a bawdy-house. However, Hilton J., writing for the majority, quashed the conviction and ordered a new trial. Drawing upon *Labaye,* Hilton J. indicated that "the need to adjust the definition of prostitution, especially the component of 'exchange of sexual favours' is constant in a rapidly changing environment" (*Marceau* para 79). Here, the judge searched for a means of prosecution when *Labaye* criteria are applied and no harm is found. In other words, a more flexible prostitution interpretation may catch conduct that the *Labaye* harm calculi missed under the indecency adjudication. As Hilton J. indicates:

> For example, should a private chat on the telephone for a fee with a person paid to arouse the caller and incite him/her to self-gratification amount to an act of prostitution and make the place where the calls are answered a common bawdy-house? Is the owner of such business a person living on the avails of prostitution of another person? What about a similar private interaction online when the person paid is performing sexually explicit acts designed to arouse the paying watcher who can masturbate in private? Is the place where the paid person is performing a common bawdy-house? Is the operator of the website who collects the fees living on the avails of prostitution? What about places where a paying client in a private booth can observe a nude dancer behind a glass while masturbating? Are they common bawdy-houses?

> These examples show that various prohibitions related to prostitution, including "having been found in a common bawdy-house", can be given either a large or a narrow scope depending on the definition of what is the provision of sexual favours for money. They also demonstrate the need to refer to objective criteria to avoid *unacceptable vagueness*. (*Marceau c R* paras 79-80 our translation and our emphasis)

Therefore, Hilton J. determined that the bar in which the appellants were found did not constitute a bawdy-house; indecency was not proven, and the services offered in the establishment did not amount to a concrete understanding of prostitution (*Marceau c R* paras 83–85). With the difficulty of establishing *Labaye*-style harms in the bawdy-house context, and given the removal of prostitution from the bawdy-house definition, it proved harder to prosecute bawdy-house offences. This has become even more acute after the repeal of s.197 of the *Code*. Investigators may choose instead to focus on prostitution-related offences drafted during the Harper era in response to the *Bedford* case.

Despite the difficulty in establishing bawdy-house violations, the legacy of *Labaye* is as much discursive as precedential as indicated by its use in other areas of the law, such as in civil, regulatory, constitutional, military sentencing, and nonindecency/obscenity criminal contexts (for a fuller discussion, see Jochelson and Gacek, "Reconstitutions"). If the prosecution of obscenity and indecency seems to have slowed in the wake of *Labaye*, its main impact may be the wide discussion of harms that courts seem to be having across a wide variety of adjudications. In effect, *Labaye* may be changing the way courts speak about harm in a general sense.

Labaye's Effect: Beyond Indecency and Obscenity Contexts?

As we demonstrate above, particular cases seem to view the *Labaye* test as a credible move towards a more nuanced approach to sexual expression and materials, and indicate in their decisions the contextual nature of finding guilt in cases of indecency and obscenity. Yet, as we have argued elsewhere (Jochelson and Gacek, "Reconstitutions"), the use of *Labaye* analytics is drawn upon in situations of speech that do not involve sexual content, and even in the constitutional context of free expression jurisprudence. This warrants further attention because on such occasions, the test is used as proxy for assessment of harm outside of the circumstances of the *actus reus* of obscenity/indecency offences. In effect, the test then becomes a precursor of harm in other, unintended contexts beyond indecency and obscenity law. In cases in which obscenity and indecency are at issue, we see the obviousness of the harm used as an excuse to do away with the evidentiary requirement in *Labaye* for expert evidence or, alternatively, objective proof. Recall that in *Labaye*, some conduct is conceived of as so risky in particular court cases that the application of the harms-based test will ask for less in the way of empirical proof to demonstrate harm. Although the *Labaye* court gave the example of a terror attack, in practice, risk is assessed in less dire circumstances as we shall see below.

For example, in *Roberts (Re)*, the issue at hand was whether the renewal of the liquor license for a cabaret providing adult entertainment would "interfere with the quiet enjoyment of neighbourhood properties" (para 1). On a balance of probabilities, the Nova Scotia

Utility and Review Board found that a significant risk of harm would occur with the opening and operation of the Sensations cabaret as it would lead to the "disturbing incidents" alluded to in the evidence—such as an increase in noise, persons urinating on the fronts of houses, women being solicited for sex or asked to expose their breasts, and women being followed by slow moving cars. Such acts are "attributable to persons who are customers leaving *Sensations,* going into *Sensations,* or attracted to the neighbourhood for similar reasons" (para 209). As a result, the Board granted the liquor license with conditions; the primary one was that the adult entertainment privileges the cabaret held would be terminated. The risk of such exposure would create obvious harms in terms of public exposure. Here, the old community standards of tolerance of harm test is linked with the test from *Labaye.* Certainly, the legacy of the community standards test is germane in the regulatory licensing context where the *Labaye* test is invoked, even in cases like *Roberts (Re).*

In *R c Colalillo,* Mr. Colalillo was charged with three counts of first-degree murder. However, the accused had died in the early morning hours prior to his appearance in court, and as a result, all criminal proceedings pending against him were terminated (para 1). The issue before Cohen J. was to determine whether the court should order a permanent publication ban on a series of letters written by the deceased accused, detailing graphic information about the accused's fantasies for murder, rape and the sexual assault of women and children (para 3). Rather than drawing upon expert evidence, Cohen J. decided that the letters, through the *Labaye* framework, should be banned from public view, as Cohen J. indicated that "unwilling viewers" would face an intolerable risk—that is, the risk of harm from the explicit content of these letters that would otherwise be unavailable here "if a publication ban were not in effect" (para 30). Here, Cohen J. is essentially using the "affronts to liberty" prong of the *Labaye* harm test to justify a publication ban, thereby further instantiating the *Labaye* calculi into the realm of court procedure. The justice contended that the letters' publication "would reasonably expect to have a corrupting effect" (para 30) on public morality and, hence, implemented the publication ban. Moreover, Cohen J. further justified the ban on the attitudinal change prong of the *Labaye* calculus.

Interestingly, the courts "I know it when I see it" approach to harm analysis is still plausible under the risk of harm evidentiary exception when the *Labaye* court noted that "the more extreme the nature of the harm, the lower the degree of risk that may be required to permit use of the ultimate sanction of criminal law" (*Labaye* para 61). Remarkably, in this case the harms-based test affected a decision to ban publication.

Furthermore, in *R v Desmarais*, the accused was charged for acts of indecency in front of a child (para 73). In his analysis, Provost J. drew upon *Labaye* to suggest that although the accused was intoxicated, his intention was clearly to frighten the girl by exposing his penis to her. Provost J. indicated that no expert evidence was necessary to demonstrate that the accused's actions were indecent and "undermine[d] the physical and psychological integrity" of children in a properly functioning society (para 73).[16] Although few would question the severity of this conduct, it would appear that this is the type of risky behavior that would be akin to the *Labaye* terror attack scenario—one that avoids the need for proof of quantum of harm, as the *Labaye* court attests. Such cases, like *Desmarais*, illustrate the obviousness of the harms in circumstances of exposed genitalia, especially when children are confronted, or at risk of being confronted, by harm. Indeed, Provost J.'s assessment seems to pull upon the harm evidentiary exception discussed above, yet, at the same time, it draws upon the special protection put in place for child victims under the *Butler* harm tiers, of which the latter is located in the attitudinal change prong of the *Labaye* test.

Clearly, a reconsideration of whether expert opinion would always be necessary to determine if harm occurred, forms the basis of the many cases we explore both here and elsewhere (Jochelson and Gacek, "Reconstitutions"). As we see from the cases above, obviations of expert opinion in place of judicial discretion do not amount to a clear definition of harm and risk within a given case. For instance, in *R v Sheikh* the Superior Court of Justice in Ontario interpreted the *Labaye* framework and its evidentiary requirements. The accused was observed by police in a high school parking lot putting a condom on his penis and was charged and convicted of indecency. The appeal concerned whether the trial judge ought to have relied upon expert opinion of harm in rendering a guilty verdict. In rendering the appeal decision, Panet J. drew upon *Labaye* to indicate that *Labaye* established that the "requirement for evidence is … only established as a 'general rule'" but that "there are *obvious* cases where no one could argue that the conduct proved in evidence is compatible with the proper functioning of society" (*Sheikh* para 33). Therefore, per Panet J., there are cases that "are exceptions to the general rule, where no evidence is required because the *nature* and degree of harm which makes it incompatible with the proper functioning of society is *obvious*" (para 33; our emphasis).

Through the *Labaye* test, what causes harm to political values is now an open-ended question, which allows the judiciary to insert their own knowledge into the evidentiary gap to criminalize certain kinds of sexual practices and materials. Those who seek to govern themselves according to the logic of the *Labaye* court are now faced with the trouble of "how to determine what degree of dangerousness will give rise to a criminal prosecution" (Jochelson and Kramar, "Governing through Precaution" 305).

Similar to how Provost J. in *Desmarais* obviates expert evidence because of how unmistakably indecent the act was in the presence of children (para 74), Panet J. downplays the need for expert opinion in *Sheikh*, as in these circumstances "opinion evidence is superfluous and unnecessary" (para 36). However, we believe that this is precisely the point of expert evidence in these cases: when a trier of fact is left to render a verdict on a sexual practice (one of many sexual practices that have changed alongside sexual mores and perspectives), expert evidence allows the fact finder "to form a correct judgment on a matter if ordinary persons are unable to do so without the assistance of persons with special knowledge" (*Sheikh* para 34). Put differently, judicial knowledge, while significant, is neither equal nor translatable to the special knowledge of experts crafted in sexual politics, and what are obvious harms to some may be contrarily viewed by others. With the *Labaye* test as conveniently amorphous as it is, positioning (risk of) harm as a threat to political values allows judicial knowledge to spread through the field of sexual politics and criminalize what interferes with their vision of a properly functioning society.

Similar corrupting and risky collateral effects were also of issue for the judiciary in terms of those in the military serving overseas. For instance, Dutil C.M.J in *Cawthorne* interestingly drew upon *Labaye* to note how the accused's participation in an international exercise outside of Canada was an aggravating circumstance to consider upon sentencing:

The fact that most of the events that led to the charges took place while he was off-duty in Pearl Harbour does not diminish his responsibility. Committing service offences outside Canada inherently causes significant disturbances for the chain of command whether or not foreign authorities are involved in the investigative process or made aware of the incident.... The commission of criminal or disciplinary offences by service persons in operational settings outside of Canada will inevitably occur on occasion, but they contribute to *erod[ing] the state of readiness* and discipline. The facts of this case indicate that some of the offender's brothers-in-arms were very troubled by the discovery of child pornography material found on his iPhone, and *that has an impact* on morale and discipline. (R v Cawthorne para 18; our emphasis)

Here, Dutil C.M.J. is placing the harm to others in the second prong of *Labaye* harms, where attitudinal change occurs in the form of damage to morale and discipline. Arguably, this is a novel and thought-provoking application of *Labaye*-style harms going beyond indecency and obscenity contexts and within the military sentencing context.

Finally, in *R v Coldin*, the accused were charged with public nudity (para 16). The first accused, Mr. Coldin, was observed by witnesses walking down a highway, at a park, near a nudist camp and at Tim Horton's drive thru with his genitals and buttocks uncovered. Coldin was charged with four counts of public nudity. Coldin and the second accused, Mr. Cropper, were observed at an A & W drive thru by a witness who claimed they were both naked (para 22). Cropper was charged with one count of public nudity. Drawing upon *Labaye*, Douglas J. determined that Cropper was not guilty of public nudity as he had been wearing a thong at the drive thru (para 27), and the witness of Cropper gave inconsistent evidence about Cropper, suggesting that there was a reasonable doubt as to the extent of his nudity (para 145). In turning to Coldin, Douglas J. indicated that Coldin was never entirely naked as he had footwear and a cell phone holder on at the time (para 12). Although near nudity was certainly not a public norm, and Coldin's conduct created a significant risk of harm to the privacy rights of those forced to observe him (paras 114, 125), Douglas J. was not convinced that "the sort of harm to the privacy interests of the clothed or to society at large is so great as to be called incompatible with the proper functioning of society" (para 87). In addition, Douglas J. recognized that "there is no direct sort of evidence that suggests ... that public displays of nudity might or might not predispose others to anti-social behaviours" (para 74); however, the justice did note "the *potential* for tensioned responses—breaches of the peace—when such confrontations occur" (para 75; our emphasis).

Although the Crown failed to prove indecency, the embedded notion of public order supported a guilty verdict for Coldin. Therefore, even though the justice did not find proof of actual physical or psychological harm to those involved (para 115), "what perhaps needs somewhat more emphasis in the application of this *[Labaye]* test to matters of public order as opposed to public indecency is the notion that harm can befall not only individuals, but society." (para 117) As Douglas J. goes on to state:

> In the context of an application of the *[Labaye]* harm test under the rubric of assessing public order, the focus is not so much on how the players hurt themselves or those who stumble onto the activity in question. It, rather, is on the significantly more *ethereal notion* of "public order," or the "King's peace" etc. Given the very real and difficult philosophical issues of whether it makes any real sense to talk of the welfare of society as distinct from anything other than a consideration of the welfare of many particular individuals.
>
> The real issue, thus, in the context of applying a harm test developed in a significantly different context to the notion of public order is whether I can conclude that the Crown has proven a degree of harm incompatible with public order.... I believe they have. Here, I agree and have found in the context of the indecency test that the harm to the participants did not rise to the level of diagnosable psychological harm. However, these same and varied people were *clearly harmed to the degree that the social order or milieus in which they carried on their lives* was interrupted sufficiently to put a stop to how they were then and there carrying on their day to day business of driving on a public road, going for a swim, walking in a public park, serving coffee or selling hamburgers. In my view, our Queen's Peace was

clearly breached when the actions of the Defendants created such concern among and interference with these individuals. (paras 118–22, 126; our emphasis)

In sum, Douglas J. drew upon *Labaye* to query the harm imposed upon the public order rather than in indecency- and obscenity-based charges. Although the justice believed that Coldin did not engage in an indecent act that rose beyond the *Labaye* test's threshold, the ethereal notion of public order was used to substantiate harm done to societal welfare and to the potential risk such harm could impose upon others in society. The probable tension arising when others may be confronted, inspired or moved by near nude exposure, was deemed harmful enough by the justice to justify a public order conviction for Coldin. The court was able to use the *Labaye* calculus to establish a lower threshold of harm for public order offences, which has a striking and disturbingly similar resonance to the retired community standards of tolerance of harm test. Through the attitudinal- and liberty-based affronts of the *Labaye* harm test, Douglas J. noted that offences of public order required something less than the *Labaye* quantum of objective harm. Notwithstanding the fact that *Colden* represents another example of the pliability of *Labaye* in nonindecency/obscenity contexts, the case illustrates what happens when one lowers the harm quantum that *Labaye* attempts to create. Consequently, the harms-based test more closely resembles the community standards of tolerance of harm test, and no evidence is required to substantiate the subjective, judicial discretion imposed.

Discussion

Our analysis shows that the *Labaye* court has articulated a justification for censorship of indecency and obscenity inasmuch as the criminalization of this pair is not confined to a single logic. In other words, shifting towards the abstract values of liberalism and away from the values and opinions of the community, as the *Labaye* test has done, has the potential for the state to promote women's equality (see Craig, "Re-Interpreting")—clearly a welcomed start to fostering sex-positive narratives and the voices of sexual minorities. At the same time, however, the new test can easily be read in multiple directions, and we continue to wrestle with the ways in which broad understandings of harm and risk have been used to justify censorship or criminalization in the context of indecency and obscenity. If, as is the case in *Labaye*, society's proper functioning is constructed by reference to a universalized empirical standard, dissenting voices ultimately become obscured and the notion of the "proper functioning" of society is constructed mono-vocally; as such, it is only a court's voice that can have a true appreciation of the concerns underpinning (risk of) harms in society.

As mentioned above, indecency and obscenity jurisprudence is historically rooted in Victorian mores, often prudish when in the context of sexual expression and artistic depictions of sexuality that would corrupt the vulnerable classes; in resistance to this paradigm the doctrine of community standards emerged as a "liberalizing reaction" (Boyce 302; see also Gacek and Jochelson, "Animal Justice"; Jochelson and Gacek, "'Ruff' Justice"). Although subsequent legal evolution has diverged on a litany of issues, including "not just harm versus morality, but also national versus local standards, taste versus tolerance, and artistic merit," the overarching concern of the indecency and obscenity doctrines was to confront those acts, events, or materials that infringed upon the constitutional rights to freedom of expression and moral authority (Boyce 302-3). We remain concerned about whether such doctrines post-*Labaye* fulfill the acts they were established to serve.

Such concern also begs another question: now in the post-*Labaye* era, what is to be done about indecency and obscenity jurisprudence? Scholars, such as Bret Boyce and Julie Yan, contend that the elimination of these laws is warranted to modernize Canadian criminal law. In particular, Boyce contends that the invocation of the community standards test to suppress obscenity still has not appropriately reconciled with fundamental rights enshrined in the *Charter*, and that the substitution of a harm-based standard like the *Labaye* test merely delays a further resolution to the problem at hand. Furthermore, Yan takes an anticensorship feminist approach to the harms-based test and argues that obscenity law restricts artistic expression by "requiring an unsubstantiated risk of harm" (363) where no tangible evidence of actual harm is present, with detrimental effects to artists and their artwork. (See also Jochelson et al. for a further discussion of unsubstantiated risks of harm in relation to precautionary and precriminal ethics in the

Canadian criminal justice system.) Yan argues that by censoring materials based on intangible risks of harm, consequently, "we stop the conversation of violence and silence and those who try to confront it," and unsubstantiated evidence "limits the expression of ideas and silences the very voices that can raise awareness to social change" (365).

As we have stated elsewhere, after *Labaye,* the posited harms-based test became a legal means to assess risk, where the risk is not regarded as intrinsically real "but as a particular way in which problems are viewed or imagined or dealt with" (Jochelson et al. 53, citing Rose et al. 18). The flexibility of harm within *Labaye* allows it to act like a "veritable joker card" with certain risks being much more readily assumed to cause harm to society (Valverde 184). Once we supplant this argument with our examination of how courts have applied the harms-based test since *Labaye,* our findings could not be any closer to this reality. In the worst scenario, the *Labaye* test widens the boundaries of state intervention "because of *perceived* threats to abstract political values like autonomy, liberty and equality, irrespective of any actual or tangible harms caused" (Jochelson et al. 53). Post-*Labaye*, we are left with a jurisprudential situation in which a court's perception of what may cause harm to political values by a given sexual circumstance is a justification for state power. Risk becomes a proxy for offence—already a problematized justification for criminalization. Through the *Labaye* decision, the judiciary is provided greater discretionary power to express the obvious risk of harm within the expression, conduct, or materials in question and obviating the need for factual evidence of this outcome (Jochelson and Kramar, "Governing Obscenity").

Furthermore, at its least effective, the *Labaye* harms-based test fosters opaqueness and fogginess (Jochelson and Gacek, "Reconstitutions"). This type of abstract prudential reasoning allows courts to draw conclusions in the absence of lived experiences and in recognition of sexual identities (Jochelson and Kramar, *Sex*). If the courts' willingness is to see harm as comprised of possibilities of unformed risks, this conception of harm is once again rooted in a judge's fear of harm or in threats to political values that need to be protected for the benefit of societal good. In either case, harm is neither purely objective nor empirical. In both cases, harm becomes subjective, abstract, and concomitantly ethereal. Despite the SCC's demand in *Labaye* for positive knowledge of (risk of) harm, *Labaye* is much like its legal predecessors; it remains an autocratic test devoted mainly to "protecting a normative vision of society" (Jochelson and Kramar, *Sex* 60) rather than promoting human sexuality, freedom of expression, and the creation, production and dissemination of materials that have educational/artistic merit. After *Labaye,* when the loss of context combines with risk, greater concerns arise of whether we see a return to the determination of indecency and obscenity with the "I know it when I see it" approach to legal analysis, and the unfortunate, key discursive turn being that "it" is now a muddied conception of (risk of) harm.

In effect, the *Labaye* test links criminal regulation to liberal moral and political principles—a move that has the potential to limit freedom by appealing to uninterrogated social norms (Jochelson and Kramar, *Sex* 60). A society constructed in such a way is threatened by indecency and obscenity, and inequalities and marginalization are not seen as structural social phenomenon but rather risks to prevent at all costs. Inconsistencies in the judicial approach in applying *Labaye* and in comprehending harm and society's proper functioning was the problem that *Labaye* aimed to solve. In our view, there remains scant evidence that the case of *Labaye* succeeded in its venture.[17]

Conclusion

This chapter was an attempt to stimulate attention to the steps taken by courts to develop indecency and obscenity jurisprudence in Canada. Although we applaud the SCC's retirement of the community standards of tolerance test in favour of a modern iteration, we continue to query the direction the *Labaye* test is taking us. Where some may view the harms-based test as liberating, we would continue to urge the reader to interrogate more fully the subtexts of the *Labaye* court's reasoning. As this chapter has demonstrated, we lament how the current harms-based test has been implemented within case adjudication and treatment since its inception in *Labaye*. As we have suggested elsewhere, it is neither our intention nor desire for the discussions surrounding indecency, obscenity, and harms-based testing "to [become] stunted as we lie in wait for the next important Supreme Court of Canada case or the next activist cause" (Jochelson, "After" 744). Rather, this chapter supplements our prior research in this area of law and the oscillating relationship between society and law, asserting that since *Labaye*, we still have no clarity on the meaning of harm in the post-*Charter* era. Such an assertion also begs the question of not only what harm is but what harm could represent going forwards and what these definitions will mean to our current and prospective delineations of human decency, dignity, and sexual autonomy (Plaxton). The use of risk of harm as a factor to substantiate guilt in any case before the court creates more opportunity for state intervention to criminalize conduct and censor sexually explicit materials, yet concerns remain about the negative impact of criminalization and its effects on individuals and sexual communities of interest. As Richard Jochelson and Kirsten Kramar contend, "when we protect values rather than people, the context of sexual expression or sexual conduct is utterly lost" (*Sex* 72).

Post-*Labaye*, there continues to be a presumption of harm on the basis of risk analytics, and this occurs at a cost to evidentiary strictures (Jochelson and Kramar, *Sex* 74). In fact, the evidentiary vacuum in *Labaye* does more than protect a prospective normative vision of society. As the court itself states, if the *Labaye* vision of harm is utilized to ensure the proper functioning of society, the courts maintain a status quo that holds issues of sex and sexuality at arm's length and sublimates social concerns through overreaching constructs of harm; problematically, that same normative societal construction now becomes possible across areas of speech and conduct that transcend the sexually illicit (Gacek and Jochelson, "Placing"; Jochelson and Gacek, "Reconstitutions"). Further legal clarity and the development of jurisprudence, especially surrounding the definition of harm, should be warmly welcomed. The imagined effects of indecency and obscenity (potential attitudinal harm) as the basis for penal sanction should not empower the judiciary to expand the harms-based test to imagined threats of harm, nor should the judiciary be afforded the further luxury of avoiding any criticism of the relationship between punishment and the protection of constitutional values. Limiting the test to use in indecency and obscenity-based offences would be a good step in the right direction to ameliorate the continued obfuscation of harm in juridical analysis. In addition, it would be beneficial to see declaratory prose from the SCC that the *Labaye* harm test is not the arbiter of harm assessment in Canada. It could then be possible to recede to a more modest advocacy goal—problematizing the test in the context of sexual conduct and publications and/or materials.

Endnotes

1. The sections focusing upon the historical development of Canada's obscenity and indecency laws build on earlier versions of our work. However, this chapter adds substantially to the findings with newer data, case information, and theoretical analyses.

2. As we do not have the space here to fully engage with all applications of the *Labaye* test since 2005, we provide a more thorough discussion of post-*Labaye* applications in a twin study that resulted in a paper (Jochelson and Gacek, "Reconstitutions"). In effect, this chapter comprises some of the findings found in our sister paper.

3. Section 163(8) of the *Criminal Code* refers to the definition of an obscene publication: "Any publication a dominant characteristic of which is the undue exploitation of sex, or of sex and any one or more of the following subjects, namely, crime, horror, cruelty and violence, shall be deemed to be obscene."

4. In *Labaye* (para 55) McLachlin C.J.C. (as she then was) cited, with approval, Friedman J.'s nearly half-century old observation, suggesting that the standard of what is acceptable in interpersonal and sexual activities has evolved over time. As Freedman. J states:

    Times change, and ideas change with them. Compared to the Victorian era this is a liberal age in which we live. One manifestation of it is the relative freedom with which the whole question of sex is discussed. In books, magazines, movies, television, and sometimes even in parlour conversations, various aspects of sex are made the subject of comment, with a candour that in an earlier day would have been regarded as indecent and intolerable. We cannot and should not ignore these present-day attitudes when we face the question of whether [sexual materials] are obscene according to our criminal law. (*Dominion News & Gifts* paras 116-17)

5. As we indicate elsewhere (Jochelson, "After" 748), we propose to use the term queer to refer to and recognize any/all of the following: people who identify themselves as gay, lesbian, bisexual, questioning, transgender, transsexual, two spirit, and intersex.

6. RSC 1985, (2nd Supp.), c. 1, section 152(3), provides that "in any proceeding under this Act, the burden of proof in any question relating to ... the compliance with any of the provisions of [this] Act or the regulations in respect of any goods" lies on the importer.
7. The factums of the interveners were diverse, varied, and highly contextualized, and regrettably we could not do justice to their many arguments within the scope of this chapter. For an articulation of the specific minutiae of each intervener, see Karen Busby, "*Little Sister's v Canada*: What Did the Queer-Sensitive Interveners Argue about Equality Rights and Free Expression?" *Law in Society: Canadian Readings*, 2nd edition, edited by Brian Burtch & Nick Larsen, Thompson Canada, 2006.
8. Section 163(1) of the *Criminal Code* refers to corrupting morals: "Everyone commits an offence who (a) makes, prints, publishes, distributes, circulates, or has in his [sic] possession for the purpose of publication, distribution, or circulation any obscene written matter, picture, model, phonograph record or other thing whatever; or (b) makes, prints, publishes, distributes, sells or has in his [sic] possession for the purpose of publication, distribution, or circulation a crime comic." Section 210(1) of the *Code* then referred to the keeping of a common bawdy-house: "Everyone who keeps a common bawdy-house is guilty of an indictable offence and liable to imprisonment for a term not exceeding two years." The provision and the definition of the term "bawdy-house" were repealed in June 2019. Bill C-75, which in part sought to amend the *Criminal Code*, by repealing bawdy-house law received Royal Assent on June 21, 2019 (see https://www.parl.ca/LegisInfo/BillDetails.aspx?Bill=C75&Language=E&Mode=1&Parl=42&Ses=1.).
9. It does not indicate in *Blais-Pelletier* why the trial judge did not have *Mara* or *Tremblay* to rely upon for a decision.
10. Referred to as section 197 prior to amendment and repeal of the provision.
11. RSC, 1985, c. C-46.
12. Per McLachlin C.J.C.:

    Incompatibility with the proper functioning of society is more than a test of tolerance. The question is not what individuals or the community think about the conduct, but whether permitting it engages a harm that threatens the basic functioning of our society. This ensures in part that the harm be related to a formally recognized value, at step one. But beyond this it must be clear beyond a reasonable doubt that the conduct, not only by its nature but also in degree, rises to the level of threatening the proper functioning of our society.

Whether it does so must be determined by reference to the values engaged by the particular kind of harm at stake. If the harm is based on the threat to autonomy and liberty arising from unwanted confrontation by a particular kind of sexual conduct, for example, the Crown must establish a real risk that the way people live will be significantly and adversely affected by the conduct. The number of people unwillingly exposed to the conduct and the circumstances in which they are exposed to it are critical under this head of harm. If the only people involved in or observing the conduct were willing participants, indecency on the basis of this harm will not be made out. (*Labaye* paras 56-57)

13. Per McLachlin C.J.C.:

    Where actual harm is not established and the Crown is relying on risk, the test of incompatibility with the proper functioning of society requires the Crown to establish a significant risk. Risk is a relative concept. The more extreme the nature of the harm, the lower the degree of risk that may be required to permit use of the ultimate sanction of criminal law. Sometimes, a small risk can be said to be incompatible with the proper functioning of society. For example, the risk of a terrorist attack, although small, might be so devastating in potential impact that using the criminal law to counter the risk might be appropriate. However, in most cases, the nature of the harm engendered by sexual conduct will require at least a probability that the risk will develop to justify convicting and imprisoning those engaged in or facilitating the conduct. (*Labaye* para 61)

14. Under section 197, now repealed, of the *Code*, a "common bawdy-house means" for the practice of acts of indecency, a place that is kept or occupied or resorted to by one or more persons.

15. Section 197 (now repealed) of the *Code*, at para 67. An identical approach was also applied in the companion case, *R. v Kouri*, 2005 SCC 81, [2005] 3 SCR 789.

16. For another example see *R v Sheikh* 2008 [2008] OJ No 1544 (QL); 77 WCB (2d) 252.
17. In fact, we note elsewhere that the *Labaye* harm test seems to have moved to other areas of law unrelated to obscenity/indecency in some adjudications, which provides an interesting analytic for the measuring of harm across a variety of case treatments (Jochelson and Gacek, "Reconstitutions").

Works Cited
Secondary Sources

Boyce, Bret. "Obscenity and Community Standards." *The Yale Journal of International Law*, vol. 33, 2008, pp. 299-368.

CBC News. "Lap Dancing Legal, Top Court Says." *CBC News*, 14 December 1999, www.cbc.ca/news/canada/lap-dancing-legal-top-court-says-1.185098. Accessed 8 May 2019.

Cossman, Brenda. "Feminist Fashion or Morality in Drag? The Sexual Subtext of the Butler Decision." *Bad Attitude/s on Trial: Pornography, Feminism, and the Butler Decision*, edited by Brenda Cossman et al., University of Toronto Press, 1997, pp. 107-151.

Craig, Elaine. "Re-Interpreting the Criminal Regulation of Sex Work in Light of *R. c. Labaye*." *Canadian Criminal Law Review*, vol. 12, no. 3, 2008, pp. 327-51.

Craig, Elaine. "Laws of Desire: The Political Morality of Public Sex." *McGill Law Review*, vol. 54, 2009, pp. 355-85.

Gacek, James, and Richard Jochelson. "Placing 'Bestial' Acts in Canada: Legal Meanings of 'Bestiality' and Judicial Engagements with Sociality." *Annual Review of Interdisciplinary Justice Research*, vol. 6, 2017, pp. 236-61.

Gacek, James, and Richard Jochelson. "'Animal Justice' and Sexual (Ab)use: Consideration of Legal Recognition of Sentience for Animals in Canada." *Manitoba Law Journal*, vol. 40, no. 3, 2017, pp. 335-62.

Heath, Deana. *Purifying Empire: Obscenity and the Politics of Moral Regulation in Britain, India and Australia*. Cambridge University Press, 2010.

Jochelson, Richard. "After *Labaye:* The Harm Test of Obscenity, the New Judicial Vacuum, and the Relevance of Familiar Voices." *Alberta Law Review*, vol. 46, no. 3, 2009, pp. 741-67.

Jochelson, Richard. "Let Law Be Law, and Let Us Critique: Teaching Law to Undergraduate Students of Criminal Justice." *The Annual Review of Interdisciplinary Justice Research*, vol. 4, 2014, pp. 234-45.

Jochelson, Richard, and James Gacek. "'Ruff' Justice: Canine Cases and Judicial Law-Making as an Instrument of Change." *Animal Law Review*, vol. 24, no. 1, 2018, pp. 171-95.

Jochelson, Richard, and James Gacek. "Reconstitutions of Harm: Novel Applications of the *Labaye* Test Since 2005." *Alberta Law Review*, vol. 56, no. 4, 2019, pp. 991-1038.

Jochelson, Richard, and Kirsten Kramar. "Practicing Justice by Practicing Method: A Brief Rethinking of Feminist Analytics of Obscenity and Indecency Law in Canada." *The Annual Review of Interdisciplinary Justice Research*, vol. 1, 2010, pp. 26-44.

Jochelson, Richard, and Kirsten Kramar. "Governing through Precaution to Protect Equality and Freedom: Obscenity and Indecency Law in Canada after *R. v Labaye* [2005]." *Canadian Journal of Sociology*, vol. 36, no. 4, 2011a, pp. 283-312.

Jochelson, Richard, and Kirsten Kramar. *Sex and the Supreme Court: Obscenity and Indecency Law in Canada.* Fernwood Publishing, 2011.

Jochelson, Richard, and Kirsten Kramar. "Governing Obscenity and Indecency in Canada." *Locating Law: Race, Class, Gender, Sexuality Connections*, 3rd ed., edited by Elizabeth Comack, Fernwood Publishing, 2014, pp. 294-314.

Jochelson, Richard, et al. *Criminal Law and Precrime: Legal Studies in Canadian Punishment and Surveillance in Anticipation of Criminal Guilt.* London: Routledge, 2017.

Johnson, Kirsten. "Obscenity, Gender and the Law." *Locating Law: Race/Class/Gender Connections*, edited by Elizabeth Comack, Fernwood Publishing, 1999, pp. 289-313.

Plaxton, Michael. "What Butler Did." *Supreme Court Law Review*, vol. 57, pp. 317-35.

Rose, Nikolas, et al. "Governmentality." The University of Sydney, Sydney Law School, Legal Studies Research Paper No. 09/94.

Valverde, Mariana. "The Harms of Sex and the Risks of Breasts: Obscenity and Indecency in Canadian Law." *Social & Legal Studies*, vol. 8, no. 2, 1999, pp. 181-97.

Yan, Julie. "Art in the Dichotomy of Freedom of Expression & Obscenity: An Anti-Censorship Perspective." *Manitoba Law Journal*, vol. 40, no. 3, 2017, pp. 363-87.

Jurisprudence

Little Sisters Book and Art Emporium v Canada (Minister of Justie), 2000 2 SCR 1120, 2000 SCC 69 [*Little Sisters*].

Marceau c R, 2010 QCCA 1155 [*Marceau*].

Roberts Re, 2006 NSUARB 46 [*Roberts*].

R v Blais-Pelletier, 1999 3 SCR 863 [*Blais-Pelletier*].

R v Brodie, 1962 32 DLR (2d) SCC 39 [*Brodie*].

R v Butler, 1992 1 SCR 452, 89 DLR (4th) 449 [*Butler*].

R v Cawthorne WK (Ordinary Seaman), 2014 CM 1014 [*Cawthorne*].

R c Colalillo, 2006 QCCS 7903 [*Colalillo*].

R v Coldin, 2012 ONCJ 1009 [*Coldin*].

R c Desmarais, 2008 QCCQ 7959 [*Desmarais*].

R v Dominion News & Gifts (1962) Ltd. 1964, SCR 251, [1963] 42 WWR 65 (CA) [*Dominion News & Gifts (1962) Ltd.*].

R v Kouri, 2004 QCCA 2619 [*Kouri*].

R v Kouri, 2005 SCC 81, 3 SCR 789 [*Kouri*].

R v Labaye, 2005 SCC 80, [2005] 3 SCR 728 [*Labaye*].

R v Mara, 1997 2 SCR 630 [*Mara*].

R v Ponomarev, 2007 ONCJ 271 [*Ponomarev*].

R v Sheikh, 2008 OJ No 1544 (QL); 77 WCB (2d) 252 [*Sheikh*].

R v Towne Cinema Theatres Ltd., 1985, 1 SCR 494 [*Towne Cinema Theatres Ltd.*].

R v Tremblay, 1993 2 SCR 932 [*Tremblay*].

Regina v Hicklin, 1868 LR 3 QB 360 [*Hicklin*].

Legislation

Bill C-75. An Act to Amend the Criminal Code, the Youth Criminal Justice Act and other Acts and to Make Consequential Amendments to other Acts. 2019. c 25. 42nd Parliament, 1st Session.

Canadian Charter of Rights and Freedoms, Part 1 of the *Constitution Act, 1982,* being Schedule B to the *Canada Act 1982* (UK), 1982, c-11 [*Charter*].

Criminal Code R.S.C. 1985, C-46 [*Criminal Code*].

Chapter Two

Sex Work in Canada: Beginnings, *Bedford*, and Beyond[1]

James Gacek and Richard Jochelson

Introduction

Since the inception of the *Canadian Charter of Rights and Freedoms*, there has been an increasing debate regarding the legitimacy of sex work in Canada. Scholars have made arguments for and against sex work, underscoring this work not only as a moral issue, but also as one of safety and equality for its workers (Aprol). Although the risks associated with sex work are not a modern-day occurrence, the dangers that come with one engaging and/or participating in sex work have become more evident. This chapter examines the jurisprudence of sex work in Canada and traces out the factual, historical, legislative, and socio-political shifts in how sex work has been perceived and treated thus far. This chapter will also look at where such perceptions and treatments are taking us. Preconceived notions of sex work, whether they exist on the grounds of morality or safety, have the potential to harm those who work in this industry. Although recent attempts to reform sex work jurisprudence in Canada have incrementally shifted to try to protect sex workers from harm, such empathetic shifts by Canadian governments towards sex workers has not always been the case.

We begin this chapter by outlining the early historical and legislative developments of sex work jurisprudence in Canada; we briefly consider the vagrancy and solicitation laws existing in the years prior to and during Confederation as well as before the initiation of the *Charter*. Following this, we explore different models of sex work regulation, including a review of the Nordic model, a variant of which is currently implemented in Canadian sex work jurisprudence. We then turn our attention to the *Prostitution Reference,* the first time in Canadian history when the Supreme Court of Canada (SCC) was asked to examine the constitutionality of certain provisions of the antiprostitution *Criminal Code*. Subsequently, we trace the judicial rationale underpinning sex work jurisprudence until the ground-breaking *Bedford* case—the SCC case that infamously resulted in several *Criminal Code* provisions dealing with sex work to be deemed unconstitutional. The Harper government's legislative response to this case is discussed, coupled with our assessment of the Trudeau government's options within the new criminalization regime. A discussion of potential law reform opportunities for Canadian sex work jurisprudence going forwards concludes the chapter.

Making Sense of Sex Work

Merging the recent influence of labour studies with the sociology of sex work reveals cogent insights into how sex and sexuality discursively shift how we view ourselves as social beings within social phenomena. Indeed, reconsidering sex work jurisprudence is more than an academic exercise; it also allows us to query how sex workers make sense of their work as work. For example, Chris Bruckert and Collette Parent argue that focusing on the labour side of sex work allows researchers "to step outside of the traditional criminological analyses of deviance to examine these jobs as jobs" (97). In this light, there is significant theoretical and methodological room to manoeuvre in the sociology of sex work—room in which our perspective of the criminal law can constellate together and gain a strong foothold to critique how the law understands sex work in Canada and the sociality underpinning sex work jurisprudence.

What lies at the heart of sociological understandings of sexuality is the notion that social change shapes sexual identity and conduct.

Anthony Giddens explores this idea in his comments on what he calls "decentered sexuality": forms of intimacy that are not bound by tradition, family, gender roles, or custom. In a similar vein, Zygmunt Bauman suggests that postmodern uses of sex are "self-sufficiently erotic" insofar as sexual pleasures are sought for their own sake at one's convenience.[2] More middle-class people than ever engage in sex work, partly as a result of these understandings (for example, see Bernstein). Elizabeth Bernstein conceptualizes how broad economic shifts translate into relations between sex workers and their clientele and argues that currently sex is "available for sale and purchase as readily as any other form of commercially packaged leisure activity" (7). Such a shift towards sex work and selling sex for the middle class is a part of a move "to a recreational model of sexual intimacy" (Bernstein 141). Taken together, we see how societal shifts mitigate certain understandings of how sex and sexuality are conceived by and through the law and how such concepts are then developed into understandings of the buying and selling of sexual activities in society. Although understanding sex work as an economic activity is one way of understanding the phenomena, it does not get at the historical, social, and legal developments that have comprehensively shaped the sex work jurisprudence existing in Canada, a discussion to which we now turn.

Early Historical and Legislative Developments of Sex Work in Canada: Vagrancy and Solicitation Law

Determining what is justice and how it applies to sex work and the law is still a contentious topic (Shaver, "Sex Work and the Law"). Indeed, this is unquestionably the case for sex work, as guaranteeing justice for sex workers working in the industry is particularly problematic. Too often, such a guarantee for sex workers involves major discrepancies on moral, social, and political grounds. The buying and selling of sexual services between consenting adults continues to be an issue of contention in Canada and, unfortunately, has been for well over 250 years. Historically, sex work (prostitution)[3] was not an offence in Canadian criminal law, but this lawful work was surrounded by numerous criminal prohibitions—notably, the offences related to bawdy-houses (now mainly repealed), living on the avails of the prostitution, and communicating in public for the purpose of engaging in prostitution (as either buyer or seller) (Hamish 71-72). Grounded in British legal tradition, one of the earliest laws related to sex work was embedded within the *Nova Scotia Act of 1759* (Shaver, "The Regulation of Prostitution"; "*Bill C-36*"). This law made street solicitation a status offence of vagrancy for women unable to provide a "good account" of themselves, and annoying or disruptive behaviour did not qualify as a prerequisite for detention. Simply put, the purpose of the law was to provide police with the power to get sex workers off the street when necessary as well as to alleviate land use conflicts and problems of public order associated with the operation of brothels (Shaver, "Sex Work and the Law"). Indeed, several municipalities and provinces enacted similar laws prior to the *Criminal Code*'s passage in 1892. As Angela Campbell indicates, Canada's first *Criminal Code* "criminalized a 'nightwalker' or 'common prostitute' in a public place if she did not, when asked, provide a satisfactory account of herself" (30). In response to reformers anxious to abolish such a "social evil," in the mid-nineteenth-century, more complex provisions designed to protect women from "the procurer, pimp, and brothel keeper" were introduced at Confederation in 1867 (Shaver 2). Although there were no decisive changes in enforcement patterns, such provisions were extended and strengthened in the decades that followed. Between 1865 and 1970, officials recognized the futility of criminalizing sex workers under a moral rubric and, instead, opted to regulate sex work through a public health approach (Backhouse). Police became enforcers of the *Contagious Disease Act* and "were authorized to detain women suspected of prostitution for medical examination" (Backhouse 235). Furthermore, the sex trade was also "regarded by judges and police as a convenient outlet for male sexual needs" (Brock 82). As Frances Shaver indicates, the clients of street-based sex workers continued to fall outside the purview of the law, convictions for keepers and frequenters of bawdy-houses were sporadic, and conviction rates for procuring sex were very small. In effect, the ones in society who were the most penalized by these provisions were the street-based women workers themselves ("Sex Work and the Law"; see also McLaren). In response to a recommendation by the Royal Commission on the Status of Women, coupled with pressure from women's and civil liberties groups, in 1972, the vagrancy law was repealed and replaced by a soliciting law. Regrettably, the wording left unclear whether it applied to both sellers and buyers or just sellers. Furthermore, this unclear wording left police chiefs, criminal justice practitioners, and municipal politicians perplexed and, ultimately, made it more difficult to regulate street-based sex work, thereby increasing its visibility (Lowman).

Nevertheless, there have been several other attempts to take seriously the fundamental issues of importance to sex workers since the repealing of vagrancy law and the insertion of soliciting law, including the right to safe and secure sex work environments (Shaver, "Sex Work and the Law"). The Special Committee on Pornography and Prostitution (1985) and The House of Commons Subcommittee on Solicitation Laws (2005/2006) are two examples of such attempts. The former was struck in 1983 to investigate the economic and social determinants of sex work and provide appropriate recommendations, whereas the latter was created in 2003 to review the solicitation laws and recommend changes to improve the safety of sex workers and communities at large. Unfortunately, the outcomes of these two initiatives were not successful (Shaver, "Sex Work and the Law"). As significant as these committees were to critically discussing such issues, sex workers and their families were still at risk, and the underlying economic and social conditions had not been fully addressed (Shaver; Canadian HIV/AIDS Legal Network; Campbell).

Presenting Positions on Sex Work: Criminalization, Legalization/Decriminalization, and the Nordic Model

As with other issues pertaining to sex and sexuality, "the prostitution discourse is largely concerned with determining whether this social practice is exploitative, empowering, or a consequence of immorality" (Mathieson et al. 367-68). Three primary legislative responses to sex work emerged in response to these salient positions: (1) criminalization; (2) legalization/decriminalization; and (3) the Nordic model. Although the political regulation of sex work will vary according to each nation's underlying economic and social justice commitments, it is important to examine all three models to illustrate their relative successes and failures in greater detail.

In a criminalization regime, all aspects of sex work are considered illegal, including (1) brothel keeping or pandering (or knowingly encouraging or compelling a person to sell sex in exchange for money);

(2) pimping, which is the act of receiving something of value knowing that it was earned through a person's sex work; (3) the act of sex itself (i.e., exchanging sexual acts for money); and (4) the purchase of sexual contact. Underpinning this approach is a belief that sex work is a public nuisance and/or a consequence of immoral decision making requiring regulation through public order offences. Through the criminalization model, each aspect is technically illegal and is subject to regulation as a criminal offence. Largely treated as an issue of traditional morality, and guided by Judeo-Christian ethics, women within this regime are seen as the gatekeepers of sexual responsibility. Women are thought to wield significant sexual power over men; they choose to tempt men into committing immoral sexual acts and, therefore, should ultimately be held accountable for their criminal actions. In this context, criminalization upholds the morality of society and perpetuates a vision of sex work as a victimless crime, committed by immoral, sexual deviants. Although the onus of criminalization laws target the sellers (predominately women) rather than the buyers (predominantly men), punishment of the seller fails to acknowledge that "conscription into prostitution is overwhelmingly driven by a combination of coercive factors, including racist and heterosexist social structures, homelessness, poverty, drug addiction, unemployment, childhood sexual abuse, and experiences of violence" (Mathieson et al. 375).

Under a legalization/decriminalization[4] regime, sex work arises from a personal choice, is an indication of women's empowerment, and is a business agreement between two consenting adults with equal power. Although local ordinances may be in place to restrict sex work in certain areas or communities, the national legalization and decriminalization of sex work activities remove the legal barriers impeding the growth of the legal commercial sex industry.

In legalization regimes, such as the Netherlands and Germany, the government takes an active role in regulating sex work through labour laws that legalize the majority of brothel ownership, pimping, and the buying and selling of sex for money (Mathieson et al. 378). Legalization could include the promotion of the sex work industry from municipal and national governments, as they embed a "prostitution economy into a country's market structure," which enables the country to derive major tax and tourism revenue from the commercial sex work industry and advance profit goals for such governments (379).

In decriminalization regimes, such as New Zealand, Denmark, and parts of Australia, governments eliminate penalties within all or some parts of the commercial sex work industry, and the enforcement of laws pertaining to sex work is largely transferred from law enforcement to local council authorities. Under this approach, the objective of local councils is to dedicate funding and administrative staff to "finding ways to regulate the industry without police authority or resources to investigate, penalize, or shut down brothel owners and pimps" (Mathieson et al. 380). Countries that decriminalize may collect tax revenue through administration regulations and benefit from sex work tourism.

In the legalization/decriminalization context, a legal system that protects a woman's right to choose to work in the commercial sex industry provides access to work benefits not provided in the illicit sex work market, allegedly protects women from the violence associated with street solicitation, and normalizes and removes the social stigma of sex work at large. However, legislation in such regimes rely "on the goodwill of brothel owners and buyers, often exploiters themselves, to prioritize reporting abuse over profit margins and personal sexual satisfaction" (Mathieson et al. 387). Furthermore, the licensing and inspecting of brothels provides "no true guarantee that women will not face abuse" as brothel owners and buyers "may choose to not report the abuse that they witness" or partake in against the prostituted individual (Mathieson et al. 387). One conclusion is that the legal commercial sex industry acts as a cover for the illicit industry, making it harder to track the illegal market (Mathieson et al. 388).

Finally, under the Nordic model, a criminalization legislative objective proceeds from an understanding of sex work as gendered violence, which differs substantially from those that identify sex work as a consequence of female immorality or legal labour. First introduced in Sweden, the Nordic model penalizes "those with power who demand the prostitution transaction, [namely] the buyer with money or the pimp/brothel owner profiting" (Mathieson et al. 397). In a Nordic regime, governments view sex work as a consequence of structural injustices, such as racism, sexism, cissexism, and heterosexism; female sex workers are constantly under duress as they face violence or threat of violence by their male pimps; this risk is not incidental but rather arises from the woman's literal commodification.

Such commodification abrogates a person's subjecthood by reducing them to the status of a sex object; here, a person is comprised of sexual parts, which are purchasable and exchangeable on the market. In essence, the normalization of sex work as legal work can be significant in increasing the market potential of a sex work economy but as dictated by capitalism, male brothel owners, and pimps.

Brothel owners and pimps, acting as employers, may subject their employees, in large part women, to harms or violence in a never-ending drive to increase profit and secure clientele. This approach views the sex work industry as an unacceptable practice rather than a market opportunity, especially as this practice "thrives off of the social inequality between women and men, adults and children, white people and people of colour, [and] wealthy and colonized nations" (Mathieson et al. 397). By interweaving social and political policy, the model, in theory, attempts to advance egalitarianism, promotes social service supports to survivors of sex work, and criminalizes those abusing their greater socioeconomic power to buy sex.

In accordance with the social demographic drive to agitate for social betterment, the original intention of the Nordic model was not punitive; instead, the model intended to change social norms that promoted and enabled sex work to flourish in society. There are several directives associated with the Nordic model, including (1) the reduction of the number of sellers (predominately women) in sex work; (2) the reduction of the size of the trafficking industry; (3) the reduction of the number of buyers (predominately men); (4) the reduction of the number of pimps (also predominately men) and sex clubs; (5) the further education of other countries about the Nordic model; and (6) the promotion of women's equality more generally (Mathieson et al. 401). Although the model acknowledges that some individuals may choose to remain in sex work, the policies underpinning this model should be constructed so as to enable individuals who wish to leave the industry the opportunity to do so safely, securely and legally.[5]

In the aftermath of the *Bedford* SCC decision, the Harper government sought to pass new laws based upon the Nordic model, which would arguably address the concerns outlined in the decision and reduce the demand for sex work in Canada (as discussed below). However, whereas supporters of the new laws argue that "by targeting the buyers of sex, the laws will reduce the demand for sex work and work toward ending what they believe is a form of sexual exploitation, which disproportionally impacts women and girls," critics indicate that these laws merely criminalize sex work to an extent similar to the *Criminal Code* provisions pre-*Bedford* (Ontario Women's Justice Network).

Prostitution Reference: Challenging the *Criminal Code*'s Prostitution Provisions

An understanding of the *Prostitution Reference* (1990) is essential to appreciating the issues raised in *Bedford*. In 1990, the SCC upheld the constitutionality of both the bawdy-house and communication provisions of the *Criminal Code*. A bawdy-house was defined in section 197(1) of the *Code* (now repealed) as "a place that is kept or occupied, or resorted to by one or more persons, for the purpose of prostitution or to practice acts of indecency" and a number of actions involving bawdy-houses attracted criminal sanction. The communication provision in section 213 of the *Code* prohibited stopping or attempting to stop a motor vehicle or a person, or impeding access to or from a place for the purposes of prostitution. As a result, virtually wherever a sex worker chooses to work (whether in call or out call) may have made them responsible under the criminal law.

In the *Prostitution Reference*, the SCC was asked to determine whether the bawdy-house provision (section 193, subsequently the repealed section 210, which defines this location by virtue of its indecency component) and the provision dealing with communication for the purposes of prostitution (section 195(1)(c), now section 213(1)(c)), separately or in combination, were a violation of subsection 2(b) (free expression) or section 7 (the right to life, liberty or security of the person) of the *Charter*. Writing for the majority, Chief Justice Dickson concluded that both provisions were consistent with section 7 (para 21). While the liberty interests were engaged by the possibility of imprisonment, the provisions could not be determined to be sufficiently "unfair as to violate the principles of fundamental justice" (para 19). Furthermore, the SCC majority found that the bawdy-house provision did not infringe on a person's right to freedom of expression (para 1). With respect to the communication provision, the majority determined that although there was an infringement of section 2(b)'s right of freedom of expression, it could be upheld as a justifiable limit (para 11). Chief Justice Dickson described the legislative objective of the communicating provision as suppressing the social nuisance caused by public solicitation and keeping it out of the public view (para 2).

Justice Lamer's opinion in the *Prostitution Reference,* despite reaching similar conclusions, branched into a discussion of economic liberty, which highlights the difference between what the SCC was asked to decide in 1990 and *Bedford* (Powell). Writing for himself, Justice Lamer argued that the impugned provisions violated liberty under section 7 because sex workers were unable to "exercise their chosen profession," which violated their right to security of the person by rendering them unable to provide for themselves (*Prostitution Reference* para 49). Although Justice Lamer could not accept that the infringement was contrary to the principles of fundamental justice, he argued that section 7 would be triggered "when the state restricts individuals' security of the person by interfering with, or removing from them, control over their physical or mental integrity," (para 68) an argument similarly made in *Bedford*. Furthermore, Justice Lamer characterized the legislative objective of the communication provision differently from the majority, with a definition that goes beyond:

> ... merely preventing the nuisance of traffic congestion and general street order. There is the additional objective of minimizing the public exposure of an activity that is degrading to women with the hope that potential entrants in the trade can be deflected at an early stage and of restricting the blight that is associated with public solicitation for the purposes of prostitution." (para 97)

Indeed, his definition extended to "general confusion and congestion that is accompanied by an increase in related criminal activity such as possession and trafficking of drugs, violence and pimping" (para 95).

Finally, in her section 7 analysis, Justice Wilson (with Justice L'HeureuxDubé concurring) dissented from the majority decision, finding that while the bawdy-house provision could be considered consistent with section 7 of the *Charter*, the communicating provision constituted a *Charter* breach (*Prostitution Reference* para 158). In her dissenting view, the risk of incarceration was disproportionate to the legislative objective of curbing public nuisance, especially in light of Justice Wilson's finding that the communicating provision also violated an individual's right to freedom of expression and could not be upheld by section 1 of the *Charter* (para 157).

Bedford: The Road to Striking Down the *Criminal Code's* Prostitution Provisions

On December 20, 2013, the Supreme Court of Canada overturned three of Canada's prostitution laws in *Canada v Bedford,* in which the court ruled that these laws infringed on sex workers' security of the person rights guaranteed under section 7 of the *Charter.* The road to striking down the impugned provisions was long, winding, and faced political barriers erected by the government of the day. Notably, as *Bedford* made its way through the different levels of Canadian courts, the federal majority Conservative government continued to defend the impugned provisions. As Jordana Wright and colleagues indicate, the federal government "evoked notions of 'community safety' as a rhetorical device to suggest that communities will not and cannot be 'safe' spaces if prostitution exists within them" (265). Although it is certainly the case that sex workers can be the victims of violence, such a minute focus upon these workers does not speak to the larger societal and gendered perceptions of sex work at play; this violence perpetrated against, in the main, female sex workers, is a by-product of the legal and social structures that disregard the human rights of women by those whom construct these women as victims and those that criminalize their work and work-related activities (Lowman; Craig; Gillies). As indicated below, such a focus misses the forest for the trees, and also fails to recognize that sex workers are residents of the community (Wright et al. 269).

The Trial Decision

At trial, Bedford's position was that the criminal prohibitions make sex work more dangerous and that the SCC decision in the *Prostitution Reference* related to the communicating provision needed to be revisited in light of "new evidence and a material change in circumstances" (*R v Bedford* para 13). Contrastingly, the Attorney General of Canada argued that Bedford had not shown sufficient reasons in law or in new evidence to warrant a reevaluation of the SCC's previous ruling and that the danger inherent in the sex trade was not caused by the impugned provisions (paras 15-17). Interveners, such as the Attorney General of Ontario, the Christian Legal Fellowship, REAL Women of Canada, and the Catholic Civil Rights League all spoke to the human dignity and vulnerability of the people that the impugned provisions were enacted to protect (paras 21-24). In effect, the trial judge, Justice Himel, found the impugned provisions unconstitutional for exacerbating the harms faced by sex workers.

Justice Himel determined that the threat of violence forced sex workers to choose "between their liberty and their security of the person," and the evidence demonstrated that the impugned provisions played a "significantly contributory role" to the threat of violence by prohibiting actions that would make sex work safer (*R v Bedford* para 362). To determine if any or all of the provisions violated the principles of fundamental justice in terms of overbreadth, arbitrariness, and gross disproportionality, Justice Himel surveyed the history of each provision to determine the legislative objectives. Justice Himel found that the bawdy-house provision was aimed at "combating neighbourhood disruption and disorder and safeguarding public health and safety" (para 242). The legislative objective of the living on the avails provision was supposed to protect sex workers from those who sought to profit from their work (para 259). Finally, relying on the SCC determination in the *Prostitution Reference,* the legislative objective of the communicating provision was an attempt to "eradicate the various forms of social nuisance arising from the public display of the sale of sex" (para 374).

Taken together, Justice Himel found that the bawdy-house provision was overbroad because of the "wide geographic scope" that encompassed areas beyond a "traditional brothel" (*R v Bedford* paras 400-1), and grossly disproportionate to the intended legislative objectives as sex workers could be denied the stability and safety that a permanent indoor location would provide (para 428). The trial judge determined that the living on the avails provision was arbitrary, as sex workers were prohibited from hiring anyone who could make their work safer (para 379), overbroad for the provision's inclusion of "non-exploitive arrangements," (para 402), and grossly disproportionate, as the provision forced sex workers to choose between jeopardizing the liberty of another or their own safety (para 431). Finally, the communicating provision was determined to be grossly disproportionate in light of the evidence that it prevented client screening and dispersed sex workers to more secluded or isolated areas to do their work (para 434). Finally, in Justice Himel's weighing of the evidence, she found that because the challenged provisions were grossly disproportionate and caused more than a minimal impairment to the rights of sex workers, the breach of section 7 *Charter* rights could not be saved by an analysis under section 1 (para 441).

In addition, Bedford challenged the communicating provision under section 2(b) of the *Charter* as an unconstitutional limit on freedom of expression. Previously, this provision was determined by the SCC in the *Prostitution Reference* as a "*prima facie* infringement of s. 2(b)," a determination which Justice Himel accepted (*Bedford* para 444). Concurring with Chief Justice Dickson's finding in the *Prostitution Reference*, Justice Himel found that eliminating social nuisance represented a legitimate, substantial, and pressing objective (para 448). However, Justice Himel found sex workers' need to "safeguard their own bodily integrity through communication with customers lies at or near the core of expression section 2(b) of the *Charter* seeks to protect" (para 462). This assessment departs greatly from that of Chief Justice Dickson in the *Prostitution Reference*, who stated the following: "It can hardly be said that communications regarding an economic transaction of sex for money lie at, or even near, the core of the guarantee of freedom of expression" (*Prostitution Reference* para 5). Considering Justice Himel had the benefit of over 25,000 pages of evidence, coupled with witnesses ranging from sex workers, to police, social workers, and academics (*R v Bedford* para 84), the difference of opinion between the two justices is understandable. As Maria Powell indicates, apart from the recommendations of the Special Committee on Pornography and Prostitution, which were released in 1985, "much of the evidence relied upon in the Bedford [trial] case was not available at the time of the *Prostitution Reference*" (194).

Justice Himel determined that the communicating provision was rationally connected to the legislative objective of curbing social nuisance; however, just as Justice Wilson outlined in her dissent in the *Prostitution Reference*, Justice Himel found that the provision was more than a minimal impairment to the right of freedom of expression (*Bedford* para 481). In effect, Justice Himel found that the communicating provision adds to the risk that sex workers will become victims of violence, a notion which was "simply too high a price to pay" to curb social nuisance and represented an "unjustifiable limit" on freedom of expression (paras 504-5).

The Appellate Decision—Majority

The court of appeal was asked to consider the constitutionality of the three challenged provisions. Upon appeal, all five judges were unanimous that the bawdy-house and living on the avails provisions were unconstitutional, upholding the decision of Justice Himel (*R v Bedford* para 325). However, when it came to the constitutionality of the communicating provision with respect to section 7 of the *Charter*, there was a stark difference of opinion in the appellate court. The court of appeal majority held that the SCC decision in the *Prostitution Reference* remained binding on the trial judge, deeming the communicating provision to be a reasonable limit on the freedom of expression under section 2(b) (para 328). Although the majority disagreed with Justice Himel's finding that the communicating provision was grossly disproportionate (and did not find a section 7 violation), in dissent, Justice MacPherson agreed with the trial judge's finding that the communicating provision was grossly disproportionate.

In the majority's assessment of the communicating provision and the principles of fundamental justice, they concurred with Justice Himel that a provision is not rendered arbitrary because it is ineffective (*R v Bedford* para 287). Despite their disagreement with Justice Himel's finding that the law was ineffective in reducing street solicitation, they agreed with the trial judge that the communicating provision was not arbitrary (para 289). In addition, the appellate court majority agreed with Justice Himel's finding that the communicating provision was not overbroad (para 290), yet they concluded that her analysis of the communicating provision and principle of gross disproportionality were flawed (para 280). In balancing the legislative objective with the effects of the law, the majority found that Justice Himel gave too little weight to the objective, whereas too much weight was assigned to the effects (para 280).

Controversially, the majority agreed with the Attorney General and found that Justice Himel "underemphasized the importance of the legislative objective" (*R v Bedford* para 309). In addition, the majority also found that given the striking down of the bawdy-house provision, less weight should be accorded to harms caused by the communicating provision as sex workers would now have the option to move to indoor locations to engage in their work (para 309). The majority recognized the distinct vulnerability of sex workers and acknowledged that even with the ability to move from the streets to indoor sites many sex workers would not have the resources necessary to facilitate this move. Yet the majority remained unconvinced that the provision was a factor that when coupled with the other evidence presented would tip the balance towards a finding of gross disproportionality (*R v Bedford* para 322).

Although Justice Himel found that the ability to screen clients was an "essential tool" to enhance the safety of sex workers, the majority was not convinced that the evidence supported this determination (*R v Bedford* para 310). Rather, the majority found that Justice Himel drew her conclusion from "the anecdotal evidence [of] prostitutes" (para 311); this finding by the court is evidence of "the outdated notion that sex workers are unreliable witnesses" and shows how the majority perceived sex workers' chosen profession as undermining their credibility and the evidence they espouse (Powell 196). Although the majority felt Justice Himel's conclusion on the effectiveness of client screening as a safety tool reached "well beyond the limits of the evidence" (*R v Bedford* para 311), the support for screening was actually quite robust—from academic and expert witnesses to policy and legislative initiatives within Canada and beyond (for a review, see Powell).

Appellate Dissent—Minority

Authoring a brief but powerful dissent, Justice MacPherson (with Justice Cronk concurring) agreed with the appellate majority's reasoning on all points except for their finding that the communicating provision was not grossly disproportionate. Justice MacPherson would have upheld Justice Himel's finding of gross disproportionality in violation of section 7 of the *Charter* (*R v Bedford* para 333). Justice MacPherson queried why the majority, without reason, used a different method to assess the communicating provision—an analysis that was in stark opposition to the method and reasoning used to amend the provisions concerning bawdy-houses and living on the avails. Even with these amendments, Justice MacPherson determined that the communicating provision still prevented sex workers from using all available means to protect themselves.

Furthermore, Justice MacPherson disagreed with the change in the tone of the analysis for the communicating provision and the incorporation of the concepts of "cruel and unusual punishment" and "abhorrent or intolerable" to the analysis (*R v Bedford* para 339). Although the test for gross disproportionality under section 12 of the *Charter* requires a similar balancing test for these notions, these "touchstones" were not considered for the bawdy-house or the living on the avails provisions (para 340). If the concepts of "cruel and unusual punishment," "abhorrent," and "intolerable" are to be incorporated into the analysis, then one must consider the evidence before the appellate court, which clearly indicates that "violence is occurring and ... the impugned provisions prevent sex workers from protecting themselves and from working with the police to see that the perpetrators of violence are punished" (Powell 199). Justice MacPherson's reasons (*R v Bedford* paras 345-47) indicate a belief that Justice Himel was correct in her appraisal of the legislative objective of the communicating provision; it would be difficult to justify violence as an acceptable alternative to calm and orderly neighbourhoods, and the appellate majority by sanctioning as criminal the conduct commonly associated with street solicitation exaggerated the legislative objective more than what was accepted by the SCC majority in the *Prostitution Reference*.

Finally, Justice MacPherson took issue with the weight assigned to the importance of client screening for sex workers—an act largely prevented by the communicating provision that "denies an already vulnerable person the opportunity to protect herself from serious physical violence" (*R v Bedford* para 360). MacPherson reasoned that the appellate majority took a narrow view of the weight of client screening, and that although the majority determined a fallibility in client screening as a means of protection from violence, such fallibleness, per Justice MacPherson, does not diminish its value to the sex workers themselves (para 348). In this view, there are other risks to safety for sex workers that the appellate majority failed to consider; in agreement with Justice Himel, the dissenting judge found that the effect of the provision also displaced and dispersed sex workers, which compounded their vulnerability, and that these factors should not be discounted (para 353).

Justice MacPherson ultimately concluded that the trial judge's assessment of the communicating provision as unconstitutional was correct.

The Supreme Court Decision and the Aftermath

The SCC issued a unanimous decision in the case and largely endorsed Justice Himel's trial court decision with a few caveats. Per Hamish Stewart, a central theme of the decision "was that sex work was lawful and that, absent a very significant legislative objective, it was not constitutionally permissible for Parliament to prohibit sex workers from taking elementary precautions to protect themselves from the dangers of this lawful work" ("Constitutionality" 70). Indeed, what emerges from the evidence in *Bedford* is that "a core function of communication is to screen 'bad dates.' In other words, it is self-protective. Criminalization not only prevents this screening but ... pushes sex workers into remote and even more risky spaces" (Hughes et al. 489).

The SCC declared that the soliciting, living on the avails, and bawdy-house provisions were not constitutional and provided Parliament with one year to propose a new law before the declaration of constitutional invalidity would come into effect. The decision upheld the lower court's determinations on most accounts, noting that the trial judge was entitled to deference. The one exception was an omission on Justice Himel's finding that the solicitation provisions violated section 2(b) (freedom of expression) of the *Charter*—a finding was that was not made by the SCC in the *Prostitution Reference*. The SCC relied on the legal concepts of vagueness, overbreadth, arbitrariness, and gross disproportion to conclude that the solicitation provision violated the applicants' security of the person in a way that was too severe to align with the main goal of the laws: the prevention of public nuisance. This was too low a price to put on the lives of sex workers according to the court (*Bedford* paras 93-123).

The SCC was careful in specifying that the bawdy-house provision was invalid "as it relates to prostitution," and in striking the word "prostitution" from section 197 of the *Criminal Code,* the bawdy-house provision applies to section 210 only (*Bedford* para 123).[6] This would have meant, seemingly, that the court's test for harm in obscenity and indecency jurisprudence would continue to persist and be tacitly considered by the court to be constitutional and sufficiently precise to provide a legal standard. Ultimately, these bawdy-house provisions were repealed in 2019.

The SCC was also very careful to note that the ways in which sex work would be regulated would be up to Parliament. The court provided some insight as to how a constitutional set of laws regarding sex work could be concocted:

> Prohibitions on keeping a bawdy-house, living on the avails of prostitution and communication related to prostitution are intertwined. They impact on each other. Greater latitude in one measure—for example, permitting prostitutes to obtain the assistance of security personnel—might impact on the constitutionality of another measure—for example, forbidding the nuisances associated with keeping a bawdy-house. The regulation of prostitution is a complex and delicate matter. It will be for Parliament, should it choose to do so, to devise a new approach, reflecting different elements of the existing regime. (*R v Bedford* para 165)

At minimum, the SCC *Bedford* decision "provides [a somewhat] welcome clarification to what has been a contradictory and confusing area of [sex work] jurisprudence" (Wu 295). One of the plaintiffs, Valerie Scott, joyfully thanked the court for declaring sex workers as persons. Yet the laws that followed did not live up to the promise of *Bedford*. As Bruckert indicated, this could have been the moment when Canadian lawmakers listened to sex workers, attended to evidence, and introduced laws that "respect the human and labour rights of all citizens, including those in the sex industry" (1). However, this did not take place.

While some feminists began to advocate against the *Bedford* decision by trying to influence legislative change (Benedet), provinces weighed in on the debate. Manitoba Justice Minister Andrew Swan argued that the law should "target the demand for sexual services while helping sex-trade workers get the addiction counseling, mental health services and training they need to get off the streets" (Welch). Manitoba formally advocated for the Nordic model, which targeted pimps and customers under a criminalized and constitutional regime. Federal Justice Minister Peter MacKay acknowledged that the Nordic model was on the table, and the federal Government began a public consultation process in its drafting exercise. According to Mackay, "doing nothing is not an option. We are therefore asking Canadians right across the country to provide their input through an online consultation to ensure a legislative response to prostitution that reflects our country's values" (qtd. in Cheadle, cited in Jochelson et al. 57).

In terms of the former Conservative government's standpoint on sex work in Canada, Senator Donald Plett stated the position clearly: "Of course we don't want to make life safe for prostitutes we want to do away with prostitution. That is the intent of the bill" (qtd. in Jochelson et al. 57). Moreover, it is no secret that the former Conservative government was sceptical of academic experts and their opinions of policy choices (Lawrence). The *Bedford* case and the subsequent passage of Bill C-36, titled The Protection of Communities and Exploited Persons Act, offer a glimpse into the identification, mobilization, and reception of experts in the courts, the legislative process, and the public sphere at large (Lawrence). Now enacted, Bill C-36 is a law of questionable constitutionality, which has been argued to "almost certainly increase sex workers' vulnerability to violence" (Bruckert 1).

The Passing of Bill C-36: A Victory for Stereotypes, a Defeat for Sex Workers

The *Bedford* ruling gave the Harper government twelve months to come up with a new law, since the existing law infringed on the *Charter* rights of sex workers (Ivison). Following the SCC ruling, controversy surrounding sex work reemerged in the public domain. This was not unexpected, since the historical record of sex work in Canada shows that complex issues expose different moral values and provoke debate (see generally Craig; Shaver, "Sex Work and the Law"; Johnson).

As discussed above, the SCC in *Bedford* deemed three laws unconstitutional and struck from the *Criminal Code* the laws against bawdy-houses, living on the avails of prostitution, and communication for the purposes of prostitution (for examples of further legal discussions regarding *Bedford* see Stewart, "Bedford and the Structure"; Haak). Although the appellants' argument that the criminalization of prostitution harms sex workers defeated the Crown's argument that prostitution is inherently harmful, *Bedford* "maintained a focus on *harm* in the national conversation about sex work" (Law 44; our emphasis).

Indeed, the Harper government's moralization of prostitution post-*Bedford* demonstrated a concern with harm to the community and also moved "toward a discourse of individual harm to exploited, or trafficked, women" (Law 44). Although *Bedford* struck down the law that made clear Parliament's intention to eradicate sex work in Canada, the Harper government's response to the SCC ruling forcefully reiterates the "exploitation that is inherent in prostitution and the risks of violence posed to those who engage in it" (Bill C-36 preamble).

Bill C-36, which was introduced in June 2014 and received royal assent in November of that year, effectively criminalized communication in public for the purpose of prostitution, the purchase of sexual services, material benefit, procuring, and the advertisement of sexual services (Bill C-36). In *Bedford*, expertise about sex work and harm was accepted by the courts and formed the basis of the decision. However, when the Harper government drafted Bill C-36 and began parliamentary hearings, Sonia Lawrence argues that both the legal questions and the political sphere shifted. Although the result in the high court was a win for sex workers, the new legislation was a "crystal clear loss" for sex workers in Canada post-*Bedford* (Lawrence 5). Accordingly, Bill C-36 follows the neoliberal narrative of sex workers as innocent victims, terribly misguided, or loathsome as well as distinctly criminal, lawbreakers; it focuses on criminalizing the purchaser of sexual services. This narrative broadly serves to deny and obscure "the structural problems undergirding so much harm" (5). In so doing Bill C-36 both "responsibilizes individuals and ignores the role of the state in failing to alleviate or creating problems"—such as colonialism, poverty, and discrimination on the basis of race and gender (5).

The government purported that the new sex work law adopted the Nordic model, whereas critics argued that the new law was aligned with the criminalization approach to sex work; critics argued that although the law attempted to place the burden of criminality on purchasers of sexual services, its reach was restrictive enough that it effectively put sex workers out of business entirely. Furthermore, critics indicated that there was no separation between the law and personal moral values in Bill C-36; they contended that, ultimately, the bill brought into play a wide range of moral values concerning the personal character of those involved, the commodification of sexual services, and the visibility of such services (Shaver, "Sex Work and the Law").

As Marcus Sibley indicates, the Harper government cited the sex trade as part of a system of exploitation that capitalizes on the vulnerable and profits from the sale of those who are unable to consent, a detrimental rhetoric with two important strategies: (1) it assumes that all sex workers experience violence in the same way, ignoring the social, cultural, and economic factors that allow sex workers to manoeuvre the trade in different ways; and (2) positions sex workers "beyond the reach of any meaningful harm reduction strategies" (Shaver 2). On one hand, Bill C-36 positioned sex workers as victims in need of protection from exploitative clients and managers. On the other hand, they were criminals "bringing 'violence, drug-related crime, and organized crime' into communities, and thus should be penalized if in places where youth might be" (Wright et al. 266, citing MacKay). In effect, the corollary is that sex workers themselves were understood both as potential victims and as threats, "as at-risk and as risky" (Wright et al. 266; see also Bruckert and Hannem). Unfortunately, risk becomes "something both inevitable and non-negotiable; risk of violence is inextricably bound to the sex trade as a permanent and universal feature of sex work" (Sibley 2).

Although Bill C-36 may well be unconstitutional, its constitutional flaws are not immediately obvious. Even though Bill C-36 responded to the constitutional defects of the former sex work law that were identified in *Bedford,* according to Stewart, the bill was distinct in two ways. First, rather than abating the nuisances that sex work creates, the main policy objective of Bill C-36 was to denounce and deter sex work itself. This shift in purpose was evidenced in both the preamble to the bill and in the structure of the new offences. As Stewart indicates, "it is highly unlikely that any court will say that denouncing and deterring sex work is a constitutionally impermissible object. So ... any detrimental effects of the law must now be measured against a different and perhaps weightier legislative objective" ("Constitutionality" 71).

Notwithstanding its generally punitive approach, the second concern with Bill C-36 is its purpose of improving sex worker's safety by decriminalizing some of the activities that were of specific concern in *Bedford.* In theory, if these two stated purposes are considered separately and the law is measured against the constitutional norms that were invoked in *Bedford,* arguably Bill C-36 appears to be constitutionally valid. However, Stewart contends the following:

The bill's two policy objectives are so at odds with each other that they are likely to create a constitutional problem. On the one hand, Bill C-36 criminalizes prostitution; on the other hand, it purports to ameliorate the legal situation of sex workers. In practice, these two objectives are likely to frustrate each other, and that frustration generates a plausible constitutional argument against Bill C-36: the incompatibility of its two purposes creates arbitrary and grossly disproportionate effects on sex workers' security of the person. ("Constitutionality" 71)

We contend that portions of the law overemphasize the criminality of purchasing sexual services, underscore a focus of harm, risk, and exploitation, yet significantly reduce or cast aside entirely the structural, social, and economic conditions of sex work. These sections include the communication of sexual services in public (section 213 (1.1)); the purchase of sexual services (section 286.1 (1); the reception of "financial or other material benefit" for sex work (section 286.2) and its procurement (section 286.3); and finally, the advertisement of sexual services (section 286.4). By addressing the issues for each section, we stand by critics who call for advancing beyond the provisions as they stand and, subsequently, developing economic and social policies grounded in a harm reduction/labour rights framework (for a similar review see Jochelson et al.; for additional examples, see Lewis and Shaver; Lewis et al.).

Section 213 (1.1): "*offering, providing or obtaining sexual services for communication—in a public place, or in any place open to the public view, that is or is next to a place where persons under the age of 18 can reasonably be expected to be present.*"

Under the new section 213 (1.1), which was amended by the House of Commons Standing Committee on Justice and Human Rights, it will be possible for a sex worker to communicate in a public place for the purpose of offering sexual services, unless it is a place that is "open to public view, that is or next to a school ground, playground or daycare centre" (Section 2.13; Casavant and Valiquet 12). Similar to the communication section struck down in *Bedford*, section 213 (1.1) displaces sex workers trying to avoid detection, and further minimalizes the ability of sex workers to communicate with their clients. Moreover, this provision has the potential to increase the isolation of sex workers and maintains adversarial relations between sex workers and the police. In this context, sex workers' experiences of violence "tend to go unnoticed and disregarded by the police and others even while they and their activities are rendered hyper-visible through forms of social profiling" (Wright et al. 268; see also Bruckert and Hannem). As a result, it now becomes more difficult for sex workers to access police protection, given the risk of arrest (Shaver, "*Bill C-36*"). What is crucial to note is that the relationships sex workers develop—for example, between each other and with their clients—enhance their own security and safety, yet this provision undermines and weakens such relationships (Wright et al.; see also STAR 2005, 2006) and opens up a space of discretion that could result in police abuse (Bruckert and Hannem). Indeed, sex work literature in Canada demonstrates the significance of such relationships for these workers (for example, STAR; Lowman; Bruckert and Chabot; Wright et al.). For instance, these studies demonstrate that working in pairs or groups and sharing information, particularly among sex workers, is a strategy that not only empowers them but increases access to resources and helps identify situations of enhanced risk or security.

Furthermore, when police attention displaces sex workers far from amenities such as transportation, public telephones, restaurants (where they meet or take a break), and other services and facilities, such displacement has been shown to increase feelings of isolation for sex workers (Shaver, *Bill C-36*; see also Laing, and Campbell and O'Neill regarding the selective and geographic variability of police regulating sex workers).

Section 286 1(1): a prohibition against the purchase of sexual services

Within the new section 286 1(1) of the *Code*, clients are criminalized for purchasing sexual services "*in any place*" (Bill C-36 10, our emphasis). Although this provision is designed in part to protect sellers of sex, it reinforces stereotypes about sex workers—namely that their decisions are ill-conceived and that they are 'victims' lacking agency

(Shaver, *Bill C-36*; see also Benedet). According to Shaver, sex workers are not all victims lacking agency; they come from a wide array of cultural and social backgrounds, and can range in age from eighteen to fifty-two years (see Weinberg et al.; Jeffrey and Macdonald). The majority of sex workers have had varied work experiences outside the sex industry, with most jobs being within the service industry (Weinberg et al.; Shaver and Weinberg; Wright et al.). Indeed, many sex workers move within and about the industry, an indication that not all are victims trapped on the street (Jeffrey and Macdonald; Lewis and Shaver; Wright et al.). At the same time, understanding this mobility within the sex work industry is only part of a much larger narrative of structural inequalities at play, especially as it relates to a women-dominated service and lends itself to racialized and classed groups of individuals who are generally caught within low paid, precarious labour. Furthermore, recent studies affirm that unstable family backgrounds are common, especially among street-based sex workers. Such findings indicate that sex workers are "structurally disadvantaged" and not morally corrupt or helpless as Bill C-36 would suggest (Shaver, *Bill C-36*; see also Hallgrimsdottir et al.; McCarthy et al.; Johnson; Wright et al.).

Moreover, this subsection also suggests and strengthens stereotypes about clients. Contrary to Bill C-36, the notion that clients are violent perpetrators is ill-conceived. In fact, similar to sex workers, clients come from a wide variety of demographic backgrounds, and their motivations for buying sexual services also vary (Shaver, *Bill C-36*). Some clients have reported that they are unsatisfied with the sexual aspects of their current relationship, whereas others wish to avoid the long-term obligations in conventional relationships, or wish to seek a limited, quasi-romantic connection (Shaver; see also Milrod and Weitzer; Sanders). In effect, client violence is exaggerated (see for example Benoit et al.; Weitzer; Lowman and Atchison).

In addition to displacing sex workers and pushing them into the black market, this subsection undermines the relationships developed between sex workers and their clients; these relationships are needed in order to enhance the security and safety of sex workers themselves. In Ottawa and Montréal, Canada, for example, Sandra Ka Hon Chu and Rebecca Glass reported that anti-client measures undertaken by the police resulted in increased violence. Andrea Krüsi and colleagues' study in Vancouver found similar outcomes when a Vancouver Police Department policy to criminalize clients reproduced significant vulnerabilities of poor health and violence among sex workers at the street-based level. What is important to note is that generally client-worker transactions are not anonymous, and longer-term relationships are often developed. In effect, the ability for sex workers to have good clients increases the economic and physical security for these workers as they engage in these relationships (Shaver, *Bill C-36*). However, by arresting clients, this provision renders sex workers unable to distinguish the "predatory violence of aggressors posing as clients from clients who may be aggressive on occasion due to frustrations with the quality of the service" (Shaver, *Bill C-36* 5; see also POWER). As such, arresting clients weakens the relationships between sex workers and their clients and does not improve their working environment (Shaver).

Section 286.2: Prohibitions on receiving "financial or other material benefit" for sex work

Section 286.3: Prohibitions on procuring sexual services through recruiting, harbouring, concealing or holding a person for the purposes of sex work.

These sections of the *Code* impede relationships between sex workers and third parties, exclude sex workers from labour-site protections, and increase social and professional isolation. Contrary to the pervasive stereotype that third parties are exploitative and abusive, Shaver rightly contends that sex workers have a wide range of relationships with third parties. Similar to what is witnessed in other service industries, some third parties provide training, whereas others do not; some third parties maintain a great deal of control over their workers, while others maintain little control (Shaver, *Bill C-36*; see also Lewis et al.). Most of these relationships contribute to and help maintain secure and safe working environments, and research indicates that these relationships are in fact desirable, regardless of sex workers working independently or for someone else (Shaver *Bill C-36*; Johnson). Indeed, managers and supervisors enhance economic security, since they are often responsible for providing the work space, attracting clients, and advertising of services. Managers and supervisors can also enhance physical security through protections and precautions against aggressors (STAR; Bruckert and Law).

Taken together, we maintain the above subsections of the *Code* reinforce the stereotype that sex work is always inherently violent. However, we remain mindful that the perception of risk does vary by gender and sexual orientation. It is clear that regardless of the work environment, women worry more about their safety than men. Studies of various work environments indicate that female sex workers suffer the most with respect to insults and threats (Shaver, *Bill C-36*). Such findings suggest that the safety and health concerns of sex workers—especially those related to violence—parallel those of women and men in other occupations in Canada (Shaver, *Bill C-36*). However, other studies suggest that transgender and two-spirit sex workers experience more violence than their ciswoman counterparts (Lyons et al.).

Within the sex industry, and with respect to experiences of violence and arrest, there are also significant gender and sexual orientation differences to consider. While Shaver contends that women experience more physical violence than either transgender or male sex workers, and women are more likely to be arrested (Shaver, *Bill C-36*), other scholars indicate that transgender sex workers are disproportionately targeted by police and experience more violence than ciswomen sex workers. Cristine Rotenberg suggests that Indigenous transgender and cisgender sex workers are more likely to be subject to violence than most other sex workers. Therefore, violence within the industry is linked to "broader social and economic issues such as gender inequality, unequal education and occupation opportunity structures, poverty, exploitation, and violence," (Shaver, *Bill C-36* 6) and we recognize and contextualize this violence in relation to race, class, and sexual orientation.

Section 286.4: Prohibition against advertising of sexual services

Finally, this subsection restricts the ability for sex workers to advertise, limits the opportunities for working indoors, and increases the potential for miscommunication between workers and clients. This provision denies these workers an important security mechanism by shutting down websites that, in addition to providing space for advertising, host virtual sex worker-only spaces where information can be shared regarding security measures, clients, and third parties (Bruckert and Law). In effect, this provision ultimately prohibits working inside a fixed location, inevitably increasing the probabilities of children and youth viewing such advertisements and street solicitation within the public domain (Shaver, *Bill C-36*).

In sum, the debate surrounding prostitution as a criminalizable enterprise is well articulated in the literature (for example, see generally Bruckert and Law; Bruckert and Parent; Gorkoff and Runner; Lewis and Shaver; Lowman; Shaver; van der Meulen and Durisin). The criminalization of sex work is something about which many Canadians disagree and scores of scholarly articles and media personalities continually debate. However, as the *Bedford* case has proven, certain provisions of the *Criminal Code* and the now enacted Bill C-36 can be challenged to improve the working conditions of sex workers. Although the specific provisions outlined above have yet to stand up to judicial scrutiny, it is clear that the risk to political values (in this case the purported claim of the new law to uphold equality values for women and girls) does converge neatly with "the ascribed 'victims of sexual exploitation' master status espoused by Bill C-36, as it draws upon deeply entrenched discrediting stigmatic assumptions" about sex workers (Bruckert 2). Bruckert goes on to state this line of reasoning relies on certain assumptions:

> Specifically, that sex workers *must* be under the control of a pimp, drug addicted, mentally ill, psychologically damaged, deluded (suffering from false consciousness) or, at the very least, so disadvantaged that they are incapable of conceptualizing options—otherwise, why would they continue this demeaning, destructive, and, of course, inherently violent activity? Questions of consent and agency are [thereby] rendered irrelevant, and we are left with incompetent subjects in need of rescue rather than rights. (2)

So once again, the agency of the free individual to choose to engage in sex work disappears in Canadian jurisprudence and legislation. This line of reasoning suggests that the sexually exploited person (usually a woman) has, through her victimization, been coerced to work within the sex trade. The need to rescue the worker receives primacy over conceptions that sex workers ought to participate in safer, clean, and regulated working conditions.

In the context of the post-*Bedford* passage of Bill C-36, experts and the government avoided any suggestion of women choosing to engage in sex work: "by placing all of [sex work] in the context of coercion," the study of sex work becomes "a rich source of material for understanding the politics of later neoliberalism" as it unfolds in Canada (Lawrence 7). The legal ground shifted and selling sex in exchange for money was no longer legal; those in favour of the change argue that the criminal law now focuses more acutely on punishing the customers of sex workers. The record of the hearings revealed how a heart-breaking and stifling pathos took centre stage, insofar as "references to specific children and their futures—sometimes already lost, sometimes full of potential—[were] everywhere" (7). As a result, Bill C-36 came to represent "the grim reality of sex workers' lives, or rather, deaths," focusing the frame of the legislation predominantly on making "sex work the killer" instead of the structural disadvantages that continually plagued Canadian society (7).

Furthermore, Bill C-36 espouses a protectionist perspective, which "assumes all sex workers are victims lacking agency, hints that human dignity and sex work are incompatible, and takes for granted that viewing sex workers and clients on the street is injurious to the well-being of children and youth" (Shaver, *Bill C-36* 3; see also Benedet). It reorients discussions related to the governance of sex trade "from questions of *nuisance management* to that of *risk management*" (Sibley 2; our emphasis). Studies that have examined the adoption of protectionist approaches indicated that such approaches tend to embed negative stigmas into public discourse and debate; this has a negative impact on sex workers' health and subsequent health behaviour (Abel; Benoit et al.; Wright et al.).

Moreover, Shaver contends that Bill C-36 fails to respect the safety and security of sex working conditions; she takes issue with how this law subsequently assembles, sustains, and perpetuates "inaccurate stereotypes that seriously undermine the relationships" essential for the working conditions and spaces sex workers frequent (Shaver, *Bill C-36* 4; see also Johnson; Wright et al.). We concur with Shaver's criticism, as it is clear there exists an apparent synchronicity between personal moral values and legal opinions within the bill. We also maintain that the adoption of protectionist claims upholds dubious, ill-conceived, and misinformed notions regarding sex work, sex workers themselves, and the struggles they endure.

The recent case heard in the Ontario Superior Court of Justice is an apt example that speaks to the acceptance of a protectionist perspective at the hands of Bill C-36. In *R v Boodhoo and Others*, Justice Bale dismissed a *Charter* challenge to three provisions of the *Code*: subsection 286.2(2) (receiving material benefit from sexual services provided by a person under the age of 18 years); subsection 286.3(2) (procuring a person under the age of eighteen years); and subsection 286.4 (advertising sexual services). A jury found Deshon Boodhoo, Kemoy Chisholm, and Keon Chisholm guilty under provisions subsection 286.2(2) and subsection 286.3(2), and, in addition, Deshon Boodhoo and Keon Chisholm were found guilty under subsection 286.4 and section 163.1(3) of the *Code* (distributing child pornography). Following conviction, the applicants sought an order declaring subsections 286.2(2), 286.3(2), and 286.4 of the *Code* to be unconstitutional (para 2). The applicants argued that the objective of the legislation is aimed at enhancing the safety, security, and dignity of sex workers, but Justice Bale disagreed (para 22). Per Justice Bale, the objective of Bill C-36 should be taken from the Conservative technical paper on Bill C-36, wherein it states that the overall objective is "to reduce the demand for prostitution with a view to discouraging entry into it, deterring participation in it, and ultimately abolishing it to the greatest extent possible" (*Technical Paper—Bill C-36* para 3, cited in *Boodhoo* para 23). Therefore, Bill C-36 is not concerned with the security, safety, and dignity of sex workers (especially given the *Bedford* trial and appellate decisions we discussed above, coupled with the accepted expert and lay evidence provided in the *Bedford* SCC decision).

One could argue that it would be fair to find that the formal or official aim of Bill C-36 is to denounce and deter prostitution, as the remit of Bill C-36 indicates. However, what we find surprising is that Justice Bale seems to uncritically accept the notion that "the best way to avoid prostitution's harms is to bring an end to its practice" (*Technical Paper—Bill C-36* para 3, cited in *Boodhoo* para 23). Justice Bale's decision reflects a direct, limited, and conservative interpretation of sex work, and reveals an unwillingness to embrace reasonable hypotheticals of how the provisions arbitrarily revictimize sex workers (an already marginalized group in Canadian society—see para 52). Indeed, these issues were litigated throughout *Bedford*, wherein the parties agreed that there were inherent risks of harm or violence, yet they disagreed on whether measures could be taken to reduce the risks of experiencing identified harms. In effect, while *Boodhoo and Others* seems to raise narrow concerns about the recriminalization provisions, it does not squarely face whether recriminalization offends the SCC *Bedford* decision. Nevertheless, the acceptance of the Conservative fantasy of just ending sex work remains a pressing and substantial worry for sex workers; it remains to be seen whether the effects of the law will severely trench sex workers' freedoms of security, safety, and expression any more than the law has already accomplished.

Simultaneously, the presence of the sex worker in public is seen as a social nuisance and as a behaviour to inoculate society from—hence, the criminal restrictions of communicating for sexual purchases and of third-party advertising in media. Preventing sex work from occurring at all aligns with homeostatic conceptions of equality, insofar as such conceptions presuppose all people as entering Canadian society as substantively equal. A more radical approach would understand the societal inequalities that inure daily in Canada—inequalities that persist due to (often intersecting) reasons of poverty, gender, gender identity, sexual orientation, race, and Indigeneity (for example, see Beloso; Laing; Laing et al.; Rotenberg). Such an approach would seek to provide resources and safety to sex workers. Instead, the law aims to criminalize the work itself and to inoculate mainstream society from being affronted, indeed corrupted, by its social realities (see also Stewart; Haak).

The Pressures for and Resistance to Legalization/Decriminalization: The Trouble with the Trudeau Government

The SCC's *Bedford* decision marked a significant step in recognizing sex workers' rights in Canada. Yet as we have indicated, the Conservative government's passage of Bill C-36 provided no real victory for sex workers or those lobbying for sex work law reforms. This new law was a discursive shift that conflated sex work with human trafficking, reinvigorating the notion that all sex workers are victims to justify the continued aggression regulation of sex work in Canada (Prasad). When Bill C-36 was implemented in 2014, a decline in the rate of police-reported sex work offences, largely attributed to communicating offences (specifically section 213 of the *Code*), was evident (Rotenberg). However, it is important to note that these statistics are based on the Uniform Crime Report Survey, which considers only the incidents of criminality that come to the attention of police. The focus of criminal prosecutions shifted as well, with recent statistics showing that prostitution incidents "fell from an average of 2,800 a year prior to the new law to just 209 in 2016, while 'commodification of sexuality' incidents (prosecution of pimps and johns) rose to 708" (Ivison). Crucially, these statistics demonstrate that the new law continued to criminalize the sex work industry with a focus on the prosecution of pimps and johns while, quite likely, driving sex workers underground or deep inside the Internet.

At the time, the Liberal Party of Canada, then an opposition party, clearly denounced the law. The Liberals "took a clear stance and expressed serious concerns about the new legislation failing to adequately protect the health and safety of vulnerable people, particularly women" (Prasad). During the 2015 federal elections, the Liberals promised to review the prostitution laws in place and listen to sex workers and their concerns, recognizing that the health and safety of sex workers "needs to be given greater priority by the government" (qtd. in the Ottawa Citizen). When the Liberals won a majority government in November 2015, they pledged real change unlike what had been witnessed under the Harper government, and branded Canada's new Prime Minister, Justin Trudeau, as a feminist, and their Liberal government as a party of feminist ideals (Prasad; The Guardian). Once elected, the Trudeau government took the unprecedented step of publicly releasing all ministerial mandate letters—documents that provide a framework "for what Ministers are expected to accomplish," including specific policy objectives and challenges to be addressed (Prasad). Sex workers urged the Liberals to do for them what Trudeau had promised to do for marijuana users and decriminalize their activities (Ottawa Citizen). However, the public mandate letter received by the new Attorney General of Canada and Justice Minister, the Honorable Jody Wilson-Raybould, did not mention the passage of Bill C-36 nor the concerns of sex work in Canada.

Many were hopeful that the Trudeau government would address the bawdy-house provision in Bill C-66. The bill was concerned with addressing the historic injustices faced specifically by LGBTQ2S+ persons who were criminalized for consensual sexual relations (Leamon). Historically, many LGBTQ2S+ people were convicted under the bawdy-house provisions of the *Code*, and some advocates hoped that including the bawdy-house provision repeal as part of the bill would allow for those targeted by the provision, including sex workers, to have their records expunged. As the Canadian HIV/AIDS Legal Network and HALCO noted in their brief to the Standing Senate Committee on Bill C-66, "there is a substantial overlap between LGBTQ2S+ and sex workers communities. Many sex workers are members of the LGBTQ2S+ communities, and the venues and spaces of these two communities have often also been shared" (Canadian HIV/AIDS Legal Network & HALCO 2). The Canadian HIV/AIDS Legal Network and HALCO advocated for the expungement of criminal convictions for sex workers and clients under the bill and to create a legal framework to create safe working conditions for sex workers (5). Advocates were frustrated when Bill C-66 went unamended and received royal assent on June 21, 2018, excluding the bawdy-house provision repeal (CBC Radio; Bill C-66). The struggle resulted in further advocacy. More recently, Bill C-75, which sought to broadly amend the *Criminal Code*, would proffer some improvements. The bill proposed repealing bawdy-house law by eradicating its definition and attendant provisions. The relevant bawdy-house provisions were ultimately repealed in June 2019. Bill C-75, which in part sought to amend the *Criminal Code*, by repealing bawdy-house law, received royal assent on June 21, 2019.

Notwithstanding these recent amendments, we have still not received a timeline of whether and how sex work will be addressed by the Trudeau government, contrary to this government touting itself "as one that promotes, respects and fights for *Charter* rights" (Prasad). For a self-proclaimed progressive government, it is quite odd that the Liberals have not moved to repeal the hastily-drafted Conservative prostitution law (Ivison). The Canadian Alliance for Sex Work Law Reform states that they are "losing patience" with the Liberals, and Pivot Legal Society, a law firm set up in Vancouver to represent both marginalized and disenfranchised persons, has indicated its interest in launching a fresh constitutional challenge in late 2018 (Ivison). The

Liberal party adopted a resolution at the Liberal National Convention in April 2018 indicating their intent to work towards decriminalizing sex work. The move was welcomed by the Canadian Alliance for Sex Work Law Reform, but they urged the government to act swiftly and in consultation with stakeholders (Canadian Alliance for Sex Work Law Reform, "Public Statement to the Liberal Party"). Sex work advocates continue to challenge the government on de-criminalization as well as the impact of anti-trafficking initiatives, which in their current manifestation, significantly harm sex workers (Canadian Alliance for Sex Work Law Reform, "Current Anti-Human Trafficking Initiatives"). Although the Trudeau government continues to push its feminist credentials—especially with the recent announcement that $20 million would be earmarked for gender-based violence services (Ivison)—the foot-dragging on the current prostitution law suggests that the Trudeau government's concern with sex work is no horse of a different colour. Indeed, while the *Protection of Communities and Exploited Persons Act* is situated in the Nordic model in theory, in practice this law achieves the same criminalization of the sex work industry as its predecessor. By delaying the critical debate needed to redress this law, the legalization/decriminalization of sex work in Canada has a slim chance of coming to fruition under the Trudeau government specifically, at least for the foreseeable future.

Conclusion

There is an ongoing lack of consensus domestically and internationally concerning how to identify and respond to the problems associated with the commercial exchange of sex for money (Haak). This continues to be a present issue in Canada, and as this chapter has outlined, on more than one occasion the judiciary has been tasked to determine how Canada should interpret and adjudicate sex work. The decision of the SCC in *Bedford* could have had a monumental effect of decriminalizing some (if not all) aspects of sex work in Canada. Following a lack of consensus in the Harper government and arguably, a lack of concern for sex workers, Parliament expressly rejected the option of legalization/decriminalization/administrative regulation (which could have occurred had it failed to act) and enacted legislation with the alleged intention of protecting communities and victims of exploitation from the harms associated with adult prostitution. As we have demonstrated, the legislation shows either the contempt the Harper government held for the SCC or for sex workers; the government pushed through legislation that would likely not survive a constitutional challenge.

By examining the developments and discursive shifts of Canadian sex work jurisprudence, what becomes clear is that sex workers remain victims of the dangerous conditions created by this jurisprudence. We concur with Stewart that Bill C-36 is an incoherent piece of legislation, and that this incoherence could very well amount to the same constitutional flaws that led the SCC in *Bedford* to strike down the sex work provisions in the *Criminal Code* in the first place. Bill C-36 has two distinct policy objectives, and when considered separately, it becomes difficult to see any constitutional defect in the new sex work law. Each objective is in itself constitutionally permissible: criminalizing sex work is a rational way of discouraging the work to the public; decriminalizing sex work (or aspects of sex work) is a rational way of making the work safer for those whom engage in it. When taken together, however, the two distinct policy objectives remain irreconcilable. Although the harm created by criminalizing sex work is clear and has been recognized by Canada's highest court, "contemporary legal frameworks continue to be driven by moralistic ideology that refuses to contemplate sex work as having any legitimacy in public spaces" (Campbell 43). If we are to move beyond the current unfortunate frameworks underpinning sex work jurisprudence in Canada and the difficult situation in which sex workers find themselves, we must begin to consider potential law reforms that modestly contemplate sex work as amenable to societal existence rather than assuming it to be a nuisance that must be extinguished at all costs.

Endnotes

1. This chapter builds on earlier versions of our work (Jochelson et al.) by substantially adding to the findings with newer data and theoretical analyses.
2. This is not to suggest that obtaining sexual pleasures for their own sake are at odds with the use of sex for reproductive purposes; there are larger power dynamics and structural inequalities at play in the buying and selling of sex that we do not have the space to visit.

Nevertheless, we recognize that a greater focus on queer theory adds richness to further discussions of sex work and sexuality, which we warmly welcome and have been taken up elsewhere (for an insightful example, see Beloso; Laing et al.).

3. Under the *Criminal Code,* "prostitution" was the legal term for the act of providing or obtaining sexual services for consideration; this term is similarly used in other English-speaking legal systems (Hamish). "Sex work" is the term preferred by persons whom engage in this work and by those whom advocate for their safety and for the legalization of their work. In particular, Bill C-36 refers to obtaining and providing 'sexual services for consideration.' Similar to Hamish we will use these terms as dependent upon the context of our discussion.

4. Whereas Shaver views legalization and decriminalization as separate models to view sex work ("Sex Work and the Law"), Mathieson and colleagues indicate that legalization is too closely related to complete decriminalization in theory and in practice to not discuss in tandem (378). We concur with Mathieson and colleagues' assertion and similarly discuss legalization and decriminalization simultaneously in this chapter.

5. It is important to note that the Nordic model does acknowledge that women may choose to enter sex work; however, findings from Mathieson and colleagues' study suggests that, when speaking to Swedish law enforcement officers' experiences of the Nordic Model, the amount of women which indicate their interest in participating in sex work remains few: "only two or three women of 100 might say, 'I want to be in prostitution'" (Mathieson et al 409).

6. Section 197 of the *Criminal Code,* repealed in 2019, and altered in the Harper prostitution legislation, was at the time of *Bedford* informed by the definition of a "common bawdy-house," which then referred to a "place that is (a) kept or occupied, or (b) resorted to by one or more persons for the purpose of prostitution or the practice of acts of indecency" (Section 197(1)). Section 210 of the *Criminal Code,* also now repealed, at the time of Bedford, referred to the keeping of a common bawdy-house, which indicates that anyone who keeps a common bawdy-house "is guilty of an indictable offence and liable to imprisonment for a term not exceeding two years" (Section

21(91)). Furthermore, the old law indicated that anyone who is found "without a lawful excuse" (Section 210(2)) inside of a common bawdy-house can be charged and given a summary conviction (if found guilty) under Section 210(2) of the *Code*. Bill C-75 has now repealed the bawdy-house prohibitions and attendant definitions in 2019.

Works Cited

Abel, Gillian. "Different Stage, Different Performance: The Protective Strategy of Role Play on Emotional Health in Sex Work." *Social Science & Medicine*, vol. 72, no. 7, 2011, pp. 1177-84.

Aprol, Manpreet. "The Criminalization of Prostitution: Putting Women's Lives at Risk." *Prandium: The Journal of Historical Studies*, vol. 3, no. 1, 2014, pp. 1-10.

Backhouse, Constance. *Petticoats and Prejudice: Women and Law in Nineteenth Century Canada*. Women's Press, 1991.

Bauman, Zygmunt. *Liquid Love: On the Frailty of Human Bonds*. Polity, 2003.

Beloso, Brooke. "Queer Theory, Sex Work, and Foucault's Unreason." *Foucault Studies*, no. 23, 2017, pp. 141-66.

Benedet, Janine. "Marital Rape, Polygamy, and Prostitution: Trading Sex Equality for Agency and Choice?" *Review of Constitutional Studies*, vol. 18, no. 2, 2013, pp. 161-87.

Benoit, Cecilia, et al. *Bill C-36 and the views of people involved in the Canadian sex industry*. 2014, www.nswp.org/sites/nswp.org/files/Benoit%20Atchison%20Brief%20to%20Justice%20Committee.pdf. Accessed 8 May 2019.

Bernstein, Elizabeth. *Temporarily Yours: Intimacy, Authenticity, and the Commerce of Sex*. University of Chicago Press, 2007.

Brock, Deborah R. "Victim, Nuisance, Fallen Women, Outlaw, Worker? Making the Identity Prostitute in Canadian Criminal Law." *Law as a Gendering Practice*, edited by Dorothy E. Chunn and Dany Lacombe, Oxford University Press, 2000, pp. 79-99.

Bruckert, Chris. "*Protection of Communities and Exploited Persons Act:* Misogynistic Law Making in Action." *Canadian Journal of Law and Society*, vol. 30, no. 1, 2015, pp. 1-3.

Bruckert, Chris, and Fred Chabot. *Challenges: Ottawa area sex workers speak out.* 2010, https://www.nswp.org/sites/nswp.org/files/POWER_Report_Challenges.pdf. Accessed 9 May 2019.

Bruckert, Chris, and Collette Parent. "The In-Call Sex Industry: Classed and Gendered Labour on the Margins." *Criminalizing Women: Gender and (In)Justice in Neo-Liberal Times*, edited by Gillian Balfour and Elizabeth Comack, Fernwood Publishing, 2006, pp. 95-112.

Bruckert, Chris, and Stacey Hannem. "Rethinking the Prostitution Debates: Transcending Structural Stigma in Systemic Responses to Sex Work." *Canadian Journal of Law and Society*, vol. 28, no. 1, 2013, pp. 43-63.

Bruckert, Chris, and Stacey Hannem. "To Serve and Protect? Social Profiling and Police Abuse of Power in Ottawa." *Selling Sex: Experience, Advocacy and Research on Sex Work in Canada*, edited by Emily van der Meulen et al., University of British Columbia Press, 2013, pp. 297-313.

Campbell, Angela. "Sex Work's Governance: Stuff and Nuisance." *Feminist Legal Studies*, vol. 23, 2015, pp. 27-45.

Canadian HIV/AIDS Legal Network. *Not Up to the Challenge of Change: An Analysis of the Report of the Subcommittee on Solicitation Laws.* 2007, www.aidslaw.ca/site/wp-content/uploads/2013/04/SSLR_response-E.pdf. Accessed 4 May 2018.

Canadian HIV/AIDS Legal Network and HALCO (HIV & AIDS Legal Clinic Ontario). *Brief to the Standing Senate Committee regarding Bill C-66, An Act to Establish a Procedure for Expunging Certain Historically Unjust Convictions and to Make Related Amendments to Other Acts.* April 2018, sencanada.ca/content/sen/committee/421/RIDR/Briefs/2018-04-06_C-66_BRF_HALCO_e.pdf. Accessed 9 February 2019.

Canadian Alliance for Sex Work Law Reform. "Current Anti-Human Trafficking Initiatives Harm Sex Workers." *Media Release.* 11 January 2019, sexworklawreform.com/blog/. Accessed 9 Feb. 2019.

Canadian Alliance for Sex Work Law Reform. "Public Statement to the Liberal Party on the adopted resolution on the Decriminalization of Sex Work." *Media Release.* 23 April 2018, sexworklawreform.com/public-statement-to-the-liberal-party-on-the-passing-of-the-resolution-of-decriminalization-of-sex-work/. Accessed 9 Feb. 2019.

Casavant, Lyne, and Dominique Valiquet. "Bill C-36: An Act to Amend the *Criminal Code* in Response to the Supreme Court of Canada Decision in Attorney General of Canada v Bedford and to make consequential amendments to other Acts." *Parliamentary Information and Research Service: Legal and Social Affairs Division*, 18 July 2014, pp. 1-26.

CBC Radio, "There's a 'major contradiction' between Trudeau's apology to LGBTQ Canadians and Bill C-66, prof says." *CBC Radio.* 25 June 2018, www.cbc.ca/radio/thecurrent/the-current-for-june-25-2018-1.4720521/there-s-a-major-contradiction-between-trudeau-s-apology-to-lgbtq-canadians-and-bill-c-66-prof-says-1.4720541. Accessed 9 February 2019.

Craig, Elaine. "Sex Work By Law: *Bedford*'s Impact on Municipal Approaches to Regulating the Sex Trade." *Review of Constitutional Studies*, vol. 16, no. 1, 2011, pp. 97-120.

Cheadle, Bruce. *"Federal Government Opens up Prostitution Law Rewrite to Public Input." Winnipeg Free Press.* 17 February 2014, winnipegfreepress.com/canada/federal-government-opens-up-prostitution-law-rewriteto-public-input-245845471.html. Accessed 5 May 2018.

Chu, Sandra Ka Hon, and Rebecca Glass. "Sex Work Law Reform in Canada: Considering Problems with the Nordic Model." *Alberta Law Review,* vol. no. 1, pp. 101-24.

Giddens, Anthony. *Modernity and Self-Identity: Self and Society in the Late Modern Age.* Stanford University Press, 1992.

Gillies, Kara. "A Wolf in Sheep's Clothing: Canadian Anti-Pimping Law and How it Harms Sex Workers." *Selling Sex: Experience, Advocacy and Research on Sex Work in Canada*, edited by Emily van der Meulen et al., University of British Columbia Press, 2013, pp. 269-278.

Gorkoff, Kelly, and Jane Runner. *Being Heard: The Experiences of Young Women in Prostitution*. Fernwood Publishing, 2003.

Haak, Debra M. "The Initial Test of Constitutional Validity: Identifying the Legislative Objectives of Canada's New Prostitution Laws." *University of British Columbia Law Review*, vol. 50, no. 3, 2017, pp. 657-96.

Hallgrimsdottir, Helga et al. "Fallen Women and Rescued Girls: Social Stigma and Media Narratives of the Sex Industry in Victoria BC from 1980-2005." *Canadian Review of Sociology and Anthropology*, vol. 43, no. 3, 2006, pp. 265-80.

Prasad, Sandeep. "*Now Is the Time to Decriminalize Sex Work.*" *HuffPost*. 24 April 2017, www.huffingtonpost.ca/sandeep-prasad/decriminalizing-sex-work_b_16211160.html. Accessed 4 May 2018.

Hughes, Jula, et al. "Equality & Incrementalism: The Role of Common Law Reasoning in Constitutional Rights Cases." *Ottawa Law Review*, vol. 44, no. 3, 2013, pp. 467-506.

Ivison, John. "Liberal Foot-Dragging on Prostitution Law May Lead to Charter Challenge." *National Post*, 18 January 2018, nationalpost.com/opinion/john-ivison-liberal-foot-dragging-on-prostitution-law-may-lead-to-charter-challenge. Accessed 5 May 2018.

Jeffrey, Leslie Ann, and Gayle Macdonald. *Sex Workers in the Maritimes Talk Back*. UBC Press, 2006.

Jochelson, Richard, and Kirsten Kramar. "Essentialism Makes for Strange Bedmates: The Supreme Court Case of *J.A.* and the Intervention of L.E.A.F." *Windsor Yearbook of Access to Justice*, vol. 30, no. 1, 2012, pp. 77-100.

Jochelson, Richard et al. *Criminal Law and Precrime: Legal Studies in Canadian Punishment and Surveillance in Anticipation of Criminal Guilt*. Routledge, 2017.

Johnson, Genevieve Fuji. "Governing sex work: an agonistic policy community and its relational dynamics." *Critical Policy Studies*, vol. 9, no. 3, 2015, pp. 259-77.

Krüsi, Andrea et al. "Criminalisation of Clients: Reproducing Vulnerabilities and Poor Health among Street-Based Sex Workers in Canada—A Qualitative Study." *BMJ Open*, vol. 4, 2014, pp. 1-10.

Laing, Mary. "Regulating Adult Work in Canada: The Role of Criminal and Municipal *Code*" *Policing Sex*, edited by Paul Johnson and Derek Dalton, Routledge, 2012, pp. 166-84.

Laing, Mary et al., editor. *Queer Sex Work*. Routledge, 2015.

Law, Tuulia. "Licensed or Licentious? Examining Regulatory Discussions of Stripping in Ontario." *Canadian Journal of Law and Society*, vol. 30, no. 1, 2015, pp. 31-50.

Lawrence, Sonia. "Expert-Tease: Advocacy, Ideology and Experience in *Bedford* and Bill C-36." *Canadian Journal of Law and Society*, vol. 30, no. 1, 2015, pp. 5-7.

Leamon, Sarah E. "Canada Should Expunge All Historically Unjust LGBTQ Convictions." *HuffPost*. 15 June 2018, www.huffingtonpost.ca/sarah-e-leamon/lgbtq-bill-c-66-pride_a_23452862/. Accessed 9 Feb. 2019.

Lewis, John et al. "Managing risk and safety on the job: The experiences of Canadian sex workers." *Journal of Psychology and Human Sexuality*, vol. 17, no. 1/2, 2005, pp. 147-67.

Lewis, John, and Frances Shaver. "Rising to the Challenge: Addressing the Concerns of People Working in the Sex Industry." *Canadian Review of Sociology and Anthropology*, vol. 48, no. 1, 2011, pp. 47-64.

Lewis, Jacqueline, et al. "Going 'round again: The Persistence of Prostitution-Related Stigma." *Selling Sex: Experience, Advocacy and Research on Sex Work in Canada*, edited by Emily van der Meulen et al. UBC Press, 2013, pp. 198-208.

Lowman, John. *Submission to the Subcommittee on Solicitation Laws of the Standing Committee on Justice, Human Rights, Public Safety and Emergency Preparedness*. House of Commons, 1st Session, 38th Parliament (February 21). 2005, files.efc-canada.net/si/Prostitution/Solicitation%20-%20EFC%20Submission%2020050216%20Web.pdf. Accessed 5 May 2018.

Lowman, John, and Chris Atchison. "Men who buy sex: A survey in the Greater Vancouver Regional District." *Canadian Review of Sociology and Anthropology*, vol. 43, no. 3, 2006, pp. 281-96.

Lyons, Tara, et al. "Negotiating Violence in the Context of Transphobia and Criminalization: The Experiences of Trans Sex Workers in Vancouver, Canada." *Qualitative Health Research*, vol. 27, no. 2, 2017, pp. 182-90.

MacKay, Peter. Statement by the Minister of Justice Regarding Legislation in Response to the Supreme Court of Canada Ruling in Attorney General of Canada v Bedford et al. Department of Justice, 4 June 2014, www.canada.ca/en/news/archive/2014/06/statement-minister-justice-regarding-legislation-response-supreme-court-canada-ruling-attorney-general-canada-v-bedford-al-.html. Accessed 5 May 2018.

Mathieson, Ane et al. "Prostitution Policy: Legalization, Decriminalization and the Nordic Model." *Seattle Journal for Social Justice*, vol. 14, no. 2, 2016, pp. 367-428.

Milrod, Christine, and Ronald Weitzer. "The Intimacy Prism: Emotion Management among the Clients of Escorts." *Men and Masculinities*, vol. 15, no. 5, 2012, pp. 447-67.

McCarthy, Bill, et al. "Factors Linked to Selection into Sex Work: A Comparative Study of Three Service Occupations." *Archives of Sexual Behavior*, 2014. doi: 10.1007/s10508-014-0281-7. Accessed 5 May 2018.

McLaren, John. "Chasing the Social Evil: Moral Fervour and the Evolution of Canada's Prostitution Laws, 1867-1917." *Canadian Journal of Law and Society*, vol. 1, 1986, pp. 125-65.

O'Neil, Maggie, et al. "Living with the Other: Street Sex Work, Contingent Communities, and Degrees of Tolerance." *Criminology & Penology*, vol. 4, no. 1, 2008, pp. 73-93.

Ottawa Citizen. "Sex Workers Urge Liberal Government to Decriminalize Prostitution." *Ottawa Citizen*, 17 Dec. 2015, ottawacitizen.com/news/local-news/sex-workers-urge-liberal-government-to-decriminalize-prostitution. Accessed 5 May 2018.

Ontario Women's Justice Network (OWJN). "Sex Work and the Law in Canada: After Bedford." Ontario Women's Justice Network (OWJN), 2016, owjn.org/2016/03/sex-work-and-the-law-in-canada-after-bedford/. Accessed 5 May 2018.

Prostitutes of Ottawa, Gatineau, Work, Educate, Resist (POWER). "Sex Workers Speak about Safety, Security and Well-being." *Challenge: Ottawa area sex workers speak out*. POWER, 2012, www.powerottawa.ca/POWER_Report_Challenges.pdf, pp. 30-63. Accessed 5 May 2018.

Powell, Maria. "Moving Beyond the Prostitution Reference: *Bedford v Canada.*" *University of New Brunswick Law Journal*, vol. 64, 2013, pp. 187-207.

Rotenberg, Cristine. "Prostitution offences in Canada: Statistical trends." *Canadian Centre for Justice Studies*, no. 85-002-X, 2016, www150.statcan.gc.ca/n1/en/pub/85-002-x/2016001/article/14670-eng.pdf?st=KUBSk28G, pp. 1-24. Accessed 6 Aug. 2018.

Sanders, Jane. *Recent Changes to Police Powers of Arrest (Amendments to Section 99 of LEPRA)*. 2014, www.criminalcle.net.au/main/page_cle_pages_police_powers.html. Accessed on 23 June 2015.

Shaver, Frances. "The Regulation of Prostitution: Setting the Morality Trap." *Social Control in Canada*, edited by Bernard Schissel and Linda Mahood, Oxford University Press, 1996, pp. 204-26.

Shaver, Frances. "Sex Work and the Law: A Critical Analysis of Four Policy Approaches to Adult Prostitution." *Thinking about Justice: A Book of Readings*, edited by Kelly Gorkoff and Richard Jochelson. Fernwood Publishing, 2012, pp. 190-216.

Shaver, Frances. *Bill C-36: Entrenched in Personal Moral Values and Inaccurate Stereotypes*. 2014, www.parl.gc.ca/Content/SEN/Committee/412/lcjc/Briefs/C-36/SM_C-36_brief_Frances_Shaver_E.pdf. Accessed 5 May 2018.

Shaver, Frances, and Martin Weinberg. "Outing the stereotypes: A comparison of high track strolls in Montreal, Toronto, and San Francisco." Paper presented at the Society for the Scientific Study of Sex, Annual Meeting, Montreal, Quebec, Canada, November 2002.

Sibley, Marcus A. "Owning Risk: Sex Worker Subjectivities and the Reimagining of Vulnerability and Victimhood." *British Journal of Criminology*. doi: doi:10.1093/bjc/azy010. 2018. Accessed 4 May 2018.

Socías, María Eugenia et al. "Social and Structural Factors Shaping High Rates of Incarceration among Sex Workers in a Canadian Setting." *Journal of Urban Health*, vol. 92, no. 5, 2015, pp. 966-79.

Special Committee on Pornography and Prostitution. *Pornography and Prostitution in Canada Volume II*. Ottawa: Minister of Supply and Services Canada, 1985.

Sex Trade Advocacy and Research (STAR). *Health, Security and Sex Work Policy. Invited Presentation to the House of Commons Subcommittee on Solicitation Laws.* 2005, billreimer.net/fmshaver/research/documents/LEWIS-etal-2005-complete.pdf. Accessed 4 May 2018.

Sex Trade Advocacy and Research (STAR). *Safety, Security and the Well-being of Sex Workers.* Policy report submitted to the House of Commons Subcommittee on Solicitation Laws. 2006. web2.uwindsor.ca/courses/sociology/maticka/star/pdfs/safety_and_security_report_final_version.pdf. Accessed 4 May 2018.

Stewart, Hamish. "*Bedford* and the Structure of Section 7." *McGill Law Journal*, vol. 60, no. 3, 2015, pp. 575-94.

Stewart, Hamish. "The Constitutionality of the New Sex Work Law." *Alberta Law Review*, vol. 54, no. 1, 2016, pp. 69-88.

The Guardian. "Raise Boys as Feminists to Change 'Culture of Sexism,' Says Justin Trudeau." *The Guardian*, 11 Oct. 2017, www.theguardian.com/world/2017/oct/11/justin-trudeau-pens-essay-on-raising-feminist-sons-all-of-us-benefit. Accessed 4 May 2018.

Van der Meulen, Emily, and Elya Maria Durisin. "Why Decriminalize? How Canada's Municipal and Federal Regulations Increase Sex Workers' Vulnerability." *Canadian Journal of Women and the Law*, vol. 20, no. 2, 2008, pp. 289-311.

Weinberg, Martin S., et al. "Gendered Sex Work in the San Francisco Tenderloin." *Archives of Sexual Behavior*, vol. 28, no. 6, 1999, pp. 503-521.

Weitzer, Ronald. "Sociology of Sex Work." *American Review of Sociology*, vol. 35, 2009, pp. 213-34.

Welch, Mary Agnes. "Province Urges Feds to Use Nordic Model on Sex Trade: Targets Pimps, Johns Rather Than Workers." *Winnipeg Free Press*, 15 Feb. 2014, www.winnipegfreepress.com/local/province-urges-feds-to-use-nordic-model-on-sex-trade-245655561.html. Accessed 5 May 2018.

Wright, Jordana et al. "'It Depends on Who You Are, What You Are': 'Community Safety' and Sex Workers' Experience with Surveillance." *Surveillance & Society*, vol. 13, no. 2, 2015, pp. 265-82.

Wu, David. W.L. "Case Comment: Missing the Forest for the Trees in *Canada (Attorney General) v Bedford*." *Review of Constitutional Studies*, vol. 19, no. 2, 2015, pp. 281-302.

Jurisprudence

Bedford v Canada (Attorney General) 2010 ONSC 4264 [*Bedford Trial*].

Canada (Attorney General) v Bedford 2012 ONCA 186 [*Bedford Appeal*].

Canada (Attorney General) v Bedford 2013 SCC 72, [2013] 3 S.C.R. 1101 [*Bedford*].

R. v Boodhoo, and others 2018 ONSC 7205 [*Boodhoo and others*].

Reference re ss.193 and 195(1)(C) of the Criminal Code (Man.) [1990] 1 SCR 1123 [*Prostitution Reference*].

Legislation

Bill C-36, *An Act to Amend the Criminal Code in Response to the Supreme Court of Canada Decision in Attorney General of Canada v Bedford and to Make Consequential Amendments to Other Acts*, 2nd Session, 41st Parliament, 2013-2014 (first reading 4 June 2014).

Bill C-66, *An Act to Establish a Procedure for Expunging Historically Unjust Convictions and to Make Related Amendments to Other Acts*, 1st Session, 42nd Parliament, 2015-2018 (first reading 28 November 2017).

Bill C-75, *An Act to Amend the Criminal Code, the Youth Criminal Justice Act and other Acts and to Make Consequential Amendments to other Acts*. 2019. c 25. 42nd Parliament, 1st Session.

Criminal Code of Canada, RSC 1985, c C-46.

Criminal Code of Canada, RSC 1985, Section 197.

Criminal Code of Canada, RSC 1985, Section 210.

Criminal Code of Canada, RSC 1985, Section 213(1.1).

Criminal Code of Canada, RSC 1985, Section 286.1 (1).

Criminal Code of Canada, RSC 1985, Section 286.2.

Criminal Code of Canada, RSC 1985, Section 286.3.

Criminal Code of Canada, RSC 1985, Section 286.4.

Chapter Three

Intimate Images and the Law

Richard Jochelson, Alicia Dueck-Read, James Gacek, and Brayden McDonald

Introduction

Sharing nude or partially nude pictures of oneself is part of the modern landscape of dating and relationships. These image exchanges may be motivated by a desire to enhance intimacy, flirtation, or as a form of sexual expression (Slane 117). Yet increasingly, images that were initially shared voluntarily are being circulated without consent. Distribution may involve the recipient of the image showing another friend, posting the image on social media, or sending the sexually explicit photo directly to friends, family, and co-workers of the victim. In its most extreme manifestation, the image may be posted to one of the estimated three thousand searchable revenge porn websites along with the name, address, and phone number of the victim (McGlynn et al. 29). Canada's legal responses to the non-consensual distribution of intimate images (NCDII) has often left much to be desired in the way of understanding the gendered, violent nature of the phenomenon in a comprehensive way.

In this chapter, we discuss the social problems that undergird the phenomenon of NCDII, the legislative responses, and some of the harms that occur with the distribution of these images. The second half of the chapter discusses the initial judicial responses to the proliferation of intimate images and the legislative web of provincial and criminal statutes available to victims of NCDII. As we show, NCDII criminal prohibitions are only one way these matters can appear before courts. Voyeurism, extortion, provincial civil statutes, and various other criminal sanctions are commonly used instead of the specific NCDII criminal charges under section 162.1 of the *Code*. Ultimately, as time progresses, more jurisprudence will emerge to develop a more fulsome NCDII legal analytic. We are truly at the early stages of legal responses to this phenomenon. We end this chapter by suggesting that the phenomenon of NCDII should be viewed through a gendered lens, with attention to its inherent violence, thereby moving beyond the privacy-based approach of the current legal regime.

Framing the Issue of NCDII

In this chapter, we use the phrase "non-consensual distribution of intimate images" (NCDII)[1] to refer to the phenomenon through which nude, seminude and sexualized images—photographs or videos—are distributed electronically without the consent of the person(s) in the image. The initial photos may be taken with consent in the context of a romantic relationship. Some studies estimate that up to 80 per cent of NCDII were initially taken as selfies by the person depicted in the photo (Uhl et al. 53). Colloquially, the unauthorized sharing of these photos, sometimes occurring after a relationship ends, is referred to as "revenge porn." However, this label fails to capture the diversity of circumstances under which the initial image is captured and the intersecting factors at play in distribution. For example, the initial photos may not have been taken in the context of a relationship, such as in voyeuristic acts of "upskirting" or "downblousing," or may have been taken in the context of a relationship but without the knowledge of the person in the image, such as by hidden camera. Additionally, photos are sometimes retrieved from the victim's device through hacking or other means of theft (51). Other practices captured under the umbrella of NCDII and related terms may include when the initial image is not taken consensually such as when a victim is asleep, unconscious, or under the effects of drugs or alcohol. NCDII and related terms are also sometimes used to refer to photos taken during the course of a sexual assault (Powell and Henry, "Sexual" 400). NCDII may also encompass situations in which there was no intimate image initially shared and sexualized photoshopping was used; sexualized photoshopping delineates circumstances in which a pornographic image is superimposed onto an individual's head or body so that it looks as if that person is nude, seminude, or engaged in a sexual act. Technology has advanced to the point where it is almost impossible to tell when images have been altered in this way (McGlynn et al. 34).

Within academic literature, media, parliamentary debates, and public society, a wide variety of other terms are used to describe the gathering and non-consensual distribution of images including sexting, cyberbullying, and revenge porn. Sexting is used to describe the creation and distribution of sexually explicit text, video, and/or picture messages via mobile phones, social media, or the Internet (Powell and Henry, "Blurred" 119; Lee and Crofts; Slane 117). Problematically, it is not uncommon for the consensual and non-consensual sharing and distribution of images to be subsumed under the same umbrella term of sexting (Powell and Henry, "Blurred" 120; Lee and Crofts 454). Furthermore, the term "sexting" has been used to refer to recordings of sexual assaults and grooming of children by adult predators (Lee and Crofts). The erasure of consent in the framework of sexting, accompanied by a moral panic over young people's sexual expression, has led to sexting, even in its consensual form, being vilified in some contexts (Lee and Crofts; Karaian 283; Henry and Powell, "Embodied" 767; Henry and Powell, "Beyond" 105). Anastasia Powell and Nicola Henry note that "current debates and responses to sexting have tended to conflate consensual sexual behavior between two young people of consenting age with sexual harm in, and of, itself" (Powell and Henry, "Blurred"), even though many of the cases we discuss in this chapter occur between adults.

Cyberbullying is a broad term under which NCDII is sometimes captured and has been used frequently in Canadian discussions of intimate image sharing. Cyberbullying is defined "an act of reciprocal conflict" in an online environment, often though not exclusively involving youth who can simultaneously be a victim and an aggressor (see Coburn et al.). Cyberbullying as a term is easily recognized and to some degree understood, but it covers such a broad range of behaviours and practices that we would contend that it is unhelpful to yield a meaningful understanding of what is at issue when examining the non-consensual distribution of intimate images (Bailey, "Time").

Interestingly, cyberbullying as a concept was used substantially in media, political and popular discourse surrounding the development of section 162.1, Canada's NCDII criminal sanction. Both opponents and advocates of Bill C-13, the precursor to section 162.1, tended to associate cyberbullying with the non-consensual distribution of images (Felt 146).

The merger of the concepts of cyberbullying and NCDII is problematic for a number of reasons. For one, the lack of intersectional analysis in discussions of cyberbullying is of note. Cyberbullying as a concept has received enormous attention in scholarly and popular discourse, yet the literature on cyberbullying generally lacks an understanding of how gender, racialization, and sexuality operate as structuring principles of violence (Crooks 63, 71; West Coast LEAF, "Submission" 1). Furthermore, as noted in the definition of cyberbullying provided by Patricia Coburn and colleagues above, bullying is sometimes conceived of as "an act of reciprocal conflict," which is a gross misrepresentation of the power imbalance within which NCDII occurs.

Most commonly, NCDII is referred to as "revenge porn." In the media, revenge porn is often defined in narrow terms as when a person uploads nude or semi-nude photos, often as an act of revenge or retribution after a relationship has ended (Bates 22–23). Although this label may fit some types of NCDII, the framework fails to capture the scope and complexity of how images are distributed online without consent (Beyens and Lievens 32). For example, the term "revenge porn" ignores incidences of NCDII that are not motivated by revengeful desires or when the images do not serve the purpose of pornography (Henry and Powell, "Sexual" 400).

Even so, the label of revenge porn is concerning for a number of other reasons. First, using the terminology of revenge porn validates a victim-blaming narrative in which a woman becomes an object whose consent was unnecessary or unwarranted given the presumed betrayal in the situation (Uhl et al. 51). Evidence of how labelling the distribution of images as a result of betrayal contributes to victim blaming can be seen in a study of websites devoted to the posting of NCDII. The study found that only women whose pictures were posted alongside a rationale for the posting (i.e., because they were an ex, a slut, unfaithful) were threatened in other website user's comments. In this way, by labelling their actions as motivated by revenge or their former partner's sexual unfaithfulness, the perpetrator was able to assign culpability to their female victim (62).² Women are thereby positioned as gatekeepers of sexuality, punished for taking the photo in the first place and reducing the extent to which they are seen as victims. As noted by Henry and Powell, in their broader discussion of technology-facilitated sexual violence,

> These behaviours [of technology-facilitated sexual violence] are frequently framed in public discourse using euphemistic, titillating or narrow language that produces a paradigmatic conceptualization of the behaviour (e.g: "revenge porn") and in the process excludes other related behaviours or leads to both victim blaming and perpetrator exoneration. ("Sexual" 398)

Second, framing the image as pornography puts the focus on the content of the image, which may have the effect of conflating images that could be distributed consensually in commercial pornography with those distributed nonconsensually (Henry and Powell, "Sexual" 401). Similarly, the phrase "non-consensual pornography," which is also used to describe NCDII, is problematic, as it may incorrectly assume or legitimize other forms of pornography as consensual (McGlynn et al. 38). Third, framing NCDII as pornography may fail to recognize the impact of NCDII on victims and the way in which distribution is used by perpetrators as a tool of humiliation, exploitation, and coercion. As Clare McGlynn and colleagues note, "the language of porn risks eroticising the harms of image-based sexual abuse" (38). The term also fails to capture the fact that some of the images involved in NCDII may be taken in the context of a loving relationship (Henry and Powell, "Sexual" 401). As Henry and Powell posit, using the term pornography "has the potential both to minimize the harm done to victims and to liken the images to an acceptable and/or desirable subgenre within commercially produced online pornography" (Henry and Powell, "Sexual" 409-1; see also McGlynn et al. 39).

Scope of the Problem

Research confirms that consensually sending sexually explicit photos and videos is increasingly common in the modern dating and relationship context (Uhl et al.). Particularly among youth, the behaviour appears to be a common part of courtship (Henry and Powell,

"Technology-Facilitated" 201; Branch et al. 130). In a Canadian study analyzing over thirty different studies of youth sexting, on average, 14.8 per cent of youth were sending sexts, and 27.4 per cent were receiving sexts (Madigan et al.). Some research suggests that women and girls may engage in more consensual sexting behaviours than boys and men (Branch et al.) and that many girls engage in taking and sending intimate photos under coercion (138). Although coercion is highlighted as a factor in incidences of youth sexting, other researchers contend that female youth are no more likely than male youth to send sexts due to pressure (Madigan et al.) and that studies may be overstating the extent that pressure and coercion motivate girls' sexting due to problematic moral overtones in research design and analysis (Lee and Crofts). Rather, the desire to send a "sexy present" or responding to a sexually explicit sext received may be more salient factors for sending a sext (Branch et al. 130). An exception to this may be present in marginalized populations, which may be more likely to experience coercion as a motivating factor in sending sexts (Lee and Crofts).

Alongside the rise of the consensual sharing of intimate images has been the non-consensual distribution (Uhl et al. 50). The majority of research conducted highlights incidences of NCDII among adolescents and youth (Henry and Powell, "Technology-Facilitated" 198). In their study of college students in the United States, Kathryn Branch et al. found that 10 per cent of their sample had an intimate photo shared beyond the intended recipient; those who reported this were predominantly female, eighteen years of age, and had the photo shared by a current boyfriend or girlfriend (138). In an examination of youth studies on sexting, Shari Madigan and colleagues found that on average, one in eight youth either forwarded or had an intimate sext forwarded without consent. Several studies point to youth and young adults having a higher proportion of NCDII than adults (Eaton et al. 16; Lenhart et al.). However, Henry and Powell suggest that it is a mistake to think that the sharing of intimate images and other forms of online harassment and violence are a practice common only to youth. In fact, they argue that "there appears to be a great deal of similarity between the forms of technology-facilitated sexual violence and harassment experienced by young and adult women alike" (Henry and Powell, "Beyond" 114).

Studies in the United States have found that between 4 to 12.8 per cent of adults may have been victims of, or threatened with, the non-consensual disclosure of intimate images (Eaton et al. 11; Lenhart et al. 4). Not surprisingly, the number of websites catering to NCDII has also risen; one estimate is that there are likely three thousand in operation (McGlynn et al. 29). These websites encourage users to submit nude photos of ex-partners and allow for derogatory and salacious comments by the original poster and by other site users. These websites can also be very profitable, with one reported to bring in $13,000 USD a month (Bates). There are some indications that sexualized photoshopping is also on the rise, as some websites are marketed to produce such images (McGlynn et al. 34).

Canadian statistics on the incidence of NCDII are sparse. The Canadian Centre for Child Protection (CCCP) reported that thirteen hundred Manitobans accessed online resources to deal with problems of intimate image distribution between 2016 and 2018 and that fifty people directly contacted CCCP staff for help with nonconsensually distributed intimate images (Kubinec). The Manitoba government reported that between March 2015 and January 2016, 350 reports of non-consensual intimate image sharing from across Canada were made to the CCCP (Manitoba Government). In 2016, Statistics Canada reported that there were 815 incidences of non-consensual distribution of intimate images in Canada. These numbers are small and represent only those incidences reported and properly categorized by government officials under the NCDII label and, therefore, likely fail to represent the multitudes of people actually affected by the phenomenon.

When images are shared nonconsensually, these tend to be shared alongside identifying information. In a sample of victims of non-consensual intimate image sharing by Danielle Keats Citron and Mary Anne Franks, more than 50 per cent had their full names and links to social media profiles included with their image, and 20 per cent had their email address and phone number posted alongside their photo (Bates 23). In a study from Uhl and colleagues, 18.7 per cent of posts on revenge porn websites included the victim's first name; 17.9 per cent of these also included their last name, age, and city (57). Interestingly, when the perpetrator gave a reason for posting the image, the victim's name was more likely to be present. Furthermore, when a reason was provided, it was also more likely for the women to be threatened in comments made by other website users (63). It is not uncommon for women whose pictures are posted along with identifying information to receive threats of sexual assault, rape, and even death (Kitchen 265).

Research confirms that women are the primary victims of online sexual violence generally (Henry and Powell "Sexual" 399; Henry and Powell "Embodied" 759; Henry and Powell, "Technology-Facilitated" 198) and in the sharing of non-consensual intimate images, more specifically (Henry and Powell "Technology-Facilitated" 202; Eaton et al 12). A 2017 American study found that women were 1.7 times more likely than men to be victims of, or threatened with, non-consensual intimate image distribution (Eaton et al. 12). In an American study of photos from seven websites devoted to the NCDII, researchers found that 91.8 per cent of the images posted were of women (Uhl et al. 57). Another Canadian study of NCDII websites found that the nature of the comments and the type of intimate pictures suggested a heterosexual male perspective (Slane and Langlois, "Debunking"). This corresponds with research that shows that women and girls are the primary victims of sexual violence offline (Henry and Powell, "Sexual" 399).

Overall, there is an absence of research examining the intersection of online violence with race, age, sexuality, and socioeconomic status (Henry and Powell, "Technology-Facilitated"). An American study of college students found that those who had experienced revenge porn were more likely to be racialized (Branch et al. 138). Furthermore, women with disabilities may also be frequent targets in NCDII (Bond and Tyrrell 3). Several researchers noted that lesbian, gay, bisexual, transgender, queer, and intersex people may be disproportionately targeted by online forms of violence (Bond and Tyrell 3; Henry and Powell, "Technology-Facilitated" 198; Citizen Lab 2). In Andrea Langlois and Ganaele Slane's examination of non-consensual intimate image websites, although the majority of the pictures were of female victims, the male pictures that did exist were mainly of allegedly gay males (Langlois and Slane 123; see also Uhl et al. 61).

Interestingly, Langlois and Slane found that the majority of user comments on the NCDII websites were directed at shaming other website users, particularly the original poster; this shaming frequently involved making homophobic or racist comments about the original poster (Langlois and Slane 126). This is further evidence of the way in which racism and heteronormativity intersect with the online culture of non-consensual intimate image sharing.

Harms

Although conventional legal protections are often focused around protecting the body from harm and tend to have more credence, it would be a mistake to presume that the online harms are somehow less important or impactful than physical harms (Henry and Powell, "Embodied"). As Jordan Fairbairn discusses, "by continuing to understand safety as primarily physical, and breaches of privacy as embarrassment, law and policy ignore the complexity of our social world" (Fairbairn 244). Thinking of technological spaces in socio-spatial terms may help to undergird the far-reaching impacts of NCDII. Technological spaces are realms in which people work, play, build communities, and pursue learning; increasingly, the Internet is a sphere on which people's social interactions depend and these spheres may even be more important in some contexts than non-virtual spaces (Henry and Powell, "Embodied" 765).

Furthermore, harms perpetrated virtually can have real world, physical effects. As a result of NCDII, women may lose jobs and fall into isolation and poverty, all of which can have significant effects on physical health and safety: "It is misguided to conclude that online sexual violence has no impact on physical well-being" (Fairbairn 244). The harms experienced by victims of non-consensual pornography are wide ranging and may include damage to reputation, humiliation, and public shaming (Bates 23). This may correspond with a loss of self-confidence (33) and the decision to change names or alter appearances after the incident (Uhl et al. 51). When women hold other marginalized identities, such as being LGBTQ2S or being from a racialized community, this may also "compound ... experiences of gender-based violence" (Citizen Lab 2).

The far-reaching and all-encompassing nature of the reputation damage brought about by new technologies hold an "unprecedented power" to achieve a shaming that stretches across geographic borders to vast audiences and at great speeds (Henry and Powell, "Embodied" 759; Langlois and Slane 129). Once an image is posted, even legal avenues may prove insufficient to combat ongoing distribution given jurisdictional immunities (Langlois and Slane 131). This means that the resulting harm is continuous and long lasting (Bates 23). Furthermore, the anonymity of the Internet allows for perpetrators to undertake their actions without the corresponding social shame that may have been tied to those actions had anonymity not been as easy to establish. Within the online realm, the narrative constructed by the perpetrator by posting intimate images may become the dominant or only online story about the victim, which can in turn have personal and professional consequences (see for example Nussbaum 79-80).

The economic impacts of the reputation damage are substantial. Langlois and Slane note the following:

> What is most noticeable about revenge porn ... is not only the intense sexual violence it promotes but also the ways in which it functions within multiple information networks that enable and solidify capitalization on negative reputations. As networks, algorithms, and platforms are now in the business of collecting all information that constitutes and builds network subjects, attacks on reputation should be understood as economic attacks as well as social ones, where victims suffer and perpetrators profit both socially and economically. (133)

In short, harm can no longer be conceived of as what is done to the physical body alone but in recognition that women have "technosocial lived experience" and the online violence perpetrated against them must be understood in relation to the importance of the online realm (Henry and Powell, "Embodied" 767-68).

Other authors have labelled the NCDII as an attack on human dignity. In discussing their study of NCDII, Langlois and Slane note that "since most of the pictures on the site were taken willingly at the time, their release plays especially brutally on the victim's disempowerment, robbing her of her sexual integrity and of her dignity to inhabit her body as her own" (126). It can lead to difficulties in later trusting partners and others as well as an inability to find new romantic partners (Bates 23, 33). Many victims also experience mental health issues as a result including anxiety, depression, and PTSD (33).

More broadly, the NCDII compounds inequality for women in the electronic realm. It compromises women's "ability to share cyberspace on equal terms with men, and amplifies that sexual stereotyping and discrimination women experience in the offline world" (Franks qtd. in Uhl et al. 54). It is neither fair nor reasonable to expect women to forgo online and technological involvement in order to protect themselves. Nonparticipation is tyrannical, liberty-depriving, and contributes to an all-encompassing form of harassment (Franks 251). Unsurprisingly, because of the many harms associated with non-consensual image sharing and the extensive media coverage of several suicides that followed incidences of NCDII, legislators have crafted a range of legal responses.

The Emergence of Section 162.1

The high-profile suicides of Canadian teens Rehtaeh Parsons and Amanda Todd (Felt 147), who were bullied following the distribution of their intimate images, spurred the creation of Bill C-13 in 2013 and the resulting *Criminal Code* section (Aikenhead). Section 162.1 made it a criminal offence to knowingly and without consent distribute, publish, sell, transmit, advertise, or make available an intimate image. The bill also allowed for the court to compel Internet service providers to delete the material; it also prohibited someone convicted under the section from using the Internet for a period of time and allowed the court to order the seizure of intimate images (West Coast LEAF, "#Cybermisogny" 12). The wording of section 162.1 is gender neutral, as with the vast majority of *Criminal Code* offences. Moira Aikenhead notes that 162.1 has been framed into a choice-based narrative, similar to sexual assault (126). Elements of 162.1 contain provisions similar to those on sexual assault, voyeurism, and criminal harassment (128). The offence "occupies a notional space between criminal harassment and sexual assault" (Mathen 540). Although the word "cyberbullying" is not used within section 162.1, a number of authors argue that the section was constructed within the milieu of concerns about youth cyberbullying and framed as a social problem (Felt 137; Bailey, "Time"). Cyberbullying was also used as a justification by government ministers when discussing and debating the Bill (Felt 137).

Discussions about cyberbullying emerged in Canadian political and public discourse as early as 2003 (Felt 140) and then again in 2008 (Bailey, "Time"). In 2011, the Standing Senate Committee on Human Rights was tasked with researching cyberbullying under Canada's international obligations under the UN Convention on the Rights of the Child (Felt 144). Their report in December 2012 was followed by a study released in June 2013 by the Coordinating Committee of Senior Officials Cybercrime Working Group (144). In 2012, the first federal response to cyberbullying culminated in Bill C-30—Protecting Children from Internet Predators Act. Bill C-30 failed when Parliament was prorogued (Cartwright 21). Bill C-13 followed in the fall of 2013 and was given royal assent in March 2015 (Felt).

Parliamentary debates on Bill C-13 focused primarily on examples of cyberbullying that culminated in suicides. The main examples of those targeted included girls who experienced sexualized attacks and gay male youths (Bailey, "Time"). The content of these parliamentary debates provides evidence of how NCDII was framed as a social problem of cyberbullying (Felt 137; Bailey, "Time"). The social problem frame tended to characterize the problem in relation to its most intense circumstances and omitted discussions addressing the most common forms of the problem (Felt).

Alongside these parliamentary debates, the news coverage predominantly framed cyberbullying as a social problem with the primary remedy recommended as public attention and new legislation (Cartwright 22). The media oversimplified the stories of the youth suicides "in an effort to establish a clear pattern and construct the Canadian definition of cyberbullying as a social problem" (Felt 148). Thus, cyberbullying was framed as more of a moral issue than a legal one (Cartwright 22).

Responses to section 162.1 were mixed; in some circles it was praised for filling in a grey area in the law and assigning a moral blameworthiness that only criminal law could provide (Mathen 530). The section was also lauded for recognizing and legitimising victim experiences (Dodge and Spencer 4). Yet many academics and community organizations were sceptical of Bill C-13, which included expanded powers of state surveillance; there was also widespread advocacy for the bill to be split into two sections, separating the parts expanding surveillance powers from those specific to the NCDII offence (Bailey, "Time"; Cartwright 22; Felt 148; Citizen Lab 3; West Coast LEAF, "#Cybermisogyny" 13). The University of Toronto's Citizen Lab noted that "narratives which emphasize the vulnerability and victimhood of women and girls have been repeatedly employed in order to support claims for great generalized government powers to de-anonymize, identify, track, and surveil individuals online" (Citizen Lab 3). At the time of Ms. Parsons's complaint to police, for example, law enforcement already held the necessary search powers and grounds to investigate;

they simply failed to do so (3). Other concerns with Bill C-13, and later section 162.1, included the requirement to find a reasonable expectation of privacy at the time the image was created and at the time it was distributed in order to meet the definition of intimate image (Aikenhead). This meant that the victim must retain a reasonable expectation of privacy at both times in order for the charge to be sustained.

Such a requirement exacerbates the risk that judges would focus on the "reasonableness" of the victim's privacy expectations rather than on the severity of the offender's behaviour. An overemphasis on privacy may reduce the court's understanding of the offence as gender-based sexualized violence and instead focus a judge's attention to victim blaming—that is, the question of culpability may be reduced to the question of whether the victim's expectation of privacy was "unreasonable" (Aikenhead 133).

Scholars and civil society advocates were critical of Bill C-13's focus on criminal, punitive measures and the absence of concrete efforts to examine broader attitudes and systemic issues (Choo 72; Dodge and Spencer 4), such as rape culture and slut shaming, which allow for the distribution of such images in the first place (Shariff and DeMartini 294; Dodge 76; Choo 72-73). Some authors contend that attaching criminal penalties to non-consensual intimate image distribution deters youth from reporting incidences out of fear that they or their friends will face prosecution (Coburn et al. 571).

Since 162.1 was passed, there has not been a tremendous proliferation of cases prosecuted under the provision, but it is still in its early days. In a study of law enforcement approaches to NCDII among youth, Alexa Dodge and Dale Spencer found that the majority of officers did not even discuss the new law as an alternative to using child pornography provisions; instead of charging someone under 162.1, the officers articulated a desire to use noncriminal approaches, such as education and intimidation, including threatening to use child pornography provisions to charge youth (Dodge and Spencer 10). Part of this reluctance to charge youth under criminal provisions was due to the common-place nature of NCDII among youth (11). Arguably, part of the reluctance to use criminal sanctions has its roots in the failure of police to view NCDII as online sexual violence. In their survey, Dodge and Spencer found that police articulated some victim-blaming beliefs, such as conflating consensual and non-consensual image sharing and focusing on the behaviour of female victims, such as advocating digital abstinence (15-16). Although occurring before the advent of 162.1, a 2013 report from the Cybercrime Working Group similarly found that while Canadian law enforcement received reports of NCDII regularly, no criminal action was generally taken unless the images qualified as child pornography or there were aggravating factors (West Coast LEAF, "#Cybermisogyny" 12). However, as we shall see in the second half of this chapter, reported cases are beginning to emerge in the jurisprudence, and we may be at the beginning of a proliferation of cases and a more fulsome jurisprudence of NCDII.

To date, section 162.1 has not yet been applied to third party websites. Websites that cater to and promote the non-consensual distribution of intimate images are prolific and fueled in large part by economic incentives. As the content of the websites is primarily user generated, little investment is required on the part of the website operator (Langlois and Slane 127). Although 162.1 seems to apply to businesses that intentionally distribute such images, prosecuting businesses was not in direct contemplation when Bill C-13 was introduced, and to date, no business operator has been charged (Slane and Langlois, "Debunking" 44, 50). Additional amendments to 162.1 would better clarify business liability and, ideally, could specify that a business would not be criminally liable for user-generated content unless the business incites, invites, solicits, or counsels another person to commit an offence (61).

Multiple Legal Responses

Although NCDII has undoubtedly increased in recent years, its relatively recent explicit criminalization is arguably a testament to a "historical indifference and hostility to women's autonomy" (Citron and Franks 347). This is not to say that there were no other criminal and civil provisions that were used to combat NCDII. In fact, criminal laws on child pornography (section 163.1), criminal harassment (section 264), uttering threats (section 264.1), voyeurism (section 162), and extortion (section 346) have been used in varying degrees to combat NCDII (Khoday; Mathen; West Coast LEAF, "#Cybermisogyny"). Additional criminal provisions that could be applicable in some NCDII cases include the offences of obscene publication (section 163), false messages (section 372(1)), defamatory libel (section 300 and 301), mischief in relation to data (section 430(1.1)), identity theft and identity fraud (section 402.1, 402.2, and 403), unauthorized use of a computer (section 342.1 and 342.2), and intimidation (section 423) (West Coast LEAF, "#Cybermisogyny").

In addition, several common-law torts have been used or have the potential to be of use by victims of NCDII, including breach of confidence, invasion of privacy, intentional infliction of mental distress, misappropriation of personality, and defamation (Khoday; West Coast LEAF, "#Cybermisogyny"). Revenge porn websites, specifically, could be held liable through Canada's *Copyright Act* or the *Personal Information and Electronic Documents Act* (PIPEDA), which could be adapted easily to allow for the prosecution of businesses (Slane and Langlois, "Debunking", 57; Slane and Langlois, "Regulating"; West Coast LEAF "#Cybermisogyny" 33). As we shall discuss shortly, some of these criminal and civil alternatives continue to be used in cases of NCDII.

In addition, civil remedies under provincial privacy legislation, and specifically NCDII privacy legislation, were used in various forms over the years in response to intimate image distribution. One of the first, and most notorious provincial attempts to respond to NCDII, was Nova Scotia's *Cyber-Safety Act*. The Act was passed hastily within weeks of Rehtaeh Parsons's death. It was expansive in its provisions and purported to tackle the ability of cyberbullies to hide their identities online and limit the way in which perpetrators could enlist the help of others in their activities (Cartwright). Furthermore, the Act contained expansive powers of search and seizure for a newly formed cyber-investigative unit including the ability to enter the home of an alleged cyberbully and remove computers and cellphones, without notice (West Coast LEAF, "Cybermisogyny" 27).

The Act created a protection order regime, which included relaxed notice requirements, the ability to prohibit communications between the perpetrator and the victim, and order the temporary or permanent confiscation of electronic devices or the discontinuation of Internet service. It also gave profound powers to the court to compel anyone with information related to the computer, cell phone, IP address, website, or email to disclose information to authorities to assist with the identification of the perpetrator (Cartwright 20). If the perpetrator was a minor, the Act also allowed for the court to hold parents jointly or severally liable depending on whether the parents had provided access to the device used in the act, whether they had exercised reasonable degree of supervision, and whether they made an effort to prevent bullying upon becoming aware of its existence (20). The definition of cyberbullying within the Act was also found to be overbroad. Although the Act was written with youth in mind, the first cases pursued involved adults (20).

The Act was found unconstitutional in 2015 by the Supreme Court of Nova Scotia in *Crouch v Snell* after it was determined that the Act violated the section 2(b) and section 7 *Charter* rights of the defendant. The Supreme Court of Nova Scotia held that the Act was problematic because it provided no defence and did not require proof of harm; it was a "colossal failure" (Cartwright 20-21). Although the extensive powers of search and seizure granted to the government under the Act were later deemed unconstitutional, its attempt to curtail the ability of perpetrators to hide their identities was a laudable though formidable objective.

Indeed, some of the most difficult and pressing challenges to address within non-consensual intimate image distribution are jurisdictional (West Coast LEAF, "Cybermisogyny" 34). Canadian courts have a limited ability to enforce the removal of content from non-Canadian social media platforms or compel companies and Internet service providers to comply with their orders to remove content. Although some providers have made voluntary commitments to remove reported content from their search engines and storage platforms (Langlois and Slane 131; Slane and Langlois, "Debunking"), neither this nor the traditional justice apparatus can solve the ways in which information is shared and reshared, proliferating at vast speeds across the expansive anonymity of the Internet (Henry and Powell, "Embodied" 759, 769; Citron and Franks 350).

As our discussion above reveals, there are multiple means by which the criminal law could attempt to respond to the technological innovations that have allowed the non-consensual distribution of intimate images. Certainly, in March 2015, when Bill C-13 became law (Protecting Canadians from Online Crime Act), it was Canada's most targeted response to the phenomenon, even though policy documents have demonstrated other ways the *Criminal Code* could have been used to prosecute against the abuses of sharing digital intimate images without consent.

WestCoast LEAF, in its #Cybermisogyny report from 2014, discussed a number of ways digital crimes against women could be prosecuted. Notably, the report acknowledges the difficulty of using many of the existing provisions in the *Code*. For example, on page twenty-four of the report, in respect of defamatory libel, the report notes the following:

> While these provisions could apply in cases of cyber misogyny, it is very rare for charges to be brought under these sections. The cases considering these provisions highlight the challenges of using the criminal law in cases involving speech and expression. The Supreme Court of Canada has upheld the offence of publishing a defamatory libel known to be false (s. 300) as a reasonable limit on free speech rights under section 1 of the *Charter* ... however, several provincial courts of appeal have struck down the "simple" defamatory libel provision (s. 301) as an unjustifiable limit on freedom of expression .... The courts of BC have not ruled on this question. (West Coast LEAF, "#Cybermisogyny" 24)

The report is a thorough primer on the possibilities of the *Code* to deal more broadly with cyber-misogynistic acts. In our research, we limited ourselves to looking for application of the behaviours involved in the distribution of intimate images without consent pursuant to section 162.1 (contained in Bill C-13). We also looked for what other charges were used, either because the facts of the cases preceded the passage of Bill C-13 into law or because the court decided to use alternate routes of criminality. We focused on cases from 2014 to 2018, and we were surprised that a number of cases still use other *Code* provisions beyond section 162.1. As evidenced in the chart below, when section 162.1 was not used, charges under voyeurism (section 162) were the most common, followed by extortion (section 346) and civil, provincial statutes. Nonetheless, there is a robust trend to prosecute these matters under the new 162.1 provisions, which suggests that many more prosecutions may be on the horizon in years to come.

Table 4.0: Type of Charge Related to Intimate Image Nonconsensual Distribution 2014–2018

Type of Charge	Number of Reported Cases as of June 1, 2018*
s.162.1 Nonconsensual Distribution of Intimate Image	13
s.264 Criminal Harassment	3
s.162 Voyeurism	5
s.346 Extortion	4
s.163.1 Child Pornography	2
s.264.1 Uttering Threats	1
s.430(1.1) (5) Committing Mischief with Computer Data s.342.2 Use of device to further Computer Mischief without authorization	1
Civil Cases Discussing Intimate Images	4
Total Cases	**33**

* (includes multiple charges; does not include sentencing)

In the coming pages, we discuss the meaning of the intimate images provisions of the *Code* and consider a sample of the cases that have applied the provision. A great majority of the reported cases are sentencing decisions, and in those cases, we consider what courts are looking at in sentencing determinations. We also consider the adjudications under the more common criminal charges used in relation to NCDII, other than section 162.1. Lastly, we consider some of the civil law treatments available for victims of unlawful intimate image sharing. This area is one that continues to evolve as justices find themselves with more and more options in light of the ongoing growth in legislated torts and the common law itself. Finally, the chapter concludes by calling for NCDII to be resituated as regulating a behaviour that is rooted in gendered violence.

The *Code* and Intimate Images

Section 162.1 says the following: Everyone who knowingly publishes, distributes, transmits, sells, makes available or advertises an intimate image of a person knowing that the person depicted in the image did not give their consent to that conduct, or being reckless as to whether or not that person gave their consent to that conduct" has committed an offence. The offence is a hybrid one which means that the Crown can proceed either as an indictable offence and liable to imprisonment for a term of not more than five years; or offence punishable on summary conviction.

Section 162.1(2) defines "intimate image" as "a visual recording of a person made by any means including a photographic, film or video recording":

a) in which the person is nude, is exposing his or her genital organs or anal region or her breasts or is engaged in explicit sexual activity;

b) in respect of which, at the time of the recording, there were circumstances that gave rise to a reasonable expectation of privacy; and

c) in respect of which the person depicted retains a reasonable expectation of privacy at the time the offence is committed.

These conditions are conjunctive: all three must be demonstrated by the Crown. Section 162.2 allows for the court to impose a prohibition order on those either convicted under section 162.1 or discharged on conditions, which can prohibit the individual from using the Internet and other digital networks. Regarding the distribution of digital intimate images, a public good defence applies in 162.1(3): "No person shall be convicted of an offence under this section if the conduct that forms the subject-matter of the charge serves the public good and does not extend beyond what serves the public good."

Although section 162.1 focuses on the distribution of intimate images, including those captured with or without consent, their capturing when unbeknownst to a victim is also contemplated by the voyeurism provisions of the *Code*. Section 162 provides that everyone

> commits an offence who, surreptitiously, observes—including by mechanical or electronic means—or makes a visual recording

of a person who is in circumstances that give rise to a "reasonable expectation of privacy" if:

a) the person is in a place in which a person can reasonably be expected to be nude, to expose his or her genital organs or anal region or her breasts, or to be engaged in explicit sexual activity;

b) the person is nude, is exposing his or her genital organs or anal region or her breasts, or is engaged in explicit sexual activity, and the observation or recording is done for the purpose of observing or recording a person in such a state or engaged in such an activity; or

c) the observation or recording is done for a sexual purpose. (*Criminal Code* section 162)

The Crown must make out a reasonable expectation of privacy on the part of the victim. Note that these subsections are disjunctive; the Crown need only demonstrate that the facts match one of the three situations stipulated. Voyeurism is a hybrid offence that when prosecuted as an indictable offence carries a maximum punishment of imprisonment for a term not exceeding five years. Distributing voyeuristic materials is also an offence under 162(4) when one "prints, copies, publishes, distributes, circulates, sells, advertises or makes available the recording, or has the recording in his or her possession for" those purposes. These voyeurism provisions are applicable to situations where the victim was unaware of the images' creation in the first place. Once again, the defence of public good is available to the offender. Although voyeurism may not come to mind when one hears the term revenge porn, it encapsulates a type of behaviour that appears with some frequency in the case law and the repercussions for victims of both sets of crimes can be remarkably similar and severe.

Criminal prosecutions under section 162.1 (non-consensual distribution of intimate images) and section 162 (voyeurism) accounted for more than 50 per cent of the reported cases we found dealing with intimate image distribution in a four-year period. Reviewing some of these cases helps illuminate many of the common features of these adjudications. The constellation of facts in intimate image distribution cases is often straight forward. Thus, we see many more plea agreements than trials and therefore many of the reported decisions are sentencing decisions. Examining sentencing decisions can help elucidate elements of the substantive offence and aid us in understanding what aspects of the accused's conduct aggravates or mitigates their sentence. Nonetheless, we expect to see many more of these prosecutions proliferate as law enforcement and Crowns become better versed in the offences' constituent elements in the digital era.

Case Examples of 162.1

The early reported cases struggled to give meaning to the legislation. For example, how is the word "intimate" interpreted? Other issues that arose were identity: how does one determine the identity of the distributor of NCDII? We discuss two cases that speak to these issues.

In *R v Verner*, the complainant, M.S., and the accused, Verner, had been in a dating relationship on and off for about three years. M.S. dated B.L. for a time while she and Verner were in an off period. A conflict, which the court did not delineate, occurred between Verner and B.L. The alleged conduct occurred during one of M.S. and Verner's breaks from their relationship. An hour after this conflict, Verner sent an electronic communication, via either text message or Facebook, to B.L., containing an intimate image of M.S. that appeared to be a screenshot from a video. M.S. was with B.L. at the time and saw the image. She had been completely unaware of any such video and had never consented to it. The image depicted her and Verner having sexual intercourse. Although M.S. could not recall specifically, she testified that the image was accompanied by a message indicating that there was more of the video. The screenshot appeared to be of a Facebook page, and comments were visible, including by individuals known to M.S. It was also clear in the screenshot that Verner had posted the video. M.S. was unable to view the video, as Verner had blocked her from seeing his Facebook page. Although M.S. was visible in the image and was clearly nude, her breasts and genital or anal region were not visible.

The court was satisfied that a reasonable expectation of privacy in the images existed at the point of production and distribution of the image (*Verner* para 28). The main issue for the court was whether the nudity in question was captured by section 162.1, which required that the victim be "nude," "exposing ... her genital organs or anal region or her breasts" or "engaged in explicit sexual activity" (para 9).

The defence argued that nudity required either exposure of the genitals, breast, anus, or the depiction of explicit sexual activity. The Crown argued that any of the three scenarios would meet the definition of an intimate image: one where the depicted person is nude; another where the depicted person is exposing his or her genitals, anal region, or breasts; and one where the depicted person is engaged in explicit sexual activity.

The court considered the history of the legislation and the plain meaning of the section and concluded that the Crown's theory was correct. Alternatively, the court noted that the fact that the victim was shown bending on a bed while nude in the presence of another person constituted an explicit sexual activity (*R v Verner* paras 47, 64). The accused was, thus, found guilty.

The issue of identity arose in *R v M.R.* The complainant and the accused, M.R., were in a romantic relationship for several months in 2015. During the course of this relationship, they became engaged to be married. Both sets of parents were involved in the arrangements, in keeping with cultural custom. The complainant had provided several intimate images to the defendant during the summer months of 2015 in electronic form. Shortly before the relationship ended, M.R. texted the complainant to tell her that he had seen intimate images of her on Reddit, although the complainant was not able to find these when she accessed the site herself immediately afterwards. The relationship ended in September of 2015.

Of note is that after the end of the relationship, someone gained access to the complainant's university online account and locked her out of it. Furthermore, M.R. was in direct contact with the complainant's academic advisor without her knowledge. Her academic advisor also received anonymous correspondence alleging misconduct. After the end of the relationship, M.R. persistently contacted the complainant, despite her clear desire to have no further contact. The accused argued that the complainant had agreed to remain friends with him. In October of 2015, a number of the complainant's friends and family received an anonymous email containing an intimate image of her.

In November, the complainant's father received a further anonymous email, containing multiple intimate images of her. The prosecution alleged that the defendant—as the sole recipient of these intimate images sent by the complainant during the course of the relationship—

was the true author of the anonymous emails and committed an offence contrary to section 162.1 of the *Criminal Code*.

The most contested issue in this case was identity: it was the Crown's theory that the accused was, in fact, the source of the anonymous emails sent in both October and November. The evidence given by the complainant—that she had only sent intimate images to the accused—was accepted. It was also found that the intimate images sent by the complainant to M.R. were received by him (*R v M.R.* paras 57, 59).

The trial judge found that days after the alleged Reddit incident, the relationship ended with a meeting at a train station (*R v M.R.* para 75). The complainant's version of events was that she made it clear to M.R. during this meeting that she wanted no further contact with him and that he threatened to distribute her intimate images. This version of events was accepted by the court (para 121).

The complainant's testimony—that the shared images were a subset of the ones sent to the accused—was accepted (*R v M.R.* para 121). Furthermore, the accused possessed all of the necessary information to access the accounts of the complainant. The way that the October emails specifically targeted those closest to the complainant was also highly suggestive of someone with particular knowledge of her family and social circle. There was also evidence of messages sent by the accused to the complainant contemporaneously with the October emails, which demonstrated a discrete knowledge of what had occurred. This—taken together with the acceptance of the complainant's evidence that the accused had threatened to disseminate her intimate images at the train station—all led to a conviction (para 121).

Both of the cases above provide good examples of the way in which the court has attempted to determine questions of identity and what constitutes "intimate" under the provisions of section 162.1. Interestingly, as noted above, the bulk of the decisions we discovered dealing with section 162.1 were sentencing cases. Thus, it is worth summarizing the main sentencing principles we uncovered in the application of section 162.1.

Sentencing and 162.1

In making sentencing decisions, a judge needs to determine what constitutes the paramount sentencing objectives of the offence. Sections 718 to 718.2 of the *Criminal Code* explain the objectives and principles of sentencing and are intended to make sentencing fair and consistent (*R v Nasogaluak*). The purpose of sentencing under the *Code* is outlined in section 718:

> The fundamental purpose of sentencing is to contribute, along with crime prevention initiatives, to respect for the law and the maintenance of a just, peaceful and safe society by imposing just sanctions that have one or more of the following objectives:
>
> a) to denounce unlawful conduct;
>
> b) to deter the offender and other persons from committing offences;
>
> c) to separate offenders from society, where necessary;
>
> d) to assist in rehabilitating offenders;
>
> e) to provide reparations for harm done to victims or to the community; and
>
> f) to promote a sense of responsibility in offenders, and acknowledgment of the harm done to victims and to the community. (*Criminal Code* section 718)

In our review of the reported cases dealing with section 162.1 and sentencing, the paramount sentencing objectives were denunciation and deterrence, and, thus, incarceration was the norm (*R v P.S.D.* para 10; *R v McFarlane* para 22; *R v Greene* para 36; *R v A.C.* para 77; *A.C.* para 28; *R v J.S.* para 20). Deterrence, both specific and general, must have primacy (*R v M.R.* para 16). In situations of section 162.1 involving drug addiction or mental health factors, the principle of rehabilitation must be kept in mind, but in all cases, the principle of proportionality must be kept in mind under section 718.1 of the *Code*: a sentence must be proportionate to the gravity of the offence and the degree of responsibility of the offender (*R v O.S.D.* para 7). The gravity of the offence could result in an increased sentencing severity if a court became aware of planned action by an accused (para 13) or an accused's reduced control of the distribution chain of the image (*R v Greene* para 65;

Ly para 34). Similarly, the gravity of the offence would be reduced by the distribution of low quality images, where there was a reduced likelihood of future transmission (*R v P.S.D* para 15), and when the image is not posted on the Internet (*R v Greene* para 65). Our review of the jurisprudence in the context of section 162.1 demonstrates that a reviewing court should apply deference to the sentencing judge's weighing of aggravating and mitigating circumstances (*R v McFarlane* para 22).

Secondary sentencing principles are delineated by the *Code*, and the sentence can be aggravated or mitigated as determined by section 718.2:

> A court that imposes a sentence shall also take into consideration the following principles:
>
> a) a sentence should be increased or reduced to account for any relevant aggravating or mitigating circumstances relating to the offence or the offender, and, without limiting the generality of the foregoing,
>
>   i) evidence that the offence was motivated by bias, prejudice or hate based on race, national or ethnic origin, language, colour, religion, sex, age, mental or physical disability, sexual orientation, or any other similar factor,
>
>   ii) evidence that the offender, in committing the offence, abused the offender's spouse or common-law partner,
>
>   ii.i) evidence that the offender, in committing the offence, abused a person under the age of eighteen years,
>
>   iii) evidence that the offender, in committing the offence, abused a position of trust or authority in relation to the victim,
>
>   iv) evidence that the offence was committed for the benefit of, at the direction of or in association with a criminal organization, or
>
>   v) evidence that the offence was a terrorism offence shall be deemed to be aggravating circumstances. (*Criminal Code* section 718.2)

We have summarized the common aggravating circumstances from section 162.1 cases into victim's harms, offender's mentality, the nature of the image and its distribution, and the abandon of the accused. Victims' harms that can aggravate the sentence include when the accused's conduct was designed to harm the victim or family (*R v M.R.* para 18; *R v A.C.* para 43; *R v J.S.* para 37); the victim suffered a serious impact *(R v Greene* para 64; *R v A.C.* para 84; *R v M.R.* para 18; *R v J.S.* para 30; *R v J.T.B.* para 97), including the emotional impact (*R v A.C.* para 43); the harassment is ongoing and received from strangers (*R v A.C.* para 43); the lasting nature of the impact on the victim (*R v J.S.* para 37); the number of victims affected *(R v J.T.B.* para 97); the conduct resulted in suicide attempts by the victim *(R v J.S.* para 30); the victim's family is affected negatively (*R v M.R.* para 18); the degree of privacy violation experienced by the victim (*R v J.T.B.* para 97); and there was a clear lack of consent by the complainant regarding distribution (*R v P.S.D.* para 16; *R v B.H.* para 24).

Factors that speak to the mentality of the accused and constitute aggravating factors include when the motive of the accused was revenge (*R v A.C* para 81) or the advancement of his own sexual purpose (*R v B.H.* para 24), as well as when the accused meant to share the images so that others were able to use them for sexual gratification (*R v Ly* para 35); their behavior is part of pattern against one or more victims (para 35; *R v J.S.* para 30); their actions intersect with other co-criminal activities such as voyeurism and extortion (para 35; *R v A.C.* para 81); they deliberately objectified and degraded the victim sexually (*R v Ly* para 35); and they planned and deliberated in the commission of the offence (*R v A.C.* para 43; *R v J.S.* para 37; *R v J.T.B.* para 97). The court also considered the length of the accused's possession of the intimate images (*R v Ly* para 35) and if the offender manipulated the victim(s) to enhance further victimization (*R v J.T.B.* para 97). Aggravating factors also include when the offender's actions constitute a breach or abuse of trust (*R v Ly* para 35; *R v B.H.* para 24; *R v A.C.* para 83; *R v M.R.* para 18; *R v A.C.* para 43; *R v J.T.B.* para 97) such as when there is a gross abuse of trust (*R v M.R.* para 18) in the context of a spousal relationship (*R v J.T.B.* para 97).

Aggravating factors relating to the nature of the image and its distribution include when there were serial, numerous, and repeated distributions after seeing the initial reaction of the victim (*R v J.T.B.* para 97). Furthermore, the court considered it aggravating when the offender posted images so as to guarantee a loss of control over distribution (*R v B.H.* para 24; *R v A.C.* para 43) and when the image was posted to more than one pornography hub at a time (*R v Ly* para 35). It also considered the breadth of distribution (*R v J.S.* para 30; *R v Agoston* para 17); the permanence of the online footprint (*R v J.T.B.* para 90); the identifiability of the complainant (*J v A.C.* para 43); and the use of personal identifiers in the posting of the image, including names (*R v Ly* para 35; *R v J.S.*, para 30) age, ethnicity, place of birth (*R v A.C.* para 43), pictures of a victim's driver's license, as well as pictures of the victim's home interior (*R v J.T.B.* para 97). The court also considered when the offender used accompanying, degrading descriptions of the victim (*R v J.S.* para 30), the degree of sexual activity in pictures (*R v A.C.* para 85), and the intimate nature of the images, including whether the victim was seen to perform a range of explicit sexual acts or close up shots of private and intimate areas of the victim's body (*R v J.S.* para 30; *R v J.T.B.* para 97).

Last, behaviors that demonstrated abandon by the accused could be aggravating. This included serial posting behaviour over a period of time (*R v Ly* para 35); determining to carry out a plan to distribute images despite numerous opportunities to discontinue the behaviour (*R v J.T.B.* para 97); and continuing the conduct despite awareness of the high moral gravity of the situation as informed by offender's education or intellect (*R v B.H.* para 28). Other examples include situations when one is only prevented from uploading additional content by posting restrictions on a website but one persists (*R v A.C.* para 43) and when the offender was engaged in previous criminality or was a "mature offender" (*R v J.T.B.* para 97). Furthermore, the court considers when the posting is carried out after an offender makes threats to share the materials or after the offender was warned by police, threatened with charges, and/or has been actually charged (*R v Ly* para 38) or caught (*R v B.H.* para 24).

Mitigating factors that may reduce the sentence for the offence were less numerous in the jurisprudential review. Mitigating factors included the circumstances of the accused, the accused's consideration of the impact on the victim, cooperation with institutions of justice, rehabilitative potential for the offender, the lack of intentionality of the accused, and factors relating to the degree of distribution.

Mitigating circumstances of the accused included the relative youth of offender (*R v Greene* para 66; *R v Ly* para 41); the lack of a prior criminal record (*R v P.S.D.* para 18; *R v Greene* para 66; *R v A.C.* para 93; *R v M.R.* para 17; *R v Agoston* para 19); if the accused's sentence will affect his dependents (*R v Ly* para 42); and if the accused delivered a guilty plea at the first reasonable opportunity (*R v P.S.D.* para 18; *R v Ly* para 41; *R v B.H.* para 25; *R v A.C.* para 90; *R v J.S.* para 31; *R v Agoston* para 18; *R v J.T.B.* para 100).

Mitigating factors that showed the offender's consideration of the victim included when the accused appreciated the impact of the conduct on the victim (*R v A.C.* para 92); when the accused undertook actions which spared the victim further suffering (para 90); when the accused accepted responsibility (*R v P.S.D.* para 18; *R v M.R.* para 20); when there was credible evidence of the accused possessing a capacity for new found empathy (*R v J.T.B.* para 100); and when the accused expressed credible remorse (*R v Ly* para 41; *R v B.H.* para 26; *R v A.C.* para 91; *R v Agoston* para 20).

Cooperation with institutions of justice and the rehabilitative potential for the offender could be mitigating factors in the following scenarios: if the accused cooperated with police (*R v Ly* para 42); expressed a willingness to accept a custodial sentence (*R v J.S.* para 31); spent time in presentence custody (*R v A.C.* para 97); presented with a positive presentence report when no victim impact statement was presented (*R v Agoston* paras 20, 27); sought treatment (*R v Ly* para 41); and had strong prospects for rehabilitation (*R v P.S.D.* para 19; *R v Greene* para 66; *R v A.C.* para 96; *R v M.R.* para 20; *R v J.T.B.* para 101). Also of relevance was whether there was psychological evidence indicating that the accused was committed and motivated to improve (see *R v Ly* para 41, but note that this can be offset by past failures of rehabilitation—*R v J.T.B.* para 102). Furthermore, mitigating factors examined included if the accused consented to a sexual behaviours assessment (*R v B.H.* para 25); agreed to participate in group or individual counselling (para 25); and had not reoffended since being released (*R v A.C.* para 98).

Mitigating factors speaking to the intentionality of the offender included if the accused's actions were merely impulsive and not considered (*R v J.S.* para 37); if there was a complete lack of planning and deliberation (*R v Agoston* para 21); if the offender acted in a momentary lapse of judgment while offending (para 45); if the accused did not solicit the images himself; and if he was not responsible for the conduct that led to his receiving them (para 21).

Lastly, limited or limiting distribution or attempting to aid in minimizing distribution could also be mitigating. Examples include if there was virtually no distribution of the images (*R v Agoston* para 17); and if the accused attempted to aid in limiting distribution or in retrieval of images, even if such attempts were self-serving (*R v J.T.B.* para 105).

Unsurprisingly, sentencing ranges varied drastically. Incidences of light sentences included a conditional discharge with twelve-month probation *(R v Agoston* para 46); conditional discharge with a condition of three months of home confinement (*R v A.C.* para 118); and a suspended sentence with two-year probation (*R v P.S.D.* para 24). The main mitigating factors associated with light sentences included accidental distribution and/or very minimal distribution.

Similarly, severe sentences were also reported in the gravest of circumstances. The most severe sentence we found was in the case of *R v J.T.B.* In this case, the victim, L.B., and the offender, J.T.B., entered into a dating relationship in 2008 and began living together. Their sexual relationship included the consensual taking of intimate images. Their relationship was turbulent. In 2012, L.B. discovered that J.T.B. had posted intimate images of her online without her consent. L.B. confronted J.T.B., leading to an argument resulting in J.T.B. being found guilty of domestic violence. J.T.B. received a conditional discharge with probation and a condition that he would delete all intimate images of L.B. Nonetheless, the couple reconciled and were married for two years before separating.

In 2016, J.T.B. began orchestrating a sexual attack on L.B. through another individual. According to J.T.B., his goal was to create a situation where he could intervene to save L.B. from a sexual assault, thus winning back her affection. The details of J.T.B.'s plan were as follows: create profiles on websites that facilitate consensual sexual encounters under the guise of L.B., upload intimate images of L.B., and link the profiles to his cellphone so that he could carry on text communications with matches in pursuit of his plans.

Eventually, one of the profiles described above came to the attention of a third party who contacted J.T.B. thinking he was L.B. J.T.B., masquerading as L.B., stated that she had extreme rape fantasies that she wanted the third party to fulfill. A plan was formed for L.B. to meet the third party, completely unbeknownst to L.B. When the third party came to meet L.B, neighbours and J.T.B. intervened, and the third party stopped what appeared to be an assault on L.B. Although the third party was arrested, he was able to demonstrate his innocence through his protracted text message logs with J.T.B. (disguised as L.B.). Ultimately J.T.B. was arrested and charged with distribution of intimate images without consent, contrary to section 162.1; assault, contrary to section 266; sexual assault, contrary to section 271; and obstruction of justice, contrary to section 139(2).

The sentence in this case was very severe, consisting of imprisonment for four years in relation to the section 162.1 offence along with a number of ancillary orders. The offender was prohibited from possessing weapons for life and was required to provide DNA samples. Also, he had to comply with the *Sex Offender Information Registration Act* for twenty years and was only allowed to use the Internet in accordance with conditions requiring him to use his full legal name. He could not post anything online related to the victim for twenty years and had to pay victim surcharges totaling $800. Moreover, he could not contact the victim or anyone on a specific list of people provided, and had to have his cell phone collected and destroyed (*J.T.B.* paras 127-30).

The NCDII offence under section 162.1 is clearly an offence that carries with it a great degree of variation, which is reflected in the sentencing range and is dependent on aggravating and mitigating circumstances. Yet NCDII is not only dealt with by section 162.1 of the *Code*. Other *Code* provisions also provide some alternatives for law enforcement and the Crown.

Voyeurism Cases

As discussed above, cases involving intimate images may overlap with other criminal charges. This is especially true if elements under section 162.1 prove difficult to demonstrate with evidence, or if the facts of the case adjudicated preceded the passage of section 162.1 into law but due to various delays were adjudicated after the law was proclaimed. Similar to section 162.1, many cases involving voyeurism and intimate images are reported at the sentencing phase, since guilty pleas are common in these cases. Although section 162.1 targets the distribution aspect of revenge porn, voyeurism targets the creation or recording of intimate images in the first place, when done surreptitiously. Voyeurism also has its challenges in determining the identity of the offender and in establishing the elements of the offence.

In *R v Ravindran*, an appeal of a voyeurism conviction was heard. The complainant, S.C., was in a dating relationship with the appellate, Ravindran, which terminated in September 2010. At the beginning of October, 2010, an acquaintance of S.C., who was also a friend of Ravindran, saw images of S.C. on Ravindran's Facebook, which depicted S.C. in a state of complete undress. The acquaintance informed S.C. of the images. At the trial, S.C. testified that the images were of her and that they were taken without her knowledge or consent. The police was contacted, and Ravindran was charged with voyeurism, contrary to section 162(1)(b) of the *Criminal Code*.

The major issue on appeal was how to interpret "explicit sexual activity" for the purposes of section 162 of the *Criminal Code*, which provided the following:

> Every one commits an offence who, surreptitiously, observes—including by mechanical or electronic means—or makes a visual recording of a person who is in circumstances that give rise to a reasonable expectation of privacy, if ...
>
> b) the person is nude, is exposing his or her genital organs or anal region or her breasts, or is engaged in explicit sexual activity, and the observation or recording is done for the purpose of observing or recording a person in such a state or engaged in such an activity. (*Criminal Code*, section 162)

The appellant asserted that what was depicted in the images in question fell short of the established definition of "explicit sexual activity," which should only include depictions of sexual intercourse and other nontrivial sexual acts, and that it was not open to the trial judge to conclude that the images met this definition on the basis that there was an available inference from the images that sexual activity had occurred, was occurring, or was about to occur.

The appellate court found that most of the images depicted S.C. naked and in provocative poses. These did not rise to the level of depicting explicit sexual activity. However, one image depicted S.C.'s genital area, with her legs spread wide apart, and some body parts of another individual partially visible. The appellate court found that anyone objectively viewing this image "could not come to any other conclusion than that S.C. was engaged in explicit sexual activity." Therefore, the trial judge was not in error, the appeal was denied, and the conviction was upheld (*Ravindran* para 41).

The case of *R v Jarvis* has helped to give content and colour to the meaning of reasonable expectation of privacy in the *Code's* image sharing provisions. Jarvis was a high school teacher in London, Ontario. Between 2010 and 2011, he used a camera pen to surreptitiously record videos of female students, and one female teacher, at the school where he worked. These videos varied from six seconds to just over two and a half minutes in length. Many of the videos were recorded by Jarvis while he had conversations with those he was recording. In most of the videos, while the camera remained on the subjects' faces, the focus remained for extended periods on their chests and cleavage. The students recorded were between fourteen and eighteen years old (*R v Jarvis* 2015 paras 4-10).

The police became involved after being called by the school's principal. A teacher had informed the principal that he had frequently observed Jarvis recording students with his pen. After receiving this report, the principle observed similar conduct by Jarvis on two other occasions that same day. Following the second time, the principal took Jarvis aside and asked to see his pen. The pen, which matched the other teacher's description, was handed over to police. Before obtaining a search warrant or making an arrest, the police viewed three of the videos on the USB in the pen. This led them to obtain a search warrant. In total, the pen contained nineteen videos, two of which had been deleted. There were thirty different individuals on the videos, twenty-seven of whom were female students at the school (*R v Jarvis* 2015 para 11-13).

Jarvis was charged with voyeurism, contrary to section 162(1)(c) of the *Criminal Code*. He was acquitted at trial. The offence of voyeurism has three elements that define and limit the offence. The person who is observed or recorded must be in a place where they can reasonably be expected to be nude or engaging in sexual activity; they must actually be nude or engaged in sexual activity, or the observation or recording must have been made for a sexual purpose (*R v Jarvis* 2015 paras 20-21).

The trial judge found a section 8 breach of the right against unreasonable state searches but admitted the evidence of the videos recorded on the camera pen under section 24(2) of the *Charter*, which allows admission of evidence when the administration of justice would be brought into disrepute by its exclusion. He concluded that the students had a reasonable expectation of privacy in the circumstances. However, he was not satisfied beyond a reasonable doubt that the videos were done for a sexual purpose (*R v Jarvis* 2015 para 79).

The majority of the appellate court found that the trial judge erred in two ways. First, he erred in his interpretation of the sexual purpose provision and that the lack of nudity or sexually suggestive clothing or poses, on its own, could derogate from the sexual purpose of the videos. This was a case in which the videos focused overwhelmingly on young women's breasts and cleavage. Subsection (b) of the offence of voyeurism specifically makes it an offence to surreptitiously observe or visually record a person who is nude. Subsection (c) requires only that the observation or recording be "done for a sexual purpose" (*R v Jarvis* 2017 para 53).

Second, it was not open to the trial judge to find that Jarvis may have had another purpose in recording the videos when no such alternate purpose had been identified. In this case, given what little evidence was available, any such inference would have been speculative. Therefore, the appeal was allowed on the ground raised by the Crown. However, the court also needed to consider the grounds raised by the respondent (*R v Jarvis* 2017 para 54).

The first such ground raised by the respondent was that the trial judge erred in admitting the evidence resulting from the initial warrantless search of the camera pen by police. Although the appellate court found that the trial judge made some errors in the section 24(2) analysis, its own analysis favoured admission as well. Thus, this ground of appeal failed (*R v Jarvis* 2017 para 83).

The second issue raised by Jarvis on appeal was that the trial judge erred in finding that the subjects of the videos had a reasonable expectation of privacy at the time of recording. Section 162(1) makes it an offence to either observe or to make a video of a person, surreptitiously, where the person is "in circumstances that give rise to a reasonable expectation of privacy," in any of the three aforementioned situations. This offence is concerned solely with a complainant's privacy interest in not having their body viewed or video recorded in a sexual context. The central question is in what circumstances does this interest arise (*R v Jarvis* 2017 para 86).

Parliament created the voyeurism offence with three limitations as delineated earlier in this chapter. The appellate court took the view that these conditions are an indication by Parliament that the ability to protect individual visual sexual integrity has limits (*R v Jarvis* 2017 para 91). The court considered that one governing aspect of privacy is location. Privacy is expected in places that exclude others or places where a person feels confident that they are not being observed. However, Parliament also included the concept of "circumstances" that give rise to such an expectation. This implies that, in some situations, it is possible to have a limited expectation of privacy in public spaces.

The trial judge interpreted the privacy expectation in this case as an expectation not to be secretly recorded. Jarvis argued that this was erroneous, as it conflated the surreptitious requirement of the offence with the privacy requirement. The majority of the appellate court agreed with this argument (*Jarvis* 2017 para 108). The areas of the school where students congregate and where classes are conducted are not areas where people have any expectation that they will not be observed or watched. People at the school were not prohibited from looking at anyone in the public areas. The presence of security cameras, and associated signage, meant that no one believed that they were not being observed or recorded (paras 10, 104, 110).

The expectation of students that they will not be surreptitiously recorded by teachers arises from the nature of the student-teacher relationship, not from an expectation of privacy. It was also open to Parliament to draft the voyeurism offence more broadly, such that all surreptitious recording would be captured. Instead, Parliament chose to further limit the criminality of surreptitious recording to those instances where the subject is in circumstances that give rise to a reasonable expectation of privacy. If a person is in a public place, fully clothed, and not engaged in toileting or a sexual activity, they will normally not be in circumstances that give rise to a reasonable expectation of privacy (*R v Jarvis* 2017 paras 104, 108).

Although the judge erred in finding that the videos recorded by Jarvis were not for a sexual purpose, he also erred in finding that the videos' subjects had a reasonable expectation of privacy at the time of recording (*R v Jarvis* 2017 para 111). Therefore, the appeal was dismissed.

The dissent in the case would have found that there was a reasonable expectation of privacy and that the majority of the appellate court had improperly interpreted privacy. On this dissenting view, privacy is a normative concept, and although location is a factor in determining a reasonable expectation of privacy, it is not determinative (*R v Jarvis* 2017 para 28).

The case was subsequently heard at the Supreme Court of Canada (SCC). In LEAF's intervention at the court, it argued for a contextual interpretation of the voyeurism provisions in the *Code*. Privacy, they argued, should not be interpreted in the same way for the purposes of protection against the state's search powers as in cases of protecting the sexual integrity of young persons and women against potential predators. Prior to intervening in the case, LEAF wrote that they would "ask the SCC to adopt an expansive approach to the concept of 'reasonable expectation of privacy' that takes into account women's constitutional right to equality." They continued as follows:

> LEAF will urge the Court to adopt a contextual approach to privacy which respects women's liberty, autonomy, and bodily and sexual integrity, in both private and public spaces. Anything less risks reinforcing the discriminatory presumption that women have no place in public life, or that women who enter public spaces are "fair game" for this type of sexual violence.
>
> LEAF will further argue that this contextual analysis of privacy must take into account women and girls' subjectively held privacy expectations. In the context of this case, LEAF will argue that it is "reasonable" for girls to expect their teachers, who occupy a position of trust and authority, to respect and safeguard their autonomy and well-being. Further, equality values demand that schools be treated as places where it is reasonable for girls to expect privacy from sexual intrusion, particularly from those in positions of power.
>
> LEAF intends to identify the importance of s. 162(1) for promoting the equality of women and girls in the context of the digital era and the consequent rise of online misogyny and harassment. This case will be the first important test of the scope of the relatively new criminal prohibitions on voyeurism. It will

also have implications for the even newer criminal restrictions on non-consensual distribution of intimate images, sometimes referred to as "revenge pornography", which also apply only to images that were made in circumstances in which the complainant had a reasonable expectation of privacy. These provisions are of critical importance for women's equality in the age of camera phones and social media. A broad and contextual interpretation of their scope, including what circumstances engage a reasonable expectation of privacy, is therefore of vital importance. (LEAF, "LEAF Applies for Leave to Intervene")

In LEAF's factum as an intervenor in the case at the SCC, they argued for a contextual approach and that section 162.1 and 162 should be read as a coherent scheme of Parliament to combat image-based sexual violence (LEAF, Factum para 27). LEAF noted that the two sections of the *Code* were intimately related in that if an image is not determined to have been made in circumstances that give rise to a reasonable expectation of privacy under section 162, then section 162.1 will not criminalize its subsequent distribution (LEAF, Factum 30). Indeed, *R v Jarvis* will be definitive on the scope of reasonable expectation of privacy in the context of the sexual exploitation provisions in the *Code*.

The SCC's ruling in *R v Jarvis* held that a reasonable expectation of privacy under the voyeurism provisions may arise when "a person would reasonably expect not to be the subject of the type of observation or recording that in fact occurred" (*R v Jarvis* 2019 para 5). To determine whether a reasonable expectation of privacy exists, the court outlined an approach that requires considering "the entire context in which the observation or recording took place," including but not limited to:

1. The location the person was in when she was observed or recorded...

2. The nature of the impugned conduct, that is, whether it consisted of observation or recording...

3. Awareness of or consent to potential observation or recording...

4. The manner in which the observation or recording was done...

5. The subject matter or content of the observation or recording...

6. Any rules, regulations or policies that governed the observation or recording in question...

7. The relationship between the person who was observed or recorded and the person who did the observing or recording...

8. The purpose for which the observation or recording was done...

9. The personal attributes of the person who was observed or recorded. (para 29)

The court emphasized that the list of considerations was not exhaustive and not all factors will be relevant in every given case. Rather, to determine whether a reasonable expectation of privacy exists, a judge must engage in a contextual inquiry, considering the totality of circumstances (*R v Jarvis* 2019 para 30).

The court noted that although an expectation of privacy will be highest in traditionally private places, such as in a bedroom or bathroom stall, "a person does not lose all expectations of privacy, as that concept is ordinarily understood, simply because she is in a place where she knows she can be observed by others or from which she cannot exclude others" (*R v Jarvis* 2019 para 37). The court gave several other examples of when a person would expect some degree of privacy even while knowing that she could be viewed or recorded in public, including the video recording of a woman breastfeeding in public, high resolution photographs of sunbathers at a public pool or using a cell phone to capture up-skirt images of women on public transit (para 40). The court also noted that recording is more intrusive to privacy than mere observation, and, thus, a person's expectation regarding whether she will be observed may be different than her expectation of whether she will be recorded in a particular situation (para 29).

The court interpreted Parliament's use of the phrase "circumstances that give rise to a reasonable expectation of privacy" within section 162 as not limiting the commission of the offence of voyeurism to traditionally private spaces (*R v Jarvis* 2019 para 44). The court posited that although section 162(1)(a) specifically limited the prohibited conduct to traditionally private places, sections (b) and (c) showed that Parliament understood that a person could have a reasonable expectation of privacy in a place other than where nudity or explicit sexual activity could reasonably be expected to take place (para 46). Thus, the court held that understanding reasonable expectation of privacy in a contextual manner accords with Parliament's objective to protect the privacy and sexual integrity of individuals (para 48).

Chief Justice Wagner, writing for the majority, also looked to section 8's search and seizure Charter-jurisprudence in interpreting section 162(1) and noted that one of the principles emerging from this jurisprudence was to undertake a contextual assessment to determine whether a reasonable expectation of privacy was in existence (*R v Jarvis* 2019 para 60) and that privacy need not be an all or nothing concept (para 61). Chief Justice Wagner saw the symmetry between the section 8 approach to privacy and the approach used within the *Jarvis* decision.

In applying this contextual approach to the facts of *Jarvis,* the court determined that although the students filmed by Mr. Jarvis were in a quasi-public space and under general video surveillance, they did not expect to be the subject of targeted videos focused on their bodies, specifically their breasts; furthermore, the students did not expect to be the subject of videos recorded by a teacher for a sexual purpose (*R v Jarvis* 2019 para 6). In other words, "the students' expectation that they would be recorded by the school's security cameras tells us little about their privacy expectations with respect to the recording done by Mr. Jarvis" (para 75).

The court considered the location in which the students were recorded and noted that their expectation of privacy in common areas of the school was lower than in traditionally private locations. Yet a high school is not a completely public place, as it is subject to rules about who may be there as well as formal and informal rules with respect to behavior. The court determined that the quasi-public nature of the school did not mean that the students could not have had a reasonable expectation of privacy in relation to the recordings of Mr. Jarvis (*R v Jarvis* 2019 73).

The court also noted that Mr. Jarvis's targeted filming of students, specifically the upper portion of the students and their breasts, allowed the students to be personally identifiable and subjected to intensive scrutiny (*R v Jarvis* 2019 para 80). The recordings were of good quality and shot at close range with a secretive pen camera (para 91). The court also considered the fact that Mr. Jarvis was a teacher and in a position of trust, that the students recorded were young persons, and that there was a formal school board policy at the time that prohibited recordings such as those done by Mr. Jarvis (para 91).

LEAF responded with celebration to the ruling, arguing that the SCC's adoption of a "nuanced, contextual test" will help to advance the interests of women and girls in the digital age: "today's ruling will allow Canadian women and girls to engage in public life with greater confidence that the law will protect them from demeaning, non-consensual intrusions into their sexual integrity and autonomy" (LEAF, "LEAF Celebrates"). Indeed, the *Jarvis* ruling will ease the use of the *Code*'s voyeurism provisions to combat the production or recording of intimate images in a wider variety of locations and contexts. Furthermore, the decision is likely to profoundly shape how the reasonable expectation of privacy requirement within section 162.1 will be interpreted; foreseeably, reasonable expectation of privacy in this section will be analyzed in a more contextual manner in line with section 162, with a broader understanding of privacy rights inherent in the production and distribution of intimate images without consent.

Other *Criminal Code* Provisions

The use of intimate images without permission of the victim also came up in a number of other scenarios. Below, we briefly review some of the related charges.

Section 346 of the *Criminal Code*, dealing with extortion offences, makes it an offence to leverage a person to provide what one seeks through intimidating actions: "Every one commits extortion who, without reasonable justification or excuse and with intent to obtain anything, by threats, accusations, menaces or violence induces or attempts to induce any person, whether or not he is the person threatened, accused or menaced or to whom violence is shown, to do anything or cause anything to be done." The provision does not require that the inducement be successful. The punishment can be quite severe, in part due to its historic links to criminal organizations and firearms, and, thus, sentencing can range from a minimum sentence of four years where a firearm is involved to life imprisonment. Importantly, a threat to undertake a civil action will not constitute a threat under the *Code*, section 346(2). It is not uncommon to see charges of extortion form part of the panoply of behaviours at issue in a 162.1 offence (for example both *R v Ly* and *R v McFarlane,* above, involved charges of 162.1 and 346). Unfortunately, many cases demonstrate the link between coerced or obtained intimate images, extortion, and sexual assault

An example of a trial decision involving extortion, sexual assault, and intimate images was *R v Lauzon.* In 2014, the complainant, S.M., began communicating with a person on Facebook, Daniel Lauzon. His profile was accompanied by a picture. Lauzon convinced S.M. to produce intimate images of herself. These images did not include her face. These were sent to Lauzon.

Afterwards, Lauzon threatened to post the images publicly if S.M. did not meet him at the marina in Pembroke, ON. S.M. went to the marina. She was met there by a man, who ordered her to a secluded area, had her remove her clothes, and then had sexual intercourse with her. After this incident, S.M. told her friends that she intended to commit suicide, although she did not tell them why. They were able to convince her not to harm herself.

She saw Lauzon on two occasions afterwards. In 2016, a profile under the name "Brandon Antiraxi" began communicating with S.M. via Facebook. S.M. believed that the person behind the profile was actually Lauzon. This finally pushed her to contact police. Police took control of her Facebook profile and arranged a meeting with Antiraxi. Lauzon showed up and was arrested. He was charged with both extortion and sexual assault. Lauzon denied both charges at trial.

Despite an admission that her memory was poor and some vague descriptions of her assailant when describing the incident, S.M.'s consistent certainty that the accused was the person who assaulted her caused the judge to believe her testimony (*R v Lauzon* paras 69-74). Lauzon's testimony was often absurd. His reason for appearing on time to the meeting set up by police, for instance, was that he had a habit of walking up and down that particular street, so that was why he walked into the Dairy Queen where the meeting was arranged. Therefore, the judge accepted S.M.'s identification of the accused, and Lauzon was found guilty of both extortion and sexual assault (para 75).

Some cases have expressly noted that the pairing of intimate images and extortion is a matter that is likely to be more frequent in the era of social media. In the sentencing case of *R v Hunt,* an eerily familiar set of facts were presented. The complainant, X, and the offender, Hunt, were in a relationship. X ended the relationship. As a result, Hunt sent

X a number of text messages indicating that he would post intimate images of her on Facebook and kill himself, if X did not agree to tell her friends that they were trying to figure things out in their relationship. The images in question were of X naked and of X and Hunt engaging in sexual acts. X initially acquiesced to Hunt's request. However, after further consideration by the victim and cooperation with law enforcement, Hunt was later charged with extortion, contrary to section 346(1) of the *Criminal Code*. He entered a plea of not guilty. After the trial commenced, he changed his plea to guilty.

The sentencing judge found that the role of modern technology must be considered in sentencing (*R v Hunt* para 8). Modern technology has dramatically increased the potential impact of extortion, as social media allows for widespread, rapid dissemination of materials that cannot be limited. The increased seriousness of modern extortion must be reflected in sentencing. Similar to section 162.1 charges, denunciation and deterrence should be the key sentencing principles (para 8). The court considered factors similar to the ones discussed earlier in this chapter regarding section 162.1 adjudication but interestingly noted that the widespread accessibility of Facebook made the offence more egregious (para 45). The judge would have sentenced Hunt to twelve months but determined that nine months and probation under specialized conditions would be appropriate. He was banned from attending any place where the victim was employed or going to school; he must not access X's Facebook page or post anything online relating to her, and he must attend counselling sessions. A victim surcharge of $200 and a DNA sample were also required from the offender (paras 46, 52-54).

Other offences that are often implicated in the recording and sharing of digital images are cases of child pornography and related offences. We have paid attention to these offences in other chapters of this volume. Similarly, distributed images that are manifestly harmful under the obscenity provisions of the *Criminal Code* have also been considered in other chapters.

Intimate images need not foment physical violence to result in other actionable charges under the *Code*. Indeed, we have begun to see some cases where intimate imagery and the *Code* provisions against uttering threats intersect. This was the case in *R v Hirsch*. The case was notable also for its approach to accepting evidence of digital images. In this case, the complainant's testimony that the images in question existed was accepted, even though the evidence of this which was presented consisted of screenshots of the accused's Facebook page.

The complainant had been in a romantic relationship with the appellant, Hirsch, for eight years. During this relationship, the complainant emailed nude images of herself to Hirsch. She ended this relationship, as it was emotionally and physically abusive. Despite this, the two of them continued to see each other occasionally. The complainant had seen Hirsch each day for about a week prior to the alleged conduct.

Hirsch had unfriended the complainant on Facebook two months prior to the alleged conduct. The complainant relied on friends to tell her if he posted anything about her. On October 2, 2013, one of these friends informed the complainant that Hirsch had nude images of her on his Facebook page. The friend sent the complainant a screenshot of what was apparently Hirsch's Facebook page, showing the posted image. She recognized the page as Hirsch's and the person depicted in the image as herself. Also visible were degrading comments, including one that implied that Hirsch intended to choke the complainant and to shoot her with a shotgun.

The complainant testified at trial that she was concerned primarily by the images. She texted Hirsch and begged to have them taken down but received only increasingly threatening messages in response. In one instance, he sent her one of the nude images by text. After Hirsch indicated that he had sent further images to all of the contacts in his phone, as well as posting them to Facebook, the complainant contacted both Facebook and the police. The images on Facebook were removed shortly thereafter. Whether this was done by Hirsch or Facebook administrators was unclear.

Hirsch was charged with uttering threats for the comments made on Facebook. He was found guilty at trial (*R v Hirsch* para 12). He appealed on the basis that the trial judge had relied on evidence that had not been authenticated and incorrectly concluded that the court had jurisdiction and delivered an unreasonable verdict that was unsupported by the evidence.

Hirsch argued that the trial judge erred by admitting and relying upon the screenshots without getting the Crown to authenticate them. At trial, the Crown adduced evidence from the complainant that she recognized the depicted Facebook page as that of Hirsch (*R v Hirsch* para 15). Hirsch argued that she was not in a position to authenticate the screenshots, as he had blocked her access to his Facebook two months prior. Additionally, the Crown should have called the friend who took the screenshots as a witness.

The appellate court was not persuaded by these arguments (*R v Hirsch* para 18). Although the authentication of electronic documents is required, it is not an onerous requirement. It is sufficient, at the authentication stage, for counsel to present the evidence to a witness and for that witness to articulate some basis for authenticating what it is purported to be. The integrity or reliability of the evidence is not open to attack at this stage: such challenges are resolved under the best evidence rule. In the appellate court's view, the complainant was able to give reasons capable of authenticating the evidence. Although it might have been preferable to have had the complainant's friend testify as to authenticity, there was sufficient evidence of authentication before the trial judge for him to reach the conclusion that he did. Ultimately, the appellate court found that there was still a sufficient evidentiary basis for the trial judge to have reached the conclusion that he did. Therefore, the authentication ground of appeal failed. The appeal was denied on all grounds, and the conviction was upheld (para 54).

When digital images occur in the context of serial threats or similar behaviour, the offence of criminal harassment may also be at play. Section 264 of the *Code* describes the offence. This provision makes it an offence to knowingly or recklessly cause a person to fear for their own safety or for the safety of anyone known to them by engaging in one or more of the following activities, which are set out in subsection 264(2):

a) repeatedly following from place to place the other person or anyone known to them;

b) repeatedly communicating with, either directly or indirectly, the other person or anyone known to them;

c) besetting or watching the dwelling-house, or place where the other person, or anyone known to them, resides, works, carries on business or happens to be; or

d) engaging in threatening conduct directed at the other person or any member of their family. (*Criminal Code,* subsection 264(2))

Under subsection 264(1), the victim's fear of harm must be reasonably held, and the Crown need not necessarily prove that the accused knew that their actions were harassing, only that they were reckless as to whether they were. Under subsection 264(3) criminal harassment is a hybrid offence. On indictment, it is punishable by a term of imprisonment not exceeding ten years. Subsection 264(4) provides factors to be considered aggravating by courts, including that at the time the offence was committed, the accused was in violation of an order, recognizance, or similar provision.

A recent example of the intersection of intimate images and harassment is *R v Sim*. Sim met the complainant in 2001. He was employed in property maintenance in the complainant's apartment building. After seeing the complainant around the building several times, Sim asked her out for coffee, and they developed a friendship. At some point, Sim confessed that he had romantic feelings for the complainant, but these were not reciprocated. Their friendship continued until sometime between 2003 and 2004, when the complainant indicated to Sim that she wanted to find a romantic partner, and that because she was aware that he still had feelings for her, she thought it best if they did not continue to have contact. This frustrated Sim. Each of them moved on with their lives and started families.

Later, they resumed contact by email, and Sim began asking for images of the complainant (nonintimate ones), which were provided. In 2010, Sim established an online forum that, according to its own home page, was dedicated to the proliferating degradation of the complainant. He recruited over 150 members to the site. Sim and these members then created false sexualized commentaries about the complainant, altered images of her to sexualize them, and posted sexualized fantasies about the complainant. The home page also listed biographical details of the complainant, including her name, age, weight, height, bra size, underwear size, hobbies, education, occupation, and number of children.

The complainant discovered the site after receiving an email concerning the site, which had about fifteen hundred members by then. The complainant gained full access to the site, took screenshots of what she found, and contacted police. Sim was charged with criminal harassment and publishing defamatory libel. He was convicted of the former charge and acquitted of the latter. Sim appealed his conviction.

Sim argued that the *actus reus* of criminal harassment requires proof of subjective intent to engage in threatening conduct. The trial judge agreed that if this were the case, then Sim should be acquitted. However, the trial judge disagreed that this subjective intent was required. The appellate court agreed with the trial judge and rejected Sim's argument. In order to rise to the level of "threatening conduct" that is required by the *Criminal Code* to make out criminal harassment, conduct must amount to a "tool of intimidation designed to instill a sense of fear in the recipient" (based on *R v MacDuff* citing *R v George*). Sim argued that the word "designed" was indicative of a subjective intention requirement.

The appellate court pointed out that in a prior case it had endorsed more of an objective standard for assessing whether impugned conduct met this definition. Furthermore, the court did not read the definition in the way that Sim had because the *mens rea* component of criminal harassment could be met by an accused's knowledge or recklessness. Therefore, the suggestion that the *actus reus* of threatening conduct required a specific intent to instill fear was contrary to the plain language of section 264(1) (*R v Sim* paras 16, 18). The appeal was dismissed and conviction upheld (para 21). It is worth noting that criminal harassment offences remain difficult to prove and one can expect that the majority of cases will proceed under section 162.1 in the future. In this case, it was the alteration of the image for a sexualized purpose that likely made the Crown leery to proceed under section 162.1, since the *Code* requires that a reasonable expectation of privacy exists in the originating image.

The production of digital imagery and its manipulation by a putative offender provides another entry point for criminal liability. Two examples include the hybrid charges of using a computer system with intent to commit an offence, contrary to section 342.1 of the *Criminal Code* and with charges of mischief in relation to data, contrary to section 430(1.1) of the *Criminal Code*. Section 342.1 provides the following:

1) Everyone is guilty of an indictable offence and liable to imprisonment for a term of not more than 10 years, or is guilty of an offence punishable on summary conviction who, fraudulently and without colour of right,

a) obtains, directly or indirectly, any computer service;
b) by means of an electro-magnetic, acoustic, mechanical or other device, intercepts or causes to be intercepted, directly or indirectly, any function of a computer system;
c) uses or causes to be used, directly or indirectly, a computer system with intent to commit an offence under paragraph (a) or (b) or under section 430 in relation to computer data or a computer system; or
d) uses, possesses, traffics in or permits another person to have access to a computer password that would enable a person to commit an offence under paragraph (a), (b) or (c). (*Criminal Code* section 342.1)

Section 431.1 provides the following:

Every one commits mischief who willfully:

a) destroys or alters computer data;
b) renders computer data meaningless, useless or ineffective;
c) obstructs, interrupts or interferes with the lawful use of computer data; or
d) obstructs, interrupts or interferes with a person in the lawful use of computer data or denies access to computer data to a person who is entitled to access to it. (*Criminal Code* section 431.1)

In *R v Maurer*, the accused was charged under both offences. Maurer was knowledgeable about computers due to his completion of a two-year information technology course and his subsequent experience working in computer-related fields. He met the complainant at work, and they carried on a romantic relationship for about six months. Prior to entering into this relationship with Maurer, the complainant was in another relationship. During this relationship, the complainant sent nude images of herself via her laptop. She deleted these from her computer when that relationship ended.

Sometime after the end of her relationship with Maurer, the complainant's laptop was damaged at work. Knowing of Maurer's skills, she contacted him to see if he could help. Maurer agreed to help, and the complainant dropped off her laptop at his house. Maurer quickly realized that the laptop would not be worth fixing and indicated as much to the complainant. This turned the discussion towards the preservation of the data on the laptop. The accused testified that he explained to the complainant that he could attempt to preserve the data on the old laptop by pulling out the hard drive and processing the data through his computer, running it through antivirus software in the process. He said that he asked whether there was anything on the laptop that he should not see and that he was assured repeatedly that there was nothing.

According to Maurer, the virus scan detected suspicious files and quarantined them. Upon investigation, these files turned out to be intimate images of the complainant. Maurer testified that he called the complainant to discuss this and that the discussion concluded with her indicating that he could keep the images. The complainant's version of events was that this discovery upset her and that she asked Maurer to delete the images. Maurer refused and evaded her requests by saying that they would have further discussions.

At some point later, Maurer and the complainant got into an argument. Maurer threatened to post the images online unless the complainant was "good to him" for a month. Their relationship continued to degrade until a month later, when Maurer posted the complainant's images to a website. He distributed flyers at the complainant's work place with links to the website and filed a complaint to the Human Rights Commission about her work. This led to the complainant being suspended from her job.

It was the alleged theft of the intimate images, in the form of data, that gave rise to the charge of unauthorized use of a computer with intent to commit mischief in count one and the charge of mischief in relation to data in count two.

The SCC dealt with the similar question of whether an employee's personal information could be the object of theft in *R v Stewart*. Justice Lamer J (as he then was) concluded that there are two conditions that must be satisfied for anything to be capable of being an object of theft. First, whether tangible or intangible, the thing must be of such a nature that it can be the subject of a proprietary right. Second, the object must be capable of being taken or converted in a manner that results in the deprivation of the victim. He determined that confidential information was not anything (i.e., an object) for the purposes of theft under the *Criminal Code* (*Maurer* para 21).

Although theft was not an essential element of either offence with which Maurer had been charged, the Crown was bound to prove the charge as alleged and the Crown had described the images as the objects of theft. The Crown, therefore, was bound to prove that theft had occurred. Even if the intimate images were capable of being an object of theft, what Maurer did with them still would not have met the definition of theft, as he never intended to deprive the complainant of them (*Maurer* paras 25, 26). The accused was found not guilty on both charges, and the decision was upheld on appeal (para 26).

The *Criminal Code* landscape for dealing with issues of intimate images is, thus, potentially vast, encompassing charges of obvious application, such as the non-consensual distribution of digital images (section 162.1) and voyeurism (162). We have also seen that other areas of the criminal law may come into play: extortion (346), uttering threats (section 264.1), criminal harassment (264), mischief with computers (sections 342.1 and 431.1), and child pornography charges (e.g., 163.1). The last several years have seen an initial eruption of section 162.1 charges. Even several years ago, the only reported cases dealing with non-consensual distribution of digital images were civil cases, one of which was an unsuccessful cause of action after a second trial. We can certainly expect that the number of reported cases will continue to rise as the proliferation of digital intimate images continues to be normalized in relationships, and aggrieved partners or predators choose to use such images for criminal purposes. The criminal cases reported are bound to proliferate and provide even further fodder for explication.

Yet there is another side to the legal exploration of intimate image distribution, and it occurs under the auspices of the civil law. A number of provinces have long existing protections of the privacy rights of its citizens in its statutes (examples include British Columbia, Quebec, Newfoundland and Labrador, Saskatchewan, and Manitoba); some provinces have drafted sweeping cyberbullying legislation only to have their legislative attempts declared unconstitutional (Nova Scotia), and other provinces have adopted relatively new intimate image prohibitions, creating new standalone legislative torts in their province (examples include Manitoba, Saskatchewan, and Alberta). Even when a cause of action is not on the legislative books of a province, the potential for civil action from the common law may remain a possibility.

Privacy Legislation

Since 1996, British Columbia has enumerated protections against privacy violations in its *Privacy Act*. The Act does not deal specifically with the sharing of intimate images without consent. However, on its face, it seems that the invasion of privacy tort that the Act creates would be applicable to such a situation.

Section 1 of the *Privacy Act* establishes the tort of violation of privacy:

1) It is a tort, actionable without proof of damage, for a person, wilfully and without a claim of right, to violate the privacy of another.

2) The nature and degree of privacy to which a person is entitled in a situation or in relation to a matter is that which is reasonable in the circumstances, giving due regard to the lawful interests of others.

3) In determining whether the act or conduct of a person is a violation of another's privacy, regard must be given to the nature, incidence and occasion of the act or conduct and to any domestic or other relationship between the parties. (British Columbia *Privacy Act* section 1)

Under subsection 1(1), the plaintiff need not prove damages in order to succeed. The plaintiff must have been entitled to some degree of privacy. How this requirement relates to the reasonable expectation of privacy stipulated in the *Criminal Code* intimate images provisions and other provincial legislation is still unclear.

Section 2 provides for exceptions to the tort. These exceptions are fairly standard and include consent, lawful exercise of defence of self or property, public interest, activities of peace officers undertaken in the course of their duties, and privilege in accordance with defamation. Section 5 prevents actions under the Act from surviving death of the plaintiff.

Saskatchewan possesses similar legislation in its *Privacy Act*. Section 2 provides that "it is a tort, actionable without proof of damage, for a person wilfully and without claim of right, to violate the privacy of another person." Section 4 provides several defences in the form of exceptions to the tort. These include consent, exercise of lawful right to defence, authorization by law, reasonably necessary to news gathering, public interest, and privilege in accordance with defamation. Section 6 provides for a number of considerations the court should make in determining whether a violation of privacy has occurred. These include but are not limited to the following: the nature and degree of privacy to which the plaintiff was reasonably entitled on the circumstances; the nature, incidence, and occasion of the act; the effect of the act on health and welfare as well as the social, business, or financial position of the plaintiff or related persons; any relationship between the parties to the action; and the conduct of the parties before and after the complaint. Section 7 provides a standard list of remedies.

Similar privacy protections include those found in section 2 of the *Privacy Act* in Manitoba, section 3 of the *Privacy Act* in Newfoundland and Labrador, and section 35 of the *Civil Code* of Québec in Quebec. The *Civil Code*, while substantially similar, does go on in section 36 to enumerate a nonexhaustive list of privacy violations, including the following:

1) entering or taking anything in his dwelling;
2) intentionally intercepting or using his private communications;
3) appropriating or using his image or voice while he is in private premises;
4) keeping his private life under observation by any means;
5) using his name, image, likeness or voice for a purpose other than the legitimate information of the public
6) using his correspondence, manuscripts or other personal documents. (Civil *Code* of Quebec section 36(5)).

Notably, subsection 5 could apply to the non-consensual distribution of digital images. Indeed, this was the issue in *NG c FB*. In the context of a custody dispute, the defendant released pictures of the plaintiff and sent her a text saying "Go see milf solo on youporn" (*NG c FB* para 12). The defendant pleaded guilty to a section 162.1 offence, ultimately obtaining an unconditional discharge and admitting he had sent the intimate images to the plaintiff's current partner. Using section 36 of the *Civil Code*, the court noted that the improper dissemination of the photographs, without the consent of the plaintiff, was a wrongful infringement of her right to privacy in the intimate images (para 29).

Furthermore, by illegally transmitting the photos of the plaintiff to her partner, the defendant violated the plaintiff's right to privacy and the preservation of her dignity, honour, and reputation (para 75). The situation was an attack on the plaintiff's integrity and had the effect of denigrating her to her new spouse in order to break up their relationship (para 76).

The court found that the defendant had, in bad faith, attacked the integrity of the plaintiff by alleging he had disseminated the pictures on the Internet when, in reality, he only sent the photos to the plaintiff's partner. Thus, the court assessed the damages suffered by the plaintiff at the sum of $7,000. However, an additional $3,000 in punitive damages was assessed for the unlawful and intentional interference with the plaintiff's reputation.

Nonconsensual Image Legislation

In 2015, the Manitoba legislature passed the *Intimate Image Protection Act*. It is one of an emerging set of provincial acts specifically addressing intimate image sharing that is currently in force. Alberta has similar legislation in force, whereas Saskatchewan and Nova Scotia both have developed comparable legislation. The tort created in these Acts is functionally very similar to the *Criminal Code* but creates civil liability on a balance of probabilities, unlike the *Code* which requires proof beyond a reasonable doubt. The definition of intimate image is identical in the civil legislation to the *Criminal Code*. A unique feature of the Manitoba legislation is that it lays the foundation for a government department designed to support victims, advise government, and educate the public regarding the issue of non-consensual intimate image sharing.

The tort of non-consensual distribution of intimate images is established in subsection 11(1) of the Act: "A person who distributes an intimate image of another person knowing that the person depicted in the image did not consent to the distribution, or being reckless as to whether or not that person consented to the distribution, commits a tort against that other person." Under subsection 11(2) proof of damage is not required from the plaintiff. Section 12 provides that the plaintiff's privacy expectation is not lost if they consented to the making of the intimate image or provided the image to another person, so long as the circumstances were such that the other person knew or ought to have known that further distribution was not consented to by the victim. Section 13 provides for the public interest defence. Section 14 stipulates the usual remedies, and section 15 allows for publication bans.

The Alberta legislation, *Protecting Victims of Nonconsensual Distribution of Intimate Images Act,* largely accomplishes the same feats. Somewhat distinctly, under section 8, parents of children found to have committed a tort under the Act are not liable unless the court is satisfied that they participated directly in the in the distribution of the intimate image (s) without consent.

Saskatchewan's Bill 72, *The Privacy Amendment Act,* amends Saskatchewan's *Privacy Act* to specifically target intimate image sharing. It received royal assent on May 9, 2018. Section 7.5 is of note, as it creates a presumption on commencement of an action that distribution of the intimate image(s) was not consented to by the victim. The onus is, thus, shifted to the defendant to prove they had reasonable grounds to believe that consent for further distribution was ongoing.

In the first part of this chapter, we briefly discussed Nova Scotia's *Cyber-Safety Act,* which was Nova Scotia's original legislative response to both non-consensual intimate image sharing and to cyberbullying in general. It was found to be in violation of section 2(b) and section 7 of the *Canadian Charter of Rights and Freedoms* by the Supreme Court of Nova Scotia in the 2015 case of *Crouch v Snell*. Section 3(b) provided the following:

> Cyberbullying means any electronic communication through the use of technology including, without limiting the generality of the foregoing, computers, other electronic devices, social networks, text messaging, instant messaging, websites and electronic mail, typically repeated or with continuing effect, that is intended or ought reasonably be expected to cause fear, intimidation, humiliation, distress or other damage or harm to another person's health, emotional well-being, self-esteem or reputation, and includes assisting or encouraging such communication in any way.

In adjudicating a heated and protracted workplace dispute between two founders of a company, where one alleged that the other had engaged in cyberbullying, the court found that the legislation infringed free expression rights under section 2(b) of the *Charter* and also violated the principles of fundamental justice of arbitrariness, vagueness, and overbreadth under section 7 of the *Charter*. The judge found that the Act did not provide sufficiently clear standards to avoid arbitrary and discriminatory applications. There was no "limit prescribed by law," and the impugned provisions of the Act could not be justified under section 1 (*Crouch v Snell* para 137). The violations were such that the legislation as a whole had to be struck down (para 220).

It took some work for the Cyber-Safety Act to be replaced. However, new legislation that aims at achieving the same goals has received royal assent. This new legislation, Bill 27, *Intimate Images and Cyber-Protection Act,* addresses cyberbullying and non-consensual distribution of intimate images through creating a process where complainants can apply to the court for a form of protection order. These orders can contain a number of different requirements, from requiring the removal of the images by the defendant to a referral to dispute resolution services. There is also a catch-all clause allowing the court to make any other orders which are just and reasonable. There are provisions to allow for the establishment of an agency, similar to the one established in the Manitoban intimate images legislation. Section 3(d) defines "distribution without consent" in relation to intimate images, and the definition of "intimate image", contained in subsection 3(f), effectively uses the same definition present in section 162.1 of the *Criminal Code* and other intimate image specific legislation.

Section 6 allows the court to order damages, as in a conventional tort, as well as the ability to issue a variety of orders. The section provides a list of factors to be considered by the court in making an order under the act including an assessment of damages. These apply to both cyberbullying and non-consensual intimate image distribution situations. The factors are much more extensive than those provided in similar legislation. In making an order or a damages assessment, the court shall consider the following:

a) the content of the intimate image or cyber-bullying;
b) the manner and repetition of the conduct;
c) the nature and extent of the harm caused;
d) the age and vulnerability of the person depicted in the intimate image distributed without consent or victim of cyber-bullying;

e) the purpose or intention of the person responsible for the distribution of the intimate image without consent or the cyber-bullying;

f) the occasion, context and subject-matter of the conduct;

g) the extent of the distribution of the intimate image or cyber-bullying;

h) the truth or falsity of the communication;

i) the conduct of the person responsible for the distribution of the intimate image or cyber-bullying, including any effort to minimize harm;

j) the age and maturity of the person responsible for distribution of the intimate image without consent or cyber-bullying;

k) the technical and operational practicalities and costs of carrying out the order;

l) the *Canadian Charter of Rights and Freedoms*; and

m) any other relevant factor or circumstance. (*Intimate Images and Cyber-protection Act* section 6)

Common Law Torts

Even when statutory relief is not available, it remains a possibility that judges could turn to the common law to adjudicate the non-consensual distribution of intimate images. Originally, the case *Jane Doe 464533 v N.D.* made waves for its damages assessment in the context of civil liability for intimate image sharing. The case was one where an eighteen-year-old plaintiff was victimized when intimate videos that she had given to her boyfriend were posted on a pornographic website for three weeks. She received $75,000 in nonpecuniary damages, of which $25,000 was for aggravating factors, along with a further punitive sum of $25,000. The case was a default judgment, and, subsequently, the defendant brought a motion to set aside the default judgment. In reasons for the decision dated September 26, 2016, in *Doe 464533 v N.D.*, Justice Dow set aside the findings of liability and the assessment of damages upon payment by the defendant of legal costs of $10,000. Subsequently, Jane Doe sought leave to appeal that decision and failed. The case must now be heard from the start with both parties present.

Nonetheless, the original default judgement provided some interesting possibilities for using common law principles to adjudicate cases of NCDII. Specially, the defendant was held liable in tort for breach of confidence, intentional infliction of mental distress, and invasion of privacy.

The court recognized that the unauthorized use of confidential information to the detriment of the party communicating it, and from which damages ensue, may lead to a cause of action. The elements required to make out the tort of breach of confidence are as follows:

a) that the information must have the necessary quality of confidence about it;

b) that the information must have been imparted in circumstances importing an obligation of confidence; and

c) that there must be unauthorized use of that information to the detriment of the party communicating it. (*Jane Doe 464533 v N.D.* para 51)

The video created by the victim met the first element. The video was meant to be confidential information and had the "necessary quality of confidence about it" (*Jane Doe 464533 v N.D.* para 22). The video was to be private and personal to the plaintiff and was not publicly available, until it was shared on the Internet (para 22) and thereby met the second element. The circumstances that led to the creation of the video were clearly communicated to the defendant on the expressed basis that he would treat the video as confidential (para 23). The third element of the tort was normally considered on a commercial basis; however, the court found that there was no rational basis to distinguish between an economic harm and a psychological harm to the plaintiff in this case. The facts met the third element in the test because the recipient had misused the confidential information for commercial advantage at the expense or detriment of the other party. The impact of the defendant's actions has possible future adverse impact on the plaintiff's career and employment prospects arising from the possibility that the video may someday resurface (para 25). The plaintiff had, thus, made out a cause of action for breach of confidence.

The court also found that the test for intentional infliction of mental distress was met because the defendant engaged conduct that was flagrant and outrageous, calculated to produce harm, and resulted in a visible and provable injury (*Jane Doe 464533 v N.D.* para 26). The defendant's conduct was flagrant and outrageous because he knew that the plaintiff had been reluctant to make the video and was hesitant to share the video of herself. The defendant persuaded her to do so and assured her that only he would view the video. The defendant nonetheless posted the video online and shared it with his friends the same day (*Jane Doe 464533 v N.D.* para 29). The second element was established, since the defendant must have either wanted to produce the mental distress or known that this type of harm was likely. Posting a private intimate video on a public website, and sharing the video with peers would cause the person whose "trust had been betrayed in this fashion extreme emotional upset and understandable psychological distress" (paras 30-31). The final element of the test was established since the conduct caused significant psychological harm. Doe was taken to a crisis centre, suffered from depression, underwent extensive counselling and remains emotionally fragile and vulnerable (para 32).

The defendant also invaded Doe's privacy and, as such, she was able to prove the cause of action for invasion of privacy. The court's analysis of this tort relied heavily on *Jones v Tsige*. Invasion of privacy encompasses a number of potential situations. The one most applicable to the case was public disclosure of embarrassing facts about the plaintiff. The court adopted the elements of this tort and then modified them by stipulating that the act of publication can itself attract liability. The court noted that "one who gives publicity to a matter concerning the private life of another is subject to liability to the other for invasion of the other's privacy, if the matter publicized or the act of the publication (a) would be highly offensive to a reasonable person, and (b) is not of legitimate concern to the public" (*Jane Doe 464533 v N.D.* para 46).

By posting on the Internet a privately-shared and personal intimate video recording of the plaintiff, the court found that the defendant "made public an aspect of the plaintiff's private life" (*Jane Doe 464533 v N.D.* para 48) and that a "reasonable person would find such activity, involving unauthorized public disclosure of such a video, to be highly offensive" (para 48); furthermore, there was no public interest rationale for sharing the video (para 38).

In *Jane Doe 72511 v Morgan*, Justice Gomery of the Ontario Superior Court of Justice recognized the tort of public disclosure of private facts in a situation of NCDII (*Jane Doe 72511 v Morgan* para 93). The plaintiff,

Jane Doe, began dating the defendant, Nicholas Morgan, while in high school. The defendant was physically and verbally abusive towards the plaintiff and eventually convicted of assault after the plaintiff reported the abuse to the police. In 2016, the plaintiff learned that the defendant had posted an explicit video of her on a pornographic website without her consent. The video was posted several years earlier and was linked to ten other pornographic websites. Although Morgan's face was not visible in the video, Jane's face was clearly visible. The video was eventually removed from the website, but by that time, it had been viewed over sixty thousand times, and it was not known how many times it was downloaded and shared (para 3-6). In recognizing the tort of public disclosure of private facts, the court noted that in order to establish liability, the plaintiff must prove that "the defendant publicized an aspect of the plaintiff's private life" and that they did not consent to this publication. Furthermore, the plaintiff must show that the publication would be highly offensive to a reasonable person and that the publication was not justified by any legitimate public concern (para 99).

The court in *Jane Doe 72511* recognized the deep harm that may result from acts of NCDII, noting that the impact goes beyond one's immediate social circle: "Jane's face was clearly visible on the video. Given the amount of time it was posted and the number of times it was viewed, she may well be recognized from the video for years to come by employers, coworkers, family members, neighbours and strangers" (*Jane Doe 72511 v Morgan* para 126). The court awarded the plaintiff $50,000 in general damages, $25,000 in aggravated damages, and $25,000 in punitive damages. The court considered four factors in making the decision on the damage award: the vulnerability of the victim; the number, frequency, and nature of the assaults; the defendant's age and whether there was a position of trust; and the consequences of the wrongful behaviour on the victim, including psychological injuries (para 129). In making a total award of $100,000, the judge concluded that the damages to the plaintiff were much more significant than those that would be awarded for intrusion on seclusion or other privacy breaches. Justice Gomery noted that "the Internet never forgets. Her dignity and personal autonomy have been, and will continue to be, compromised" (para 132).

The *Jane Doe* cases, or similar cases, will undoubtedly provide fruitful possibilities for making causes of action using common law tort principles. This law will develop jurisdiction by jurisdiction, filling the gaps where criminal law or statutory relief is not sought. This is a potentially expansive source of relief for victims of intimate image exposure. Yet, undoubtedly, the legal theory underpinning the civil causes of action, whether under common law or legislation, remains rooted in conceptions of privacy. Critiques abound that a more accurate legal lens would be to consider NCDII a form of sexualized violence, mainly against women. We conclude this chapter by considering a critical and gendered lens of the NCDII legal regime.

Discussion and Concluding Remarks: Providing a Critical, Gendered Lens

With the majority of victims being women, NCDII can be seen as part of a continuum of gendered, sexualized violence against women (McGlynn et al 26; Dodge and Spencer; Powell 77) and as a manifestation of sexism (Dodge and Spencer) or cyber misogyny (West Coast LEAF, "#Cybermisogyny"). Although there is a growing awareness of NCDII and other forms of online harassment as acts of violence against women, categorizing the NCDII as sexual violence still involves "working against a strong social current of resistance" (Fairbairn 235). As we have seen, the non-consensual sharing of intimate images is still frequently placed within the framework of a privacy violation (McGlynn et al. 36). Interestingly, in an analysis of Canadian and America media coverage of NCDII between 2011 and 2014, the word "violence" was only used once in reference to NCDII; rather, NCDII was more commonly described with words labelling it as an experience of "harassment," "humiliation," and "cyberbullying" (Fairbairn). As Powell notes, "there is arguably a false distinction currently operating in law, policy and public debates between unauthorized sexual imagery as distinct from sexual violence. One is seen as merely a distasteful violation of privacy ... and the other a criminal violation of bodily integrity" (Powell 80).

Framing NCDII as a privacy issue is problematic for a number of reasons (Franks 259). Notably, privacy fails to account for the structural inequality and gendered nature of the phenomenon. A privacy framework also fails to recognize the NCDII's disproportionate impact on women as well as LGBTQ2S+, racialized, and disabled people.

Privacy as a legal concept itself is gendered and racialized, and has not always met the needs of marginalized populations (Bailey, "Towards"). Powell notes that "by framing the issue [unauthorized sexual images and videos] as one of privacy violation, mainstream media and indeed legal discussions have largely taken place at a relative distance from the broader issues of gender and sexual violence" (77). In her critical analysis of section 162.1, Aikenhead notes that the requirement under the section for the complainant to hold a reasonable expectation of privacy at the time the image was taken and at the time of distribution is premised on the idea that somehow a person's privacy interest in their intimate image could be lost; the issue of NCDII, however, is not a manner of privacy alone (129): "Given that intimate images will depict a person who is naked, or involved in sexual activity, and the substantive offence requires those images be nonconsensually distributed, it is troubling to think that a person's privacy interest in their intimate images can somehow be lost" (129). In a similar vein, Lise Gotell in her discussion of sexual violence more generally notes that "the judicial focus on privacy encourages a legal analysis that is both degendered and decontextualized" (141).

There are several reasons to consider NCDII within the frame of violence against women. First, the harms experienced by victims of NCDII are not dissimilar to those experienced by victims of physical sexual violence, and, in fact, some women who have been the subjects of NCDII experience it as a form of sexual assault (McGlynn et al. 36; Bates 39; West Coast LEAF, "#Cybermisogyny" 15). Second, the discursive tendencies surrounding NCDII within media, popular culture, and criminal justice responses are similar to those found in cases of sexual assault and sexual harassment (Fairbairn 239).

One such discursive tendency is for consensual and non-consensual intimate image sharing to be conflated in terminology as well as in popular discourse (Dodge 15). Some perpetrators and their supporters may explicitly conflate the two and argue that the initial consent of a woman to have her photograph taken is consent to subsequent distribution (Citron and Franks 348). Indeed, the conflation of consensual and non-consensual intimate image sharing may be more common than one would think. In a 2015 study by Shaheen Shariff and Ashley DeMartini, they presented teens with a scenario in which a girl consensually shared a sexually explicit photo with a boy, who later distributed it. Forty-six per cent of respondents did not feel that the girl in the scenario had the right to object to the subsequent distribution because she sent the initial photograph consensually (Shariff and DeMartini 294). Less explicit manifestations of this erasure of consent is manifested in the victim-blaming orientation of some public education campaigns. For example, campaigns that focus on the behaviour of the victim rather than the perpetrator (Karaian 284) and promote digital abstinence or a risk management approach to the problem of NCDII are examples of this erasure of consent (Bates). Lara Karaian notes the following:

> Anti-sexting initiatives that reify and mobilize a culture of sexual shame in order to responsibilize certain girls for their own, and others', safety constitute meaning-making projects that reproduce and reify gendered, racialized, classed and heteronormative ideas of sexual value, propriety, privilege and blameworthiness, often "regardless of intention, power differences and goodwill." (284)

Within such a frame, men are viewed as inevitable perpetrators, and victims are held responsible to avoid violence. This is not unlike what commonly happens in discourses of sexual assault (Fairbairn 239). Feminist scholars have long documented the tendency to both blame women for the sexual violence they experience and then hold them responsible for avoiding sexual assault through certain activities (Grant 563).

Another discursive tendency found within NCDII, which is similar to those found within sexual assault, is the construction of the perfect victim. In examining a Canadian Centre for Child Protection (CCCP) digital abstinence-oriented campaign on sexting, Karaian argued that the campaign privileged white, heterosexual femininity and idealized and fetishized it. In the process, the campaign reproduced the very objectifying and sexualizing contexts it purported to fight against (Karaian 291). Similarly, other authors have pointed to the popular narrative that women in the context of the NCDII are supposed to be chaste, passive, and lacking in sexual agency (Dodge 74; Hasinoff 211-212). The idealized victim, therefore, is not a woman who has engaged in overt sexual expression outside of the bounds of acceptable femininity, such as voluntarily sending sexually explicit pictures. Such a victim is often blamed for inviting her own victimization (Hasinoff 211-212; Shariff and DeMartini 286). In Dodge and Spencer's 2017 study of police responses to NCDII, the construction of the ideal victim was evident in police attitudes, whereby women expressing themselves sexually by sending sexually explicit photos were sometimes deemed to be somewhat deserving of the non-consensual distribution of their photo and boys were framed as simply being boys for engaging in non-consensual distribution (15). A study of media responses to NCDII found that the media tended to engage in blaming teenage girls for sharing pictures of themselves (Hasinoff 203).

The erasure of consent and construction of the idealized victim are most obviously demonstrated in mainstream media representations of girls' use of technology, which generally falls into one of two categories: either girls are in constant danger from online predators or girls are dangerous loose cannons when it comes to technology (Crooks 47; Lee and Crofts). Their participation in consensual sharing of intimate images becomes conflated with non-consensual distribution and subsumed under the moral panic over young women's sexuality. This erasure of consent is reflected in research on sexting and cyberbullying. As Murray Lee and Thomas Crofts argue "research into sexting often begins with an adult oriented moral agenda and unproblematically takes sexting on board as a negative risk" (Lee and Crofts). Furthermore, in cyber safety campaigns and public discourse, non-consensual distribution is positioned as being rooted more in user naiveté than gender-based violence (Henry and Powell, "Beyond" 105). Such a moral panic over young women's sexuality and focus on youth naiveté fail to capture the gendered nature of the harms at play (Lee and Crofts).

The imbalance in power relations, as well as the way in which non-consensual intimate image distribution accompanies other forms of violence, suggests that NCDII should be considered under the umbrella of violence against women. The anonymity of the Internet provides the perfect opportunity for hegemonic masculinities to operate (Henry and Powell, "Embodied" 769). Amar Khoday discusses this power imbalance and notes that when one person possesses and controls images of a sexual nature "the person who possesses the material clearly exercises power over that individual." He continues: "This dominant power is then exercised oppressively when such video or photographic material is then posted online or otherwise shared with others without the consent of those within the material" (62). Through NCDII, men can exert sexual dominance over women (Bates 25) and use non-consensual intimate image sharing as a way to harass, humiliate, objectify, blackmail, and coerce women (Henry and Powell, "Sexual" 398). Specifically, NCDII is sometimes used in the context of domestic abuse to coerce, control, threaten, and harass current and former partners (Bond and Tyrrell 2; Citron and Franks 351; Henry and Powell, "Sexual" 113). Studies also suggest that the non-consensual sharing of intimate images sometimes accompanies acts of physical sexual violence (Dodge and Spencer) or other offences (Henry and Powell "Embodied"). It is increasingly common for photos of a sexual assault to be taken and circulated (Dodge), sometimes with a threat of distribution used as blackmail to keep the victim quiet about the assault (Powell and Henry, "Blurred" 122). Dodge examined comments made on the photos of three high profile cases of images of sexual assault, which were distributed in Canada and the United States; she notes that many people who commented on the images did not read the photographs as evidence of sexual assault but rather that the girls pictured within the photos were sluts, deserving of having their bodies violated (Dodge 68). The NCDII can also lead to further violence, with many victims experiencing online harassment and stalking (Bates 23).

In short, the NCDII removes the freedom of women to control their own destiny: "sexual pleasure is found in the ability to exert control over the woman's options, removing her ability to refuse consent, to depart from the situation"(Nussbaum 72). As we await the proliferation and stabilization of the emerging jurisprudence of NCDII in Canada, perhaps courts and legislatures will begin to consider the sexualized violence that inhabits the core of the distribution of these images instead of focusing solely on privacy related concerns. Only time will demonstrate whether Canada's justice system is capable of this turn.

Endnotes

1. Alternative phrases utilized within academic scholarship to capture NCDII, and under which a wider range of online violence directed at woman is also captured, include "image-based sexual exploitation" (Powell and Henry "Blurred"), "technology facilitated sexual

violence" (Henry and Powell, "Beyond"), "cyber misogyny" (LEAF, "Submission to standing committee"), and "cyber harassment" (Franks; Citron and Franks).

2. Of the photos studied, 35.8 per cent included reasons given by the perpetrator for why the photo was posted; 21.6 per cent of perpetrators indicated that the reason for posting was that the person was an ex; 21.6 per cent indicated that the reason for posting was because the person was hot/sexy; 6 per cent posted because the person was unfaithful; and 14.9 per cent posted because the person was a slut (Uhl et al. 57). Removing the hot/sexy category from this analysis suggests that 42.5 per cent of the photos that provided a reason for posting assigned a negative, victim-blaming culpability to the victim.

Works Cited

Secondary Sources

Aikenhead, Moira. "Non-Consensual Disclosure of Intimate Images as a Crime of Gender-Based Violence." *Canadian Journal of Women and the Law,* vol. 30, no.1, 2018, pp. 117-42.

Bailey, Jane. "Time to Unpack the Juggernaut?: Reflections on the Canadian Federal Parliament Debates on 'Cyberbullying;?" *Dalhousie Law Journal,* vol. 37, no. 2, 2014, pp. 661-707.

Bailey, Jane. "Towards an Equality-Enhancing Conception of Privacy." *Dalhousie Law Journal,* vol. 31, no. 2, 2008, pp. 267-63.

Bates, Samantha. "Revenge Porn and Mental Health: A Qualitative Analysis of the Mental Health Effects of Revenge Porn on Female Survivors." *Feminist Criminology,* vol. 12, no. 1, 2017, pp. 22-42.

Beyens, Jolien, and Eva Lievens. "A Legal Perspective on the Non-consensual Dissemination of Sexual Images: Identifying Strengths and Weaknesses of Legislation in the US, UK and Belgium." *International Journal of Law, Crime and Justice,* vol. 47, 2016, pp. 31-43.

Bond, Emma, and Katie Tyrrell. "Understanding Revenge Pornography: A National Survey of Police Officers and Staff in England and Wales." *Journal of Interpersonal Violence,* 2018, pp. 1-16, doi: doi-org.uml.idm.oclc.org/10.1177/0886260518760011.

Branch, Kathryn, et al. "Revenge Porn Victimization of College Students in the United States: An Exploratory Analysis." *International Journal of Cyber Criminology*, vol. 11, no. 1, 2017, pp. 128-42, doi: 10.5281/zenodo.495777.

Canada. Statistics Canada. *Nonconsensual Distribution of Intimate Images.* Ottawa, Ont.: Statistic Canada, 2018, www150.statcan.gc.ca/t1/tbl1 /en/tv.action?pid=3510017701&pickMembers%5B0%5D= 1.1& pickMembers%5B1%5D=2.257. Accessed 30 July 2018.

Cartwright, Barry. "Cyberbullying and 'The Law of the Horse': A Canadian Viewpoint." *Journal of Internet Law*, vol. 20, no. 10, 2017, pp. 14-26.

Choo, Hannah. "Why We Are Still Searching for Solutions to Cyberbullying: An Analysis of the North American Responses to Cyberbullying under the Theory of Systemic Desensitization." *University of New Burnswick Law Journal*, vol. 66, 2015, pp. 52-77.

Citizen Lab. "Submission of the Citizen Lab (Munk School of Global Affairs, University of Toronto) to the United Nations Special Rapporteur on Violence against Women, Its Causes and Consequences, Ms. Dubravka Simonovic." *Citizen Lab: Munk School of Global Affairs*, 2 Nov. 2017, citizenlab.ca/wp-content/uploads/2017/11/Final-UN-SRVAG-CitizenLab.pdf. Accessed 14 June 2018.

Citron, Danielle Keats, and Mary Anne Franks. "Criminalizing Revenge Porn." *Wake Forest Law Review*, vol. 49, 2014, pp. 345-91.

Coburn, Patricia, et al. "Cyberbullying: Is Federal Criminal Legislation the Solution?" Canadian *Journal of Criminology and Criminal Justice*, vol. 57, no. 4, 2015, pp. 566-79.

Crooks, Hayley. "An Intersectional Feminist Review of the Literature on Gendered Cyberbullying: Digital Girls." *Jeunesse: Young People, Texts, Cultures*, vol. 8, no. 2, 2016, pp. 62-88.

Dodge, Alexa. "Digitizing rape culture: Online sexual violence and the power of the digital photograph." *Crime Media Culture*, vol. 12, no. 1, 2016, pp. 65-82, doi: 10.1177/1741659015601173.

Dodge, Alexa, and Dale Spencer. "Online Sexual Violence, Child Pornography or Something Else Entirely? Police Response to Non-Consensual Intimate Image Sharing Among Youth." *Social & Legal Studies*, vol. 20, no. 10, 2017, pp. 1-22, doi: 10.1177/0964 66391772 4866 1.

Eaton, Asia A., et al. "2017 Nationwide Online Study of Nonconsensual Porn Victimization and Perpetration: A Summary Report." *Cyber Civil Rights Initiative*, June 2017, www.cybercivilrights.org/wp-content/uploads/2017/06/CCRI-2017-Research-Report.pdf. Accessed 14 June 2018.

Fairbairn, Jordan. "Rape Threats and Revenge Porn: Defining Sexual Violence in the Digital Age." *eGirls, eCitizens*, edited by Jane Bailey and Valerie Steeves, University of Ottawa Press, 2015, pp. 229-51.

Felt, Mylynn. "The Incessant Image: How Dominant News Coverage Shaped Canadian Cyberbullying Law." *University of New Brunswick Law Journal*, vol. 66, 2015, pp. 137-60.

Franks, Mary Anne. "Unwilling Avatars: Idealism and Discrimination in Cyberspace." *Colum. J. Gender & L.*, vol. 20, 2011, pp. 224-61.

Gotell, Lise. "The Discursive Disappearance of Sexualized Violence: Feminist Law Reform, Judicial Resistance, and Neo-Liberal Sexual Citizenship" *Reaction and Resistance: Feminism, Law and Social Change*, edited by Dorothy E Chunn et al., UBC Press, 2007, pp. 127-63.

Grant, Isabel. "Intimate Partner Criminal Harassment through a Lens of Responsibilization." *Osgood Hall LJ*, vol. 52, 2015, pp. 552-600.

Hasinoff, Amy Adele. "Sexting and Privacy Violations: A Case Study of Sympathy and Blame." *International Journal of Cyber Criminality*, vol. 11, no. 2, 2017, pp. 202-217, doi: 10.5281/zenodo.1037391.

Henry, Nicola, and Anastasia Powell. "Beyond the 'sext': Technology Facilitated Sexual Violence and Harassment Against Adult Women" *Australian & New Zealand Journal of Criminology*, vol. 48, no. 1, 2015, pp. 104-18, doi: 10.1177/0004865814524218.

Henry, Nicola, and Anastasia Powell. "Embodied Harms: Gender, Shame and Technology-Facilitated Sexual Violence." *Violence Against Women*, vol. 21, no. 6, 2015, pp. 758-779, doi: 10.1177/1077801215576581.

Henry, Nicola, and Anastasia Powell. "Sexual Violence in the Digital Age: The Scope and Limits of Criminal Law." *Social & Legal Studies*, vol. 25, no. 4, 2016, pp. 397-418.

Henry, Nicola, and Anastasia Powell. "Technology-Facilitated Sexual Violence: A Literature Review of Empirical Research." *Trauma, Violence & Abuse*, vol. 19, no. 2, 2018, pp. 195-208.

Jochelson, Richard, and Kirsten Kramar. *Sex and the Supreme Court: Obscenity and Indecency Law in Canada*. Winnipeg and Halifax: Fernwood Publishing, 2011.

Karaian, Lara. "Policing 'Sexting': Responsibilization, Respectability and Sexual Subjectivity in Child Protection/Crime Prevention Responses to Teenagers' Digital Sexual Expression." *Theoretical Criminology*, vol.18, no.3, 2014, pp. 282-99.

Khoday, Amar. "Resisting Revenge Pornography: When Victims Strike Back." Case Comment on *Jane Doe 464533 v D(N.)*, *Canadian Cases on the Law of Torts*, vol. 25, no. 4, 2016, pp. 45-67.

Kitchen, Adrienne. "The Need to Criminalize Revenge Porn: How a Law Protecting Victims Can Avoid Running Afoul of the First Amendment." *Chi-Ken L Review*, vol. 90, no. 1, 2015, pp. 247-99.

Kubinec, Vera-Lynn. "More than 1,300 Manitobans Seek Help after Intimate Images Shared." *CBC News*, 27 Apr. 2018, www.cbc.ca/news/canada/manitoba/revenge-porn-help-online-1.4637615. Accessed 14 June 2018.

Langlois, Ganaele, and Andrea Slane. "Economies of Reputation: The Case of Revenge Porn." *Communication and Critical/Cultural Studies*, vol. 14, no. 2, 2017, pp. 120-38, doi: 10.1080/14791420.2016.1273534.

LEAF. "LEAF Applies for Leave to Intervene at the Supreme Court of Canada in *R v Jarvis*." *LEAF: Women's Legal Education and Action Fund*, 2018, www.leaf.ca/leaf-applies-for-leave-to-intervene-at-the-supreme-court-of-canada-in-r-v-jarvis/. Accessed 26 July 2018.

LEAF. *Factum of the Intervenor, Women's Legal Education and Action Fund in the Supreme Court of Canada: R v Jarvis*, 2019 SCC 10, www.leaf.ca/wp-content/uploads/2018/04/Factum-of-the-Intervener-Womens-Legal-Education-and-Action-Fund-Inc.-....pdf. Accessed 15 February 2019.

Lee, Murray, and Thomas Crofts. "Gender, Pressure, Coercion and Pleasure: Untangling Sexting between Young People." *The British Journal of Criminology*, vol. 55, no. 3, 2015, pp. 454-73.

Lenhart, Amanda, et al. "Nonconsensual Image Sharing: One in 25 Americans Has Been a Victim of 'Revenge Porn'" *Centre for Innovative Public Health Research: Data and Society Research Institute*, December 2016, datasociety.net/pubs/oh/Nonconsensual_Image_Sharing_2016.pdf. Accessed 14 June 2018.

Madigan, Shari, et al. "Prevalence of Multiple Forms of Sexting Behavior Among Youth: A Systemic Review and Meta-analysis." *JAMA Pediatrics*, vol. 172, no. 4, 2018, pp. 327-35.

Manitoba Government. "Province Announces New Law in Force Helps Victims of Revenge Porn, Unwanted Distribution of Sexual Pictures" *News Release, Manitoba Government*, 18 January 2016, news.gov.mb.ca/news/index.html?item=37330. Accessed 12 May 2019.

Mathen, Carissima. "Crowdsourcing Sexual Objectification." *Laws*, vol. 3, 2014, pp. 529-52, doi:10.3390/laws3030529.

McGlynn, Clare, et al. "Beyond 'Revenge Porn': The Continuum of Image-Based Sexual Abuse." *Fem Leg Stud*, vol. 25, 2017, pp. 25-46.

Nussbaum, Martha. "Objectification and Internet Misogyny." *The Offensive Internet: Speech, Privacy, and Reputation*, edited by S. Levmore and M. C. Nussbaum, Harvard University Press, 2010, pp. 68-90.

Powell, Anastasia. "Configuring Consent: Emerging Technologies, Unauthorised Sexual Images and Sexual Assault." *The Australian and New Zealand Journal of Criminology*, vol. 43, no. 1, 2010, pp. 76-90.

Powell, Anastasia, and Nicola Henry. "Blurred Lines? Responding to 'Sexting' and Gender-based Violence among Young People." *Children Australia*, vol. 39, no. 2, 2014, pp. 119-24, doi:10.1017/cha.2014.9.

Shariff, Shaheen, and Ashley DeMartini. "Defining the Legal Lines: eGirls and Intimate Images." *eGirls, eCitizens*, edited by Jane Bailey and Valerie Steeves, University of Ottawa Press, 2015, pp. 281-305.

Slane, Andrea. "Sexting and the Law in Canada" *Canadian Journal of Human Sexuality*, vol. 22, no. 3, 2013, pp. 117-122.

Slane, Andrea, and Ganaele Langlois. "Debunking the Myth of 'Not My Bad': Sexual Images, Consent and Online Host Responsibilities in Canada." *Canadian Journal of Women and the Law*, vol. 30, no. 1, 2018, pp. 42-81.

Slane, Andrea, and Ganaele Langlois. "Regulating Business Models that Capitalize on User Posted Personal Information of Others: How Can Canada's Privacy Regime Protect Victims of Online Shaming Businesses?" *Office of the Privacy Commissioner of Canada*, Submissions received for the consultation on online reputation, August 2016, www.priv.gc.ca/en/about-the-opc/what-we-do/consultations/consultation-on-online-reputation/submissions-received-for-the-consultation-on-online-reputation/or/sub_or_01/. Accessed 12 May 2019.

Uhl, Carolyn A., et al. "An Examination of Non-consensual:Pornography Websites." *Feminism & Psychology*, vol. 28, no. 1, 2018, pp.50-68.

West Coast LEAF. "#CyberMisogyny: Using and Strengthening Canadian Legal Responses to Gendered Hate and Harassment Online." *West Coast LEAF (Women's Legal Education and Action Fund)*, 2014, www.westcoastleaf.org/wp-content/uploads/2014/10/2014-REPORT-CyberMisogyny.pdf. Accessed 19 June 2018.

West Coast LEAF. "Submission to the Standing Committee on Justice and Human Rights on Bill C-13: An Act to amend the *Criminal Code*, the Canada Evidence Act, the Competition Act, and the Mutual Legal Assistance in Criminal Matters Act." *West Coast LEAF (Women's Legal Education and Action Fund)*, 2014, www.westcoastleaf.org/wp-content/uploads/2014/11/2014-05-13-SUBMISSION-Standing-Committee-on-JHR-on-Bill-C-13.pdf. Accessed 18 June 2018.

Jurisprudence

Crouch v Snell, 2015 NSSC 340, [2015] N.S.J. No. 536, 2015 CarswellNS 995.

Jane Doe 464533 v N.D., 2016 ONSC 541 (CanLII), <http://canlii.ca/t/gn23z>, retrieved on 2018-05-14.

Jane Doe 464533 v N.D., 2016 ONSC 4920.

Jane Doe 464533 v N.D., 2017 ONSC 127.

Jane Doe 72511 v Morgan, 2018 ONSC 6607.

Jones v Tsige, 2012 ONCA 32.

L. (T.K.) v P. (T.M.), 2016 BCSC 789.

N.G. c F.B., 2017 QCCS 5653, 2017 CarswellQue 11341, 287 A.C.W.S. (3d) 194, EYB 2017-288158.

R v A.C., 2017 ONCJ 129 (CanLII), http://canlii.ca/t/h0nzz, retrieved on 2018-05-11.

R v A.C., 2017 ONCJ 317 (CanLII), http://canlii.ca/t/h42q9, retrieved on 2018-05-11.

R v Agoston, 2017 ONSC 3425 (CanLII), http://canlii.ca/t/h4dlr, retrieved on 2018-05-22.

R v B.H., [2016] O.J. No. 7080.

R c Bradette, 2009 QCCQ 20918, [2009] J.Q. no 23391.

R v B.Z., 2016 ONCJ 547 (CanLII), http://canlii.ca/t/gt89m, retrieved on 2018-05-21.

R v C.N.T. [B.M.S.], 2016 NSCA 35, [2016] N.S.J. No. 163, 2016 CarswellNS 354, 130 W.C.B. (2d) 316, 373 N.S.R. (2d) 298.

R c D.G., 2016 QCCQ 6167, [2016] J.Q. no 7730.

R v Greene, 2018 CanLII 25580 (NL PC), http://canlii.ca/t/hr7cd, retrieved on 2018-05-14.

R v Hirsch, 2017 SKCA 14, [2017] S.J. No. 59, 2017 CarswellSask 77, 136 W.C.B. (2d) 555, 353 C.C.C. (3d) 230, 36 C.R. (7th) 216.

R v Hunt, 2017 CanLII 86655 (NL PC), http://canlii.ca/t/hpgqn, retrieved on 2018-05-23.

R v Jarvis, 2015 ONSC 6813.

R v Jarvis, 2017 ONCA 778, 2017 CarswellOnt 15528, 142 W.C.B. (2d) 850, 356 C.C.C. (3d) 1, 41 C.R. (7th) 36.

R v Jarvis, 2019 SCC 10.

R v J.S., 2018 ONCJ 82 (CanLII), http://canlii.ca/t/hq7nk, retrieved on 2018-05-11.

R v J.T.B., 2018 ONSC 2422 (CanLII), http://canlii.ca/t/hrj5m, retrieved on 2018-05-22.

R v Kennedy, [2017] N.J. No. 162.

R v Lauzon, 2017 ONCJ 937, [2017] O.J. No. 7044.

R v Ly, [2016] O.J. No. 7196.

R v Maurer, 2014 SKPC 118, [2014] S.J. No. 286, 113 W.C.B. (2d) 498, 447 Sask. R. 76, 2014 CarswellSask 319.

R v Maurer, 2015 SKQB 175, [2015] S.J. No. 332, 2015 CarswellSask 388, 123 W.C.B. (2d) 404, 477 Sask. R. 272.

R v M.B., 2016 BCCA 476 (CanLII), http://canlii.ca/t/gvvln, retrieved on 2018-05-22.

R v McFarlane, 2018 MBCA 48 (CanLII), http://canlii.ca/t/hrwhl, retrieved on 2018-05-21.

R c Mercier, 2017 QCCQ 4347, 2017 CarswellQue 3929, EYB 2017-279366.

R v M.R., 2017 ONCJ 558, [2017] O.J. No. 4233.

R v M.R., 2017 ONCJ 943 (CanLII), http://canlii.ca/t/hr4l8, retrieved on 2018-05-08.

R v Nasogaluak, 2010 SCC 6.

R v P.S.D., 2016 BCPC 400 (CanLII), http://canlii.ca/t/gw378, retrieved on 2018-05-14.

R v Ravindran, 2016 ONSC 6228, [2016] O.J. No. 5139.

R v Sim, 2017 ONCA 856, 2017 CarswellOnt 17179.

R v Trinchi, 2016 ONSC 6585, [2016] O.J. No. 6719.

R v Tunney, 2018 ONSC 961, 2018 CarswellOnt 2157, 145 W.C.B. (2d) 524.

R v Stender, 2005 SCC 36, [2005] 1 S.C.R. 914, 2005 CarswellOnt 2336, 2005 CarswellOnt 2337, 201 C.C.C. (3d) 319, 201 O.A.C. 136, 258 D.L.R. (4th) 577, 336 N.R. 21, 67 W.C.B. (2d) 174.

R v Verner, 2017 ONCJ 415, [2017] O.J. No. 3206.

Legislation

Bill 72: The Privacy Amendment Act 2017.—Amendment to The Privacy Act, RSS 1978, c P-24.

Canadian Charter of Rights and Freedoms, Part I of the *Constitution Act, 1982*, being Schedule B to the *Canada Act 1982* (UK), 1982, c 1.

Canada Evidence Act, RSC 1985, c C-5.

Civil Code of Québec, CQLR c CCQ-1991.

Criminal Code (R.S.C., 1985, c C-46).

Bill 27: Intimate Images and Cyber-protection Act, 2013, c. 2, s. 1, 1st Session, 63rd General Assembly, Nova Scotia, 66 Elizabeth II, 2017.

Privacy Act, RSBC 1996, c 373.

Privacy Act, RSNL 1990, c P-22

Protecting Canadians from Online Crime Act, SC 2014, c 31.

The Intimate Image Protection Act, CCSM 2015 c I8.

The Privacy Act, C.C.S.M. 2008 c P125.

The Privacy Act, RSS 1978, c P-24. *Distribution of Intimate Images Act,* RSA 2017, c P-26.9.

Chapter Four

Technologies of Regulating Sexual Offences against Youth

Lauren Menzie and Taryn Hepburn

Introduction

Child sexual abuse invokes a particularly strong condemnation from most people, certainly all reasonable people. The regulation of sexual offences that target and harm youth is part of the fabric of most societies, including Canada. Canada's governance of these types of offences has a long history in law that has seen a dramatic change since its inception. This chapter chronicles the changes in legislation and problematizes the current articulation of law under a society that continues to evolve and grow through technology.

Changes to legislation are often brought about through social anxieties surrounding the protection of children, and, as such, they are remarkably expansive. In Canada, the primary point of inquiry for sexual offences against youth would fall under two sections of the *Criminal Code of Canada*: section 163.1 (child pornography) and section 172.1 (luring a child). This chapter considers the historical shift in legislative governance of sexual crimes against youth, tracing its expansion through various bills and acts. It establishes the current legal interpretation of both sections 163.1 and 172.1 by noting changes occurring through the common law. Finally, it moves to consider how technological innovation poses challenges to the law. The commission of offences under these sections predominantly takes place online, and the difficulty in preventing sexual offences and punishing perpetrators in virtual space prompts further social anxieties and, we argue, a confused sense of harm.

Representations of child sexual abuse—whether through artistic renderings, online fantasy, or life-sized silicone constructions—have been indistinguishable from real harm under the law. Although we argue that the representation of harmful acts should not be considered interchangeable with actual acts, in many cases, the law views these as one and the same. This approach is risk averse and precautionary; in viewing a representation as akin to an act, the law makes a moralistic argument and attempts to characterize these offences as posing both an ongoing moral harm and future risk of harm (see Jochelson et al.). This chapter exemplifies this logic by examining the proactive investigations of child luring and the possession of child sex dolls. Both of these have generated a great deal of debate within legal cases, much of which is still ongoing and likely to continue.

Child Luring: A Brief History of Legislative Governance

To determine how any system operates, it is important to consider from where it is has developed and how it has grown. Historical understanding (even recent historical understanding) aids us in developing the ongoing narrative, which, in turn, serves to place the utility and social value of systems at the forefront. Historical considerations allow researchers to question why a system is in place, what it is necessary for, and what end it serves (Fairclough, *Critical Discourse Analysis*; Hsieh and Shannon). In particular, examining the progressing changes in language and content allows researchers to develop cohesive arguments on the purpose and goals of the systems as well as to demonstrate systematic problems and issues.

For these purposes, this section examines the recent history of child luring legislation in Canada and considers how the legislation governs Canadian citizens. It also explores the changes to section 172.1 of the *Criminal Code* from its inception in 2002 until its most recent amendment in 2015. As section 172.1 has undergone many changes since 2002, this section focuses most specifically on the amending bills: Bill C-15A (2002), Bill C-277 (2007), Bill C-2 (2008), Bill C-10 (2012),

Bill C-36 (2014), and Bill C-26 (2015). It is important to note that the current legislation has gone through many amendments to date and will likely be subject to many more.

In 2002, a Liberal government under then-Prime Minister Jean Chrétien enacted Bill C-15A, the *Criminal Law Amendment Act*. Parliament enacted the bill in an atmosphere of growing public concern over the dangers of technology for young people and in light of the recent Supreme Court of Canada decision in *R v Sharpe* (Benedet; Gotell; Jenkins; Casavant and Robertson). The Supreme Court of Canada (SCC)'s ruling in *Sharpe* was highly contentious and led to a great deal of outcry by the public, the House of Commons, and in academia (see Benedet for example). In 1999, the Supreme Court of British Columbia ruled that section 163.1 (4) of the *Criminal Code,* possession of child pornography, contravened the *Canadian Charter of Rights and Freedoms*. This ruling was upheld by a majority at the SCC, with a dissenting minority. The ruling spurned the House of Commons to hold a vote to invoke the notwithstanding clause, and section 163.1 (4) remained. Public concern over the outcome of *Sharpe* had the most impact on section 163.1, child pornography legislation, but the effects of this case have also coloured the amendments to section 172.1 and their purpose.

It was against the backdrop of *Sharpe* that the Chrétien administration advanced Bill C-15A. Generally, the bill was aimed to address the dangers associated with the Internet and was particularly concerned about the sexual exploitation of young people. The first listed objective of Bill C-15A was to amend the *Criminal Code* by "(a) adding offences and other measures that provide additional protection to children from sexual exploitation, including sexual exploitation involving use of the Internet," followed by amendments to reform and "modernize" criminal procedure "with respect to ... (iv) electronic documents and remote appearances." Section 8 of the Bill C-15A introduced a new section immediately following section 172 labelled "Luring a Child." The new section 172.1 introduced a new offence into the *Criminal Code*, specifically penalizing the use of "a computer system" to communicate with "a person who is, or who the accused believes is, under the age of eighteen years, for the purpose of facilitating the commissions of an offence under subsection 153(1), section 155 or 163.1, subsection 212(1) or (4) or section 271, 272 or 273 with respect to that person" (*Criminal Code of Canada,* section 172.1, 2002). The amendment makes it a hybrid offense to lure children under sixteen years of age and under fourteen years of age over the Internet. The offence is originally punishable as an indictable offence for a term of no more than five years or as a summary offence. The court is required to view evidence that the accused was knowledgeable of the child's age. The court may not entertain the defence of mistaken belief that the person was at least eighteen, sixteen, or fourteen years of age "unless the accused took reasonable steps to ascertain the age of the person." It is important to recognize that the legislation does not indicate what constitutes a "reasonable step."

The first amendment to the child luring section of the *Criminal Code* came in 2007, enacted by Bill C-277. The sole object of the bill was to increase the penalties in section 172.1 (2)(a) and (b). The indictable offence's penalty increased from no more than five years to a term of no more than ten years. The summary offence was imprisonment for a term of no more than eighteen months. This amendment was the first of two in quick succession targeting the sentencing of the offence of child luring; it was an attempt to deter crime through harsher punishment. In 2008, the Harper government enacted Bill C-2, the *Tackling Violent Crime Act,* a bill intended to provide "more effective sentencing and monitoring of dangerous and high-risk offenders." The changes to section 172.1 (1)(a) and (b) expanded the relevant sections and subsections of the *Criminal Code,* expanding the range of the offence.

The next changes to section 172.1 were significant, when the Harper government introduced their omnibus crime bill in 2012. Bill C-10, the *Safe Streets and Communities Act,* featured nine separate measures for amendment, many of which focused on regulating sex and sexually explicit information. These included regulating communication "by any means" with a person under the age of sixteen years (sections 161(1)(c) and 172.1(1)), which served to strengthen the regulation of Internet communications as they relate to section 172.1. The omnibus bill also removed any possibility of discharged, suspended, or conditional sentences by revising the statute to read that punishment is for "*every person* who commits an offence under subsection 1" (our emphasis). Further changes to the sentencing provisions introduced mandatory minimum sentences of no shorter than one-year imprisonment for an indictable offence and no shorter than ninety days imprisonment for a summary offence, with no allowance for standalone fines.

In 2014 and 2015, there was another quick succession of amendments: Bill C-36 (Protection of Communities and Exploited Persons Act, 2014) and Bill C-26 (Tougher Penalties for Child Predators Act 2015). In the tradition of section 172.1's introduction, Bill C-36 was a response to a SCC ruling. The 2014 Bedford decision led to Parliament putting forth the Protection of Communities and Exploited Persons Act to prevent the decriminalization of all adult prostitution-based activities. The bill contained amendments to section 172.1 that expanded upon the relevant *Criminal Code* sections. Notably, the "Luring a Child" section of the *Code* was amended and placed within a bill legislating adult sex work; this demonstrates a perceived connection between sex work and exploitation. This conflation calls into question the underlying moral structure that attempts to regulate the ability of both sex workers and young people to exercise sexual agency. This legislation is a response to perceived "grooming" activities enacted to regulate future outcomes.

The most recent amendment, Bill C-26, amended section 172.1 (2) by increasing the punishment. Indictable offences are currently punishable by a term no less than one year and no more than fourteen years. Summary offences are punishable by a term no less than six months and no more than two years less a day. The most recent change is an example of an ongoing trend through the development of section 172.1, as the activities the section governs become more heavily regulated and punished. The areas of the *Criminal Code* connected to child luring continued to expand past its inception and the punishments for offences became increasingly severe.

Child Luring: Authoritative Cases

In its original form, section 172.1 of the *Criminal Code* reads as follows:

Luring a child

1) Every person commits an offence who, by a means of telecommunication, communicates with

    a) a person who is, or who the accused believes is, under the age of 18 years, for the purpose of facilitating the commission of an offence with respect to that person under subsection 153(1), section 155, 163.1, 170, 171 or

279.011 or subsection 279.02(2), 279.03(2), 286.1(2), 286.2(2) or 286.3(2);

b) a person who is, or who the accused believes is, under the age of 16 years, for the purpose of facilitating the commission of an offence under section 151 or 152, subsection 160(3) or 173(2) or section 271, 272, 273 or 280 with respect to that person; or

c) a person who is, or who the accused believes is, under the age of 14 years, for the purpose of facilitating the commission of an offence under section 281 with respect to that person.

Punishment

2) Every person who commits an offence under subsection (1)

a) is guilty of an indictable offence and is liable to imprisonment for a term of not more than 14 years and to a minimum punishment of imprisonment for a term of one year; or

b) is guilty of an offence punishable on summary conviction and is liable to imprisonment for a term of not more than two years less a day and to a minimum punishment of imprisonment for a term of six months.

Presumption re: age

3) Evidence that the person referred to in paragraph (1)(a), (b) or (c) was represented to the accused as being under the age of eighteen years, sixteen years or fourteen years, as the case may be, is, in the absence of evidence to the contrary, proof that the accused believed that the person was under that age.

No defence

4) It is not a defence to a charge under paragraph (1)(a), (b) or (c) that the accused believed that the person referred to in that paragraph was at least eighteen years of age, sixteen years or fourteen years of age, as the case may be, unless the accused took reasonable steps to ascertain the age of the person.

This section details and forms the offence of, through means of telecommunication, communicating with children for the purpose of facilitating the commission of determined sexual offences. In paragraphs (1)(a), (b), and (c), the section sets out the various sexual offences dependent on the child's age. Here, either the child's age or the accused's belief in the age stated by the communicant will establish the offence. In *R v Alicandro,* Doherty J.A. held that the accused's belief that the child was under age makes up the *actus reus* (the action or conduct forming part of the offence) and that their intention to facilitate the commission of a sexual offence would form the *mens rea* (the intention or the mental element of the offence). However, more recently in *R v Legare,* Fish J. noted that it was unnecessary to establish the accused's belief in the age of the communicant in either the *mens rea* or *actus reus* of the offence (*R v Legare* paras 39-41).

Subsection (3) was determined to be of no force and effect by the SCC in *R v Morrison* 2019. Prior to this, subsection (3) had been read to establish a presumption that the accused believed the communicant was under the relevant age if they had represented themselves to the accused as being under that age. This could only have been rebuttable if there had been evidence to the contrary. While it was in effect, subsection (3) created further evidentiary burdens upon an accused by requiring that reasonable steps be taken pursuant to subsection (4). Indeed, these sections were described by the court to be "close companion[s]" (*R v Levigne* para 3). Subsection (4) states the defence that the accused believed the person to be over the relevant age is not valid, unless there had been reasonable steps taken to ascertain the age of that person. These steps must be reasonable considering the circumstances, and the evidentiary burden is placed on the accused. The evidence must constitute both "evidence to the contrary" within the meaning of subsection (3) and "reasonable steps" under subsection (4). Simply having evidence to the contrary without taking reasonable steps, or taking steps and not establishing evidence to the contrary, is insufficient (*R v Levigne*). The combined effect of these subsections paves two pathways to conviction when a communicant represents themselves as underage to the accused: the Crown can prove that the accused believed the communicant was underage or that they failed to take reasonable steps to ascertain the age of the communicant. With respect to proactive investigations of child luring, both pathways are available to the trier of fact (*R v Morrison* 2019 para 49). In *R v Morrison* 2019, the SCC found subsection (3) to be inoperable and unconstitutional, as the presumption conflicted with the section 11(d) *Charter* rights of the accused. This case is discussed further below along with the court's decision to uphold subsection (4) and its clarification of how this section should operate.

Subsection (1)(c) forms an inchoate or preparatory offence, which requires proof that there was an intentional communication through use of a cell phone or computer with a person under the relevant age (or who the accused believes is under that age) for the purpose of facilitating the commission of a specified secondary offence with respect to the underage person. The content of the communication is not determinative; the accused may be found guilty without making sexually explicit comments, as the communication may be found to be an attempt to groom or create trust. Here, facilitating means helping to make the secondary offence easier or more probable. The accused does not have to be objectively capable of committing the secondary offence.

Challenging Proactive Investigations and Legislative Assumptions Under section 172.1

There are many challenges that could be leveraged at proactively investigating offences under section 172.1 of the *Criminal Code*. Proactive investigations, using an undercover police officer posing as a child, are a means of circumventing possible harms that an offender may pose to actual children in future communications. They are rooted in a precautionary, precriminal logic, in which an expansion of governance is permitted due to the difficulties posed by investigating online offences and a social interest in protecting the vulnerable from harm (Jochelson et al.). In practice, however, police tactics to curb child luring online is comprised of two adults having a consensual conversation in which the police officer's age and identity are misrepresented. Here, the law is able to suggest that the accused believed to be communicating with someone under the age of consent, and should they not have taken reasonable steps to establish the age of the officer, they will be found guilty of child luring.

Here, we suggest four possible challenges to section 172.1; some of them have previously been raised before the courts. Constitutionality issues have been heard by the SCC, most recently in *R v Morrison* (2019). These challenges have seen some success, but have not been wholly accepted. Prior to this, some accused have raised a defence of entrapment. Outside of these legal issues, we consider the nature of harm in both the investigatory tactics of child luring and in the assumptions made about those who communicate with youth online. We argue that these assumptions are risk averse and possibly do further harm in limiting or restricting communication between youth and their past support workers, teachers, and counsellors. Finally, we suggest that investigatory tactics and practices can be seen as kinkphobic. By targeting adult role-play advertisements that solicit consensual age play or by investigating adult fantasy chat rooms, child luring legislation is used as a means of governing kink communities. How this legislation is operationalized by police should be looked at critically for its pejorative treatment of adults who seek consensual play.

Entrapment

Despite the nature of police investigative tactics, the issue of entrapment is rarely raised in court. In law, entrapment is not seen as a defence to criminal responsibility; rather, it emerges from the court's inherent jurisdiction to control procedures and safeguard against abuses of process. A finding of entrapment does not result in an acquittal but a stay of proceedings. It does not negate guilt on the part of the accused, but it is used to deter police conduct that is deemed unacceptable and, possibly, the root and source of criminality on the part of the accused. With this in mind, the accused must be found guilty by the court before using the doctrine of entrapment. Entrapment is assessed on a balance of probabilities, where the burden of proof is on the accused. It has been suggested that this is why very few Canadian criminal cases, particularly child luring cases, use entrapment as a defence (Kettles). Furthermore, it is suggested that the use of entrapment to defend against child-luring offences will likely prove unsuccessful (Kettles).

In *R v Mack*, the leading Canadian case on the doctrine of entrapment, the SCC found the following:

There is entrapment when

a) the authorities provide a person with an opportunity to commit an offence without acting on a reasonable suspicion that this person is already engaged in criminal activity or pursuant to a bona fide inquiry;

b) although having such a reasonable suspicion or acting in the course of a bona fide inquiry, they go beyond providing an opportunity and induce the commission of an offence. (*R v Mack* para 126)

There are, therefore, two branches to the doctrine of entrapment: presenting an opportunity to offend absent a legitimate investigation or reasonable suspicion, or the actual inducement. Only in two cases, *R v Gerlach* and *R v Chiang*, has the accused suggested that actual inducement occurred, and in each case, both branches of entrapment were argued. There has only been one instance where the doctrine of entrapment was successfully used by the accused, and this decision was ultimately overturned on appeal (*R v Bayat*). However, with respect to child-luring offences, the court is predominantly concerned with the first branch of entrapment: there must exist a reasonable suspicion rooted in either a targeted person or location to justify preemptive or proactive investigations if police were not previously engaged in a *bona fide* inquiry. Anything else can be understood as random virtue testing, where police present an opportunity to commit an offence without a reasonable suspicion that criminal activity is likely to occur (*R v Ghotra*; *Mack* para 129). In *R v Ghotra*, the accused suggests that appointing officers to routinely drift through chat rooms is random virtue testing; these spaces are indistinct and ill-defined, and cannot be seen as a targeted location. "Here, Parliament created an offence which is akin to a search and seizure power which results in individuals giving into temptation. Internet luring in this context is a totally police-created crime" (*R v Ghotra* para 10).

However, in *R v Ghotra*, relying on judgments made in *R v Clothier*, Dunro J. held that there was no entrapment in proactive investigations without a clear, targeted person. These investigations are seen as *bona fide*, and officers are permitted to target areas where criminal activity can be reasonably suspected (*R v Ghotra* para 34). Police can, in these identified spaces, provide the opportunity to any person to commit an offence. In *R v Levigne*, the SCC also affirmed the nature of these spaces as inherently criminal:

> In structuring the provision as it did, Parliament recognized that the anonymity of an assumed online profile acts as both a shield for the predator and a sword for the police. As a shield, because it permits predators to mask their true identities as they pursue their nefarious intentions; as a sword (or, perhaps more accurately, as a barbed weapon of law enforcement), because it permits investigators, posing as children, to cast their lines in Internet chat rooms, *where lurking predators can be expected to take the bait.* (*R v Levigne* para 25; our emphasis)

The anxiety surrounding online space, particularly with respect to the safety of children, is demonstrated through these decisions. The Internet is suggested to be a space rife with criminal activity and a targeted location for police investigatory practices.

Although the doctrine of entrapment has yet to be successful, it poses a challenge to proactive investigations of child luring. The wide net cast around the Internet as a location of inquiry should be critically examined as a valid exercise of law and governance. The scope afforded to officers to conduct these inquiries is vast, and there has yet to be any empirically demonstrated reduction in harm to actual children. Many offenders charged with child luring through a proactive investigation assert, perhaps advantageously, that this was the first time they had communicated with a child online (see *R v Morrison* 2015; *R v Pengelley*; *R v Mermer*; *R v Mills*; *R v Gowdy*). These assertions must be considered against the legislative aims of section 172.1. In extending legislative reach and governance to those who have yet to harm, and perhaps have no intention to harm, an actual child, it becomes difficult to see the justification for tactics employed through section 172.1.

Harm

The intentions underlying section 172.1 rest on preventing harm to youth. Past scholarship has demonstrated that harm cannot be considered a self-evident category within the law (Khan). Having a malleable conception of harm in law—one that is unobservable and immeasurable—opens the law up to unjust exercises of power and governance.

Considering, for instance, the law's evolving governance of obscenity and indecency, previous work has theorized a growing, mutant conception of harm in Canadian law (Jochelson and Kramar; see also Gacek and Jochelson, this volume). Criminalization that is not confined to a single logic or a self-evident harm may be able to justify governance through a risk of harm or harm-to-community ideology and curtail many liberal critiques that might otherwise demonstrate unjust exercises of power. Perhaps the clearest liberal understanding of harm and state interference was set forth in John Stuart Mill's *On Liberty*. Mill argues that the sole purpose that power can be rightfully exercised over any member of a civilized community against their will is to prevent harm to others; one's own good, either physical or moral, does not sufficiently warrant power's exercise.

With respect to section 172.1 and proactive investigations, the prevention of harm is based on state prediction, not a physical or tangible harm. It is further based in a harm-to-community ideology through drawing clear legal lines for the age of consent and regulating behaviours seen as unusual or suspicious, such as an adult establishing a close friendship or relationship with someone underage. Here, it is particularly interesting to note that conversations with youth, or even conversations with undercover police officers, do not need to be sexually explicit in nature to result in convictions under section 172.1. The court in *R v Legare* ruled the following:

> Section 172.1(1) makes it a crime to communicate by computer with underage children or adolescents for the purpose of *facilitating* the commission of the offences mentioned in its constituent paragraphs. In this context, 'facilitating' includes *helping to bring about* and *making easier or more probable*—for example, by 'luring' or 'grooming' young persons to commit or participate in the prohibited conduct; by reducing their inhibitions; or by prurient discourse that exploits a young person's curiosity, immaturity or precocious sexuality.
>
> I hasten to add that sexually explicit language is not an essential element of the offences created by s. 172.1. Its focus is on the intention of the accused at the time of the communication by computer. Sexually explicit comments may suffice to establish the criminal purpose of the accused. But those who use their

computers to lure children for sexual purposes often groom them online by first gaining their trust through conversations about their home life, their personal interests or other innocuous topics. (*R v Legare* paras 28-29; our emphasis)

As harm is not self-evident and, indeed, a person's intentions may not be immediately or fully apparent to the court, there is a prediction being made as to the purpose of online communication. This prediction is necessarily risk averse and relies on precautionary, incalculable logics. It is difficult to see a tangible harm that occurs by simply cultivating trusting relationships with youth through innocuous conversations, and, here, the law borders on criminalizing conversations taking place between adults and youth entirely. This may have deleterious effects on the ability of counsellors or teachers to keep in touch with youth that in the past they had supported. In fact, this is something that an author of this chapter has had personal experience with while employed in public education.

Furthermore, there has been demonstrable harm caused by police investigatory tactics justified through this legislation. As discussed later in this chapter, officers will target adult fantasy chat rooms or adults who may be seeking consensual age play with other adults. Outside of this, however, police have also attempted to justify public disclosures about the accused prior to conviction, even though no tangible harm was caused by his actions. This ensuing disclosure had detrimental effects on his job and relationships with family and friends. Officers were concerned about the risks posed to a fictitious youth that they had created to respond to the accused's Craigslist advertisement.

In this case, a proactive investigation determined upon a search incident to arrest that the accused, Mr. Gowdy, was HIV positive. Despite being a pastor of the Free Methodist Church and posting an ad that sought men "under 35... college guys, skaters young married guy[s]" who were interested in receiving fellatio, the police chose to also charge him with attempted aggravated sexual assault, contrary to section 273(2) of the *Criminal Code* as well as inviting sexual touching by means of telecommunication contrary to section 172.1(b) (*R v Gowdy* para 1). This charge, withdrawn shortly before the trial, presumed that Mr. Gowdy intended to expose a fictitious youth to HIV. Following his arrest, officers put out a press release that disclosed Mr. Gowdy's HIV status, criminal charges, and professional work history. This was absent any consideration of his privacy, the severity of his medical condition and viral load, or the lawfulness of this action. Although this was found at trial to have been unlawful indifference to the privacy rights of Mr. Gowdy, and Mr. Gowdy himself testified the substantial effect that this disclosure would have on his relationships with friends and family along with his livelihood, it was found that the integrity of the justice system would not be compromised by these actions. The trial judge instead suggested that "the stern judicial rebuke reflected in this judgement" and a reduced sentence could address the discriminatory practices of the police officers and the suffering they caused Mr. Gowdy (*Gowdy* para 51).

The justification for these actions is ethically problematic at best and discriminatory—both to Mr. Gowdy's HIV status and sexual orientation—at worst. It is even harder to justify this practice absent any risk to a real child, particularly after considering Mr. Gowdy's repeated concern with whether the fictitious child would be able to consent and his persistent line of questioning regarding the legality of a sexual interaction. The trial judge found that the media release violated Mr. Gowdy's section 7 *Charter* rights by police conduct. Although the abuse of rights can be seen in case-by-case analyses of police practices, *R v Morrison* 2019 also demonstrated how section 172.1 was found to violate certain constitutional rights and protections guaranteed under the *Charter*.

Constitutional Issues

Mr. Morrison, a sixty-seven-year-old man with no prior criminal record, attracted the attention of local police after posting a personal ad on an eighteen-plus section of Craigslist. The ad read as follows: "Daddy looking for his little girl—m4w—45 (Brampton)" (*R v Morrison* 2017 para 13). Upon seeing this ad, a police officer concluded that Mr. Morrison was looking to meet with a young girl and responded to his ad as "Mia," who identified herself to be fourteen. Mr. Morrison submitted that the ad was intended to solicit a consenting adult party for a specific, established role play scenario: Daddy/daughter or Daddy/little girl. Within this script, it was submitted that Mr. Morrison would be unable to reasonably believe the age of any female communicant as misrepresenting age is a fundamental component of playing out the fantasy.

Mr. Morrison also maintained that reasonable steps had been taken to support his belief that "Mia" was an adult. The ad was posted in an eighteen-plus section on Craigslist; his language was consistent with that role play scenario; the language used in the ad would not attract interest from underage women; and, finally, there was no attempted grooming prior to initiating a sexual conversation, one that Mr. Morrison believed the respondent had been receptive to (*R v Morrison* 2017 para 12). In the trial, Mr. Morrison also brought a *Charter* application asking that subsections (3) and (4) be declared unconstitutional.

As discussed earlier, section 172.1 (3) was written to allow the court to presume belief on the part of the accused regarding the age of the communicant or the age represented to them. Simply put, if evidence had been found that a communicant represented their age to be under the age of consent, it would have been considered proof that the accused believed them to be under the age of consent. Furthermore, section 172.1 (4) sets out no available defence to an accused who believed the communicant to be at least the age of consent unless reasonable steps were taken by the accused to ascertain the age of that person.

In *R v Morrison* 2015, the trial judge found that section 172.1(4) was, in part, intended to support the Crown, as it would otherwise be difficult to establish the accused's subjective belief. With this in mind, the trial judge held that this was a constitutionally valid requirement to allow for a defence. However, subsection (3), which presumes belief on the part of the accused, was found by the trial judge to infringe upon section 11(d) of the *Charter* (the presumption of innocence):

> The idea that a representation as to age will necessarily be believed by the recipient strikes me as tenuous. In the context of the Internet, that notion is rendered even frailer. In the online world, the anonymity furnished by the Internet virtually ensures that much is not as it seems. Rightly or wrongly, pseudonyms and falsehoods are a pervasive part of online communication. Given this, it does not follow, in my view, that an online representation as to age would necessarily be believed by the person to whom it is made. It is therefore far from certain that even a rational or logical connection is established between the representation and the presumption of belief as to age, much less an inexorable connection. (*R v Morrison* 2015 para 26)

Furthermore, the infringement was found to be not justifiable under section 1 of the *Charter*. Although section 172.1 (3) was not applied, the trial judge found that the Crown had proven elements of the offence without the benefit of the presumption of Mr. Morrison's belief (*R v Morrison* 2015 para 8).

Both the Crown and Mr. Morrison appealed this sentence. Mr. Morrison submitted that both subsections (3) and (4) infringed upon his section 11(d) and section 7 *Charter* rights. The appellate court, after considering the evidence, reached the same conclusion as the trial judge. There were strong legal arguments that section 172.1 (3) should be of no legal effect, as it infringed upon the accused's right to be presumed innocent under section 11(d). This was exacerbated when applied in concert with subsection (4). Subsection (4) was found to be "sufficient to eliminate specious claims of innocent belief or ignorance" without subsection (3) in effect (*R v Morrison* 2017 para 34). These interactions were the subject of adjudication in the SCC ruling in 2019.

In their decision, the SCC ruled that section 172.1(3) offended section 11(d) of the *Charter* and declared it to be of no force and effect. In the its eyes, jurisprudence demonstrates that where there is a statutory presumption argued to offend the presumption of innocence, the test must be stringent and find that there is no possibility of the substitution resulting in conviction where there would otherwise be a reasonable doubt (*R v Morrison* 2019 paras 52-53). The substituted fact supported by a statutory provision must align perfectly with the facts of the case; there is no room for rational inference or common sense to support the substituted fact, and the connection between the substituted fact and the essential element must hold true in all cases. When confronted with the nature of sexual offences on the Internet, cases have demonstrated how commonplace deception and deliberate misrepresentations can be (see *R v Pengelley* 2010). Morrison himself represented his age as forty-five when he was in his sixties; it is somewhat "expected that true personal identities are concealed" (*R v Morrison* 2019 para 59). Furthermore, section 172.1(3) was not saved by section 1 of the *Charter* because the Crown failed to establish that the child-luring provision would be rendered inoperable without the presumption of the section (para 69). The court declared that the presumption be removed and that future prosecutorial efforts must invite "the trier of fact to find, based on a logical, common sense inference drawn from evidence, that the accused believed the other person was underage" (para 70). This process of inferential reasoning is well practiced by judges and juries and ensures that there are no legislated limitations to an accused's right to be presumed innocent.

The court did not find that section 172.1(4) violated section 7 of the *Charter*; it noted that in the absence of the presumption under section 172.1(3), subsection (4) would then operate alone as a means to limit the defences available—mainly the defence that the accused believed that the person was of legal age where they failed to take reasonable steps to ascertain age (*R v Morrison* 2019 para 82). The court went on to clarify the test to be applied in relation to section 172.1(4), and it noted that the provision does not require that the accused's belief be both honest and reasonable but rather that there is some objective evidence that supports an honest belief (para 103). This test has an objective and a subjective component, requiring reasonable steps "that a reasonable person, in the circumstances known to the accused at the time, would take to ascertain the other person's age" (para 105). The court offered a nonexhaustive list of reasonable steps, including the following:

> asking for the other person's age and receiving a response that supports that accused's asserted belief; noting the other person's representation, whether solicited or unsolicited, that he or she is of legal age; asking for and receiving proof of identification indicating that the other person is of legal age; asking for and receiving a photograph or reviewing profile pictures suggesting the other person is of legal age; observing conduct or behaviour suggesting the other person is of legal age; choosing to communicate through a website that enforces age restrictions; and, in the case of a personal ad, including language indicating that the accused is looking to speak only with adults. The ultimate question is whether, in the totality of the circumstances, the accused's steps to ascertain the other person's age were sufficient to constitute "reasonable steps"—namely, those that provide information that is reasonably capable of supporting the accused's belief that the other person was of legal age. (*R v Morrison* 2019 para 112)

In short, in the context of a proactive investigation by police where there was no actual underage person, the SCC determined that section

172.1, without subsection (3) required the Crown to show either that the accused believed the other person was underage or was wilfully blind as to whether the other person was underage (para 97). The SCC ordered a new trial for Mr. Morrison, noting that the Crown's case was strong and that numerous factors appeared to point to the fact that Mr. Morrison believed that the girl was underage or was wilfully blind as to whether she was underage (para 141).

Policing Kink

The limited attention given to Mr. Morrison's explanation of a Daddy/little girl role play in all levels of adjudication suggests reluctance on the part of the court to uphold rights when confronted with non-normative sexual behaviours and kink. Indeed, the law has a demonstrable history ignoring the rights of sexual minorities and alternative expressions of sexuality, from queer pornography to BDSM consensual kink (Jochelson and Kramar; Khan). Outside of targeting posts that solicit adult consensual role play scenarios, police tactics have also included monitoring and communicating with individuals on adult fantasy sites. Although the Internet has been identified as a targeted location where children are susceptible to harm and victimization, these spaces are typically safeguarded from youth involvement and allow for fantasy, role play, and experimentation. In these spaces, concerns surrounding officers misrepresenting their age are further amplified, as other adults may misrepresent their age with no ulterior purpose outside of sexual pleasure.

An example of this was seen before the court in *R v Pengelley*. Mr. Pengelley was charged under section 172.1 of the *Criminal Code* after communicating in a hard-core, adults-only fantasy chat room with a male police officer claiming to be a twelve-year-old girl. The accused had visited this chat room frequently, playing out a very specific sexual fantasy that had nothing to do with age play or underage sex. He submitted that he believed the communicant to have a specific age play, virginity loss fantasy and that he had participated in this dialogue in the interests of the communicant so that she may be more likely to reciprocate. Due to the nature of the chat room, he found it very unlikely that he was communicating with someone underage. The chat room, Whip Cream, advertised itself as "mild to wild and part of kinky land" (*R v Pengelley* para 31). Notably, the room is intended only for sexual discussions and fantasy and not intended to facilitate real-world meetups or dating. There was no evidence given as to why the officer had chosen this chat room above others, as it was unlikely that "underage persons or predators" would use this forum (*R v Pengelley* para 32).

The officer also chose to send Mr. Pengelley a posed photo of a thirty-two-year-old policewoman just before he disclosed his age. Another photo was later sent that the trial judge noted was "obviously" not of a twelve-year-old girl (*R v Pengelley* para 50). Doing so ran contrary to his training, as officers are instructed to use photos of children. He also had taken on the persona of Stephania Cacciatore, who used the online handle "Stephania_kittycat." It was noted by the trial judge and the defence that "cacciatore," an Italian word meaning "hot," and "kittycat" both could be said to have sexual connotations. The profile also presented Stephania's age as eighteen in order to access the adult only chat room. "Stephania," particularly near the end of the exchange, initiated most of the conversations, and, at a certain point, Mr. Pengelley stopped responding due to a reported lack of interest.

The trial judge found that both the first and third element of the offence had been met unquestionably. Mr. Pengelley had sent the communicant pictures of his genitals, suggesting an underlying sexual purpose to the communication. He had also communicated online with someone who had represented herself to be under the age of fourteen. The case then hinged on whether the second element of the offence had been proven—that is, could Mr. Pengelley have reasonably believed that the communicant was underage. The trial judge found that the evidence was not sufficient to persuade him that Mr. Pengelley's held a subjective belief that "Stephania" was above the age of consent. However, the nature of the chat left him with reasonable doubt that Mr. Pengelley believed he was communicating with someone under the age of fourteen. Therefore, the primary consideration had to be whether reasonable steps were taken to determine the communicant's age, a burden on Mr. Pengelley.

In this case, the trial judge noted that neither *Levine* nor *Legare* presented a clear understanding of what is meant by "reasonable steps," and he also found that there was limited case law to rely upon. However, he ultimately concluded that reasonable steps had been taken in consideration of the photograph, the context of the chat room, and Mr. Pengelley's request to communicate using a webcam. Mr. Pengelley also testified that the language used by the officer appeared artificially "dumbed down," providing further belief that he was communicating with an adult. Here, the trial judge noted the lack of care taken by the officer.

The targeting of a fantasy adult chat room was a particularly problematic practice undertaken by police in this case. It is further troubling that the trial judge was unable to believe Mr. Pengelley's subjective belief grounded both in his appreciation of a popular role play scenario and being presented with photos of a thirty-two-year-old woman. His demonstrated history of a specific fantasy that fell outside of age play, along with his lack of interest in communicating with "Stephania" about innocuous topics, could also have served as indicators. There was no attempted grooming or delicacy when discussing sex, and the defences available to Mr. Pengelley were limited, and an evidentiary burden was placed upon him. The investigative tactics here confuse and subvert the aims of the legislation with little clear purpose outside of policing non-normative sex. The practice of targeting all online space as a potentially risky or dangerous space where youth might be exploited holds consequences for these communities and with the legislation as it currently stands offers insufficient protections.

Child Pornography: A History of Legislative Government

The legislation on child pornography follows a similar trajectory as the legislation on child luring, as the punishments continue to become more severe and the scope of governance becomes more expansive. Bill C-128, *An Act to Amend the Criminal Code and the Customs Tariff* (child pornography and corrupting morals), introduced child pornography legislation in 1993; prior to its introduction, section 163 of the *Criminal Code*, was concerned with "offences tending to corrupt morals." The original section is related to the production, reproduction, or distribution of anything obscene or glorifying criminal activity. Bill C-128 repealed and replaced the general moral corruption section with the offence of child pornography in 1993. The location of the child pornography legislation as a replacement for a general morality section demonstrates the moral assumptions and basis upon which the regulation of child pornography rests.[1] The section defines the offence as follows:

a) a photographic, film, video or other visual representation, whether or not it was made by electronic or mechanical means,

   i) that shows a person who is or is depicted as being under the age of eighteen years and is engaged in or is depicted as engaged in explicit sexual activity, or

   ii) the dominant characteristic of which is the depiction, for a sexual purpose, of a sexual organ or the anal region of a person under the age of eighteen years; or

b) any written material or visual representation that advocates or counsels sexual activity with a person under the age of eighteen years that would be an offence under this Act. (*Criminal Code of Canada* section 163.1, 1993)

It is necessary to note that included in the list of material constituting child pornography are materials that do not involve any actual children, such as physical representations or depictions. The section lists separate hybrid punishments for making, distributing, and possession. The making and distributing of child pornography are both punishable as an indictable offence of imprisonment of no more than ten years or by a summary conviction. A person charged with possession of child pornography faces an indictable offence and imprisonment of no more than five years or a summary conviction. For the making of child pornography, there is no available defence of mistaken belief that the child or depicted child was over the age of eighteen, unless the accused "took all reasonable steps to ascertain the age of the person." As is the case with child luring, there is no definition given of "reasonable steps" or an exhaustive list.

The child pornography section of the *Criminal Code* remained untouched until Bill C-15A in 2002 amended section 163.1 in response to *R v Sharpe*. The most direct response to *Sharpe* was the inclusion of a defence when the "material ... has artistic merit or an educational, scientific or medical purpose." Other changes to section 163.1 by Bill C-15A included adding the accessing of child pornography as a separate charge (section 163.1 (4.1)), with a hybrid punishment: an indictable sentence is punishable by imprisonment of no more than five years or as a summary offence. The accessing of child pornography is qualified with an interpretation stating that a person who is to be charged under section 163.1 (4.1) includes someone who "knowingly causes child pornography to be viewed by or transmitted to, himself or herself." Finally, the amendment added an order of forfeiture to section 163.1. The order stipulates that should the court be satisfied "on a balance of probabilities" that any offence under subsection (1) earned a profit for the accused, the proceedings are forfeited to the Crown. The forfeiture order is an initial example of the extending reach of the criminal charges of the section, bridging space between legal and economic considerations.

> November 2005 saw the introduction of Bill C-2, *An Act to amend the Criminal Code (protection of children and other vulnerable persons) and the Canada Evidence Act,* which introduced many changes throughout the *Criminal Code*, specifically related to sex and children. These changes included adding a new category of sexual exploitation offences of young people, deeming child abuse an aggravating factor, and creating an offence of voyeurism and distribution of voyeuristic materials. Including introducing child abuse as a aggravating factor, the amendment made several significant changes through section 163.1, including expanding the definition of child pornography, increasing the punishment for every charge under child pornography, expanding actions considered distribution of child pornography, and adding a second allowable defence. The definition of child pornography was expanded to include audio recordings and to include the following:
>
> c) any written material whose dominant characteristic is the description, for a sexual purpose, of sexual activity with a person under the age of eighteen years that would be an offence under this Act; or
>
> d) any audio recording that has as its dominant characteristic the description, presentation or representation, for a sexual purpose, of sexual activity with a person under that age of eighteen years that would be an offence under this Act. (*Criminal Code of Canada* section 163.1, 2005)

The punishment for each offence was given a minimum indictable sentence: a one year minimum for making child pornography and for distribution of child pornography, and a forty-five-day minimum for possession and accessing child pornography. All summary convictions of the offences were now limited to imprisonment: for a term no longer than eighteen months and no less than ninety days for making child pornography and for distributing child pornography, and for a term of no more than eighteen months and no less than fourteen days for possessing and accessing child pornography. Distribution was expanded to include advertisement as a form of distribution for the purposes of punishment.

The additions to the legislation added significant and new meanings to the existing section. The addition of section 163.1 (4.2), "aggravating factor," indicated that any intention to make a profit on child pornography is an aggravating factor. This claim implies that it is more reprehensible to gain economically from child pornography than to engage in child pornography for one's own private purposes or pleasure, strengthening the regulations of the forfeiture order introduced in 2002. Bill C-2 expanded the allowable defences to allow for actions that do not constitute an undue risk of harm to minors under eighteen years of age. The question arising from this addition is what forms or uses do not pose an undue risk of harm. As discussed previously, the offence under child pornography regulation includes forms that do not involve any actual children (i.e., illustrations, dolls), which makes us consider what constitutes risk of harm and to what degree is harm: real or imagined (for example, see Jochelson et al.).

The 2012 omnibus crime bill, Bill C-10, introduced changes to child pornography legislature and served to increase the punishments for each of the separate offences. Making and distributing child pornography both faced increased summary offences of no more than two years less a day and no less than six months. Possessing and accessing child pornography both included indictable sentences of no more than five years and no less than six months, or summary sentences of no more than eighteen months and no less than ninety days. The trend of increasing punishment did not end in 2012 but was instead repeated in 2015 by Bill C-26, the *Tougher Penalties for Child Predators Act*, which removed the option for summary charges for subsections (2) and (3), leaving making and distributing offences as solely indictable offences.

Punishments increased once again. Making and distributing offences were liable to imprisonment for no more than fourteen years and no less than one year. Indictable possession and accessing punishments increased to no more than ten years and no less than one year, and summary punishments increased to no more than two years less a day and no less than six months.

Child Pornography: Authoritative Cases

Section 163.1 of the *Criminal Code* reads as follows:

Definition of child pornography

163.1 (1) In this section, "child pornography" means

a) a photographic, film, video or other visual representation, whether or not it was made by electronic or mechanical means,

   i) that shows a person who is or is depicted as being under the age of eighteen years and is engaged in or is depicted as engaged in explicit sexual activity, or

   ii) the dominant characteristic of which is the depiction, for a sexual purpose, of a sexual organ or the anal region of a person under the age of eighteen years;

b) any written material, visual representation or audio recording that advocates or counsels sexual activity with a person under the age of eighteen years that would be an offence under this Act;

c) any written material whose dominant characteristic is the description, for a sexual purpose, of sexual activity with a person under the age of eighteen years that would be an offence under this Act; or

d) any audio recording that has as its dominant characteristic the description, presentation or representation, for a sexual purpose, of sexual activity with a person under the age of eighteen years that would be an offence under this Act.

Making child pornography

2) Every person who makes, prints, publishes or possesses for the purpose of publication any child pornography is guilty of an indictable offence and liable to imprisonment for a term of not more than 14 years and to a minimum punishment of imprisonment for a term of one year.

Distribution, etc. of child pornography

3) Every person who transmits, makes available, distributes, sells, advertises, imports, exports or possesses for the purpose of transmission, making available, distribution, sale, advertising or exportation any child pornography is guilty of an indictable offence and liable to imprisonment for a term of not more than 14 years and to a minimum punishment of imprisonment for a term of one year.

Possession of child pornography

4) Every person who possesses any child pornography is guilty of
   a) an indictable offence and is liable to imprisonment for a term of not more than 10 years and to a minimum punishment of imprisonment for a term of one year; or
   b) an offence punishable on summary conviction and is liable to imprisonment for a term of not more than two years less a day and to a minimum punishment of imprisonment for a term of six months.

Accessing child pornography

4.1) Every person who accesses any child pornography is guilty of
   a) an indictable offence and is liable to imprisonment for a term of not more than 10 years and to a minimum punishment of imprisonment for a term of one year; or
   b) an offence punishable on summary conviction and is liable to imprisonment for a term of not more than two years less a day and to a minimum punishment of imprisonment for a term of six months.

Interpretation

    4.2) For the purposes of subsection (4.1), a person accesses child pornography who knowingly causes child pornography to be viewed by, or transmitted to, himself or herself.

Aggravating factor

    4.3) If a person is convicted of an offence under this section, the court that imposes the sentence shall consider as an aggravating factor the fact that the person committed the offence with intent to make a profit.

Defence

    5) It is not a defence to a charge under subsection (2) in respect of a visual representation that the accused believed that a person shown in the representation that is alleged to constitute child pornography was or was depicted as being eighteen years of age or more unless the accused took all reasonable steps to ascertain the age of that person and took all reasonable steps to ensure that, where the person was eighteen years of age or more, the representation did not depict that person as being under the age of eighteen years.

Defence

    6) No person shall be convicted of an offence under this section if the act that is alleged to constitute the offence

        a) has a legitimate purpose related to the administration of justice or to science, medicine, education or art; and(b) does not pose an undue risk of harm to persons under the age of eighteen years.

Question of law

    7) For greater certainty, for the purposes of this section, it is a question of law whether any written material, visual representation or audio recording advocates or counsels sexual activity with a person under the age of eighteen years that would be an offence under this Act.

    This section creates various offences related to child pornography, defined in subsection (1). Offences under section 163.1 of the *Criminal Code* are concerned with the making, distribution, possession, and access to or of child pornography. Subsections (5) to (7) set out various defences—for instance, in subsection (5), a reasonably held mistake of fact as to the age of persons depicted. Subsection (6) recognizes an available defence if the materials are used in a legitimate purpose relating to the administration of justice or to science, medicine, education, or art, but only provided that there is no undue risk of harm to persons under the age of eighteen.

In *Sharpe*, it was found that subsections (1)(a), (b), and (4) violate section 2(b) of the *Charter*, but the SCC ruled this violation was justifiable under section 1. Moreover, the SCC found that a "person" includes both actual and imaginary human beings. The court argued that these materials may serve to counsel that sex with children could be pursued or, at the very least, make visible an idea that children are possible sexual partners. Encouragement or active inducement may come from a message implicit within the stories themselves. For instance, materials that describe or represent children as willing or consenting or that describe sex with children as normal, enjoyable, or beneficial may present children as sexually available despite not explicitly advocating commission of criminal acts against children (see *R v Beattie* for example). Parliament sought to prevent not only the harm that flows from the use of children in pornography but also the harm that arises from the mere existence of images and words which degrade and dehumanize children, which may increase the demand or appetite for child pornography (*R v Sharpe*).

Subsection (2) of the offence does not include private recordings of lawful sexual activity. The court describes this as a private use exception, which requires that (1) the recording must depict lawful sexual activity; (2) the persons depicted must consent to the recording; and (3) the recording must be held for private use. However, if the sexual activity occurred within the context of an exploitative relationship, section 153 of the *Criminal Code* will negate the legality and the private recording will not fall under a private use exception (*R v Barabash*). Outside of cases of private use, an accused may be convicted under subsection (2) provided they (1) have knowledge of the character of the object; (2) knowingly place or keep the object in a particular place; (3) intend to have the object for their use or benefit or that of another person. The possession of pornography online then will only be constituted through saving or caching the file to the hard drive of a computer, if the

Crown has satisfied the *mens rea* by demonstrating that the file was knowingly retained by the accused (*R v Morelli*). Possession also requires the accused to maintain control or authority of the objects in question; should the accused have taken control of child pornography with the intention to destroy it, they cannot be found guilty of possession (*R v Chalk*).

Defences under subsection (6) should be liberally construed and based on an objective test (*R v Sharpe*). An artistic merit defence allows for any expression that may reasonably be viewed as art. If artistic value is objectively established, it may be used to support this defence. Furthermore, materials may be defended if they have an established medical, educational, and scientific purpose or if they are involved in the justice system where their purpose is associated with prosecution or relevant research. In order for these to be considered legitimate, there must be a demonstrable connection between the accused's actions and purpose as well as an objective relationship between their purpose and one or more of the protected activities. An assessment of the value is not in question, once a degree of value has been established. Under this section, an "undue risk of harm" requires the risk to be significant and objectively ascertainable. The harm cannot just be to the moral views of the community and must be in line with the current laws governing obscenity (*R v Katigbak*).

Child Pornography and Harm 'All Dolled Up'

This section examines and problematizes the current legislation governing child pornography. It questions the nebulous character of harm that section 163.1 uses to justify regulation and takes the position that moral corruption is an anachronistic stance unable to bear the weight of constitutional rights. Here, rather than repeating arguments made in other academic work concerned with artistic merit and sexual expression, the nature of harm in child pornography offences is exemplified through the case of Kenneth Harrisson. Mr. Harrisson's case resulted in not guilty verdicts across all charges; the case is illustrative of the dangers of entertaining sexual kinks outside of the norm, even in victimless cases.

Under section 163.1, child pornography is considered harmful simply by existing. This hearkens back to a Victorian conception of obscenity, where non-normative sexuality was said to cause moral harm to those susceptible to depravity and corruption (Jochelson and Kramar; see also Gacek and Jochelson, this volume). By suggesting that these materials might counsel or advocate for others to perpetrate violence, child pornography governance adopts a similar stance to that of the Victorian era, where intrusion was justified in upholding the proper functioning of a moral society. Contemporary legislative governance has begun to attach objective importance to the risk of harm or future harms that acts and materials may cause (Jochelson et al.). Although this understanding of harm is presented as objective, it allows for the courts to mobilize political and moral value judgments on the basis of a precautionary logic.

Child pornography then operates in an interesting grey space between contemporary and past governances of obscenity. Obscenity governance is understood as a response to clear social harms. Sexual contact between adults and children, regardless of how it might be depicted or represented, is considered to pose harm both to children and to the moral fabric of societies. Unlike queer or kinky pornography, child pornography is rooted in a socially observable moral harm— that is, producing pornographic materials featuring youth who, under the law, cannot provide consent in the filming of an assault. Furthermore, the distribution of this production may create a further risk of emotional harm to the youth involved. Productions of child pornography, however, do not need to involve any actual assault. They may be depicted in literature, art, or through electronic renderings. In this sense, the consumption of pornographic materials that depict children is assumed to always harm both children and society. The imposition of legal and carceral consequences for those who may strategically consume child pornography with no real victim (i.e., erotic literature or artistic depictions) is not considered as a harm but rather a response to harm. Here, the court continues to govern proper morality and continues to consider pornography as a corruptible influence.

Child pornography legislation has been critiqued by some scholars as trespassing legal governance into youth sexuality—for instance, through regulating and policing sexting (Karaian; Slane). There is also evidence that the availability of sexual images and representation may positively influence children's welfare, safety, health, and physical and psychological wellbeing; academic work has attempted to unpack the contentions between freedom of expression, artistic merit, and child pornography (Ross; Yan). It has been described as confused, incoherent, and in need of reconsideration (Ryder). Finally, there is a body of work that calls into question the harms of obscenity, including virtual child pornography (Woo; Danay); empirical evidence is often cited as inconclusive in this regard. Without clear evidence of harm caused by virtual child pornography or other depictions that do not involve real children, rationalizing the governance of child pornography rests solely on arguments of moral corruptibility and a demeaning representation of youth. As neither of these arguments can be demonstrated, this is a potentially problematic articulation of law that polices uncertain harms.

Canada has few cases that consider offences under section 163.1 where no children are involved. The clearest case to date is *R v Beattie*, where an accused possessed thirty-three pornographic stories featuring children. While he was acquitted at the trial level, the appellate court ordered a new trial, as the materials could be said to counsel or advocate that "sex with children can and should be pursued" (*R v Sharpe* para 56). Effectively, this is a moral corruptibility argument, even though there was no evidence that Mr. Beattie had planned on sharing this binder of stories with any other person. Kenneth Harrisson seems to have beat the initial charges. Mr. Harrisson ordered a sex doll from Japan that was concluded to represent a prepubescent depiction of a child. Though Harrissson was acquitted at trial, the doll was considered child pornography in part based on the site where Mr. Harrisson ordered the doll and the doll's height of under 120 centimetres. This was the first case in Canada where the courts were asked to assess whether a sex doll may constitute child pornography.

A similar case in the UK occurred in 2017, where David Turner was charged with the possession of a doll around the same height as in the case of Mr. Harrisson (BBC News). Mr. Turner pled guilty to the charges and admitted to having sex with this doll and, in addition to the doll, possessed more than thirty-four thousand pornographic images depicting children. Conversely, Mr. Harrisson's sex doll was immediately seized by the Canada Border Services Agency, and he was charged with, though acquitted of child pornography offences as well as number of federal customs offences. The similarities between Harrisson and Turner, then, begin and end with the doll. With the first landmark decision setting precedent that child sex dolls constitute child pornography, Mr. Harrisson's case, with its confirmation that a sex doll can be child pornography echoes the decision reached in the UK (BBC News). A sex doll can be classified as child pornography because section 163.1 (1)(a)(i) states that depictions of children, real or imagined, would fall under the scope of this legislation.

Conclusion

Canada has a long history of governing sexual offences involving children, a history that has been subject to significant changes. These changes address the ongoing progress of technology by both regulating online interactions and reinterpreting the nature and availability of materials that we may find morally offensive. Many of those changes also see the expansion of governance through further legislation and precedent. This chapter has traced the historical development of sections 163.1 and 172.1 of the *Criminal Code* and the precedent set by relevant legal cases to examine and problematize the current legal articulation of laws governing adult sexual contact and fantasy with children.

Our chapter has considered legislation and case law related to luring a child and to child pornography. These areas of legislation are ever expanding, serving to regulate sexuality alongside public morals. Much of the regulations of sexual offences involving children are based on anachronistic moral structures that presume all possible representations of adult sexual contact with children, including imaginary representations, are morally reprehensible without consideration of actual harm. The basis of these outdated moral structures serves to confuse and conflate the object of current legislation as addressing future risks while keeping moral reservations of the past.

The interplay between law, regulation, and technology will continue to test conceptions of morality and harm, and expose anxieties underlying youth sexuality and vulnerability. Legal practitioners should be cautious of this and attentive to the rapid shifts in common law. As innovation continues, it is likely that these cases and constitutional challenges will grow along with the scope of what we consider to be harmful.

Endnote

1. Much of the moral assumption is based on outdated moral positions, including the notion that any depiction of an act risks influencing others to commit the act. An example of this is found in sections 163 and 163.1, which regulate the production and distribution of "crime comics." A moralist bill passed in the mid-1940s banned any comics depicting the time immediately prior, during, or immediately after the commission of a crime on the premise that young men reading the comics would choose to commit those crimes themselves. Under this legislation, comics such as those by Marvel and DC are considered illegal. The legislation remains in effect under section 163.1.

Works Cited

Secondary Sources

BBC News. "Ex-school Governor Who Imported Child Sex Doll Is Jailed." *BBC News*, BBC, 8 Sept. 2017, www.bbc.com/news/uk-41203239. Accessed 16 July 2018.

Benedet, Janine. "Children in Pornography after Sharpe." *Les Cahiers de Droit*, vol. 43, no. 2, 2002, pp. 327-50.

Casavant, Lyne, and James R. Robertson. *The Evolution of Pornography Law in Canada*. Law and Government Division, 2007.

Danay, Robert. "The Danger of Fighting Monsters: Addressing the Hidden Harms of Child Pornography Law." *Review of Constitutional Studies*, vol. 11, no. 1, 2006, pp. 151-92.

Fairclough, Norman. "Critical Discourse Analysis as a Method in Social Scientific Research." *Methods of Critical Discourse Analysis*, edited by Ruth Wodak and Michael Meyer, SAGE, 2001, pp. 121-38.

Fairclough, Norman. *Critical Discourse Analysis: The Critical Study of Language*. 2nd ed. Routledge, 2013.

Good, Sarah D. *Understanding and Addressing Adult Sexual Attraction to Children: A Study of Paedophiles in Contemporary Society*. New York, Routledge, 2010.

Gotell, Lise. "Inverting Image and Reality: R. v Sharpe and the Moral Panic around Child Pornography." *Constitutional Forum*, vol. 12, 2001, pp. 9-22.

Hsieh, Hsiu-Fang, and Sarah E. Shannon. "Three Approaches to Qualitative Content Analysis." *Qualitative Health Research*, vol. 15, no. 9, Nov. 2005, pp. 1277-88. *SAGE Journals*, doi:10.1177/1049732305276687.

Jenkins, Philip. *Beyond Tolerance: Child Pornography on the Internet*. New York University Press, 2001.

Jochelson, Richard, et al. *Criminal Law and Precrime: Legal Studies in Canadian Punishment and Surveillance in Anticipation of Criminal Guilt*. New York, Routledge, 2018.

Jochelson, Richard, and Kirsten Kramar. *Sex and the Supreme Court: Obscenity and Indecency Law in Canada*. Winnipeg, Fernwood, 2011.

Karaian, Lara. "Policing 'Sexting': Responsibilization, Respectability and Sexual Subjectivity in Child Protection/Crime Prevention Responses to Teenagers' Digital Sexual Expression." *Theoretical Criminology*, vol. 18, no. 3, 2014, pp. 282-99.

Kettles, Brent. "The Entrapment Defence in Internet Child Luring Cases." *Canadian Criminal Law Review*, vol. 16, no. 1, 2011, pp. 89-101.

Khan, Ummni. *Vicarious Kinks: S/M in the Socio-Legal Imaginary*. Toronto, University of Toronto Press, 2014.

Mill, John Stuart. *On Liberty*. Auckland, The Floating Press, 1909.

Ross, June. "R. v Sharpe and the Defence of Artistic Merit." *Constitutional Forum*, vol. 12, no. 1, 2001.

Ryder, Bruce. "The Harms of Child Pornography Law." *UBC. Law Review*, vol. 36, no. 1, 2003, pp. 101-36.

Slane, Andrea. "From Scanning to Sexting: The Scope of Protection of Dignity-Based Privacy in Canadian Child Pornography Law." *Osgoode Hall Law Journal*, vol. 48, no. 3/4, 2010, pp. 543-93.

Woo, Jisuk. "The Concept of 'Harm' in Computer-Generated Images of Child Pornography." *The John Marshall Journal of Information Technology & Privacy Law*, vol. 22, no. 4, 2004, pp. 717-30.

Yan, Julie. "Art in the Dichotomy of Freedom of Expression & Obscenity: An Anti- Censorship Perspective." *Manitoba Law Journal*, vol. 40, no. 3, 2017, pp. 363-87.

Jurisprudence

R v Alicandro, 2009 ONCA 133.

R v Barabash, 2015 SCC 29.

R v Bayat, 2011 ONCA 778.

R v Beattie, [2005] O.J. No. 1302.

R v Chalk, 2007 ONCA 815.

R v Chiang, 2010 BCSC 1770.

R v Clothier, 2011 ONCA 27.

R v Gerlach, 2014 ONCJ 646.

R v Ghotra, 2016 ONSC 5675.

R v Gowdy, 2014 ONCJ 592.

R v Harrisson, 2019 Unreported.

R v Katigbak, 2011 SCC 48.

R v Legare, 2009 SCC 56.

R v Levigne, 2010 SCC 25.

R v Mermer, 2015 ONSC 2715.

R v Mills, 2015 CanLII 13412.

R v Morelli, 2010 SCC 8.

R v Morrison, 2019 SCC 15.

R v Morrison, 2017 ONCA 582.

R v Morrison, 2015 ONCJ 599.

R v Mack, [1988] 2 S.C.R. 903.

R v Pengelley, 2009 CanLII 19936.

R v Sharpe, [2001] 1 S.C.R. 45.

Legislation

An Act to Amend the Criminal Code and the Customs Tariff (Child Pornography and Corrupting Morals). Statutes of Canada, c 46. Canada. Department of Justice, 1993.

An Act to Amend the Criminal Code (Luring a Child). Statutes of Canada, c 20. Canada. Department of Justice, 2007.

An Act to Amend the Criminal Code (Protection of Children and Other Vulnerable Persons) and the Canada Evidence Act. Statutes of Canada, c 32. Canada. Department of Justice, 2005.

Criminal Law Amendment Act. Statutes of Canada, c 13. Canada. Department of Justice, 2002.

Protection of Communities and Exploited Persons Act. Statutes of Canada, c 25. Canada. Department of Justice, 2014.

Safe Streets and Communities Act. *Statutes of Canada, c 1.* Canada. Department of Justice, 2012.

Tackling Violent Crime Act. Statutes of Canada, c 6. Canada. Department of Justice, 2008.

Tougher Penalties for Child Predators Act. Statutes of Canada, c 23. Canada. Department of Justice, 2015.

Chapter Five

Rethinking Bestial Regulation

Richard Jochelson, Alicia Dueck-Read, and James Gacek

Introduction

Bestiality. Today, the word itself generally conjures up silence, nervous giggles, and sentiments of disgust or incredulity. In Renaissance law textbooks, bestiality was "the offense the very naming of which is a crime" (Adams, "Woman-Battering" 68). Indeed, for the most part, in a relative sense, bestiality is a scarcely studied or talked about phenomenon (Beirne 113). Unsurprisingly, its emergence within the law has been shrouded in silence and conflated in legal discourse with a wide variety of other "sexual acts against nature" under the label of sodomy (Delaney 260). What has resulted from this historical progression are criminal laws on bestiality that are broadly worded, rooted in a moral prerogative, and intimately implicated with the creation of human subjectivity.

In this chapter, we seek to place modern understandings of bestiality law in Canada in context. Doing so requires that we first understand bestiality and its definitions, its occurrences in society, and the degree to which it is a social problem. Second, we delve into the historical antecedents of bestiality law, its historic link with same-sex prohibitions, and the way this played out historically in Canada and throughout the twentieth century. Then we consider the modern legal landscape governing bestiality in Canada and look at some case examples, some legislative possibilities, and some broad commonalities in the modern jurisprudence. Following a critique of the modern applications of the law, we conclude the chapter by considering critical perspectives that provide alternate lenses in conceptualizing bestiality as a social problem and that may untether bestiality from its Judaeo-Christian and Victorian roots.

Understanding Bestiality and its Occurrence

Bestiality is most commonly used to refer to sexual activity between a person and an animal (Stern and Smith-Blackmore 1058) and may also be used to capture sexual activity in which one party is portrayed as an animal (Boggs, *Animalia* 48). Narrow definitions of bestiality contrast the practice with that of zoophilia; some scholars argue that bestiality refers to the use of animals as sex objects, whereas zoophilia refers to sexual relationships with animals carried out within the context of consent and mutual emotional attachment (Stern and Smith-Blackmore 1058; Rudy 606). Those who label all sexual encounters with animals as inherently abusive prefer the term animal sexual abuse over either bestiality or zoophilia (Stern and Smith-Blackmore 1057; Beirne) and compare its impact on the animal as similar to that of child sexual abuse (Stern and Smith-Blackmore 1058-1059) or human sexual assault (Beirne).[1]

Initially, zoophilia was considered a mental disorder under the DSM III but was later removed and relegated under the DSM-5 to the category of "other specified paraphilic disorder," as it is not considered a clinically significant problem by itself. This category recognizes situations in which a person's preferred sexual object of desire is animals and in which this causes significant distress and impairment in other important areas of function (Aggrawal 258; Lesandric et al. 27–28; Beirne 121). Proponents of zoophilia argue that there is nothing inherently wrong about sex with animals and that their actions are rooted in love and the consent of animals, ascertained through the reading of body language. Within the zoophile conception, animals hold a robust subjectivity and they can consent or refuse sex, initiate sex, and communicate desires for particular kinds of pleasure (Rudy 607). The story of the zoophile is self-presented as a story of love conquers all, intermixed with fervent hope of social progress (Delaney 241,

252). One church is even reported to have performed weddings between animals and humans (Senjo 331). Exactly where the line between bestiality and zoophilia lies is difficult to determine and subject to "slippage and condensation" (Rudy 609).

Bestialists and zoophiles may engage in a broad number of sexual activities with animals—ranging from penetration to fondling genitalia, oral-genital contact, penetration with an object, or anal sex (Stern and Smith-Blackmore 1057; Beetz, "New" 107-8). Sex with animals is also commodified, and there exists a large online pornography industry devoted to human-animal sex (Klein; Beirne). Many of these images involve women forced to have sex with animals or to harm or kill animals (Beirne 118; Adams, "Woman-Battering" 67). There is also evidence of animals being placed into animal sex work rings (Beirne). The notorious death of a man near Enumclaw, Washington, in 2005 prompted the discovery of an animal brothel in operation at a farm (Senjo 329). There have been reported deaths and injuries to humans following interspecies sex (Stern and Smith-Blackmore 1058). Sexual contact with animals has been found as a risk factor for penile cancer as well as various other diseases, such as urological diseases (Nature Reviews Urology; Singg 25). Though often not highlighted, animals may sustain various injuries as a result of sexual contact, including damage to sexual organs, internal organs, and sometimes even death (Stern and Smith-Blackmore). A variety of animals may be part of sexual encounters, including dogs, sheep, goats, llamas, pigs, rabbits, chickens, cows, horses, and guinea pigs (Stern and Smith-Blackmore 1057). Some research indicates that dogs may be the most frequently involved animals, followed by horses (Beetz, "New" 106).

The frequency of human-animal sex is largely unknown (Stern and Smith-Blackmore). Alfred C. Kinsey's famous study on sexuality found that 8 per cent of males and 3.6 per cent of postpubescent women had some sexual experience with animals (Stern and Smith-Blackmore 1059; Beirne 122-23; Holoyda "Bestiality") and that as many as 40 to 50 per cent of all farm boys had some sexual experience with animals (Beirne 122–23). Kinsey suggested that much of the incidence of bestiality arose due to the sheer opportunity of being in rural farm settings and that prohibitions against premarital sex might have increased the number of people practicing bestiality (Johnson 56-57). Arguably, society has changed dramatically and become increasingly urbanized since Kinsey's studies. In 1974, a study by Morton Hunt reported a bestiality prevalence rate of 5 per cent among men and 2 per cent among women (qtd. in Beetz, "Bestiality" 48). A study of primarily heterosexual German men and women conducted in 2000 found that 4.4 per cent of the sample had sexual fantasies about animals sometimes; another 7.4 per cent of the sample indicated that they seldom fantasized about being sexually aroused by an animal (Beetz, "Bestiality" 49). Since Kinsey and Hunt's respective studies, there are no known studies examining the prevalence of human-animal sexual contact in the general population. Rather, most studies focus on self-identified zoophiles or incarcerated populations (Holoyda; Holoyda and Newman 129). There has also been an increasing rise in the number of online social groups for zoophiles that provide a therapeutic outlet within which zoophiles can receive self-validation, camaraderie, and a sense of normalcy in practices not available offline (Maratea 920). One such online social group examined in a study by R.J. Maratea had over 550,000 users. Data seems to support that those engaging in sex with animals had their first sexual encounter with animals during adolescence, at the average age of thirteen (Beetz, "New" 109-10).

The interrelationship between bestiality and interpersonal violence is still largely unexplored (Stern and Smith-Blackmore 1059). It is often posited that sexuality and aggression are developmentally fused when people or animals are objectified (Stern and Smith-Blackmore 1059). Carol Adams, in her seminal work, *The Sexual Politics of Meat*, argues that the socio-cultural positioning of the animal body allows for a cycle of objectification that distances people from the animals they eat, which is intimately linked with sexual violence against women (Adams, *The Sexual* 69-73). The link between interpersonal violence and meat production, as well as animal abuse, has been made by many different philosophers over time (Stern and Smith-Blackmore 1059; Beirne 167; Adams, *The Sexual*). However, it is premature to suggest that there is a progression that takes place between violence against animals and interpersonal violence—that once someone has engaged in animal abuse it leads to interhuman violence. We do not know definitively whether animal violence precedes, accompanies, or proceeds incidences of interpersonal violence (Beirne 182).

There are a limited number of studies specifically examining bestiality's intersection with interpersonal violence (Holoyda and Newman 129). Of note is that human-animal sex is likely underreported due to the fact that it is usually committed in private, rarely seen by eyewitnesses, and may endanger significant shame or stigma; therefore, bestiality's link with interpersonal violence is even more difficult to characterize (Levitt). The studies that do exist suggest a correlation between the two, although to what degree and for what type of offenses are unclear (Holoyda and Newman 129). Andrea Beetz, in a comprehensive review of a number of studies, suggests that there is a higher incidence of sexual contact with animals among people who were sexually abused earlier in life and among violent and sexual offenders (Beetz, "Bestiality" 65). In a study of inmates, those who had engaged in sexual acts with animals were found to be more likely than inmates without animal sexual experience to have been also convicted of a personal crime, such as rape, sexual assault, robbery, or assault (Holoyda and Newman 132). In an examination of 150 adult men charged with abusing animals—either physically, sexually, or through neglect—41 per cent were arrested for another act of interpersonal violence, 18 percent of which (i.e., of the 41 per cent) were arrested for rape or child molestation (Levitt). In a study of 261 prison inmates, 16 per cent reported having engaged in bestiality. Among those who reported animal sexual contact, 75 per cent had been convicted of a personal crime, compared with 47 per cent of the sample who had not reported animal sexual contact. Furthermore, 31 per cent of those who admitted animal sexual contact had been convicted of a personal crime more than once, compared with 5.4 per cent of the sample who reported having no animal sexual contact (Hensley et al. 921). In a study of 84 criminals, all of whom were sexual offenders and suffered from psychiatric disorders, the incidence of bestiality was 6 per cent (Holoyda).

Animal sexual contact may have a higher correlation with sexual assault against humans than other forms of animal abuse. In one study, one-third of those arrested for animal sexual abuse were also arrested for sexually assaulting a person, compared with 18 per cent of those arrested for physical animal abuse and 9 per cent of those arrested for animal neglect (Levitt). Furthermore, more than one-half of the victims of sexual assault were under the age of eighteen, suggesting a correlation between animal sexual abuse and sexual offenses against minors (Levitt).

It is well established that different forms of family violence tend to coexist and that if a man is battering his spouse, he is also more likely to abuse or neglect children. There is increasing evidence that sex with animals may be used as an instrument of psychological or physical terror in the context of domestic abuse (Beirne 169-70; Levitt; Beetz, "Bestiality" 55). Sex with an animal may be done to control or humiliate a partner or to demonstrate sexual dominance over a passive animal (Levitt). Women may also be forced to have sex with animals in familial contexts. Furthermore, coerced sex with animals may be largely unreported, given the immense unspeakableness of these encounters. Adams notes that forced sex with animals is "so horrifying it almost guarantees the silence" ("Woman-Battering" 68). There are no known studies specifically examining the incidence of bestiality in domestic abuse.

Some authors have pointed out that caution must be exercised in sweeping together all sexual contact between animals and humans as linked with interpersonal violence. Brian Holoyda and William Newman propose that there are a variety of different motivations for engaging in sexual contact with animals and that individuals who engage in sex with animals out of affection or intimacy, such as those who identify specifically as zoophiles, would be unlikely to fall into the category of being at higher risk for interpersonal violence (Holoyda and Newman 133; Beetz, "Bestiality" 56). Similarly, Andrea Beetz posits that there is some sexual contact with animals that does not cause pain or injuries and that does not involve coercion; therefore, caution must be exercised in presuming that these practices are also linked to interpersonal violence (Beetz, "Bestiality" 56). Furthermore, few studies, in questioning their research participants, delineate the specific types of behaviours included under the label of bestiality or zoophilia and what degree of violence was involved. This makes it more difficult to ascertain what type of sexual touching with animals may or may not correlate with interpersonal violence (Beetz, "Bestiality" 55-56).

Various theories are posited for why some individuals engage in sex with animals, but, again, there are a lack of concrete studies to understand motivating or contributing factors. Some early studies and popular conceptions suggest that those engaging in sex with animals did so because of a lower level of education (Brown and Rasmussen 166; Raina 969; Hensley et al. 912) or because they were situated rurally

(Rosenberg 480; Rydström, "Sodomitical Sins" 254; Brown and Rasmussen 166; Raina 969; Hensley et al. 912). Later studies have found that bestiality may be more common among lower educated individuals (Lesandric et al.), although there may continue to be a correlation with rural residence (Hensley et al. 918). Other researchers have posited that having sex with animals may be used as an alternative to molesting a child (Stern and Smith-Blackmore 1059) or that people having sex with animals may themselves have suffered emotional abuse or neglect as children (Holoyda and Newman; Hensley et al. 914; Beetz, "Bestiality" 53). Other motivating or contributing factors may include an affection or intimacy for animals, curiosity, cultural norms, lack of access to human partners, secondary gain through participation in online animal sex pornography industry, an enjoyment of sexual violence or cruelty, psychosis, social disorders, autism, schizophrenia, bipolar disorder, medications, cognitive impairment, or intoxication (Holoyda and Newman 133; Raina et al.; Chandradas and Champika 486; Hensley et al. 913; Lesandric et al. 29). One study suggests that there may exist a neurobiological relationship whereby elevated hormone levels may contribute to a sexual interest in animals (Lesandric et al. 28).

Interestingly, research suggests that persons engaging in sex with animals may be more likely to have another paraphilic or psychiatric disorder, with the most common co-occurring disorders being pedophilia, sexual sadism, and frotteurism (Holoyda and Newman 132; Holoyda). In a small study of psychiatric inpatients, there was a 30 per cent incidence of zoophilia compared with a 0 per cent incidence within a small nonpsychiatric inpatient control group (Holoyda). There are also studies suggesting a strong correlation between those engaging in sex with animals and sadomasochism (Holoyda and Newman 132; Hensley et al. 915; Sandnabba et al.; Blinter et al.), with a rate of bestiality within sadomasochistic communities of between 6 to 7 per cent (Sandnabba et al.; Bineter et al.).

Laws against Bestiality and Sodomy: Historical Perspectives

Conceptual Link between Bestiality and Same-Sex Relationships

Laws on bestiality are intimately tied up with laws against sodomy and buggery. Throughout Europe and other areas of the Christian world, "same-sex sexuality and sexual intercourse with animals were conceptually connected as two aspects of the sodomitic sin, or crime against nature" (Rydström, *Sinners* 2). Tracing the interconnection of bestiality and same-sex sexuality is important, not because the sexual practices are similar but rather because of the ongoing discursive and epistemological connection between the two in law (12). Trying to understand the laws prohibiting bestiality is impossible without reference to those laws that also sought to control same-sex sexuality and vice versa (30).

Throughout history, the words "sodomy" and "buggery" were used interchangeably to describe bestiality as well as a number of other sexual practices, including same-sex sexual relationships and oral sex between men and women (Beirne 106; Davidson 66; Boes 29). The label of sodomy was not always used consistently; its meaning changed depending on time and place (Beirne 106; Davidson 66). In some instances, labels such as sodomy were not used at all, and both human-animal sex and gay sex were regarded with such trepidation that they were only referred to as that unmentionable vice or sin (Beirne 106; Rydström, *Sinners* 1). Canada is no exception: laws on same-sex sexuality and bestiality hold an intimate, though rarely examined, interrelationship with each other. To understand this interrelationship, it is helpful to understand the roots of antibestiality sentiments, and how these intersect with the beliefs undergirding prohibitions on gay sex. Piers Beirne points to three common beliefs grounding views of bestiality as wrong: it ruptured nature or God-given order, violated the procreative intent of sex, and produced monstrous offspring (Beirne 101; Doniger 712; Maxwell-Stuart 83; Murrin 10).

Bestiality, oral and anal sex, masturbation, and pedophilia were often labeled as crimes against nature (Beirne 104). Condemned within the Bible and throughout early Christian theology, unnatural sexual acts, such as bestiality and anal sex between men, were widely censured (Murrin 8; Davidson 66; Beirne 100). The way in which same-sex sexuality and bestiality were grouped together within the Bible and in St. Augustine's work strongly suggests that the church's position on both subjects was similar (Ben-Atar and Brown 15). But evidence of bestiality predates Biblical times. In folklore and myths, to some extent, bestiality is glorified (Beirne 99–100), and myths abound of humans masquerading as animals and vice versa (Doniger 711). Mythical bestial unions pervade major religions, including Christianity. Yet, by and large, evidence overflows of societies since ancient times practicing and prohibiting human-animal sex, often cumulating in harsh punishments, such as death (Beirne 100; Ben-Atar and Brown 12; Miletski 1-4).

David Delaney posits that what is central to antibestiality sentiment is not that one of the participants in the sexual act is an animal but more so that human-animal sex crosses the species line and has the potential to blur the boundaries between the human and animal world, challenging the human exceptionalism around which subjectivity is built (Delaney 264; Boggs, "American" 121). Colleen Boggs similarly notes the following:

> The subject produced by compulsory heterosexuality under the rules of patriarchy is doubly man and mankind—there is a dual operation here of androcentrism and anthropocentrism: at the site of bestiality, the discourse of species and the construction of gender conjoin to create a notion of subjectivity that mandates physical behavior for the construction of the human. ("American" 104)

Thus, animality becomes a position of nonsubjectivity and "social sanctioned abjection" (Boggs, "American" 99), bestiality, was more than just a sinful practice, "it erased the boundary between man and beast, confusing categories and violating injunctions against the sanctity of God's distinction between man and animal" (Ben-Atar and Brown 18). Boggs argues that antibestiality laws function to regulate the boundary between human beings and animals. Prohibiting human-animal sex "simultaneously defines the difference between human beings and animals as absolute and yet fungible," and, thus, human subjectivity emerges through the criminalization of bestiality (Boggs, "American" 102).

What conceptually linked same-sex sexuality and bestiality in a powerful way was also the nonprocreative nature of the sex and the centrality of the phallus (Davidson 66; Ben-Atar and Brown 15; Miletski 5-6). Although in late Roman and early medieval Europe, bestiality was linked with masturbation rather than sodomy; by the late medieval period and early modern period, legislation treated bestiality and same-sex sexual relations as different aspects of the same sin (Rydström, "From Sodomy" 23; Boggs, *Animalia* 51; Ben-Atar and Brown 16-17). Thomas Aquinas, whose ideas permeated thinking until the end of the medieval period, classified any kind of nonprocreative sexual behaviour as deviant with the most egregious form being bestiality followed by homosexuality (Miletski 6). Indeed, bestiality and sodomy often functioned as synonyms for each other (Boggs, *Animalia* 51).

Delaney notes that the cultural and political history of desire is deeply embedded in nature, and although it seems to connote a positive assessment of what is natural and, therefore, laudable, it is limited to genital-to-genital (and face-to-face) heterosexual intercourse for the purpose of procreation (Delaney 244). Most of the concern related to these unnatural acts was that they did not lead to procreation. Interestingly, this may have contributed to a hyper focus on the practical and symbolic significance of the phallus throughout sexual discourse in Western society.

Most cases involving crimes against nature, argues Delaney, are not necessarily about animals; rather, "what seems to matter most is where a man puts his penis" (Delaney 264). Law's job was to punish the unnatural and control what was deemed disgusting. Disgust was among the "most culturally significant resources for making sense of nature- and of ourselves in relation to nature" (247). It was on the basis of disgust that many sexual practices were considered unnatural and criminalized on that basis. Arguably, this criminalization was an attempt to contain and destroy what was disgusting, and bestiality, in the cultural hierarchy of disgusting practices, was arguably one of the lowest (248). Indeed, Alan Young notes the pervasive role of disgust in Canada's antisodomy laws and in determining what was regulated under criminal law. Young notes that "there is little doubt that visceral response plays some role in the official construction of deviancy" (215).

Development of Antibestiality Laws in Canada

Thus, the problem of bestiality in Western society has never been one of law alone, and it is intimately intertwined with Judeo-Christian religious sexual mores. As Gabriel Rosenberg notes "sexual contact between human and nonhuman was not merely a juridical problem but also a profound religious one: a grievous form of fornication" (Rosenberg 477). Unsurprisingly, bestiality was initially managed under ecclesiastical laws, and it was not until the thirteenth century that there emerged a sharp growth in criminal laws throughout Europe prohibiting human-animal sex (Beirne 114; Pierceson 63). Many of these laws relied heavily on religious mores.

Canada's antisodomy laws of the twentieth century were direct remnants of the English crime of buggery, which was adopted, initially, by the British Parliament in 1533. The English offense of buggery was interpreted to include anal sex between men, between women and men, or between humans and animals (Pierceson 63). In 1821, the offence of buggery under English law carried a punishment of the death penalty, which was later lowered to life imprisonment (Miletski 8). Elise Chenier has noted the Canadian sexual regulation laws "were artefacts of an earlier age, rooted in medieval ecclesiastical law that made no distinction between different types of moral offenses" (Chenier, *Strangers* 26). Furthermore, Victorian ideas "to keep sexuality within tight boundaries" was paramount in the creation of Canada's *Criminal Code* and "still informs and animates contemporary law" (Young 205).

In 1869, buggery was codified in Canada as an offence in *An Act Respecting Offences against the Person* (Gacek and Jochelson, "Placing" 240). In 1892, bestiality and anal sex were incorporated into Canada's *Criminal Code*, drawing on the English offence of buggery almost word for word (*R v DLW* para 25) as the following offence: "Everyone is guilty of an indictable offence and liable to imprisonment for life who commits buggery, either with a human being or with any other living creature" (S.C. 1892, c. 29, section 174, 55-56). (Gacek and Jochelson, "Placing" 241). Buggery was interpreted to mean both male same-sex sexual relations as well as human-animal sex (Pierceson 63). In 1954, amendments to the *Criminal Code* led to the explicit naming of bestiality separate from buggery: "everyone who commits buggery or bestiality is guilty of an indictable offence and is liable to imprisonment for fourteen years" (S.C. 1953-54, c. 51) (Gacek and Jochelson, "Placing" 241).

Much of the discussion in the 2016 Supreme Court of Canada (SCC) case of *R v DLW* revolved around these 1954 amendments and whether they indicated Parliament's intention to adopt a less phallocentric definition of bestiality (i.e., must the offence of bestiality include penetration). The court ultimately found that penetration was a required element of the historic and modern versions of the offence. Animal Justice, a nonprofit animal welfare organization and an intervenor in the case, argued that the 1954 amendments demonstrated Parliament's intention to separate bestiality from its historical links to buggery and the penetrative paradigm, which linked same-sex sex and bestiality (Animal Justice 2). The majority was unconvinced and posited that the change in language from "buggery ... [with a] living creature" to "bestiality" was simply to bring more precise terms to the offense (*R v DLW* para 77). Interestingly, the text of the French version of the offence remained unchanged by the amendments, and the terms "buggery" and "bestiality" remained undefined in the *Criminal Code* (para 77). Although bestiality was named apart from buggery, the continued merger of the two within the same offense reflects the intimate interrelationship of the concepts, at least from a socio-legal perspective.

In 1978, the Law Reform Commission of Canada's *Report on Sexual Offences* argued for the repeal of the offence of bestiality, as they believed that it was covered by laws dealing with the protection of animals and that buggery, when accomplished by force, was already covered under sexual assault provisions (Hooper 64). No reference was made to suggest that the definition of bestiality was understood to have changed from requiring to not requiring penetration with the 1955 amendments. In fact, the *Report* defines bestiality as involving penetration (*DLW* para 92).

It was not until 1988 that separate offences were created for anal intercourse (section 159) and bestiality (section 160) (Gacek and Jochelson, "Placing" 241). In *R v DLW*, the Crown contended that the 1988 amendments and the separation of the offences of anal sex and bestiality demonstrated the way in which bestiality was intended to encompass any type of human-animal sexual activity not only penetration (*R v DLW* para 11). Certainly, lower courts had adjudicated the matter. For example, in *R v Ruvinsky* (1998), an Ontario trial court had ruled that penetration was a required element of the offence of bestiality; the trial judge ruled that upon review of his sources, bestiality meant intercourse with an animal, *per anum* or *per vaginum* (para 36). *DLW* was the first time the SCC had to adjudicate the issue and had to determine whether the Crown's expansionist interpretation of bestiality offences should persist.

The majority of the SCC would not agree with the Crown's position. The majority noted that there was nothing suggesting that the definition traditionally attributed to bestiality which required penetration had changed. Furthermore, bestiality remained formally undefined in the *Criminal Code* (*R v DLW* para 106). Within the current iteration of antibestiality provisions under section 160 of the *Code*, there are three different bestiality offences including the commission of bestiality, compelling bestiality, and bestiality in the presence of a child, and all would on the majority's reasoning require penetration (Gacek and Jochelson, "Animal" 344; Gacek and Jochelson, "Placing" 241). In October 2018, the Liberal government introduced Bill C-84, which sought to expand offences related to animal fighting and define bestiality more broadly, a direct response to the court's ruling in *R v DLW*. The proposed change defines bestiality as "any contact by a person, for a sexual purpose, with an animal" (Bill C-84). As of June 21, 2019, these amendments are finally in force and are codified in the *Criminal Code* in section 160. The Minister of Justice at the time, Jody Wilson-Raybould, noted that the bill:

> would increase protections for children, as well as other vulnerable individuals who may be compelled to engage in or witness bestiality, and animals, by ensuring the criminal law captures all sexual acts with animals, not just those involving penetration. By virtue of the definition's "sexual purpose" focus, legitimate animal husbandry and veterinary practices would continue to be excluded from the scope of the offence. (Bill C-84 Hansard)

Attempts to define bestiality more broadly had been pursued before. In 2017, Member of Parliament Michelle Rempel introduced a private member's bill which defined bestiality in the exact same way as Bill C-84. Although Rempel's bill received a first reading, it has been stalled since (Bill C-388).

Canada's laws on bestiality have developed in a similar manner to other countries. In eighteenth-century Sweden, bestiality was encompassed under the same section of their criminal code and subject to the same punishment as other sodomitical sins, such as masturbation and same-sex sex (Rydström, "Sodomitical" 244). Likewise, the sexuality laws emerging in the United States in the nineteenth century were holdovers from colonial-era British statutes that codified common-law prohibitions on sex and biblical injunctions (Rosenberg 479; Pierceson 63). These laws also attempted to combat supposed crimes against nature, often merging together offences of bestiality and sodomy. For much of the nineteenth century, within many Western societies, sodomy laws were not explicitly intended to regulate same-sex sexuality but reinforced attitudes against all nonprocreative sex (Pierceson 63).

The antibestiality statutes emerging in the United States were often broad and covered a wide variety of sexual transgressions. Again, this is not dissimilar to Canada's laws on bestiality, which were encompassed under antibuggery provisions sanctioning other penetrative acts. Rosenberg notes that "the statutes seldom parsed the relevant distinctions between the different categories of sexual transgress and, instead, exhibited broad, vague, and florid language consistent with nineteenth-century statutory construction" (Rosenberg 479). Many of these broad statutes persisted well into the twentieth century, and some are still in existence (479). The broad and indistinct nature of antibestiality laws is evident in the range of labels and different types of statutes in the United States under which human-animal sex is captured as well as the challenge in defining what counts as an animal entitled to protection under different statutes (Senjo 330; Beirne 9). The broad nature of laws on bestiality is a reflection of the pervasive disgust and unspeakableness of bestiality and non-normative sexualities.

Anti-bestiality Laws in the Twentieth Century: Shifting Parameters

In the United States and Sweden, the general trend before the 1900s was that bestiality was more commonly prosecuted than other sodomitical sins (Pierceson 63; Rydström, "Sodomitical" 262). This continued after 1900, as crimes of bestiality were the dominant prosecuted crimes there until the 1930s and 1940s (Rydström, *Sinners* 323).

In British Columbia, Gordon Ingram suggests that the charge of buggery was rarely used in rural areas against male same-sex sex, but it was rather used primarily to pursue charges against men who had sex with animals (Ingram).

During the 1930s and 1940s, there emerged a growing number of prosecutions under antisodomy laws for homosexual sex rather than bestiality (Rydström, "Sodomitical" 246). Bestiality was "replaced by homosexuality as the main concern with the rise of the urban gay culture" (Rydström, *Sinners* 97). Boggs goes as far to say that it was the colonial persecution of bestiality that became the founding moment in the oppression of gays, as it established the precedent for subsequent laws denying the right to practice sodomy and demonstrated the limits of liberalism (Boggs, *Animalia* 51). Indeed, the 1930s and 1940s saw the recriminalization and persecution of same-sex sexuality in Nazi Germany, France, and the Soviet Union. In the United States and Canada, gay men were singled out as objects of sodomy laws in the late nineteenth century, after the rise of gay subcultures in large cities (Pierceson 63; Rydström, *Sinners* 3). This rural-urban divide was also evident in rural British Columbia, where men were generally not arrested for homosexual activity before 1969. Rather, indications are that homosexuality between men was conceived of as an urban phenomenon (Ingram).

After World War II, the rise of the fear of the criminal sexual psychopath in Canada resulted in a wide range of sex-related offenses being treated as psychiatric problems (Chenier, "The Criminal" 78-79). In fact, psychiatrists in Ontario were some of the first in North America to conceive of sodomy and buggery as a form of mental disease (Chenier, "The Criminal" 80). In 1948, a section on criminal sexual psychopaths (CSP) was added to the *Criminal Code*, and if an individual was convicted of one of the triggering offenses, an application could be made in sentencing for the individual to be designated as a CSP, which carried with it the penalty of indefinite incarceration (Kinsman and Gentile 72). In 1953, buggery, including bestiality, was added to the list of offences that could trigger a CSP procedure (Kinsman and Gentile 73; Chenier, *Strangers* 82). Likewise, in the United States between the 1930s and 1950s, there emerged a national obsession with sexual deviants, specifically homosexuals, as a direct threat to the wellbeing of the nation and linked to the sexual abuse of children (Pierceson 64).

By the end of the 1950s, twenty-nine states had adopted sexual psychopath legislation (Chenier, *Strangers* 82). Although both homosexuality and bestiality were medicalized, they were dealt with distinctly, and homosexuality rose to the forefront of public moral panic. In Sweden, bestiality had largely disappeared from legal and medical discourse by the 1950s (Rydström, "Sodomitical" 244), and a focus on the illness of homosexuality came to the forefront (250).

In the latter half of the twentieth century, the laws on sodomy began to change. In the case of same-sex sexuality, the medicalization of same-sex sexuality transformed into same-sex desire being conceived of as a sexual orientation, but this same transformation did not occur for bestiality. Accordingly, "the sodomitic paradigm gradually was weakened and only slowly gave way to the modern homosexual paradigm" (Rydström, *Sinners* 330). Indeed, several authors have noted the rise of concern with the urban homosexual, which shifted societal discourse from a blanket condemnation of all nonprocreative sexuality to a focus on the homosexual-heterosexual binary (Brown and Rasmussen 167; Rydström, "From Sodomy" 28).

In the latter half of the twentieth century, bestiality was decriminalized in a number of places, including Sweden and several American states, but almost by accident (Rydström, "Sodomitical" 254). The union of bestiality and prohibitions on same-sex sexual relationship under the banner of sodomy meant that when one was decriminalized, the other one was too. As Rydström notes, "when bestiality was decriminalized it was not as a result of some concerted effort, but as a side-effect of the legalization of homosexuality" (254). Lawmakers, often centred within urban spaces, may have been removed from the realities of rural society and incidences of bestiality (252). The urban elite in Sweden hardly knew bestiality existed, and they did not put energy towards arguing for its abolition (210).

In most states, as in Canada, laws against gay same-sex sexual relations were under the same provisions as those against bestiality. Deeming such laws archaic in light of the growing recognition of queer relationships, many legislatures in the United States removed the anti-sodomy laws without considering their dual purpose of criminalizing same-sex and interspecies sexual contact (Rosenberg 481). In fact, between 1960 and 2017, only ten states had laws in place continuously that criminalized interspecies sexual contact. Interestingly, most statutes in the United States prohibiting human-animal sexual contact were only enacted since the 1970s with seventeen passing into law after 2000. By 2017, forty-two states had laws criminalizing human-animal sexual contact (481).

In Canada, this same accidental decriminalization of bestiality did not occur—perhaps in part due to the separation of bestiality from anal sex into separate offences in the 1980s and the remaining criminalization of anal sex, which has only recently been repealed (Canada, Dpt. of Justice, "Section 159"). The latest iteration of the *Code* in Canada, as of June 21, 2019, no longer continues to criminalize anal penetration between consenting adults within the *Code*, with a higher age of consent required for anal sex than other kinds of sexual activity. Courts in five provinces had found that the age differential for anal penetration compared with other sexual activities did not comply with the *Charter* (Canada, Dpt. of Justice, "Bill C-32"). The government explained the following in its *Charter* statement on the section 159 repeal:

> The repeal of section 159 of the *Criminal Code* would promote the equality rights protected by subsection 15(1) of the *Charter*, which provides that everyone is equal before and under the law. Section 159 prohibits anal intercourse, except by a husband and wife or two persons who are both 18 years or older, and where the act is consensual and takes place in private. The offence has had a disparate impact on homosexual males, whose consensual sexual activities have been uniquely targeted for prohibition. (Canada, Dpt. of Justice, "*Charter*")

In addition, the Government noted the following: "The repeal of section 159 would also promote the liberty interests protected by section 7 of the *Charter*. Liberty is promoted both because a prosecution under section 159 could result in a sentence of imprisonment, and because section 159 captures consensual sexual activities" (Canada, Dpt. of Justice, "*Charter*").

The bestiality prohibition persisted in Canadian law in relative stasis until the 2019 amendments by the Trudeau government. Given the previous history of bestiality, it is hardly surprising that the SCC in *R v DLW* defined bestiality as requiring penetration. Boggs, in a survey of bestiality in the United States, notes that bestiality was fundamentally defined in relation to penetration (Boggs, *Animalia* 53).

Throughout history, penetration was a key component of prohibitions against human-animal and same-sex sexuality. In early modern English law, for example, sworn testimony of penetration was required in order to find that a bestial act had occurred; this emphasis on penetration continued within North American and English law throughout the eighteenth century, and in many cases, until the present day (Ben-Atar and Brown 18, 26). As a result of the focus on penetration, women were almost never tried for same-sex or interspecies sex (Murrin 9; Pierceson 63; Rydström, "Sodomitical" 250; Lamble 125). Arguably, the focus of antisodomy laws on the phallus is indicative of the way in which transgender, bisexual, and lesbian bodies and sexualities remained unthinkable within law (Lamble 125). In an examination of British Columbia trial dossiers for the offenses of sodomy, gross indecency, and buggery, Ingram finds that the common proscription linking legal concern over these practices was genital contact, in which one or more penises were touching or were inside an orifice other than a vagina (Ingram). Here again, we see the primacy of the phallus and penetration within antisodomy laws and the centrality of masculinity to the law (Rydström, "Sodomitical" 250).

Scholars posit any number of reasons for the fact that human-animal sex never became a recognized sexual orientation in the same way that same-sex sexuality did. Michael Brown and Claire Rasmussen argue that the concern with nonprocreative sex is tied up with the idea that sex should not be undertaken solely for pleasure. Same-sex relationships have been able to be recognized as grounded in a sexual orientation, in part, because they have been recognized as being about more than just sex (Brown and Rasmussen 167). Brown and Resmussen suggest the following: "While zoophiles have made the claim that zoophilia is a sexual orientation, sex with animals is not generally understood to constitute an identity, and certainly not one that fosters the kinds of long-term relationships that are conducive to society. Instead, this mere sex is considered degrading and, well, animalistic" (167-68).

Within an historical framework, the divergence in law between same-sex intercourse and bestiality may be due to the urban-rural divide and the predominance of urban discourses of modernity emerging in the latter half of the twentieth century. Jens Rydström notes the following: "Bestiality was considered, when considered at all, as a vestigial and rural phenomenon, an individual sin or revolting habit. It did not constitute a threat to society, and it was not dealt with on a structural level" (Rydström, "Sodomitical" 254). In other words, in Sweden and other jurisdictions where bestiality fell off the books, "bestiality was so distant from a modern discourse that it was simply ignored" (Rydström, *Sinners* 326). The highly publicized Enumclaw incident, in which a man died after being penetrated by a horse and an animal sex ring was uncovered, was often portrayed in media as an example of urban corruption in a rural setting. The idea of urban sexual deviance infecting rural environments is a new phenomenon and "one that reflects a model of homosexuality as the primary model of sexual deviance" (Brown and Rasmussen 166).

Furthermore, scholars point to the rise of the dichotomy of the homosexual and heterosexual as leaving no room for conceiving of a desire for animals as a sexual orientation. As Rydström states, "the most important reason that zoophilia was not recognized as a sexual orientation ... was the rise of the normative distinction between the heterosexual and the homosexual, which has become such an important regulating principle for modern life. In the dichotomy homosexual/ heterosexual, there was simply no place for other deviant practices" (Rydström, *Sinners* 325). The threat to human subjectivity that bestiality presented further distinguished it from homosexuality in a unique way (325). Finally, those engaging in bestiality never organized or claimed their right to bestiality in the same way that the gay rights movement did (326). Regardless of the reasons, it is indeed fascinating to note the rise of homosexuality and its storied rights discourse compared with the relative disappearance of bestiality (Rydström, *Sinners* 9). As we shall see when we take a deeper dive into the Canadian law, bestiality remains relatively rare in the reported cases, and even then, judges prefer not to speak in much detail about it. Indeed, many of the lessons the cases provide are contextual rather than legal. The cases tell us about the way courts in Canada speak about bestiality and how the offences are often part of a larger pattern of offending before the courts, supporting the links with child abuse and sexual violence discussed above.

A Deeper Dive into Canadian Law and Reported Cases

Currently, the *Criminal Code of Canada* deals with bestiality through section 160. It creates three separate offences. Section 160(1) deals with the basic offence of bestiality by the accused: "160 (1) Every person who commits bestiality is guilty of an indictable offence and liable to imprisonment for a term not exceeding ten years or is guilty of an offence punishable on summary conviction." Section 160(2) criminalizes situations where the accused has compelled another person to commit bestiality: "(2) Every person who compels another to commit bestiality is guilty of an indictable offence and liable to imprisonment for a term not exceeding ten years or is guilty of an offence punishable on summary conviction." Section 160(3) criminalizes situations where an accused either commits bestiality in the presence of someone under the age of sixteen or who causes a person under the age of sixteen to commit bestiality themselves. It is of note that the punishment for this offence is greater than under the other two; this offence has a mandatory minimum sentence as well as a maximum sentence.

Importantly, for offences under section 160, courts are required to consider a prohibition or restitution order in sentencing. Only in 2019, was bestiality defined in the *Code* as any contact with an animal for sexual purposes. Prior to this amendment, courts did their best to define meanings for prohibited bestial conduct.

Other *Criminal Code* sections contemplate offences upon animals, but it is less clear whether bestiality can amount to the degree of harm required to find an offence under these sections—for example, "445.1 (1) Every one commits an offence who (a) wilfully causes or, being the owner, wilfully permits to be caused unnecessary pain, suffering or injury to an animal or a bird."

The punishment under this section is set out in section 445.1(2):

(2) Everyone who commits an offence under subsection (1) is guilty of

- a) an indictable offence and liable to imprisonment for a term of not more than five years; or

- b) an offence punishable on summary conviction and liable to a fine not exceeding ten thousand dollars or to imprisonment for a term of not more than eighteen months or to both.

The difficulty with applying this provision in situations of bestiality is well set out in the factum of Animal Justice, an intervener in *R v DLW*. These provisions require proof of harm to the animal, which could be very difficult to establish without the presence of an obvious injury or expert examination of the animal close in time to the alleged act. Arguably, this means that this provision could capture an even narrower range of sexual conduct than bestiality under section 160.

It could perhaps be argued that sexual conduct involving an animal could be captured under "suffering"; however, this would be difficult to prove in court and, ultimately, would probably fail for the same reasons that the more expansive interpretation of section 160 did in the *DLW* case: it is usually not open to the courts to expand the scope of an offence under the common law.

Although the facts are quite detailed and disturbing, *R v KDH* is an example of a relatively common case context that we found in our case review. The offender, KDH, was charged with forty sexual offences. One of these was a charge of bestiality contrary to section 160(1) of the *Criminal Code*. The other offences were committed against several complainants. These included his biological daughter and son, KH1 and KH, the daughter of a girlfriend, JA, and the two daughters of his fiancé, MA and TM. At the material times, KH1 was six to sixteen years old; KH was ten to fifteen; JA was ten to twelve; MA was fourteen or fifteen; and TM was twenty or twenty-one. The agreed statement of facts was extensive and organized by the complainant. The offences ranged from sexual touching of a young person to sexual assault with a weapon, various incest charges, and child pornography charges, to name a few. His fiancée, the mother of MA and TM, was involved in and had knowledge of many of these offences.

One of the charges against the offender was a charge of bestiality. KDH convinced JA's mother to allow a dog to lick her genitals, made MA engage in bestiality, and made MA watch her mother engage in bestiality. The agreed upon facts disclose nothing about KDH engaging in bestiality personally. However, the charge against KDH was that he had engaged in bestiality himself. As the judge notes, although no facts were disclosed supporting the charge, KDH pled guilty (para 180). Due to the guilty plea, bestiality was not analyzed. However, this case was emblematic of some typical trends in what we found.

Bestiality is often part of a much wider pattern of sexual abuse of another person or persons, including incest and child sexual abuse. The subjugation of vulnerable persons and the use of bestiality in grooming victims seem to be a prevalent theme in many of the bestiality cases we uncovered. Also of note is how little the bestiality plea is analyzed, especially considering the detailed analysis dedicated to the other charges. Courts seem reluctant to discuss the details of bestiality charges when a constellation of other numerous sexual offences accompany it (see *R v LMR* below as well as *R v JJBB* for examples). Bestiality, as the social science research indicates, is often part of a pattern of sexual offending against children, young persons, and vulnerable persons. The *R v KDH* case indicates that bestial charges ought to be dealt with severely. At one point the Court noted that the case law demonstrates that even single instances of bestiality have attracted significant penalties (para 346) and could also be considered an aggravating factor in sentencing in relation to sexual interference charges (paras 337, 342).

The use of technology is another emerging theme in modern cases dealing with bestial offences. *R v LMR* was an appellate case in Alberta involving the abuse of a child. LMR lived with her biological father in Edmonton for several months. During this time, the father convinced the respondent to sexually exploit the infant while he filmed it. Shortly afterwards, the respondent moved out, leaving her daughter in the father's care.

The father retained custody of the child until 2007, when police discovered that he was using the Internet to find women to have sex with him and the child. As a result, police searched his residence, where they found the original child pornography made with the respondent as well as video of the respondent attempting to sexually engage a dog. The respondent was charged with sexual interference, making child pornography, and bestiality. She pled guilty to all charges and received a global sentence of 4.5 years imprisonment. The Crown appealed the sentence.

Forensic and psychiatric assessments of the respondent were conducted prior to sentencing. These indicated that the respondent was serially a victim of emotional, physical, and sexual abuse in her formative years. She was found to have a limited intellectual capacity and was unable to write or understand big words. She had started drug use at fourteen and entered into sex work at seventeen. She had five children from four different fathers, all of whom were estranged. The court of appeal did not change the duration of the sentence following these assessments (para 16). Despite the facts not indicating any penetrative bestial acts, the Court did not discuss the bestiality charge.

The case is illustrative of a number of factors that are common in the reported cases. First of all, the case context involved an offender who was described forensically as vulnerable and who was compelled to participate in a series of sexual offences against her children and animals. Although she was capable of being responsible, she was portrayed as someone who had herself been victimized. Second, the case constellation involved the sexual abuse of children and child pornography. Third, the father was involved in using the Internet to lure accomplices and victims to further victimize the children—the father was the initiator of the abuses.

One of the most extreme and systematic examples of rampant sexual victimization overlapping with bestial acts was a trial decision in *R v DeJaeger* in the Nunavut Court of Justice. The accused, DeJaeger, was charged with eighty offences against forty complainants, both male and female, between the ages of four and twenty. There was a wide range of charges, including indecent assault, unlawful confinement, rape, sexual assault, assault, gross indecency, threatening, buggery, and bestiality. Four of these counts alleged bestiality with a dog. The offences were historical, occurring between 1976 and 1982, in and around the community of Igloolik. The accused was a priest and part of a Roman Catholic mission that was established in the community.

The case was a rare example of bestiality adjudication at trial rather than a sentencing after a plea deal. Most of the decision is spent on assessing the accuracy and truth of witness testimony—not establishing the elements of the offence. A number of counts were dismissed due to lapses in the memory and testimony of the victims, a common problem in cases that involve events from many years before (paras 668-69, 704-07, 922-23, and 933-36).

The final bestiality charge, count fifty-seven, was alleged by the complainant CP. During testimony, CP frequently broke down in tears, consistent with someone severely traumatized. The sequence of events described was both logical and complete, and was internally consistent. There were no obvious gaps in CP's memory in so far as the events were concerned. CP's description of the events was very graphic in its detail and included childlike, age-appropriate descriptions of his reaction to the events as well as his interactions with the accused. The court found no rational basis to doubt CP's memory of the alleged events (paras 947-49). CP's detailed description of the room and recollection was contradicted by the accused's general denial of the incident as well as his assertion that he had not allowed children into that area of the mission church. There was no basis to conclude that CP might have been mistaken about what he saw happening to the dog. The incident with the dog led directly to the alleged anal rape of the victim (paras 950-51). Therefore, the court found that count fifty-seven, along with the associated counts for the rape, had been proven beyond a reasonable doubt.

One of the very few examples of isolated acts of bestiality we found in our case review was the case of *R v Pye*, which involved a sentencing hearing. Although the accused was also facing sentencing for the sexual assault of a young girl, that matter was unrelated to the bestial acts in question. On July 31, 2004, at approximately 9:30 a.m., Kamloops police got a complaint in relation to activity at a park. It was alleged that a man was trying to grab a dog or dogs, that he was observed with his jeans around his ankles, and that a dog was yelping or crying. The same person was seen to have a roll of paper towel in his hand and was cleaning himself and the dog with the paper towel. The dog then ran off again. The vehicle being driven by the subject of interest was subsequently moved, and the person was observed either catching or attempting to catch the same dog.

Another person called in a complaint to police. She was a nurse who regularly walked through the park when on break from a nearby hospital. She complained that she had heard a dog yelping in pain and had observed a van nearby, which she described to police. Outside the van, she observed a male holding a dog leash and speaking very harshly. She approached to within six to eight feet from the male and further observed that he had his underwear down and was trying to hold a dog. She spoke to him but was ignored. She then called 9-1-1 and reported that the dog was running away near an embankment.

Police attended the area to investigate. Several days later, their investigation led them to speak with the offender. The offender denied any involvement but agreed to provide a statement. His original story to police was that he had not been involved and that he had been in the area at the time with a dog. The police then indicated to Pye that they had incriminating security camera footage depicting him, which was a deception (paras 1-9). Pye then revised his account of events. He admitted to police that he had taken the dog to the park, and that he had attempted anal intercourse with the dog three times, but said regarding penetration that "it did not fit" (para 10). The dog belonged to a friend of his, which he had offered to walk that morning. There was some indication that alcohol may have been a factor (paras 11-19). Also of note was that Pye was on a recognizance at the time, including an alcohol ban, as he was awaiting sentencing for his other sexual assault conviction. The court sentenced him to six months to be served concurrently to eighteen months for his separate sexual assault offence (para 90). Even in this reported case of an isolated bestiality charge, the offender had other predilections towards sexual offence.

Another rare example of bestiality as a standalone offence occurred in the application to a court to admit similar fact evidence for adjudication at trial. In *R v Alton*, the Ontario Superior Court had to determine whether past evidence of bestial acts could be admitted as sufficiently probative for a trial for a second set of bestial acts.

Ronald Alton was charged with three counts of breaking and entering relating to the barns of two different farmers, B and E. B alleged that he confronted an individual believed to be Alton in his barn in October 2005. At the time, Alton had explained his presence by indicating that he was looking for work. Count one alleged that on November 2, 2005, Alton broke into the barn of B and stole B's dog, Golden, who was later retrieved. Count two alleged that Alton again broke into B's barn on February 6, 2006, this time committing bestiality with Golden. Count three alleged that Alton broke into the barn of E on December 5, 2005, with intent to commit bestiality with a goat (para 8).

A number of facts were salient in the court's determination of the first two charges, including that a neighbour who had found Golden a significant distance from B's barn but very near to the home of Alton following the November 2005 theft. The neighbour's description of Alton matched B's recollection. Furthermore, DNA evidence placed Alton in B's barn, and B observed an individual leaving the barn after the February 2006 incidence, whom B was able to identify as the same person that he had confronted in the barn in October 2005 (para 8).

The details surrounding the third charge were less clear. It appears that E discovered Alton in her barn at night, very near to one of her goats, which had been tied up. Alton attempted to explain his presence by indicating that he was a hitchhiker trying to escape the cold outside (para 13).

The court held that past bestial acts, in and of themselves, may give rise to an inference of a generic propensity for such behaviour (paras 15-16). However, such a general propensity may fall short of the focused and specific propensity required to admit similar fact evidence as being probative of guilt at trial (para 19). The Crown asserted that sexual contact with a dog was evidence of intent to engage in sexual contact with a goat in the context of Alton breaking into a barn where animals are penned and being found near the tied-up goat. The court framed the inference that the Crown was proffering as follows: that an individual who demonstrates sexual interest in one animal has a similar propensity with another animal (para 20).

The court found that this inference relied on two assumptions that were not supported by evidence. The first was that sexual interest in animals is rare. Although the court recognized that this was the only reported case of this nature in that area in a decade, this was not sufficient to support the first assumption. The second assumption made by the Crown was that a sexual interest in animals is not specific to a certain animal, which meant that the court would have to accept that since the dog Golden was an animal, Alton must also have a sexual interest in goats. The court had no evidence before it that would support this assumption. Thus, the Crown failed to make out, on a balance of probabilities, that Alton had a propensity to bestiality that justified the admission of similar fact evidence as to his intention to commit bestiality with the goat (paras 20-27).

In our case law search, we found one case, which occurred prior to the *DLW* precedent that found that penetration should not be considered as required for a bestiality charge. Although the *DLW* case expressly overruled this case, the reasoning of the lower court decision still contains some compelling elements. In some ways, given the 2019 amendment of the law and the addition of a section 160(7) bestiality definition, the lower court decision may provide more compelling reasoning than DLW for future proceedings. In the Quebec case of *R c MAGI*, the accused was charged with sexual assault contrary to section

271(1)(a); assault contrary to section 266(a); and compelling bestiality contrary to section 160(2) of the *Criminal Code*.

The accused and the complainant entered into a relationship from April 1995 until December 1999. The complainant testified that the accused had many unusual sexual fetishes that he disclosed to her. An alleged offence of bestiality occurred sometime in 1995. The complainant testified that she woke one morning to see the accused had brought the family dog into the bedroom and was stimulating its penis. The accused expressed to the complainant a fantasy of watching a dog penetrate a woman. The complainant expressed a desire to leave. In response, the accused punched the wall and made her stay. She testified that the accused forced her to get onto her hands and knees, then placed the dog on her back, and attempted to insert the dog's penis into her. The complainant testified to feeling the dog's penis against her vagina.

The issue facing the court was whether the case should go to trial given the preliminary evidence. The court found there was sufficient evidence to proceed to trial (para 48). The judge began by reviewing several cases and legal dictionary definitions, which indicated that penetration had long been considered an essential element of bestiality. However, the judge noted that these sources came from the time when penetration was also still an essential element of sexual assault. On the judge's view, the 1988 *Criminal Code* revisions separating bestiality from buggery—taken with the statements of the SCC in its sexual assault jurisprudence in *R v Chase* (which indicated that the courts should adopt broader understandings of the requisite elements of sexual offences including that the sexual nature of the offence should be determined according to a reasonable person test rather than the presence of penetration)—indicate that the law has since evolved past the strict penetration requirement (paras 43-44). Additionally, and alternatively, the court noted that Black's Law Dictionary indicated that for penetration to occur "it [was] not necessary that the vagina be entered or that the hymen be ruptured; the mouth of the vulva or labia is sufficient" (para 44). On this basis, the judge concluded that the testimony of the complainant disclosed sufficient information that a jury could convict on the bestiality charge (para 47).

This sort of reasoning ultimately proved unconvincing for the SCC majority in the DLW case (which we have discussed earlier in this chapter). Perhaps most compelling for the SCC was that there should be no new common law offences under the *Criminal Code* and that an expansionist definition of bestiality would de facto create one (para 57). The majority noted the following (para 116):

> It defies logic to think that Parliament would rename, redefine and create new sexual offences in a virtually complete overhaul of these provisions in 1983 and 1988 and yet would continue to use an ancient legal term with a well-understood meaning bestiality without further definition in order to bring about a substantive difference in the law. The new bestiality offences added in the 1988 revisions, while not changing the definition of the underlying offence, added protections for children in relation to that offence. There is nothing inconsistent with the purpose of these new provisions in the conclusion that the elements of bestiality remained unchanged. There is nothing "absurd" about protecting children from compulsion or exposure to this sort of sexual conduct. And, contrary to what Justice Abella writes, it does not follow that all sexually exploitative acts with animals that do not involve penetration are "perfectly legal" (para 142). Section 160 is not the only protective provision; there were (and still are) other provisions in the *Code* which may serve to protect children (and others) from sexual activity that does not necessarily involve penetration: see, e.g., the current ss.151, 153, 172 and 173.

Conversely, Justice Abella in a scathing dissent notes the following:

> We are dealing here with an offence that is centuries old. I have a great deal of difficulty accepting that in its modernizing amendments to the *Criminal Code*, Parliament forgot to bring the offence out of the Middle Ages. There is no doubt that a good case can be made, as the majority has carefully done, that retaining penetration as an element of bestiality was in fact Parliament's intention (para 126) ...

> Section 160(3) is, in my respectful view, inarguably a reflection of Parliament's purpose to protect children from witnessing, or

being compelled to commit, bestiality. If all Parliament intended was that children be protected from seeing or being made to engage in acts of *penetration* with animals, one could reasonably wonder what the point was of such an unduly restricted preoccupation. Since it is a "well established principle of statutory interpretation that the legislature does not intend to produce absurd consequences"… surely what Parliament must have intended was protection for children from witnessing or being forced to participate in *any* sexual activity with animals, period. (para 147)

The tensions between liberty and protection of victims, both human and animal, are not a divide easily bridged. In this section of the chapter, we have discussed how bestiality law inculcates other sexual offences in the case law. Child sexual abuse, child pornography, or sexual offences in general are intertwined with bestiality in the relatively few reported cases we found. Most of the offenders are men, and even in cases of female offenders, the offences are often initiated by another male perpetrator. The cases reviewed represent a small sampling of what is likely a more widespread phenomenon of human-animal sex, incidences of which likely remain unknown or unreported. Interestingly, most of the reported cases do not deal with the question of whether the bestial offence is penetrative, though now, thanks to the 2019 amendments, the law is clear in that contact for a sexual purpose with an animal will suffice in providing a definition for bestiality.

One critique of the majority's decision in the *DLW* case is that the majority's reasoning placed animals as property by defining bestiality as requiring penetration. That is, by favouring the accused and defending them against an expansionist definition of bestiality, the court failed to weigh the potential sentience of the animal in assessing the damage done. Unsurprisingly, lower courts will try to use the status of animals as property to their advantage when bestiality charges cannot be made out due to a lack of penetration.

The offence of sexual exploitation is one example of such a possibility. Section 153 of the *Criminal Code* prohibits the touching of a person for a sexual purpose if under sixteen years of age and done with a part of the body or with an object. The prohibition applies when there is some type of relationship between the victim and the perpetrator that renders the sexual touching exploitative:

153 (1) Every person commits an offence who is in a position of trust or authority towards a young person, who is a person with whom the young person is in a relationship of dependency or who is in a relationship with a young person that is exploitative of the young person, and who

a) for a sexual purpose, touches, directly or indirectly, with a part of the body or with an object, any part of the body of the young person; or

b) for a sexual purpose, invites, counsels or incites a young person to touch, directly or indirectly, with a part of the body or with an object, the body of any person, including the body of the person who so invites, counsels or incites and the body of the young person.

In a bestiality situation, where penetration cannot be made out, application of section 153 requires that the animal be considered an object. This provision was applied to an instance of compelled bestiality in *R v PV* and its companion case *R v VJ*, below. Punishment for these sexual exploitation offences is set out in section 153(1.1):

a) is guilty of an indictable offence and is liable to imprisonment for a term of not more than 14 years and to a minimum punishment of imprisonment for a term of one year; or

b) is guilty of an offence punishable on summary conviction and is liable to imprisonment for a term of not more than two years less a day and to a minimum punishment of imprisonment for a term of 90 days.

In *R v VJ*, the Ontario Court of Justice convicted the accused and a co-accused (the parents of the victims) of a variety of sexual offences. The alleged sexual abuse included sexual touching, oral sex, vaginal and anal penetration, and bestiality. The alleged physical abuse included severe beatings, sometimes with a range of objects such as crowbars, electrical cords or hammers; burning with lighters and stove elements; and tossing the girls onto beehives. In support of the abuse, the two accused allegedly embarked on a systematic campaign to blame and isolate the girls from others.

The abuse occurred when KV was between the ages of five and seventeen, and KIV was between four and sixteen. Both victims testified that abuse occurred almost daily during this period. The matter finally came before the court as a result of disclosure by KV in the wake of a suicide attempt by KIV, which put her into a short coma.

The victim of the bestiality count was KIV. It seems from that case that she suffered more sexual abuse than KV, who was more prone to resisting. KIV was subjected to sexual intercourse with JV, her father, on an almost daily basis. According to her testimony, on a number of these occasions, PV, her mother, would bring the family dog to the room where she was being sexually assaulted. JV would then stimulate the dog and cause it to penetrate KIV. When the dog was finished, JV would then resume intercourse with KIV (para 176, paras 230-237, 248-250).

In this case, the judge did not deal with the bestial acts in isolation, which seems to be a common tactic in our review of bestiality cases in Canada. Rather, considering the testimonies of the victims as a whole, the judge found that eleven of the sexual offences had occurred beyond a reasonable doubt. Thus, there was no particular insight offered into the court's consideration of the bestiality offence. However, the sentencing decision of JV's wife, PV (see *R v PV* below), clarifies that the accused were not charged with compelling bestiality. Rather, the charge against them for forcing the bestial acts upon their children was sexual touching of a person under fourteen with an object under section 153 of the *Criminal Code*. In the *R v PV* companion sentencing case, it was made clear by the court that the dogs were considered the objects under the analysis. The court accepted this framing of the law. Clearly this reasoning supports conceptions of animals as property, but it also shows certain flexibility in Canada's courts to mete out guilt. Indeed, in our examination of Canadian cases prosecuting bestial acts, there is an overabundance of bestial acts implicated in cases of child sexual abuse, sexual abuse, incest, and child pornography. In every case we reviewed but two, bestial acts were used in actions directed at children or vulnerable populations, and almost all cases involved a gendered dynamic of male perpetration.[2] Although some cases we reviewed involved penetration, which would have triggered section 160 prosecution prior to the 2019 legislative amendments, roughly half did not, indicating that courts took other creative approaches to prosecution. Often the acts of bestiality were barely dealt with by courts and raised as aggravating factors in sentencing for other offences, and often times the courts spent as little time as possible discussing bestial conduct (see the case list at the end of the Chapter for some examples).

Canada has a number of provincial and civil animal protection pieces of legislation, and although many of them speak to animal protection from suffering or harm, none delineate specifically bestial harms. A common formula is seen in Alberta's *Animal Protection Act* (RSA 2000, c A-41). The legislation targets animal cruelty generally, making no specific mention of bestiality. The legislation could apply to a bestiality situation in theory, but we do not see any reported cases in practice. Section 1(2) of the *Act* sets out when an animal is "in distress":

(2) For the purposes of this Act, an animal is in distress if it is
   a) deprived of adequate shelter, ventilation, space, food, water or veterinary care or reasonable protection from injurious heat or cold,
   b) injured, sick, in pain or suffering, or
   c) abused or subjected to undue hardship, privation or neglect.

The subsequent section then creates a prohibition on causing distress or permitting an animal to be in distress:

2(1) No person shall cause or permit an animal of which the person is the owner or the person in charge to be or to continue to be in distress.

(1.1) No person shall cause an animal to be in distress.

The phrases "abused" and "subjected to undue hardship, privation or neglect" are not defined in the Act, although it seems possible that a case could be made that engaging in an act of bestiality with an animal could fit this definition. Yet how can one prove that any or all bestial acts cause these effects? Perhaps some acts would, whereas others would not. If pain or suffering could be demonstrated on the part of the animal as a result of a bestial act, then that conduct may be covered by this legislation. Distress-based animal protection legislation is the norm in provinces and territories, including Newfoundland and Labrador, Nova Scotia, Nunavut, Ontario, Prince Edward Island, Quebec, Saskatchewan, Northwest Territories, and the Yukon.

Some provinces seem to provide somewhat wider protections than is the norm. Quebec's Animal Welfare and Safety Act, CQLR c B-3.1 establishes legal duties owed by animal owners and custodians. For example, section 5 provides the following: "5. The owner or custodian of an animal must ensure that the animal's welfare and safety are not compromised. An animal's welfare or safety is presumed to be compromised if the animal does not receive care that is consistent with its biological needs."

This section includes several examples of conduct that would constitute a violation of the duty set out, including abuse. What makes this duty so much more expansive than duties found in other legislation is the definition of "biological needs," on which the duty relies. This definition can be found in section 1(5):

(5) "biological needs" means the basic physical, physiological and behavioural needs related to such factors as the animal's species, race, age, stage of growth, size, level of physical or physiological activity, sociability with humans and other animals, cognitive abilities and state of health and those related to the animal's capacity to adapt to the cold or heat or to bad weather

Based on this definition, establishing that an act of bestiality would violate the above duties seems plausible.

Additionally, persons are not permitted to cause an animal to be in distress under section 6, which defines an animal as being in "distress" if:

1) it is subjected to conditions that, unless immediately alleviated, will cause the animal death or serious harm;
2) it is subjected to conditions that cause the animal to suffer acute pain; or
3) it is exposed to conditions that cause the animal extreme anxiety or suffering.

Contravention of either of these sections is made an offence under section 68, which stipulates punishment of a fine of between $2500 and $62,500. In the case of subsequent offences, section 70 stipulates a doubling of the minimum and maximums for second offences and a tripling of said values for offences thereafter. Section 70 also allows for the possibility of terms of imprisonment on subsequent offences of between six and twelve months.

The development of a duty-based approach according to the biological needs of the animal represents an interesting halfway house between the "animals as property" approach to bestiality versus the recognition of animals as sentient creatures. The Liberal government successfully achieved its interest in creating more fulsome protections for animals with Bill C-84, which successfully closed Canada's bestiality loop¬hole of requiring penetration for conviction. The change defines bestiality as "any contact by a person, for a sexual purpose, with an animal" (Bill C-84).

This reasonable amendment is now in force in the *Criminal Code*. In the coming sections of this chapter, we provide a more fulsome critique of the decision in *DLW* before concluding the chapter with critical and animal-centric approaches to bestiality law.

Critical Perspectives on Canadian Bestiality Law[3]

A central question that may plague the reader is as follows: Why would a court not use the *Labaye* harm test from obscenity and indecency law as the arbiter of harm for a bestiality offence instead of the penetration requirement? After all, the *Labaye* harm test was a court-generated test for elements of the indecency and obscenity offence that was developed by the court in order to give meaning to the term indecency in the case. If a court can essentially draft a harm test for one Victorian crime (indecency), why can it not do the same for another one (i.e., bestiality)?

As we have seen in previous chapters, the development of indecency and obscenity law in Canada leads to several observations about the SCC's approach to a moral law rooted in Victorian sensibilities. First, the court is sensitive to identity politics concerns as illustrated by the types of harm articulated (i.e., the *Labaye* harms originated at least partly in response to harms to equality articulated in other *Charter* era cases). Second, the court, while purporting to require more stringent proof from the Crown, allows that risky behaviours may require less proof. Thus, the court is animated by a precautionary logic that loosens evidentiary thresholds in more threatening scenarios. Third, this precautionary logic aligns with a late modern anxiety, which views society as facing threat and in need of protection. Fourth, this precautionary logic is produced in the name of what is required to best serve the proper functioning of society. The proper functioning of society is something that courts have been guarding since the early moral corruptibility approach, and, thus, it is interesting to observe that despite the differing social eras, the judiciary in both cases is interested in ensuring that society functions properly. This functionalist account of the social world—together with the risk-based logics that emerged in late modernity—allows for the creation of the harm test, which serves both of these rationales. In effect, filling the legislative lacunae would be to apply a harms-based test, such as the one the court developed in Labaye.

In Labaye the majority noted that obscenity and indecency provisions could be made out when the nature of harms is identified and when the quantum of harm is significant enough to be incompatible with society's proper functioning. This approach identified prospective types of harms as actual physical or psychological harms to persons involved in indecency or obscenity as well as affronts to liberty and harms to society through a predisposition to antisocial conduct. In effect, only when these harms were so severe that they interfered with the proper functioning of society would the sanction of criminality be established.

However, a harm-based approach based on obscenity and indecency principles faces some real legal limits, and it is easy to see why the majority of the SCC in DLW would not have been interested in using a similar analytical approach in the context of bestiality law. The harms-based test in Labaye was developed as the court tried to interpret the meaning of the community standards test that was the long-time arbiter of criminality in obscenity and indecency law. This opaque test required judicial clarification, as the courts tried to give the judicial analysis contour and boundaries.

In contrast, the bestiality prohibitions do not have a long-term judicial history of being queried using such parameters. As the judicial history of DLW makes clear, few cases have struggled with the meaning of bestiality, and most of the nonpenetrative convictions have occurred in the context of plea agreements. Thus, the use of the Labaye calculus as a measure of bestiality seems tortured, given the different interpretive histories of indecency, obscenity, and bestiality. Moreover, the harms articulated by the Labaye Court only contemplate harms to humans, harms of which are reflected in the constitutional order of

Canada: protections of human liberty, equality, dignity, and security of the person. Without formal constitutional or otherwise legislated recognition for the sentience of animals, understanding similar harms for animals would be a major philosophical leap for a court (Gacek and Jochelson, "Animal" 355).

Nevertheless, there still exists a means of linking the *Labaye* harm-based style of reasoning to the interpretation of bestiality prohibitions. Without a definition of bestiality in the *Criminal Code* in 2016, it could have been open to the SCC to consider that bestiality refers to sexual harms against an animal. Such a definition would link with the moral history of the prohibition. If obscenity and indecency originated in Victorian morality and its prevention of corruption of morals—and it is now interpreted as a prohibition of harms that interfere with the proper functioning of society—would it not be appropriate to make similar claims about bestiality? Prohibitions on bestiality originated in Judeo-Christian, early-modern prohibitions against immoral or unnatural sex and persisted through the Victorian era; depictions of sexual activities that would corrupt the lower classes, particularly men, and children were prohibited.

Could it be that the current bestiality prohibitions are similarly aimed at sexual conduct with animals that interferes with the proper functioning of human society? The SCC has already argued that disrupting the proper functioning of society is the same as disturbing the political fundamentals underscoring the Canadian democratic system. Sexual conduct with animals would trouble Canadian political values—such as interfering with vulnerable populations, obtaining fulfillment with a being that may not be able to consent, and causing profound harms for vulnerable human and nonhuman victims. In order to make such an argument work, it would certainly require that a fundamental value of Canadian society be the prevention of animal suffering and the support of animal agency. These underlying values would be difficult for any level of court to assert, as the commodification of animals is directly linked to the Canadian economy and the food and agricultural industry. The argument would also require that the *Labaye* test be directly imported into the bestiality prohibitions, and given that the former relates to performance and expression-based offences and that the latter relates to an offence directly against an animal, the importation would be difficult for a court to accept. It is unsurprising that no member of the SCC elected to rely on obscenity and indecency law for guidance.

Using either a harm-based discourse, such as the law of obscenity and indecency, or developing a reasonable person standard for the assessment of sexual touching of animals (as the SCC did in *R v Chase*, as discussed above) would have been an opening salvo towards the social construction of animals-as-sentient beings and deserving of legal entitlements. Although the *DLW* case itself may have done little to create vast protections for animals, the decision could have been a progressive step. This kind of incrementalism could then have contributed to societal conceptions of animal rights and entitlements that may pave the way for more sweeping legislative reforms in the future. The addition of a more expansive bestiality definition to the *Code* in 2019, has helped to support this incrementalism, but only modestly. There is little in the amendments to foster a message of legal protections for animals as sentient beings.

Gender and Racism

There are other considerations that Canada's courts have failed to address respecting its bestiality provisions. Specifically, recognizing the interplay of gender and racism with prohibitions on bestiality may help to highlight how an expansionist view of the bestiality provisions would, in fact, be justified. The court in *DLW* failed to ask fundamental questions of how the creation of Western human subjectivity is interrelated with societal and legal conceptions of bestiality. Bestiality and the law have an often neglected history that is racialized and gendered.

The human exceptionalism undergirding much of the panic about bestiality is tied up with white exceptionalism (Boggs, *Animalia*). Human exceptionalism is the idea that each human being is fundamentally different from animals, and this notion has played an important role in the creation of human rights and modern Western subjectivity (Boggs, "American" 99). Animality has often been positioned in opposition to civilized humanity in the civilizing process (Traïni). Indeed, by criminalizing the crossing of the species barrier epitomized in bestiality, the law attempts to establish ontological categories and help to create human subjectivity—a process that is intimately tied up with heteropatriarchy and racism (Boggs, "American" 101-2). In short, "human subjectivity emerges via the criminalization of bestiality"

(102). Colleen Boggs posits the following:

> Human exceptionalism does not protect human beings from abjection, but it enables abuse by creating animality as a position of nonsubjectivity and of socially sanctioned abjection. Abjection takes on many forms, but one thing "interlocking oppressions" such as racism, sexism, and homophobia have in common is that their mechanisms of shame and violence revolve around literal and figurative animals. (Boggs, "American" 99)

The history of racism embedded in prohibitions against bestiality extends into the animal rights movement; the first nationalistic animal rights movements in the twentieth century perceived foreigners as a threat to animal rights and attributed bestiality to foreigners; such practices were viewed with disgust and animal rights movements evoked narratives of pride in the gentle treatment of animals by white people (Traïni 62).

According to Boggs, "images of bestiality and practices of bestialization lie at the crux of colonial violence and legal formation" (Boggs, Animalia 80). It is disturbing and illuminating to note that in early Christianity, sex with a Jew, Turk, or Muslim was considered a form of bestiality (Beirne 102; Boes 29). In early modern Germany, churches featured carvings of hideous Jews engaged in sexual acts with pigs, and a Catholic was burned for being in relationship with a Jew because "coitus with a Jewess is exactly the same as if a man were to copulate with a dog" (qtd. in Ben-Atar and Brown 17). Throughout many periods in history, bestiality was used as a label to discredit and "other" groups of people (Traïni 61; Ben-Atar and Brown 25). Widespread rumours of bestiality among North America's Indigenous peoples also existed during early periods of colonization (Ben-Atar and Brown).

Some of the dominant narratives of slavery in the United States positioned non-European races as similar to animals, and polygenesists spouted theories that Black people were a separate species from white men, with a degree of animality that whites lacked (Boggs, Animalia 85). Slaves' bodies, particularly those of Black women, were hypersexualized, and efforts were made to animalize women's bodies through the use of analogies between slave owning and animal husbandry, which allowed for the denial of women's subjectivity and wide spread sexual abuse (85). Indeed, sexual relations between white masters and

Black female slaves were often either labelled as a bestial act or portrayed as animalistic (Ben-Atar and Brown 31). The word "mulatto," used to describe biracial peoples, originated from the Spanish word for young mule, suggesting that sexual contact between people of African and European descent was similar to cross-species intercourse between horses and donkeys (31).

Although some of these more explicit forms of animalization have faded into the background, people of colour continue to be dehumanized in popular culture and in law, often with subcurrents implying animality and human-animal sexual unions (Hund and Mills; Feagin 104, 114). This animalization has supported stereotypes of Black men as criminals, as researchers have found that the "visual and verbal dehumanization of black Americans as apelike assists in the process by which some human groups become targets of societal 'cruelty, social degradation, and state-sanctioned violence'" (Feagin 105). Hortense Spiller contends that slavery and its legacy helped to construct Black women as "an animalistic other, 'the principal point of passage between the human and non-human world,'" and Amber Jamilla Musser contends that this animalization of black women continues to this day.

Not only have women been animalized by labelling their biracial sexual encounters as bestial, but women have also been controlled by men who have used animals as a tool of patriarchal domination and shaming through rape and assault (Adams, "Woman-Battering"; Adams, *Sexual*); for example, Nazi physicians forced Jewish and Polish women to have sex with animals in an attempt to create human-animal hybrids for the purpose of labour, and dogs have been used to rape women held as political prisoners (Miletski 8; Adams, "Woman-Battering" 68). This animalization of women, particularly racialized women—and the correlating feminization of animals involved in bestial acts (Adams, "Woman-Battering" 80)—highlights the profound intersections of gender and race with Western understandings of bestiality and the need to reconsider how the common duality posited between animal and human may reify racist and sexist undercurrents.

Thinking about the harms of bestiality exclusively through a penetrative lens seems especially absurd in light of this gendered, racialized history of bestiality discourses. Needless to say, the racialized history of bestial depictions was the furthest thought from the court's analysis in its *DLW* decision.

Animal Husbandry and Modern Farming

Modern bestiality law is subject to other critiques of hypocrisy. Some authors have pointed out that inherent in antibestiality laws is a profound contradiction given the other ways in which Western society condones the sexual abuse and misuse of animals. Katy Rudy notes the following:

> The act of sex with animals is so prohibited in contemporary American culture that it is often difficult to speak of such things in public. This is interesting. Humans can kill animals, force them to breed with each other, eat them, surround them, train them, hunt them, nail them down and cut them open for science, and for the most part, the humans who perform those acts can be thought of as normal, functioning members of society. Yet having sex with animals remains an almost unspeakable anathema. (Rudy 601)

Rosenberg similarly problematizes the way in which society categorizes meat agriculture and bestiality as separate phenomenon (497-98). Artificial insemination in meat production and forcible mating between animals is categorized as licit sexual contact, whereas other types of human-animal sex is categorized as illicit. Arguably, "the capital-intensification of meat agriculture has produced a range of contacts between humans and animals indistinguishable from legal definitions of sexual contact" (474). Rosenberg contends that there has been a type of revival of the logic of antisodomy laws, which are focused on prohibiting sexual contact that is not procreative. "The bestial interdiction with an agricultural exemption makes allowances for a kind of procreative sexual contact, but one that no longer conceives of procreation as confined rigidly by the boundaries of species" (488). Likewise, Brown and Rasmussen suggest that the prohibitions against sex with animals are premised on the long-standing interdictions against sex for pleasure or nonprocreative purposes. However, "purposes such as commercial gain, aesthetics, or science are acceptable justifications for sexual contact with animals. Human pleasure makes the actions illegitimate" (Brown and Rasmussen 168).

Of the twenty-one American states since 1990 that have recriminalized human-animal sex, eighteen have incorporated animal husbandry and veterinary medicine exemptions (Rosenberg 486). The way in which the boundary between illicit bestiality and licit artificial insemination and animal husbandry is an illusion argues Rosenberg:

> Agricultural exemptions to bestiality laws demonstrate that the decisive difference between a bestialist and a farmer is about a difference in *relation to capital*, not in *relation to animals*. We see this difference in the juridical articulation of what constitutes licensed sexual acts for humans: the conditions under which bodies may be licensed to entwine. It is a biopolitical difference, and it directs the destiny of some animals toward companionship and others toward meat, just as it produces both farmers and sex offenders. (Rosenberg 475)

Although the *DLW* case, and especially the dissent, engages in some discussions about the rights of animals, clearly the court did not delve deeply into the critical literature dealing with animal rights and bestial offences. Critiques are levied that laws on human-animal sex often fail to recognize the subjectivity of animals. Within the study of law, animals are largely conceived of as property (Beirne 5). This failure to recognize a sort of subjectivity of animals beyond unfeeling chattels is evident in the SCC's decision in *R v DLW* in which the majority fails to recognize the harms inflicted upon animals in agricultural and bestiality contexts and "rigidly categorize animals as effectively inanimate and non-sentient.... Animals under this approach continue to be unfeeling chattels, and the sexual violation of animals is only relevant when it crystalizes harm or moral corruptibility to humans involved or conscripted" (Gacek and Jochelson, "Placing" 255). Animals within this conception are mere items to be regulated (255). Indeed, on a local and historical level, bestiality was not only conceived of in moral terms but often as a crime against property. Rydström argues that it was because animals were considered worthless and defiled property after bestial acts that they were put to death (Rydström, *Sinners* 78). In contrast, Boggs argues that the merger of bestiality with same-sex sexuality in law changed the way in which people conceived of animals in bestial acts; instead of conceiving of animals as irrelevant objects of property, they became an important participant in the act, and, therefore, killing an animal involved in a bestial act was an attempt to erase the memory of the act (Boggs, *Animalia* 51).

So while historically animals were put to death following bestial acts—whether because they were seen as worthless property or co-conspirators—the animal rights movement recast the narrative; instead of occupying the position of co-conspirator, animals were cast as victims, sexless, penetrated, and devoid of desire (Rosenberg 482). Animal rights advocates have called for laws to protect animals from bestiality, not because of the harms to humans or property that may result but rather for the sake of the animals themselves. Within an animal rights conception, a diverse range of human-animal sexual contact is fit into one particular narrative in which human-animal sex is always exploitative and if not contained forms a "vortex of perverse and violent behavior" (Rosenberg 483; see also Rudy 607). Unintentionally, this blanket conception of animals as always lacking agency or desire may reify the understanding of animals as without subjectivity. Rosenberg suggests that we should be careful in accepting discourses of animal sexual abuse that contest that the law now recognizes "an enlightened sensibility about animals," (491) particularly since the meat agriculture industry is still condoned. As Rosenberg notes, "[the] common story is that the animal has moved from premodern role as conspirator to its current position as a vulnerable victim of sexual abuse –but within this are two ideas-uncovering innocent animal nature and law as protective of animals- but neither of these live up to these ideals" (491).

The failure of the law to consider the complexities of animal subjectivity is, no doubt, in part due to the pervasive silence surrounding bestiality. Collective disgust with bestiality is so profound that it has by and large "invited hurried bewilderment rather than sustained intellectual inquiry" (Beirne 113). Delaney notes that within the law, it was demanded that the wrongful act of bestiality be named by way of silence for describing the act in law "runs the risk of defiling law itself" (260). This has also been described as the "politics of silence," whereby legislators seek to avoid spreading knowledge of such things by failing to mention them in the law (Rydström, *Sinners* 2). Within the recriminalization of bestiality in the United States during the 2000s, Rosenberg notes that bestiality was so taboo that legislators did not always want their names associated with legislation (483). The silence surrounding bestiality was clearly evident in the SCC's deliberations in *R v DLW*, in which the majority of the court continually commented on the absence of an explicit definition of bestiality within the *Criminal*

Code. However, it would be misleading to assume that such pervasive silence somehow demonstrates a static or neutral conception of bestiality.

As discussed, bestiality as a concept is intimately connected with racism, patriarchy, and heterosexism. Thus, although silence is a common theme around bestial discourses, curiously, within debates about same-sex marriage in the United States and Canada, "the menace of bestial desire" was widely spoken about, with opponents of same-sex marriage implying a link between an approval of same-sex marriage and bestiality (Rosenberg 483-484; Corvino 501; Warner 49; 204). This is an example of how bestiality as a concept operates in order to set the parameters on human subjectivity and intelligibility. As Rosenberg notes, "the bestialist occupies the structural position of the abject and inassimilable that Lee Edelman (2004) designates as queer: a sexual contact that swears off any hope of reproduction" (489). Finally, Canadian Parliament in 2019 defined bestiality as "any contact, for a sexual purpose, with an animal" in section 160(7). This clearly signaled Parliament's intention as to the breadth of bestiality offences. It does not however solve larger problems of animal mistreatment in Canada, nor does it provide clarity in respect of how legal regimes in Canada will deal with emerging understandings of animal sentience in future cases.

Conclusion

In this chapter, we sought to complicate understandings of bestiality law in the Canadian context. The SCC's decision in *DLW* left Canada's bestiality law to wither in its vestigial form as a penetrative act and as prohibited in a comparable manner to laws of the same era that criminalized gay male sex. Ultimately, in June 2019, Parliament finally acted decisively to make clear bestiality was more than a coital offence. The evolution of bestiality law in Canada is unique in that it managed to stay on the books even as prohibitions against same-sex relationships began to be repealed through cultural and legal shifts. We explored the current legal regime in Canada and saw that the reported cases support the social science-based observations that bestiality is implicated in crimes against the vulnerable, mainly children, in child pornography, as essentially aggravating of a panoply of sexually abusive behaviours. We also reviewed the rarer reported cases dealing with isolated bestial incidents. These decisions—alongside the use of critical race, gender, and animal rights frames—demonstrate a certain naiveté by Canada's high court in its insistence that penetration must be part of the offence. At best, the entire regime of harms to animals should be rethought to include the consideration of the reasonable sexual inviolability of other species in respect of humans. At the least, in *DLW*, the regime should not have been interpreted so restrictively so as to forgive nonpenetrative human-animal sex that still does real harm to victims, child observers, and the animal and that reconstituted a patriarchal, homophobic, and racialized history of oppression. Thankfully, Canadian Parliament must have considered at least some of these conceptions in its modest amendments to bestiality law in 2019.

Endnotes

1. Other terms used to describe various types of human-animal sexual encounters include zoosexualist which sometimes is used synonymously with zoophile or may designate people who engage in human-animal role play (Stern and Smith-Blackmore 1058; Aggrawal). Other terms used to refer to human-animal sex include zooerastry, zoosadism, necrozoophile, or necrobestialist (Stern and Smith-Blackmore 1058; Aggrawal).
2. Searches on CanLII, Lexis Advanced, and Westlaw were undertaken for the terms "160", "160(1)," "160(2)," "160(3)," "160(4)," "bestiality," as well as a note up exercise for each section.
3. Contains excerpts from Gacek and Jochelson, "Animal" 354-58.

Works Cited
Secondary Sources

Adams, Carol. *The Sexual Politics of Meat: A Feminist-Vegetarian Critical Theory*. 20th edition. Continuum International Publishing Group, 2010.

Adams, Carol. "Woman-Battering and Harm to Animals." *Animals & Women: Feminist Theoretical Explorations*, edited by Carol Adams and Josephine Donovan, Duke University Press, 3rd edition, 2006, pp. 55-84.

Aggrawal, Anil. *Medico-legal Aspects of Sexual Crimes and Unusual Sexual Practices*. CRC Press, 2009.

Animal Justice. *Factum of the Intervenor, Animal Justice in the Supreme Court of Canada: R v DLW,* 2016, SCC 22, www.scc-csc.ca/WebDocuments-DocumentsWeb/36450/FM030_Intervener_Animal-Justice.pdf>. Accessed 3 Aug. 2018.

Beetz, Andrea. "Bestiality and Zoophilia: Association with Violence and Sex Offending." *Bestiality and Zoophilia: Sexual Relations with Animals,* edited by Andrea Beetz and Anthony Podberscek, Berg, 2009, pp. 46-70.

Beetz, Andrea. "New Insights into Bestiality and Zoophilia." *Bestiality and Zoophilia: Sexual Relations with Animals,* edited by Andrea Beetz and Anthony Podberscek, Berg, 2009, pp. 98-119.

Beirne, Piers. *Confronting Animal Abuse: Law, Criminology and Human-Animal Relationships.* Rowman & Littlefield Publishers, 2009.

Ben-Atar, Doron S., and Richard D. Brown. *Taming Lust: Crimes against Nature in the Early Republic.* University of Pennsylvania Press, 2014.

Bill C-84 Hansard, An Act to amend the Criminal Code (Bestiality and Animal Gighting) House of Commons Debates, 42nd Parliament 1st Session, volume 148, issue 344 (29 October 2018) (Jody Wilson-Raybould), www.ourcommons.ca/DocumentViewer/en/42-1/house/sitting-344/hansard. Accessed 3 Aug. 2018.

Binter, J., et al. "Prevalence of Zoophilia in Czech Sado-Masochistic Community." *The Journal of Sexual Medicine,* 2015, vol. 12, no. S1, presented at the 16th World Meeting on Sexual Medicine, São Paulo, Brazil (2014), doi: doi-org.uml.idm.oclc.org/10.1111/jsm.1282.

Boes, Maria R. "On Trial in Early Modern Germany." *Sodomy in Early Modern Europe,* edited by Tom Betteridge, Manchester University Press, 2002, pp. 27-45.

Boggs, Colleen. *Animalia Americana: Animal Representations and Biopolitical Subjectivity.* Columbia University Press, 2013.

Boggs, Colleen. "American Bestiality: Sex, Animals, and the Costruction of Subjectivity." *Cultural Critique,* vol. 76, 2010, pp. 98-125.

Brown, Michael, and Claire Rasmussen. "Bestiality and the Queering of the Human Animal." *Environment and Planning D: Society and Space*, vol. 28, 2010, pp. 158-77.

Canada, Department of Justice. "Bill C-32: An Act Related to the Repeal of Section 159 of the *Criminal Code*." 2016, www.justice.gc.ca/eng/csj-sjc/pl/charter-charte/cs_s159-ec_s159.html. Accessed 2 Aug. 2018.

Canada, Department of Justice."Charter Statement- Bill C-75: An Act to Amend the *Criminal Code*, Youth Criminal Justice Act and other Acts and to Make Consequential Amendments to Other Acts." Tabled in the House of Commons, 29 Mar. 2018, 2018, www.justice.gc.ca/eng/csj-sjc/pl/charter-charte/c75.html. Accessed 2 Aug. 2018.

Canada, Department of Justice. "Section 159 of the *Criminal Code* (Anal Intercourse)." 2016, www.justice.gc.ca/eng/csj-sjc/pl/s159/index.html. Accessed 2 August 2018.

Chandradasa, Miyuru, Layani Champika. "Zoophilia in an Adolescent with High-Functioning Autism from Sri Lanka." *Australasian Psychiatry*, vol. 25, no. 5, 2017, pp. 486-88.

Chenier, Elise. *Strangers in Our Midst: Sexual Deviancy in Postwar Ontario*. University of Toronto Press, 2008.

Chenier, Elise. "The Criminal Sexual Psychopath in Canada: Sex, Psychiatry and the Law at Mid-Century." *Canadian Bulletin of Medical History*, vol. 20, no. 1, 2003, pp. 75-101.

Corvino, John. "Homosexuality and the PIB Argument." *Ethics*, vol. 115, no. 3, 2005, pp. 501-34.

Davidson, N.S. "Sodomy in Early Modern Venice." *Sodomy in Early Modern Europe*, edited by Tom Betteridge, Manchester University Press, 2002, pp. 65-81.

Delaney, David. *Law and Nature*. Cambridge University Press, 2003.

Doniger, Wendy. "The Mythology of Masquerading Animals, or Bestiality." *Social Research*, vol. 71, no. 3, 2004, pp. 711-32.

Feagin, Joe. *The White Racial Frame: Centuries of Racial Framing and Counter-Framing*. Routledge, 2013.

Gacek, James, Richard Jochelson. "'Animal Justice' and Sexual (Ab)use: Consideration of Legal Recognition of Sentience for Animals in Canada." *Manitoba Law Journal*, vol. 40, no. 3, 2017, pp. 335-62.

Gacek, James, and Richard Jochelson. "Placing 'Bestial' Acts in Canada: Legal Meanings of "Bestiality" and Judicial Engagements with Sociality." *The Annual Review of Interdisciplinary Justice Research*, vol. 6, 2017, pp. 236-61.

Hensley, Christopher, et al. "Exploring the Possible Link Between Childhood and Adolescent Bestiality and Interpersonal Violence." *Journal of Interpersonal Violence*, vol. 21, no. 7, 2006, pp. 910-23.

Hooper, Thomas. "'More Than Two Is a Crowd': Mononormativity and Gross Indecency in the *Criminal Code*, 1981-82." *Journal of Canadian Studies*, vol. 48, 2014, pp. 53-81.

Holoyda, Brian. "Bestiality in Forensically Committed Sexual Offenders: A Case Series." *Journal of Forensic Sciences*, vol. 62, no. 2, 2016, pp. 541-44.

Holoyda, Brian, and William Newman. "Childhood Animal Cruelty, Bestiality, and the Link to Adult Interpersonal Violence." *International Journal of Law and Psychiatry*, vol. 47, 2016, pp. 129-35.

Hund, Wulf, and Charles Mills. "For Centuries the West Has Found It Useful to Compare Black People to Monkeys." *Quartzy*, 14 Jan. 2018, qz.com/quartzy/1179366/hm-monkey-hoodie-why-have-black-people-been-compared-to-monkeys-by-racists/ Accessed 3 Aug. 2018.

Ingram, Gordon Brent. "Returning to the Scene of the Crime: Uses of Trial Dossiers on Consensual Male Homosexuality for Urban Research, with Examples from Twentieth-Century British Columbia." *GLQ: A Journal of Lesbian and Gay Studies*, vol. 10, no. 1, 2003, pp. 77-110.

Johnson, Colin. *Just Queer Folks: Gender and Sexuality in Rural America*. Temple University Press, 2013.

Kinsman, Gary, and Patrizia Gentile. *The Canadian War on Queers: National Security as Sexual Regulation*. UBC Press, 2010.

Klein, Carolina A. "Digital and Divergent: Sexual Behaviors on the Internet." *Journal of the American Academy of Psychiatry and the Law Online*, vol. 42, no. 4, 2014, pp. 495-503.

Lamble, Sarah. "Unknowable Bodies, Unthinkable Sexualities: Lesbian and Transgender Legal Invisibility in the Toronto Women's Bathhouse Raid." *Social & Legal Studies*, vol. 18, no. 1, 2009, pp. 111-30, doi: doi-org.uml.idm.oclc.org/10.1177/0964663908100336.

Lesandric, Vinka, et al. "Zoophilia as an Early Sign of Psychosis." *Alcoholism and Psychiatry Research*, vol. 53, 2017, pp. 27-32, doi: 10.20471/apr.2017.53.01.03.

Levitt, Lacey. "Criminal Histories of a Subsample of Animals Cruelty Offenders." *Aggression and Violent Behavior*, vol. 30, 2016, pp. 48-58.

Maratea, R. J. "Screwing the Pooch: Legitimizing Accounts in a Zoophilia On-line Community." *Deviant Behavior*, vol. 32, no. 10, 2011, pp. 918-43, doi: 10.1080/01639625.2010.538356.

Maxwell-Stuart, P.G. "'Wild, Filthie, Execrabill, Detestabill and Unnatural Sin': Bestiality in Early Modern Scotland." *Sodomy in Early Modern Europe*, edited by Tom Betteridge, Manchester University Press, 2002, pp. 82-93.

Miletski, Hani. "A History of Bestiality." *Bestiality and Zoophilia: Sexual Relations with Animals*, edited by Andrea Beetz and Anthony Podberscek, Berg, 2009, pp. 1-22.

Murrin, John M. "'Things Fearful to Name': Bestiality in Colonial America." *Pennsylvania History: A Journal of Mid-Atlantic Studies*, vol. 65, 1998, pp. 8-43.

Musser, Amber Jamilla. "Queering Sugar: Kara Walker's Sugar Sphinx and the Intractability of Black Female Sexuality." *Signs: Journal of Women in Culture and Society*, vol. 42, no. 1, 2016, pp. 153-74.

Nature Reviews Urology. "Penile cancer: Association Between Penile Cancer and Zoophilia." *Nature Reviews Urology*, vol. 8, 2011, pp. 650.

Pierceson, Jason. *Courts, Liberalism, and Rights: Gay Law and Politics in the United States and Canada*. Temple University Press, 2005.

Raina, Gabriela, et al. "Zoophilia and Impulse Control Disorder in a Patient with Parkinson Disease." *Journal of Neurology*, vol. 259, no. 5, 2012, pp. 969-70.

Rosenberg, Gabriel. "How Meat Changed Sex: The Law of Interspecies Intimacy after Industrial Reproduction." *GLQ: A Journal of Lesbian and Gay Studies*, vol. 23, no. 4, 2017, pp. 473-507.

Rudy, Kathy. "LGBTQ...Z?" *Hypatia*, vol. 27, no. 3, 2012, pp. 601-15.

Rydström, Jens. "From Sodomy to Homosexuality: Rural Sex and the Inclusion of Lesbians in Criminal Discourse." *NORA- Nordic Journal of Feminist and Gender Research*, vol. 13, no. 1, 2005, pp. 20-35.

Rydström, Jens. *Sinners and Citizens: Bestiality and Homosexuality in Sweden, 1880-1950.* University of Chicago Press, 2003.

Rydström, Jens. "'Sodomitical Sins Are Threefold': Typologies of Bestiality, Masturbation, and Homosexuality in Sweden, 1880-1950." *Journal of the History of Sexuality*, vol. 9, no. 3, 2000, pp. 240-76.

Sandnabba, N. Kenneth, et al. "Demographics, Sexual Behaviour, Family Background and Abuse Experiences of Practitioners of Sadomasochistic Sex: A Review of Recent Research." *Sexual and Relationship Therapy*, vol. 17, no. 1, 2002, pp. 39-55, doi: 10.1080/14681990220108018.

Senjo, Scott. *Sexual Deviance and the Law: Legal Regulation of Human Sexuality.* Kendall Hunt Publishing Company, 2011.

Singg, Sangeeta. "Health Risks of Zoophilia/Bestiality." *Journal of Biological and Medical Sciences*, vol. 1, no. 1, 2017.

Stern, AW and M Smith-Blackmore. "Veterinary Forensic Pathology of Animal Sexual Abuse." *Veterinary Pathology*, vol. 53, no. 5, 2016, pp. 1057-66.

Traïni, Christophe. *The Animal Rights Struggle: An Essay in Historical Sociology.* Amsterdam University Press, 2016.

Warner, Tom. *Never Going Back: A History of Queer Activism in Canada.* University of Toronto Press, 2002.

Young, Alan. "The State is Still in the Bedrooms of the Nation: The Control and Regulation of Sexuality in Canadian Criminal Law." *The Canadian Journal of Human Sexuality*, vol. 17, no. 4, 2008, pp. 203-20.

Jurisprudence

CDS v HSS, [2010] B.C.J. No. 310, 2010 BCSC 236, 82 R.F.L. (6th) 333, 2010 CarswellBC 388, 186 A.C.W.S. (3d) 448.

Directeur des poursuites criminelles et pénales c Fortier, 2016 QCCQ 12046 (CanLII).

HMTQ v Gibbon, 2005 BCSC 935 (CanLII), canlii.ca/t/1ps4n, Accessed 3 Aug. 2018.

R c Champagne, [2013] J.Q. no 10333, 2013 QCCQ 9221, 2013EXP-3325.

R c MAGI, 2002 CanLII 45200 (QC CQ), http://canlii.ca/t/1c0kf. Accessed 3 Aug. 2018.

R v AB, 2007 SKPC 46 (CanLII), canlii.ca/t/1rrf3. Accessed 3 Aug. 2018.

R v Alton, 2007 CanLII 54082 (ON SC), canlii.ca/t/1v5d4. Accessed 3 Aug. 2018.

R v CDB, 2003 CanLII 46666 (MB PC), canlii.ca/t/1bv0s. Accessed 3 Aug. 2018.

R v DeJaeger, 2014 NUCJ 21 (CanLII), canlii.ca/t/g8zh5. Accessed 3 Aug. 2018.

R v DLW, 2016 SCC 22, [2016] 1 S.C.R. 402.

R v JJBB, 2007 BCPC 426 (CanLII), canlii.ca/t/1vpqz. Accessed 3 Aug. 2018.

R v KDH, 2012 ABQB 471 (CanLII), canlii.ca/t/fs78w. Accessed 3 Aug. 2018.

R v KT, [2016] O.J. No. 2045, 2016 ONCJ 222.

R v LMR, 2010 ABCA 286 (CanLII), canlii.ca/t/2ct05. Accessed 3 Aug. 2018.

R v Lund, 2016 CarswellOnt 21532, 2016 ONCJ 858, 137 W.C.B. (2d) 192.

R v PV, 2016 ONCJ 64 (CanLII), canlii.ca/t/gn7wl. Accessed 3 Aug. 2018.

R v Pye, 2005 BCPC 355 (CanLII), canlii.ca/t/1ljt4. Accessed 3 Aug. 2018.

R v Ruvinsky, [1998] O.J. No. 3621.

R v SW, [2000] O.J. No. 5101.

R v V (J), 2015 CarswellOnt 20862, 2015 ONCJ 815, [2015] O.J. No. 7735, 131 W.C.B. (2d) 429.

R v Wight, 2011 ONCJ 414 (CanLII), canlii.ca/t/fnln8. Accessed 3 Aug. 2018.

X, Re, 2005 CanLII 50699 (QC CQ), canlii.ca/t/1mkg7. Accessed 3 Aug. 2018.

Legislation

Animal Health and Protection Act, SNL 2010, c A-9.1, canlii.ca/t/5205q. Accessed 3 Aug. 2018.

Animal Protection Act, RSA 2000, c A-41, canlii.ca/t/kxct. Accessed 3 Aug. 2018.

Animal Protection Act, SNS 2008, c 33, <canlii.ca/t/52kgv. Accessed 3 Aug. 2018.

Animal Protection Act, RSY 2002, c 6, <canlii.ca/t/525j0/ Accessed 3 Aug. 2018.

Animal Welfare Act, RSPEI 1988, c A-11.2, canlii.ca/t/52x7t. Accessed 3 Aug. 2018.

Animal Welfare and Safety Act, CQLR c B-3.1, <canlii.ca/t/52rq0. Accessed 3 Aug. 2018.

Bill C-388: An Act to amend the Criminal Code (bestiality), 2017, First Reading, 1st Sess, 42nd Parl, 64-65-66 Elizabeth II, 2015-2016-2017.

Bill C-84, An Act to amend the Criminal Code (bestiality and animal fighting), 2018, First Reading, 1st Sess, 42nd Parl, 64-65-66-67 Elizabeth II, 2015-2016-2017-2018.

Dog Act, RSNWT (Nu) 1988, c D-7, canlii.ca/t/12tk. Accessed 3 Aug. 2018.

Dog Act, RSNWT 1988, c D-7, < canlii.ca/t/520dn. Accessed 3 Aug. 2018.

Criminal Code, RSC 1985, c C-46.

Ontario Society for the Prevention of Cruelty to Animals Act, RSO 1990, c O.36, canlii.ca/t/52gg6>, accessed 3 August 2018.

Prevention of Cruelty to Animals Act, RSBC 1996, c 372, <canlii.ca/t/52x45. Accessed 3 Aug. 2018.

Society for the Prevention of Cruelty to Animals Act, RSNB 2014, c 132, canlii.ca/t/533gp. Accessed 3 Aug. 2018.

The Animal Care Act, CCSM c A84, canlii.ca/t/52kvk. Accessed 3 Aug. 2018.

The Animal Protection Act, 1999, SS 1999, c A-21.1, canlii.ca/t/10f3. Accessed 3 Aug. 2018.

Chapter Six

Our Pronouns Are Protected But Not Our Bodies: How Gender-Based Protections Fail Criminalized Trans People

Leon Laidlaw

Introduction

The transgender population is one of the most marginalized groups in Western society, experiencing discrimination in nearly all aspects of social and institutional life. Recognizing the vulnerable status of trans communities, on May 17, 2016, the Trudeau government proposed legal protections for gender diverse Canadians through the introduction of amendments to federal law, Bill C-16, *An Act to Amend the Canadian Human Rights Act and the Criminal Code*. On June 19 of the following year, the bill received royal assent and came into force, resulting in "gender identity" and "gender expression" being officially safeguarded from discrimination in the *Human Rights Act* and the *Criminal Code*.

Although Bill C-16 was intended to further advance gender equality in Canada, it was ultimately a subject of heated debate. Jordan Peterson, professor of psychology at the University of Toronto, was at the heart of such controversy when he uploaded three contentious videos to YouTube. In one of these videos, Peterson stated his opposition to the proposed antidiscrimination legislation, Bill C-16, and speculated the effects that Bill C-16 would have in relation to Canadians' *Charter* right to freedom of expression. In his online lecture, "Professor against Political Correctness: Part 1," Peterson poses his concerns regarding human rights policies surrounding Bill C-16 and conveys his unwavering refusal to use trans individuals' chosen[1] pronouns, such as the gender-neutral pronoun "they." The amendments to law, as Peterson understood them, would enforce compelled speech by mandating that individuals refer to others in their chosen pronoun, thus risking criminalization and even the potential violation of the hate speech provisions of the *Criminal Code.* While advancing such erroneous legal claims, Peterson soon became an emblem of the opposition to trans rights and represented his position before the Senate at the hearings of Bill C-16.

Reflecting on the discourses that have been used in the past to oppose the formalization of trans rights in the law, legal scholar Brenda Cossman ("Gender Identity") noticed a recent shift in dialogue. Although in the past opponents to trans rights largely relied on myths surrounding women's safety in washrooms in attempts to prevent their legitimation in the law—such as the trope of the predatory man dressed as a woman in order to gain access to women's only spaces—Peterson's controversial statements gained publicity revolved around concerns over freedom of expression. Ultimately, those who suggest Bill C-16 could violate our freedom of expression by compelling individuals to adopt chosen pronouns to refer to trans people are not simply misunderstanding the law; they are also attempting to prevent the formalization of gender-based protections in the law (Cossman "Gender Identity"). Claims that Bill C-16 may violate individuals' freedom of expression manifest in a context in which trans rights are positioned as merely an issue of political correctness, thereby undermining the material reality of cisgenderism[2] and the need for gender-based protections. Although opposition to trans legal rights and protections is not new, it is only by further examining the history of transgender activism, which laid the groundwork for the contemporary rights movement, that it becomes evident why the emphasis given to the legal implications of misgendering is particularly harmful.

In this chapter, I suggest that the prominence given to the pronoun debate purposefully detracts from the material reality of oppression that trans communities experiences, such as issues addressed by early trans activists and those that continue to impact the most vulnerable sectors of trans communities today. After debunking the myth that misgendering a trans person can result in criminalization, I seek to refocus the discussion of trans rights to more pressing issues, such as how some of the most vulnerable trans people continue to be unprotected by law and how the state is in fact implicated in the violence that they experience.

I begin this chapter by relaying a brief history of transgender activism and resistance in North America. Here, it becomes evident that trans history is deeply enmeshed with anticriminalization efforts. I then provide an overview of the development of gender-based protections in human rights legislation in Canada. At this point, I analyze the Senate hearings that ultimately determined whether Bill C-16 would in fact pass into law. I highlight how pronoun use in relation to freedom of expression became a prominent issue in the debates, while even among supporters of the bill, the experiences of the most vulnerable sectors of trans communities, namely criminalized populations, remain highly invisibilized. Viewing the debate regarding pronouns and the law as potentially harmful to trans communities, as it has been advanced to reduce trans oppression to the matter of political correctness, I attempt to shift the discussion away from pronouns by demonstrating that misgendering cannot be criminalized under either the *Criminal Code* or human rights legislation. It is here that concerns over freedom of expression must be contextualized in relation to power. Erroneous legal claims, such as those advanced by Jordan Peterson, must be conceptualized as a strategic attempt to delegitimize trans people's lived experiences of oppression and ultimately thwart trans legal rights and protections from being formalized in the law. Although protections for gender diversity ultimately did pass into law, I remain critical of the law's effectiveness in protecting trans communities as a whole. Reflecting on the history of trans activism and the issues plaguing the most marginalized trans people, I explore how Bill C-16 fails to protect trans sex workers and trans prisoners, and I go on to present the ways in which these groups experience additional harm at the hands of the state through criminalization and imprisonment. With respect to the limits of the law and the inability to protect the most vulnerable sectors of trans communities, I conclude that the fight for trans rights is incomplete without the decriminalization of sex work and the work towards prison abolitionism.

Contextualizing the Trans Rights Movement: The History of Trans Activism

Although it is only recently that trans issues have entered mainstream discussions, the contemporary trans rights movement was born out of decades of trans activism that unfolded across North America. Perhaps the most prominent instance of trans activism in North American history was that of Stonewall. Although reflections on the Stonewall riots today have largely framed the protests in the context of gay liberation, the three-night-long riots were, in fact, spearheaded by racialized transfeminine women, such as Sylvia Rivera and Marsha P. Johnson, who were fighting against police oppression at the time in which crossdressing was criminalized (Duberman; Feinberg; Gan; Stryker). Even though it was not uncommon for police to raid gay bars during that time, when police began lining up gender non-normative patrons of Stonewall for identification that summer evening of 1969, patrons of the bar were joined by nearby gender diverse people and street-involved youth to resist the police brutality directed towards the transgender community (Duberman; Feinberg; Gan; Stryker). After the riots, Sylvia Rivera and Marsha P. Johnson went on to dedicate their lives to activism at the intersection of trans rights and sex worker rights. Such activism included the founding of a community organization aimed at helping sex-work-involved youth, STAR (Street Transvestite Action Revolutionary), in 1970, with the little means that they had (Feinberg). In effect, it was the actions of racialized and low-income trans women who laid the groundwork for the trans rights movement of today.

On the one-year anniversary of the Stonewall uprising, the first celebratory march was held in New York City—what we now refer to as "gay pride" (Stanley et al.). Marchers eventually made their way to the Women's House of Detention, where the crowd chanted "Free our sisters! Free ourselves!" and in doing so, it became evident that the lives of queer and trans people were inextricably linked in the fight against the prison industrial complex (Stanley et al. 155). Trans activism in Canada has likewise been deeply enmeshed with a resistance to criminalization—of trans identities and expressions as well as sex work engagement (Clamen et al.; Namaste, *Sex Change*). Indeed, sex work has been integral to the cultural identity of many trans people, and trans women have been central to sex worker activism in Canada, such as establishing the nation's first sex workers' rights march in Vancouver and developing important peer-run social services for sex workers from the 1980s onwards (for example, see Arthur et al.; Cole and Dale; Clamen et al.; Crago and Clamen; Forrester et al.; Laframboise).

Reflecting on her experiences working in an outside brothel in Vancouver during the 1970s and 1980s, trans sex worker and political activist Jamie Lee Hamilton described sex workers as beneficial to neighbourhoods and communities because of their strong political mobilization. Hamilton was an avid member of the Alliance for the Safety of Prostitutes in the early 1980s, and later she established her own drop-in centre for sex workers, called Grandma's House (Arthur et al.). In the late 1990s, in response to the disappearances and murders of sex workers from the Downtown Eastside, Hamilton dumped sixty-seven stiletto shoes on the front steps of City Hall as a symbolic effort to raise consciousness and demand action from the government (Hamilton). Yet when Hamilton opened the doors of Grandma's House to sex workers who needed a safe place to solicit their clients, police organized a sting operation where she was charged with keeping a common bawdy-house, and although charges were eventually dropped, Grandma's House was ultimately closed (Arthur et al.).

Recognizing that "trans advocacy that did not centrally address sex workers' rights would likely do more harm than good," Trish Salah, trans activist and now gender studies professor at Queen's University, worked with her local union, CUPE 3903, during her time as a teaching assistant at York University in order to advocate for trans and sex worker rights (Clamen et al., 115). The local union sent representation and resolutions to CUPE's national convention in 2001, among which, resolution 189 expressed the need for solidarity with trans sex workers and for the decriminalization of sex work (Clamen et al.). Even though resolution 189 was adopted and CUPE finally recognized the need to support marginalized populations who could benefit from unionization, the criminalization of the sex industry ultimately limited the ability to unionize sex workers and CUPE made little efforts to help challenge the laws surrounding sex work (Clamen et al.).

Although what has been presented here is simply a snapshot of trans activism throughout the years, these events demonstrate that trans activism has been deeply enmeshed with anticriminalization efforts. More recently, activism has taken the form of advocating for formal protections, such as hate crime and antidiscrimination laws, which have been sought in attempts to achieve equality and protection for gender diverse Canadians. In the next section, I outline the development of legal protections for gender identity and/or gender expression in human rights legislation in Canada.

Trans Rights in the Law

As of June 2017, all Canadian provinces and territories have enacted antidiscrimination protections in their human rights legislation to safeguard trans rights, whether it be protecting gender identity, gender expression, or both (Canadian AIDS Society). In 2002, the Northwest Territories became the first territory or province to add "gender identity" as a characteristic protected from discrimination in its territorial human rights legislation (Canadian AIDS Society). A decade later, in 2012, Manitoba followed suit by protecting "gender identity" (Canadian AIDS Society). Meanwhile, Ontario and Nova Scotia added protections for both "gender identity" and "gender expression" in 2012. Newfoundland and Labrador and Prince Edward Island added protections in 2013, Saskatchewan in 2014, Alberta in 2015, Quebec and British Columbia in 2016, and Nunavut, the Yukon, and New Brunswick in 2017 (Canadian AIDS Society). All provinces and territories now prohibit gender-based discrimination in some form. Prior to these developments, of course, safeguards for transgender rights have been recognized by various tribunals and arbiters through the laws that prohibited discrimination on the basis of sex and/or disability.[3]

At the federal level, transgender rights had been introduced quite some time ago, albeit unsuccessfully. Proposed legislation can be traced back to 2005, when NDP Member of Parliament Bill Siksay introduced Bill C-392, *An Act to Amend the Canadian Human Rights Act (Gender Identity)*. Siksay reintroduced the proposed amendment to law in 2006 as Bill C-326, and again in 2009 as Bill C-389, when it eventually died in the Senate due to the election call. In 2013, two bills were introduced, the Liberal's Bill C-276 and the NDP's Bill C-279, which again sought to amend the *Human Rights Act* and the *Criminal Code* to add "gender identity" and "gender expression" as characteristics protected from discrimination. Unfortunately, both bills ended in summer of 2015 with the election call. Following these previous failed attempts, Bill C-16 was proposed by the Trudeau government on May 17, 2016; it ultimately passed Senate and receiving royal assent on June 19, 2017, when it immediately came into force.

Despite Bill C-16 successfully passing into law, it was not without controversy. In the next section, I explore the Senate debates regarding Bill C-16 and problematize the attention afforded to the issue of pronoun use in relation to freedom of expression as well as the missed opportunity to present the challenges existing among the trans people who are most vulnerable to discrimination and violence.

The Senate Debates and the Issue of Pronouns

Over the course of three days—May 4, May 10, and May 11 2017—expert testimonies were heard from those with various backgrounds, experiences, and investments in the proposed changes to law. A fundamental concern arising within the Senate debates was the issue of gender pronouns—specifically whether Bill C-16 could be found to violate our *Charter* right to freedom of expression by compelling individuals to adopt chosen pronouns to refer to trans people, such as the gender-neutral pronoun "they." Before the Senate, Jordan Peterson expressed his concern that Bill C-16 will ultimately do more harm than good:

> I would say that the very idea that calling someone a term that they didn't choose causes them such irreparable harm that legal remedies should be sought, rather than regarding it as a form of impoliteness, that legal remedies should be sought, including potential violation of the hate speech codes, is an indication of just how deeply the culture of victimization has sunk into our society. ("Proceedings of the Standing Senate Committee")

Through his sensationalized fear of the hypothetical criminalization for refusing to adopt gender-neutral pronouns, Peterson attempts to delegitimize the rights claims of trans communities—as if misgendering is the epitome of trans oppression and that trans people will be so harmed by misgendering that they will seek to hold perpetrators criminally responsible.

Of course, because of the way in which arguments surrounding freedom of expression became so central to the debate, supporters of the bill also spent much time responding to these accusations. Marni Panas, a diversity and inclusion consultant, addressed the fear-mongering associated with the free speech debate:

> Framing amendments to the *Criminal Code of Canada* as a free speech issue is a straw man argument used to instill fear where there is nothing to fear. This amendment will protect one of our most marginalized groups of people. It does not take away your right to say what you wish any more than protections added for race, religion, sexual orientation and disability have. Purposely using incorrect pronouns does not make you a criminal; it only makes you disrespectful, but assaulting us, killing us or inciting others to do the same simply because of who we are, and that we do not fit how some in society define gender, is a different matter. Do not let those who oppose this bill on fabricated grounds and hypotheticals cause you to leave a section of your population vulnerable to the very real risks that we face every single day. ("Proceedings of the Standing Senate Committee")

Alongside defending the bill against false accusations that misgendering could be criminalized, proponents also took the opportunity to demonstrate the necessity to protect the trans population. For example, Minister of Justice and Attorney General of Canada, The Honorable Jody Wilson-Raybould, who sponsored Bill C-16, highlighted trans people's disproportionate rates of victimization and discrimination:

> As you are all aware, trans, gender-diverse and two-spirited persons face elevated levels of violence and risk of violence, including physical and sexual assault and verbal, physical and sexual harassment. They also face significant obstacles in obtaining and advancing in employment, and not because of lack of qualifications. ("Proceedings of the Standing Senate Committee")

Although transgender people are certainly at risk of transphobic violence within a society that erases and marginalizes gender variance, framing violence and discrimination as a result of gender bias alone also risks decontextualizing their experiences of oppression and violence. Such framing appeals to claims that the new amendments to law, Bill C-16, will be a saving grace to the lives of all trans people. Yet transgender studies scholars emphasize that violence against trans people cannot be separated from the way in which oppressions interact—for instance, rendering racialized trans women and trans sex workers as the disproportionate victims of violence and homicide within trans communities (Namaste, *Sex Change*; Saffin; Waters; Waters et al.). To generalize the trans experience is to erase how experiences of cisgenderism are fundamentally linked to race, class, and labour. Through discussions of violence and discrimination against trans communities that centre solely upon transphobia, the image of a white, middle-class trans person is constructed in the law (Saffin).

At the same time, those who supported the bill at times accounted for the experiences of racialized and low-income trans people as seemingly "worse off" than their white counterparts (Frankenberg). For instance, after acknowledging her family's "privilege of whiteness," Kimberly Manning alluded to the heightened disadvantage that racialized and low-income trans people face: "Indeed, although we experienced some very real challenges, these challenges cannot compare to those struggling at the margins of poverty and/or those facing the combined oppressions of transphobia and racism" ("Proceedings of the Standing Senate Committee"). While certainly well intentioned, even proponents of the bill sometimes decentred the trans people most affected by violence. As a whole, the debates garnered more concern for unsubstantiated legal implications of misgendering than for the issues that have been historically most pressing among the most vulnerable and disadvantaged sectors of transgender communities.

Considering that the fundamental issue presented at the Senate was that of pronouns in relation to the right to freedom of expression, the next section outlines the legal implications of Bill C-16. Here, I debunk the myth that misgendering can result in criminalization, first, by identifying the limited availability of charges under the hate propaganda provisions in the *Criminal Code* and, second, by discussing the possibility of applications under the *Human Rights Act*.

Misgendering and the Law

The *Criminal Code*

Freedom of speech is protected under section 2 of the *Charter*, instituted as a guaranteed right to freedom of expression. At the same time, freedom of speech is not absolute; limitations may be imposed under section 1 of the *Charter* when reasonably justified. For instance, hate speech has long been considered a reasonable and constitutional limit to free speech for the purposes of preventing harm *(R v Keegstra)*. Accordingly, the hate speech provisions of the *Criminal Code*, section 318 and 319, are considered constitutional limits to freedom of speech that prohibit advocating for genocide and the public incitement of hatred against an identifiable group, respectively. Following Bill C-16, "gender identity" and "gender expression" are now protected characteristics within these provisions.

Section 318(1) of the *Criminal Code* prohibits advocating or promoting genocide. Section 319(1) prohibits "communicating statements in any public place [which] incites hatred against any identifiable group where such incitement is likely to lead to a breach of the peace." It is also an offence to wilfully promote hatred through communication other than in private conversations (section 319(2)). Moreover, it is noteworthy that charges under these provisions of the *Criminal Code* must be agreed to by the attorney general. Because advocating genocide is defined as "killing members of the group" or "deliberately inflicting on the group conditions of life calculated to bring about its physical destruction," (section 318(2)) when applying this provision to the topic of misgendering, it is quite obvious that charges could not be substantiated for simply failing to use a correct gender pronoun.

It is also unreasonable to suggest that misgendering could result in a charge under section 319. In order to achieve a conviction under section 319(1), the Crown must prove beyond a reasonable doubt that the expression, first, constituted hatred and, second, resulted in a breach of peace. Here, the Supreme Court of Canada in *R v Keegstra* clearly explained that hatred must be construed as encompassing only the "most severe and deeply felt form of opprobrium" (para 137). A high threshold of what can be defined as hatred is designed to ensure that only the most egregious forms of expression will be regulated by law and, as such, misgendering would not meet the definitional requirements of hatred.

Moreover, in the context of section 319(2), even if the expression is deemed to constitute hatred, the Crown must prove that the hatred was wilful. The court in *R v Keegstra* explained that there must be evidence of either intent to promote hatred or knowledge of the likely certainty of such an outcome. In other words, hatred is wilfully expressed if there was intent or if a reasonable person would have foreseen that the consequences of his expression would promote hatred. Finally, four defences are available to an accused under section 319(3) of the *Criminal Code* in order to further limit the scope of expressions that are prohibited. Accordingly, an accused shall not be charged if he establishes that (a) his statements were true; (b) he, in good faith, was expressing an opinion based on a religious topic or based on a religious text; (c) the statements were relevant to a topic of public interest or for the public's benefit, as long as he reasonably perceived the statements to be true; or (d) he, in good faith, was attempting to point out, in order to resolve, matters that incite feelings of hatred.

The sections of the *Criminal Code* that protect against hate propaganda and hate speech constitute constitutional limits to freedom of expression and are intended to capture only the most egregious expressions of hatred. The narrow interpretation of what constitutes hatred, the defences available to an accused under section 319(3), and the requirement for the Attorney General to consent to the charges profoundly limit the feasibility of substantiating a charge. As such, seeking a charge under the hate crime provisions for the sole basis of misgendering simply cannot be substantiated, despite what some of those who opposed Bill C-16 asserted. In fact, the Canadian Bar Association refers to claims that Bill C-16 would violate individuals' freedom of expression as a blatant "misunderstanding of human rights and hate crimes legislation" (3). The next section demonstrates how misgendering also cannot be criminalized under human rights legislation.

The Human Rights Act

Following Bill C-16, the *Human Rights Act* was amended to prohibit gender-based discrimination that results in an individual's denial of goods, services, access to facilities, or accommodation customarily available to the public (section 5). An individual is also prohibited from denying gender diverse people from occupying residential accommodations or commercial premises (section 6) and discriminating against them in the context of employment (sections 7-12). Finally, the new amendments to the *Act* also prohibit harassment on the basis of gender identity and expression (section 14). Although provincial or territorial human rights legislation may have already addressed such discrimination falling within the scope of their corresponding jurisdiction, Bill C-16 prohibits discrimination that falls within the federal jurisdiction. In order to interpret the potential implications of the new amendments to the *Act*, I explore provincial human rights policy and case law for guidance.

Following the 2012 amendments to the *Ontario Human Rights Code*, the Ontario Human Rights Commission released policy recommendations in 2014 to assist institutions and organizations in interpreting and adhering to the changes to the *Code*. In their *Policy on Preventing Discrimination Because of Gender Identity and Gender Expression*, the Commission explains that an individual's pronouns are a common means of expressing gender, and thus the refusal to use an individual's self-identified name and pronoun could constitute harassment. The Commission describes harassment on the basis of gender identity or expression in terms of pejorative language directed toward the trans population, insults or offensive comments about an individual's gender identity or expression, or the refusal to use an individual's chosen pronoun. In other contexts, the Commission likens the increasing use of the gender-neutral pronoun "they" to the use of the term "Ms" for a woman who chooses to not disclose her marital status (Ontario Human Rights Commission). At the same time, it is important to note that the policy is not binding by law but acts as a guide to interpret the law.

In light of the recommendations made by the Ontario Human Rights Commission, critics of Bill C-16 suggested that they will be compelled to adopt chosen pronouns, lest risking claims of discrimination or harassment. Although Ontario Human Rights Commission recommends adopting individuals' chosen pronouns, Brenda Cossman, before the Senate at the hearings of Bill C-16, pointed out that pronouns are always optional:

> Bill C-16 has no specific requirement of using any particular pronouns. There is no particular requirement to use any particular gender-neutral pronoun. There is a requirement that people not be intentionally misgendered. It is not a right to a particular gender-neutral pronoun, and I believe that it does not

even mandate the use of gender-neutral pronouns. If people oppose that, they can simply abide by the law by using a person's name. ("Proceedings of the Standing Senate Committee")

As such, for those who wish to not adopt an individual's chosen pronouns, names can be used in their place. In other words, no one is compelled under the *Human Rights Act* or any other human rights legislation to adopt any specific pronoun.

Even though compelled speech is not evoked, there is potential that misgendering a trans person could result in a human rights violation on the basis of gender-based discrimination or harassment. In order to understand the circumstances in which this may manifest, I provide an overview of two relevant cases related to pronouns: the first of which draws upon claims of systemic discrimination in the context of an organization, and the second refers to misgendering between individuals.

In the case of *Dawson v Vancouver Police Board (No. 2)*, a transgender woman, Angela Dawson, alleged discrimination by the Vancouver Police Board on the basis of sex (prior to "gender identity" and "gender expression" being protected characteristics). Her case concerned six independent incidents, part of which involved her accusation that the police department engaged in systemic discrimination by referring to her in male pronouns and her legal (male) name. She argued that she has the right to be treated as a woman and that police must adopt her female name and pronoun. The tribunal concluded that Dawson was subject to discrimination on two bases, one of which was when officers referred to her as male. During her arrest, the officer indicated her sex designation as "F(?)" on the arrest form. The officer did so, he claimed, because he was unsure of what to indicate and did not know which jail she would be placed in.

Furthermore, although the officer had interacted with Dawson in the past and knew that her current name was Angela, the officer used her legal (male) name and male pronouns throughout the arrest form. The tribunal ultimately accepted Dawson's submission that the Vancouver Police Board had engaged in systemic discrimination in terms of their identification processes regarding trans people. The Vancouver Police Board was then ordered to refrain from additional or similar contraventions of the *Code*, to adopt new policies to allow for trans people to identify in manners that are not discriminatory, and to train its officers to ensure the implementation of the policy.

Not only does the issue of misgendering concern the way in which institutions must accommodate trans individuals, but human rights legislation can also govern social interactions. For instance, in the case of *Halton Children's Aid Society v G.K.*,[4] the Halton Children's Aid Society sought an order to temporarily place children, S.M. and B.M, in the custody of their father, subject to their supervision, on the premise that the children were at risk of emotional harm from their mother. The society submitted that the mother was forcing the eldest child—an assigned male referred to as "S."—to dress as a girl against S.'s wishes and was referring to S. in the female pronoun. The society submitted that no gender should be forced upon the child, but the mother refuted this assertion, claiming that S. had long displayed gender variant tendencies and that she was supporting her child's choices. Expert testimony provided by Dr. Bonafacio, a paediatrician who specializes in gender, determined that the child was not being forced by either parent to express a certain gender, but S. felt as though they must regulate their gender in front of their parents, particularly their father.

Dr. Bonafacio concluded that S. did not have an interest in changing gender (at least at this point in time); rather, S. performed fluid gender expressions. In line with Dr. Bonafacio's recommendations, the tribunal ordered that S. should be allowed to express gender in a variety of manners and should not be referred to in female pronouns or unilaterally dressed as a girl or forced to adopt specific gender roles unless S. expresses a desire to do so. The implication is that an individual should not adopt pronouns to refer to others that they see fitting, even when doing so in good faith. Rather, an individual should adopt the pronouns to which the other self-identifies. In order to do so, an individual should simply be asked which pronoun they use or simply use their name in place of pronouns.

Despite the sensationalism surrounding the pronoun debate, the implications of Bill C-16 are quite simple: the law is not compelling the use of any pronoun because everyone has the option to not use pronouns altogether. What human rights policy directs us to do, however, is to not misgender someone. Although Human Rights Tribunals have clarified their stance on misgendering, it should be noted that these cases derive from broader claims of discrimination—that is, misgendering was not advanced as the sole basis of the application.

Furthermore, it should be noted that in the event that a human rights application does arise, there is no potential for criminalizing misgendering, as opponents of Bill C-16 have asserted. Rather, remedies for human rights applications are typically monetary in order to compensate for injury to dignity, feelings, and self-respect, or there are public interest remedies, such as those that mandate workplace policies to correspond with human rights legislation to ensure no future code violations.

Reflecting on the Pronoun Debate

In debating the potential legal effects of misgendering, Jordan Peterson made a seemingly plausible yet inherently deceptive claim that Bill C-16 would enact compelled speech and could result in the criminalization of misgendering (Cossman, "Gender Identity"). In her analysis of the Senate debates on Bill C-16, Cossman concluded that the appeal to freedom of expression was merely an avenue for conservative opposition to trans rights. Analyzing how Peterson's claims became so powerful, Cossman suggests that the attack on chosen pronouns was in fact an attack on political correctness. Cossman explains that the attribution of pronouns to a matter of political correctness fosters a milieu in which concerns over the violation of freedom of speech gain traction. That is, the right has constructed political correctness as a liberal stance in which the censorship of certain words or phrases is warranted because they are simply too offensive and, in light of perceived regulation of words or phrases, they suggest that free speech is under attack (Cossman). Although the context of political correctness and the purported attack on free speech was one of the ways in which Peterson's claims was provided traction, Cossman also attributes Peterson's publicity to his assumed expert authority as a clinical psychologist and professor. Yet with respect to Peterson's lack of legal training and blatant misunderstanding of the law, one may wonder why he was chosen to testify on these issues before the Senate.

Peterson's concerns that free speech was in jeopardy were amplified through speaking invitations and panel presentations at various universities and venues (Houston; Hunter; Martin). Yet, as Sara Ahmed reminds us, "Whenever people keep being given a platform to say they have no platform, or whenever people speak endlessly about being silenced, you not only have a performative contradiction; you are witnessing a mechanism of power" (27). It is unclear as to whether Peterson truly believed he would be criminalized for misgendering, but it is evident that his refusal to adopt chosen pronouns had been mobilized through power.

By the way in which pronoun use has become central to the debate on trans rights, trans oppression has been reduced simply to misgendering. At the same time, this is not to suggest that pronouns are insignificant. Misgendering or refusing to use a trans person's pronoun is first and foremost a denial of trans existence or trans authenticity; rather than acting as an attack on an individual, misgendering constitutes an invalidation of trans existence more broadly (Ashley). Yet the fact that the hypothetical case of criminalizing misgendering garnered so much attention is deeply harmful to the trans rights movement because it undermines the material reality of cisgenderism—particularly among the most marginalized members of trans communities who may be more concerned with living a life free of violence and criminalization rather than being addressed in the correct pronoun.

Organizing around singular axes of identity in law and politics has long been deemed inadequate because it negates the way in which identity categories are co-constituted (Crenshaw). In this case, the focus on gender as a singular and primary identity fails to meaningfully engage with difference such that the image of a universalized (white, middle-class) trans subject has been constructed in the law (Saffin), and it is through this focus on gender that cisgenderism could be strategically reduced to a matter of pronouns. Of course, this understanding of cisgenderism bears resemblance to the white feminist movement who trumped the voices of, and did not challenge themselves to consider, the experiences of racialized and low-income women (Carby). Of course, the life chances of the trans population must be understood in relation to their racial and class identity. By looking to the issues affecting the most vulnerable sectors of trans communities, it becomes apparent how access to legal protections guaranteed under Bill C-16 are extremely limited.

The Limits of the Law

In this section, I explore the limits of hate crimes protections and antidiscrimination laws in order to illustrate some of the ways in which those most marginalized among trans communities remain unprotected under the law and are, in fact, further harmed by state practices of criminalization and imprisonment. Therefore, it can be argued that formal legal protections for "gender identity" and "gender expression" create an illusion that gender equality has been achieved, meanwhile structural oppressions and state-enforced gendered violence continues to flourish (Spade, *Normal Life*).

Hate Crime Protections

Critical trans scholars have conceptualized the fight for trans rights as a form of neoliberal ideology; antidiscrimination protections and hate crime laws are based on an individualizing logic that ultimately fails to protect all trans people (Ashley; Spade, "Keynote Address"; Spade, *Normal Life*; Vipond). Hate crime designations are criticized on the basis of their inability to address the intersections of identity, thus framing an individual act of violence as the result of prejudice rather than a complex web of structural injustices (Ashley; Lamble; Spade, "Keynote Address"; Spade, *Normal Life*; Saffin; Vipond). Relying on the 'bad apple' narrative, hate crime laws fail to address issues of cisgenderism, racism, and classism. At best, the reactive nature of hate crimes protections punishes individual perpetrators while doing very little to address the root causes of violence to begin with (Spade, *Normal Life*; Vipond). Even then, personal biases are often difficult to prove in court—for instance, not all cases of transphobic violence are accompanied by blatant transphobic slurs—and as such, these laws are conceptualized as "more symbolic than effective" (Vipond 17). Moreover, there is no evidence to suggest that hate crimes protections actually reduce the amount of hate crimes that occur because they are known to have no deterrent effect (Spade, "Keynote Address"). In 2009, in the United States (U.S.), antitransgender crimes were officially recognized as hate crimes following the implementation of the *Matthew Shepard and James Byrd, Jr., Hate Crimes Prevention Act* (The United States Department of Justice). Yet in light of this legislation, Sarah Lamble notes that antitrans hate crimes have not reduced in frequency. On the contrary, some have critiqued the mainstream hypervisibility of transness due to the fact that it has actually increased the violence directed at trans people of colour (Griffin-Gracy et al.).

Not only are hate crime laws unable to prevent violence, but they are also limited due to low rates of reporting. As many of us in the academy are aware, only a fraction of crimes are reported to police. The same is true of hate crimes. For instance, between 2013 and 2015, only nine antitrans hate crimes were reported by police to Statistics Canada (Leber). The relatively low rate of transphobic hate crimes is not only indicative of the general underreporting of hate crimes (Dauvergne and Brennan; Leber), but also the systemic erasure of trans people through official statistics that rely on sex designations rather than collecting information on gender (Namaste, *Invisible Lives*). Official hate crime statistics, therefore, do not provide an accurate representation of the number of transphobia-motivated offences. Indeed, the 2014 General Social Survey on Canadians Safety (Victimization) indicates that approximately two-thirds of hate crimes go unreported (Leber). Yet when we look to U.S.-based research conducted by the National Coalition of Anti-Violence Programs (NCAVP), it is noteworthy that of the 1,036 anti-LGBTQ*[5] incidents reported by twelve antiviolence programs across the U.S. in 2016, 32 per cent were directed at trans individuals (Waters). Even though antitrans crimes are prevalent, they are not being reported or accurately recorded by police.

One reason for the vast underreporting of hate crimes is the complicated relationship that transgender communities have with the police; a lengthy history of police oppression, criminalization, and cisgenderism has created reluctance towards seeking redress or reporting victimization. Evidence from a national U.S. study surveying 27,715 trans people across all fifty states indicates that over half of trans people (57 per cent) would be uncomfortable seeking assistance from law enforcement (James et al.). The relationship between police and trans communities is troubled due to the history of targeting and surveillance of trans bodies. Police profiling of racialized and gender non-normative trans people as criminals, and particularly racialized transfeminine people as sex workers for simply being present in the public sphere, has been so prevalent that trans scholars have coined the term "walking while trans" (Carpenter and Marshall; Vitulli, "The Prison-Industrial Complex"). Furthermore, the systemic racism embedded in policing (Chan and Chunn; Comack) combined with the heightened surveillance and profiling of racialized gender non-normative trans bodies (Carpenter and Marshall; James et al.; Vitulli, "The Prison-Industrial Complex") renders racialized trans people in a particularly precarious position in relation to criminalization. Hate crime laws fail to account for the intersections of identity and ultimately marginalize trans subjects outside of the white, middle class, who may be less able to rely upon police for protection or are blamed for their victimization (Vipond).

The relationship between law enforcement and racialized members of the LGBTQ* community has a troubled history that, by and large, continues today. For example, in July of 2016, Black Lives Matter (BLM) Toronto held the Toronto Pride Parade at a stand-still for thirty minutes, making a number of requests including a ban on uniformed and armed police officers in future participation of the parades (Walcott). This request was later followed through with by Toronto Pride, despite controversy from the broader LGBTQ* community (Walcott). One year later, at the Toronto Pride Parade in 2017, BLM made another unannounced appearance, holding signs such as those that read, "May we never again need to remind you that WE built THIS" (Gray). At the same time as Toronto Pride took place, however, gay pro-police activists responded to the ban on uniformed police by initiating their own alternative Pride event in a downtown Toronto park, inviting police and other emergency personnel to attend (Gray). Although few ultimately showed up to the alternative Pride event (Gray; Wang), the divide illustrates the ways in which the LGBTQ* community continues to be fractured along the lines of politics (Spade, *Normal Life*; Ware). The BLM protests at Pride signals attention to how the history of police oppression and brutality directed at the racialized LGBTQ* community is neither forgotten nor relegated to the past. Reflecting on Stonewall, Morgan Bassichis and colleagues question whether the frontrunners of the riots would have imagined that the gay rights agenda today would abandon its historical roots and support prisons, police, and war.

Alongside evident limitations on accessing hate crime protections, it is also important to reflect upon the concerns associated with fuelling an oppressive criminal justice system. Legal scholar Dean Spade warns against the implementation of hate crime protections because of the violence that occurs at the hands of the criminal justice system: "By articulating it as the place we turn to stop transphobia, we obscure the fact that the criminal punishment system is probably the most significant perpetrator of violence against trans people" (*Normal Life*, 359). Further, Syrus Ware illustrates how the achievement of rights is not necessarily the vision of substantive change among racialized trans people:

> Trans lives of color follow a different temporality: we fail the progress narrative espoused by the white trans movement, as advancement is typically reduced to acquiring "rights" that are inaccessible to most and in fact are wielded against so many on the margins of the margins through the prison industrial complex, the war on terror, and the aid development industry. (172)

As opposed to advancing neoliberal inclusion strategies that only protect a few at the expense of fuelling an oppressive system, more revolutionary ways of protecting the transgender population are warranted. Even though criticisms of hate crimes protections for trans people are numerous and multifaceted, so too are the ways in which antidiscrimination protections fail some of the most vulnerable segments of trans communities.

Gender-Based Protections

Reflecting on the history of trans activism, this section focuses on the limits of antidiscrimination protections for criminalized trans people and documents some of the ways in which criminalization and imprisonment generate additional harms to trans individuals. First, I explore how trans sex workers are not protected under antidiscrimination legislation due to the criminalization of sex work. Second, I look to recent changes adopted as a response to Bill C-16—specifically, changes to Correctional Service Canada's (CSC) trans prisoner policy—to reveal how no amount of policy reform can adequately protect trans bodies within the prison.

Trans Sex Workers

Sex work has increasingly become a mainstream topic of debate following the 2013 case of *Canada (Attorney General) v Bedford,* in which three provisions of the former sex work legislation were struck down by the Supreme Court of Canada (for a further review, see Gacek and Jochelson, this volume). The court ultimately found that subsection 2.13(1)(c) (communication), 212(1)(j) (living off the avails of prostitution), and 210 (keeping a bawdy-house as it pertains to prostitution) were unconstitutional because they interfered with sex workers' section 7 *Charter* right to safety and security of the person. The court granted the Parliament of Canada one year to revise these provisions, lest they become of no force and effect. The following year, Bill C-36, *Protections of Communities and Exploited Persons Act,* was introduced. Whereas the bill aims to target clients and exploitive third parties in sex work, sex workers can still be criminalized in public places. Activists and scholars ultimately fear that the new laws will mimic, or perhaps even exacerbate, the same harms that were caused by the previous provisions (British Columbia Civil Liberties Association; Canadian Bar Association; Shaver).

Sex work scholars have long emphasized the negative effects that criminalization and sex work stigma have on the lives of sex workers. It is through the stigma surrounding sex work and the fact that aspects of sex work remain criminalized that violence against sex work can flourish (Bruckert and Chabot). Because sex work is not perceived as a viable job, it is not granted the same benefits as mainstream employment, and sex worker's legal rights and protections are profoundly limited through criminalization (Benoit and Millar; Bruckert and Parent; Jochelsonet al; O'Doherty).

Although sex workers risk criminalization and are denied their right to protection and the same employment benefits as mainstream jobs, trans people who sell sex are further disadvantaged by their inability to access protections such as those guaranteed by human rights protections for gender identity and gender expression. A U.S. national survey has indicated that nearly one in five trans people have sold sexual services in their lifetime (James et al.). Yet trans people in the sex industry are at particular risk of violence due to the way in which transphobia and sex work stigma interact (James et al.; Namaste, *Sex Change*; Lyons et al.). Accordingly, if violence occurs in the context of selling sex, trans people cannot report victimization due to the same concerns expressed by sex workers generally—including the risk of criminalization and future surveillance of their work (Bruckert and Parent; Krüsi et al.; O'Doherty). Thus, in the event that transphobic violence occurs in the context of their work, seeking a hate crime charge is limited because of the way that sex work is criminalized. While the implementation of hate crime protections are protecting trans people, ironically those most susceptible to violence cannot access these legal protections.

Although trans sex workers would be unable to access hate crime protections guaranteed under Bill C-16—not only because of sex work criminalization but because of the complex web of reasons outlined above—trans sex workers will additionally be limited in their ability to make claims of discrimination. For instance, if an escort agency denies a trans person employment or fires them because of their trans identity, their claims of discrimination on the basis of "gender identity" or "gender expression" would not be seen as legitimate until sex work is conceptualized as a viable job choice.

In her book *Sex Change, Social Change*, Viviane Namaste takes a "critical position *against* transgender rights" as they are currently mobilized in the political context in North America because they are embedded in oppressive logics (139). Even though segments of trans communities have worked towards, and are now celebrating the passing of, human rights protections, the movement to formalize trans rights in the law has not helped to improve the working conditions of trans sex workers or to decriminalize sex work generally (Forrester et al.; Namaste, *Sex Change*). Trans people may have now been granted formal rights under the law, but it is not until sex work is decriminalized that those more vulnerable sectors of trans communities can better reap the benefits of such legal protections.

Trans Prisoners

Not only should we be cognizant of how criminalization impedes access to gender-based legal protections for trans sex workers, but we must also be critical of recent changes that have been implemented as a response to Bill C-16. In January of 2017, the Trudeau government announced interim changes to CSC's policy as it relates to housing federal transgender prisoners (Harris, "Trudeau Promises to House Transgender Inmates"). New CSC policy mandates that trans prisoners can now be housed on the basis of gender identity, as opposed to sex, pending individual assessments. Because the former policy was based on an individual's sex, or more specifically genitalia, transgender people who had not undergone, or do not wish to undergo, genital reconstruction were housed incorrectly—that is, contrary to their gender identity and/or expression. For example, pre- and/or nonoperative trans women would be held in prisons with men and only postoperative trans women would be held in women's prisons. This sudden change in correctional policy, which challenges the sex-divisive nature of prisons that has prevailed for well over a century, can be read as an attempt to prevent claims of discrimination in light of the (at the time) impending protections for gender diverse Canadians, Bill C-16.

In the spirit of the new housing policy, transgender prisoner, Fallon Aubee, was transferred to a women's penitentiary on July 27, 2017. Aubee's case was celebrated as the first time that a pre- and/or nonoperative transgender prisoner would be housed on the basis of gender, not sex, in a Canadian federal institution (Harris, "Historic 1st"). Despite Aubee's win, ambiguous wording in CSC's interim policy suggests that not all trans people may be as successful. Indeed, CSC outlines their "duty to accommodate based on gender identity or expression, regardless of the person's anatomy (i.e. sex) or the gender marker on identification documents ... unless there are overriding health or safety concerns which cannot be resolved." The interim policy requires CSC to make individual assessments of trans prisoners, and while taking into consideration the prisoner's wishes, CSC has the ultimate authority regarding their placement. Despite espousing gender affirmation for trans prisoners, there are a number of limitations that must be outlined.

For one, CSC's interim policy reifies the history of differentiating trans bodies based on surgical status. Whereas it is explicit that postoperative trans people will be housed in accordance with their gender identity, the policy does not guarantee the gender-based placement of those who have not undergone genital surgery. CSC states that the gender-affirming placement of trans prisoners may be overruled when there are "health or safety concerns" that cannot be resolved.

Whereas postoperative trans bodies are guaranteed gender-based placements, the placement of pre- and/or nonoperative trans bodies remain subject to individual assessments. However, distinguishing between trans people who have undergone sex reassignment and those who have not has been conceptualized as discrimination by human rights tribunals in other contexts. For example, in *XY v Ontario (Government and Consumer Services)*, a case was heard before the Human Rights Tribunal of Ontario to determine whether or not the surgical requirement in order to change one's sex designation on their birth certificate was discriminatory. The tribunal concluded that taking surgical status into consideration was, indeed, discriminatory because it disadvantaged pre- and/or nonoperative trans people and perpetuated the stereotype that postoperative trans bodies are more real or authentic than those who do not undergo surgery. Ultimately, Vital Statistics was mandated to strike down their surgical requirement, therefore permitting pre- and/or nonoperative trans people to change their sex marker on official documents. What this means, with respect to the placement of trans prisoners, is that there may be grounds for a complaint under the *Human Rights Act* if CSC does in fact continue to differentiate between pre- and postoperative trans bodies based on gender stereotypes. However, the limitations outlined in CSC's interim trans prisoner policy may, in fact, suggest the continuation of this discriminatory practice.

The limitations on CSC's trans prisoner policy, with respect to safety and privacy, are troublesome considering the prison's historical legacy of constructing trans bodies as exceptionally risky. The prison and legal system alike have constructed trans prisoners as threatening – to themselves, others, and institutional order – in order to justify a denial of gender-affirming treatment and care (Vitulli, *Carceral Normativities*). First, trans prisoners pose a significant risk in terms of their individual safety. U.S.-based research highlights the high rates of victimization among trans prisoners (Arkles; Brown, "Qualitative Analysis"). In fact, in 2011 and 2012, 39.9 per cent of trans prisoners incarcerated in the U.S. experienced sexual victimization within the last year (Beck). However, prisons and courts have demonstrated that the safety of trans prisoners is often disregarded and that the safety of other prisoners is prioritized over their own. For example, when trans women are placed in men's prisons, prison staff sometimes believe that they are purposefully eliciting sexual attention from male prisoners, which they then use to delegitimize any claims of sexual victimization (Buchanan; Vitulli, "Racialized Criminality"; Vitulli, *Carceral Normativities*). Yet if prisons do respond to trans women's claims of sexual violence, trans women are often held in administrative segregation

—sometimes known as 'protective custody'—which scholars suggest is a means of isolating and disciplining the 'threat' associated with gender non-normativity (Arkles; Sumner and Sexton). In other words, the trans person is isolated in attempts to maintain the gender normative environment of the prison. For example, during her incarceration in a men's institution, Fallon Aubee was reportedly held in segregation for a period of six months, making her feel, in her own words, like a "junkyard dog" (Harris, "Historic 1st"). Even though the institutions' response to victimization is to isolate the victim, the UN conceptualizes the use of solitary confinement past fifteen days as torture (Human Rights First).

Although incarcerated trans women are constructed as eliciting, and thus deserving of, sexual violence at the hands of cis men, they are likewise constructed as an aggressor when placed among cis women. Consider the case of *Kavanagh v Canada (Attorney General)*, which constituted the first legal challenge regarding the placement of trans prisoners in Canada. The case was brought before the Canadian Human Rights Tribunal in 2001 by Synthia Kavanagh, a trans woman who was incarcerated in a men's penitentiary. The tribunal was left to consider two issues pertaining to federally incarcerated trans prisoners: the housing placement of those who were pre- and/or nonoperative and whether access to sex reassignment surgery should be available during incarceration. Although the tribunal acknowledged trans women's exceptional vulnerability to sexual violence when held with cis men, they ultimately appealed to the need to protect cis women; because incarcerated cis women have unique histories of sexual abuse at the hands of men, the tribunal reasoned that placing trans women with cis women would simply be too risky.

What this threatening construction of trans prisoners means, with respect to prison placements, is that gender stereotypes have been used by prisons in order to justify discriminatory and oppressive practices. Although CSC has a new gender affirming policy, which seemingly aligns with federal human rights legislation on gender identity and gender expression, the limitations of this policy—with respect to issues of security and privacy—are precisely the constructs used to deny gender affirming treatment to trans prisoners in the past. For example, it may be argued that pre- and/or nonoperative trans women remain a security or privacy risk to cis women (Smith), which may be better managed in a men's prison. Likewise, it may be argued that pre- and/or nonoperative trans men pose too high of a risk of sexual violence when placed in a men's prison (Shah), thereby justifying their placement in women's prisons. Considering the fact that trans people are often positioned as disruptive to the sex-segregated structure of the prison, CSC's trans prisoner policy may function not to accommodate the breadth of gender diversity, but rather, to manage the threat associated with gender non-normativity.

Finally, it should be noted that policy reforms cannot prevent experiences of transphobia within the prison. Regardless of prison placement, there is the potential for transphobic victimization, especially if one's trans identity becomes known. Although the housing policy for trans prisoners attempts to account for the inclusion of trans men and women within men and women's prisons, it is fundamentally flawed because it fails to challenge the way in which prisons remain structured according to the gender binary. Trans identities can be defined as those that move away from the gender they were assigned at birth (Stryker), thereby including not only trans men and women but also nonbinary, two-spirit, and gender non-normative identities and expressions. Yet the prison is an institution designed to only accommodate femininity or masculinity, in which ideals of white middle-class gender normativity underpin the prison's vision of 'rehabilitation' and where gender is used as a tool to discipline bodies (Davis; Hannah-Moffat; Pemberton; Stanley and Smith). For those who do not identify as a normative gender, or whose expressions are not exclusively masculine or feminine, their inclusion in either prison is problematic. Trans bodies threaten the very structure and intent of the modern prison system, and, as such, they bear the brunt of the violence of this system.

With respect to the dilemmas of housing trans prisoners, the construction of trans-only prisons is not a viable solution. Analyzing reports of sexual victimization in prisoners from 2009 to 2011, the Bureau of Justice Statistics report that half of the incidents of sexual misconduct or sexual harassment against prisoners were perpetrated by staff. In fact, one in five trans prisoners have experienced sexual violence from correctional staff (James et al.). Considering that it is staff, not simply other prisoners, who are a primary source of violence against imprisoned trans people (Arkles; Sylvia Rivera Law Project), violence would not subside by housing trans prisoners together.

Finally, building more prisons is not the answer. Because prisons are structured according to rigid and binary expectations of gender and the criminal justice system has been a fundamental source of violence and oppression among trans communities, some suggest that there is no way for transgender people to be protected within the prison (Lamble; Spade, "Racialized Gender Violence"; Stanley et al.). Rather than attempting to fix a broken system, Eric Stanley and colleagues argue that we should deconstruct claims in support of caging and exiling people—which can be achieved by taking a critical stance toward the criminal justice system's ability to protect, rehabilitate, and reduce harm. Put simply, if we think about "imprisonment as gender violence," then we can relinquish the belief that the government endorses gender equality (Stanley et al. 122). While trans people are perhaps best illustrative of the ways in which the prison is a site of gendered violence, calls for prison abolitionism derive from the activism and scholarship of people of colour who have connected the contemporary surveillance, policing, and imprisonment of Black communities to past practices of slavery and racial segregation (Alexander; Davis; Maynard). Additionally, scholars such as Lisa Monchalin have likewise traced how Canada's history of colonialism has informed the targeting and disproportionate incarceration of Indigenous peoples. When listening to the voices of those most affected by the prison industrial complex, the need for prison abolitionism becomes obvious.

Conclusion

Reflecting on the anticriminalization efforts present throughout the history of trans activism in North America and the way in which trans sex workers and trans prisoners remain unprotected by law today, regardless of gender-based protections, it becomes evident why the prominence afforded to the discussion of pronoun use and the law is particularly problematic. Debates over Bill C-16's effects on Canadians' right to freedom of expression have gained considerable publicity since Jordan Peterson released his controversial YouTube video against political correctness. Specious legal claims that Bill C-16 would enforce compelled speech, potentially violate the hate speech provisions in the *Criminal Code,* and result in the criminalization of those who fail to adopt gender-neutral pronouns incited unnecessary and harmful concerns over the amendments to law. Although Peterson's erroneous claims may have gained traction in light of the critiques of political correctness and the perceived attack on freedom of speech (Cossman, "Gender Identity"), trans rights cannot be reduced to a matter of political correctness.

Although the purpose of Bill C-16 was to protect gender diverse Canadians from discrimination and hate-motivated violence, these changes will do very little to improve the living conditions of the most vulnerable trans people. A fundamental issue with legal rights is that they provide a guise of equality while allowing structural oppressions and state-enforced discrimination and violence to flourish (Spade, *Normal Life*; Stanley et al.; Vipond). Through criminalization and imprisonment, the most vulnerable sectors of trans communities are denied access to such protections and are swept into an oppressive criminal justice system that ultimately generates much of the harms that they experience. Guided by the belief that the criminal justice system is embedded in oppressive logics that will continue to harm marginalized communities, we must be critical of the state's superficial endorsement of gender equality through antidiscrimination and hate crime protections. Because the criminal justice system is an active source of violence towards trans people, protection for trans communities may only be possible through abolitionist efforts, such as those that seek to decriminalize sex work and end imprisonment.

Endnotes

1. In this paper, the term "chosen pronoun" is used over the more popular term "preferred pronoun" because the latter implies that trans people's pronouns are less real or authentic than their cisgender counterparts.
2. Cisgenderism is the system of oppression that disadvantages transgender individuals. Cisgenderism operates through the denial, belittlement, or pathologization of gender variance (Lennon and Mistler) and occurs when gender norms of masculinity and femininity are rigidly enforced (Serano).
3. For examples of tribunal rulings that protect transgender individuals under "sex" and/or "disability" see C.F. v Alberta (Vital Statistics), 2014 ABQB 237; Nixon v Vancouver Rape Relief Society,

2002 BCHRT 1; XY v Ontario (Government and Consumer Services), 2012 HRTO 726.

4. Trans people have long challenged the medical and psychiatric system to recognize their autonomy in determining their genders (Spade, "Mutilating Gender"). I use this case not to demonstrate faith in the medical profession in diagnosing gender or to suggest that gender should only be accepted following 'expert' opinion, but because this case exemplifies how we should never *assume* another person's gender.

5. LGBTQ* is a standard acronym representing lesbian, gay, bisexual, trans, and queer identities. The asterisk is intended to represent inclusion of other non-normative sexual and gender identities and expressions (e.g., pansexual, asexual, agender, and two-spirit).

Works Cited
Secondary Sources

Ahmed, Sara. "An Affinity of Hammers." *TSQ: Transgender Studies Quarterly*, vol. 3, no. 1/2, 2016, pp. 22-34.

Alexander, Michelle. *The New Jim Crow: Mass Incarceration in the Age of Colorblindness*. The New Press, 2010.

Arkles, Gabriel. "Safety and Solidarity Across Gender Lines: Rethinking Segregation of Transgender People in Detention." *Temple Political and Civil Rights Law Review*, vol. 18, no. 2, 2009, pp. 515-60.

Arthur, Joyce et al. "Overcoming Challenges: Vancouver's Sex Worker Movement." *Selling Sex: Experience, Advocacy, and Research on Sex Work in Canada*, edited by Emily Van der Meulen, Elya M. Durisin, and Victoria Love, University of British Columbia Press, 2013, pp. 130-46.

Ashley, Florence. "Don't Be So Hateful: The Insufficiency of Anti-Discrimination and Hate Crime Laws in Improving Trans Well-Being." *University of Toronto Law Journal*, vol. 68, no. 1, 2018, pp. 1-36.

Bassichis, Morgan et al. "Building an Abolitionist Trans & Queer Movement with Everything We've Got." *Captive Genders: Trans Embodiment and the Prison Industrial Complex* edited by Eric A. Stanley and Nat Smith, KA Press, pp. 15-40.

Beck, Allen J. "Sexual Victimization in Prisons and Jails Reported by Inmates, 2011–12: Supplemental Tables: Prevalence of Sexual Victimization Among Transgender Adult Inmates." U.S. Department of Justice, 2014.

Benoit, Cecilia, and Alison Millar. "Dispelling Myths and Understanding Realities: WorkingConditions, Health Status, and Exiting Experiences of Sex Workers." PEERS, 2001.

British Columbia Civil Liberties Association. "Re: Public Consultation on Prostitution-Related Offences in Canada," 17 Mar 2014, bccla.org/wp-content/uploads/2014/03/BCCLA-sex-work-submission-to-Justice-Canada-March-17-2014.pdf. Accessed 10 Feb. 2018.

Brown, George R. "Qualitative Analysis of Transgender Inmates' Correspondence: Implications for Departments of Correction." *Journal of Correctional Health Care*, vol. 20, no. 4, 2014, pp. 334-42.

Bruckert, Christine, and Frederique Chabot. "Challenges: Ottawa-Area Sex Workers Speak Out." *POWER*, 2010, powerottawa.ca/POWER_Report_Challenges.pdf&gt. Accessed 4 May 2018.

Bruckert, Christine, and Collette Parent. "The Incall Sex Industry: Gender, Class, and Racialized Labour in the Margins." *Criminalizing Women: Gender and (In)Justice in Neo-liberal Times* (2nd edition), edited by Gillian Balfour and Elizabeth Comack, Fernwood Publishing, 2014, pp. 92-112.

Buchanan, Kim Shayo. "Our Prisons, Ourselves: Race, Gender and the Rule of Law." *Yale Law & Policy Review*, vol. 29, no. 1, 2010, pp. 1-82.

Bureau of Justice Statistics. "Sexual Victimization Reported by Adult Correctional Authorities, 2009-11 and Survey of Sexual Violence in Adult Correctional Facilities, 2009-11—Statistical Tables" *Office of Justice Programs*, 23 Jan 2014, www.bjs.gov/content/pub/press/svraca0911pr.cfm. Accessed 15 Feb. 2018.

Canadian AIDS Society, "Trans Rights Legislation in Canada" 1 Sept. 2017, www.cdnaids.ca/trans-rights-legislation-in-canada/. Accessed 1 Mar. 2018.

Canadian Bar Association. "RE: Bill C-16, An Act to Amend the Canadian Human Rights Act and the *Criminal Code* (Gender Identity or Expression)." 20 May 2017, www.cba.org/CMSPages/GetFile.aspx?guid=be34d5a4-8850-40a0-beea-432eeb762d7f. Accessed 10 Feb. 2018.

Carby, Hazel V. "'White Women Listen!' Black Feminism and the Boundaries of Sisterhood." *Black British Feminism: A Reader,* edited by Heidi S. Mirza, Routledge, 1997, pp. 45-53.

Carpenter, Leonore F., and R. Barrett Marshall. "Walking While Trans: Profiling of Transgender Women by Law Enforcement, and the Problem of Proof." *William & Mary Journal of Women and the Law,* vol. 24, no. 1, 2007, pp. 5-38.

Chan, Wendy, and Dorothy E. Chunn. *Racialization, Crime and Criminal Justice in Canada.* University of Toronto Press, 2014.

Comack, Elizabeth. *Racialized Policing: Aboriginal People's Encounters with the Police.* Fernwood Publishing, 2012.

Cossman, Brenda. "Gender Identity, Gender Pronouns, and Freedom of Expression: Bill C-16 and the Traction of Specious Legal Claims." *University of Toronto Law Journal,* vol. 68, no. 1, 2018, pp. 37-79.

Clamen, Jenn, et al. "Working for Change: Sex Workers in the Union Struggle." *Selling Sex: Experience, Advocacy and Research on Sex Work in Canada* edited by Emily Van der Meulen et al., UBC Press, 2013, pp. 113-29.

Cole, Janis, and Holly Dale, directors and writers. *Hookers on Davie.* Spectrum Films, 1984.

Correctional Service Canada (CSC). "Interim Policy Bulletin 584 Bill C-16 (Gender Identity or Expression)" *Government of Canada,* 14 Dec. 2017, https://www.csc-scc.gc.ca/policy-and-legislation /584-pb-en.shtml. Accessed 15 Jan. 2018.

Crago, Anna-Louise, and Jenn Clamen. "Ne Dans le Redlight: The Sex Workers' Movement in Montreal." *Selling Sex: Experience, Advocacy and Research on Sex Work in Canada* edited by Emily Van der Meulen, et al., UBC Press, 2013, pp. 147-64.

Crenshaw, Kimberlé. "Mapping the Margins: Intersectionality, Identity Politics, and Violence Against Women of Color." *Stanford Law Review,* vol. 43, no. 6, 1991, pp. 1241-99.

Davis, Angela. *Are Prisons Obsolete?* Seven Stories Press, 2003.

Di Fiore, James. "Black Lives Matter Toronto Co-founder Needs to Resign." *The Huffington Post (The Blog),* 8 Feb. 2017, www.huffington post.ca/james-di-fiore/black-lives-matter-toronto-yusra-khogali _b_14635896.html. Accessed 11 May 2019.

Dauvergne, Mia, and Shannon Brennan. *Police-Reported Hate Crime in Canada, 2009.* Statistics Canada, 2011.

Duberman, Martin B. *Stonewall.* Plume, 1994.

Feinberg, Leslie. *Trans Liberation Beyond Pink or Blue.* Beacon Press, 2007.

Forrester, Monica, et al. "Statement for Social Service Agencies and Transsexual/Transgender Organizations on Service Delivery to Transsexual and Transvestite Prostitutes." *Sex Change, Social Change: Reflections on Identity, Institutions, and Imperialism (second edition)* edited by Viviane Namaste, Women's Press, 2005/2011, pp. 103-8.

Frankenberg, Ruth. *White Women, Race Matters: The Social Construction of Whiteness.* University of Minnesota Press, 1993.

Gan, Jessi. "'Still at the Back of the Bus': Sylvia Rivera's Struggle." *Centro Journal,* vol. 19, no. 1, 2007, pp. 124-139.

Gray, Jeff. "Black Lives Matter Toronto Makes Surprise Appearance at Pride Parade." *The Globe and Mail,* 25 June 2017, www.theglobeandmail.com/news/toronto/black-lives-matter-toronto-makes-surprise-appearance-at-pride-parade/article35460305/. Accessed 11 May 2019.

Griffin-Gracy et al. "Cautious Living: Black Trans Women and the Politics of Documentation." *Trap Door: Trans Cultural Production and the Politics of Visibility* edited by Reina Gossett, Eric A. Stanley, and Johanna Burton, The MIT Press, 2017, pp. 23-37.

Hamilton, Jamie Lee. "The Golden Age of Prostitution: One Woman's Personal Account of an Outdoor Brothel in Vancouver, 1975-1984." *Trans Activism in Canada: A Reader,* edited by Rupert Raj and Dan Irving, Canadian Scholars' Press, 2014, pp. 27-32.

Hannah-Moffat, Kelly. *Punishment in Disguise: Penal Governance and Federal Imprisonment of Women in Canada.* University of Toronto Press, 2001.

Harris, Kathleen. "In Historic 1st, Transgender Inmate Wins Transfer to Women's Prison." *CBC News,* 21 July 2017, www.cbc.ca/news/politics/fallon-aubee-transgender-inmate-1.4215594. Accessed 20 Dec. 2017.

Harris, Kathleen. "Trudeau Promises to House Transgender Inmates Based on Gender Identity." *CBC News*, 12 Jan 2017, www.cbc.ca/news/politics/prison-transgender-inmates-policy-1.3932466. Accessed 20 Dec 2017.

Houston, Jacqueline. "Lost in Translation: Understanding the Campus Free Expression Debate." *Canadian Journalists for Free Expression*, 11 Oct 2017, www.cjfe.org/lost_in_translation_understanding_the_campus_free_expression_debate. Accessed 8 Dec 2017.

Human Rights First. "International Human Rights Law on Solitary Confinement." *Prison Legal News*, 2015, www.prisonlegalnews.org/media/publications/International%20Human%20Rights%20Law%20on%20Solitary%20Confinement%2C%20HRF%2C%202015.pdf. Accessed 10 Dec 2017.

Hunter, Brad. "Jordan Peterson Fans Pack Free Speech Discussion." *Toronto Sun*, 11 Nov. 2017, torontosun.com/news/local-news/jordan-peterson-fans-pack-free-speech-discussion. Accessed 10 Dec. 2017.

James, Sandy E., et al. *The Report of the 2015 U.S. Transgender Survey*. National Center for Transgender Equality, 2016.

Jochelson, Richard, et al. *Criminal Law and Precrime: Legal Studies in Canadian Punishment and Surveillance in Anticipation of Criminal Guilt*. Routledge, 2017.

Juang, Richard. "Transgendering the Politics of Recognition." *The Transgender Studies Reader* edited by Susan Stryker and Stephen Whittle, Routledge, 2006, pp. 706-19.

Krüsi, Andrea, et al. "Criminalisation of Clients: Reproducing Vulnerabilities for Violence and Poor Health among Street-Based Sex Workers in Canada—A Qualitative Study." *British Medical Journal Open*, vol. 4, no. 6, 2014, pp. 1-10.

Laframboise, Sandy L. "Finding My Place: The High Risk Project Society." *Trans Activism in Canada: A Reader* edited by Rupert Raj and Dan Irving, Canadian Scholars' Press, 2014, pp. 51-56.

Lamble, Sarah. "Retelling Racialized Violence, Remaking White Innocence: The Politics of Interlocking Oppressions in Transgender Day of Remembrance." *Sexuality Research and Social Policy*, vol. 5, no. 1, 2008, pp. 24-42.

Leber, Ben. "Police-Reported Hate Crime in Canada, 2015." *Juristat, Statistics Canada*, 14 June 2017, www.statcan.gc.ca/pub/85-002-x/2017001/article/14832-eng.htm. Accessed 10 Jan. 2018.

Lennon, Erica, and Brian J. Mistler. "Cisgenderism." *TSQ: Transgender Studies Quarterly*, vol. 1, no. 1-2, 2014, pp. 63-64.

Lyons, Tara et al. "Negotiating Violence in the Context of Transphobia and Criminalization: The Experiences of Trans Sex Workers in Vancouver, Canada." *Qualitative Health Research*, vol. 27, no. 2, 2017, pp. 182-90.

Martin, Allen. "Peterson Rallies for Free Speech at Sold Out Western Event." *The Gazette*, 19 Mar. 2017, www.westerngazette.ca/news/peterson-rallies-for-free-speech-at-sold-out-western-event/article_1a5ae052-0c45-11e7-9dce-7b6739f92da9.html. Accessed 8 Dec. 2017.

Maynard, Robyn. *Policing Black Lives: State Violence in Canada from Slavery to the Present*. Fernwood Publishing, 2017.

Miller, Adam. "Prison Health Care Inequality." *Canadian Medical Association. Journal*, vol. 185, no. 6, 2013, pp. 249-50.

Monchalin, Lisa. *The Colonial Problem: An Indigenous Perspective on Crime and Injustice in Canada*. University of Toronto Press, 2017.

Namaste, Viviane. *Invisible Lives: The Erasure of Transsexual and Transgendered People*. The University of Chicago Press, 2000.

Namaste, Viviane. *Sex Change, Social Change: Reflections on Identity, Institutions and Imperialism* (2nd edition). Women's Press, 2011.

O'Doherty, Tamara. "Criminalization and Off-Street Sex Work in Canada." *Canadian Journal of Criminology and Criminal Justice*, vol. 53, no. 2, 2011, pp. 217-45.

Ontario Human Rights Commission. "Questions and Answers About Gender Identity and Pronouns," www.ohrc.on.ca/en/questions-and-answers-about-gender-identity-and-pronouns. Accessed 20 Dec 2017.

Pemberton, Sarah. "Enforcing Gender: The Constitution of Sex and Gender in Prison Regimes." *Signs*, vol. 39, no. 1, 2013, pp. 151-175.

Peterson, Jordan. "Professor against Political Correctness: Part 1." *YouTube*, 27 Sept. 2016, www.youtube.com/watch?v=fvPgjg201w0. Accessed 20 Dec. 2017.

Ross, Michael W. et al. "The Relationships of Prison Climate to Health Service in Correctional Environments: Inmate Health Care Measurement, Satisfaction and Access in Prisons." *The Howard Journal of Criminal Justice,* vol. 50, no. 3, 2011, pp. 262-74.

Saffin, Lori A. "Identities under Siege: Violence against Transpersons of Color." *Captive Genders: Trans Embodiment and the Prison Industrial Complex* edited by Eric A. Stanley and Nat Smith, KA Press, 2011, pp. 141-62.

Scruton, Sue. Trans Needs Assessment Report. Canadian AIDS Society, 2014.

Serano, Julia. *Whipping Girl: A Transsexual Woman on Sexism and the Scapegoating of Femininity.* Seal Press, 2007.

Shah, Benish. "Lost in the Gender Maze: Placement of Transgender Inmates in the Prison System." *Journal of Race, Gender and Ethnicity,* vol. 5, no. 1, 2010, pp. 39-56.

Shaver, Frances. "Bill C-36: Entrenched in Personal Moral Values and Inaccurate Stereotypes." A Brief to the Standing Committee on Justice and Human Rights House of Commons 41st Parliament, 2nd Session, *Understanding Sex Work,* 7 July 2014, www.understandingsexwork.ca/sites/default/files/uploads/Shaver-Brief-re-Bill-C-36-July-7-2014-English.pdf. Accessed 8 Mar. 2018.

Smith, Allison. "Stories of Os: Transgender Women, Monstrous Bodies, and the Canadian Prison System." *Dalhousie J. Legal Studies,* vol. 23, 2014, pp. 149-71.

Spade, Dean. "Keynote Address: Trans Law & Politics on a Neoliberal Landscape." *Temple Political & Civil Rights Law Review,* vol. 18, no. 2, 2009, pp. 353-373.

Spade, Dean. "Mutilating Gender." *The Transgender Studies Reader,* edited by Susan Styker and Stephen Whittle, Routledge, 2006, pp. 315-32.

Spade, Dean. *Normal Life: Administrative Violence, Critical Trans Politics, & rhe Limits of Law.* Duke University Press, 2015.

Spade, Dean. "The Only Way to End Racialized Gender Violence is to End Prisons: A Response to Robinson's 'Masculinity as Prison.'" *California Law Review Circuit,* vol. 4, no. 3, 2012, pp. 184-95.

Stanley, Eric A., et al. "Queering Prison Abolition, Now?" *American Quarterly*, vol. 64, no. 1, 2012, pp. 115-27.

Stanley, Eric A., and Nat Smith. *Captive Genders: Trans Embodiment and the Prison Industrial Complex*. Oakland, CA: KA Press, 2011.

Stryker, Susan. *Transgender History*. Seal Press, 2008.

Sumner, Jennifer, and Lori Sexton. "Same Difference: The "Dilemma of Difference" and the Incarceration of Transgender Prisoners." *Law & Social Inquiry*, vol. 41, no. 3, 2015, pp. 616-42.

Sylvia Rivera Law Project. *"It's War in Here:" A Report on the Treatment of Transgender and Intersex People in New York State Men's Prisons*. SRLP, 2007.

United States Department of Justice. "The Matthew Shepard and James Byrd, Jr., Hate Crimes Prevention Act of 2009." 2015, www.justice.gov/crt/matthew-shepard-and-james-byrd-jr-hate-crimes-prevention-act-2009-0. Accessed 20 Dec. 2017.

Vipond, Evan. "Trans Rights Will Not Protect Us: The Limits of Equal Rights Discourse, Antidiscrimination Laws, and Hate Crime Legislation." *Western J Legal Studies*, vol. 6, no. 1, 2015, pp. 1-20.

Vitulli, E. Carceral Normativities: Sex, Security, and the Penal Management of Gender Nonconformity. University of Minnesota, 2014.

Vitulli, Elias. "Racialized Criminality and the Imprisoned Trans Body: Adjudicating Access to Gender-Related Medical Treatment in Prisons." *Social Justice*, vol. 37, no. 1, 2010, pp. 53-68.

Vitulli, Elias. "The Prison-Industrial Complex in the United States." *TSQ: Transgender Studies Quarterly*, vol. 1, no. 1-2, 2014, pp. 162-64.

Walcott, Rinaldo. "Black Lives Matter, Police and Pride: Toronto Activists Spark a Movement." *The Conversation*, 28 June 2017, theconversation.com/black-lives-matter-police-and-pride-toronto-activists-spark-a-movement-79089. Accessed 10 Dec. 2017.

Wang, Yanan. "The Controversies Surrounding Black Lives Matter in Canada." *The Washington Post*, 14 July 2016, www.washingtonpost.com/news/worldviews/wp/2016/07/14/the-controversy-surrounding-black-lives-matter-in-canada/?utm_term=.f95e5d50a1ab. Accessed 11 May 2019.

Ware, Syrus M. "All Power to All People? Black LGBTTI2QQ Actiism, Remembrance, and Archiving in Toronto." *TSQ: Transgender Studies Quarterly*, vol. 4, no. 2, 2017, pp. 170-180.

Waters, Emily. *Lesbian, Gay, Bisexual, Transgender, Queer, and HIV-Affected Hate Violence in 2016*. National Coalition of Anti-Violence Programs, 2016.

Waters, Emily et al. *A Crisis of Hate: A Report on Lesbian, Gay, Bisexual, Transgender and Queer Hate Violence*. National Coalition of Anti-Violence Programs, 2018.

Jurisprudence

Canada (Attorney General) v Bedford, 2013 SCC 72, [2013] 3 S.C.R. 1101.

C.F. v Alberta (Vital Statistics), 2014 ABQB 237.

Dawson v Vancouver Police Board (No. 2), 2015 BCHRT 54.

Halton Children's Aid Society v G.K., 2015 ONCJ 307.

Kavanagh v Canada (Attorney General), 2001 CHRD 21.

R v Keegstra, 1990 3 SCR 697.

Nixon v Vancouver Rape Relief Society, 2002 BCHRT 1.

XY v Ontario (Government and Consumer Services), 2012 HRTO 726.

Legislation and Hearings

Bill C-16: An Act to Amend the Human Rights Act and the Criminal Code, 1st Sess, 42nd Parl, 2016.

Bill C-276: An Act to Amend the Canadian Human Rights Act and the Criminal Code (Gender Identity and Gender Expression), 2nd Session, 41st Parliament, 2013.

Bill C-279: An Act to Amend the Canadian Human Rights Act and the Criminal Code (Gender Identity), 1st Session, 21st Parliament, 2013.

Bill C-326: An Act to amend the Canadian Human Rights Act (Gender Identity), 1st Session 39th Parliament, 2006.

Bill C-389: An Act to Amend the Canadian Human Rights Act and the Criminal Code (Gender Identity and Gender Expression), 3rd Session 40th Parliament, (Previously introduced 2nd Session, 40th Parliament), 2009.

Bill C-392: An Act to amend the Canadian Human Rights Act (Gender Identity), 1st Session, 38th Parliament, 2005.

Cossman, Brenda. "Proceedings of the Standing Senate Committee on Legal and Constitutional Affairs, Issue 28." Senate of Canada, 1st Session, 42nd Parliament, 4 May 2017.

Manning, Kimberly. "Proceedings of the Standing Senate Committee on Legal and Constitutional Affairs, Issue 28." Senate of Canada, 1st Session, 42nd Parliament, 4 May 2017.

Panas, Marni. "Proceedings of the Standing Senate Committee on Legal and Constitutional Affairs, Issue 28." Senate of Canada, 1st Session, 42nd Parliament, 11 May 2017.

Peterson, Jordan. "Proceedings of the Standing Senate Committee on Legal and Constitutional Affairs, Issue 29." Senate of Canada, 1st Session, 42nd Parl, 17 May 2017.

Wilson-Raybould, Jody. "Proceedings of the Standing Senate Committee on Legal and Constitutional Affairs, Issue 28." Senate of Canada, 1st Session, 42nd Parliament, 4 May 2017.

Chapter Seven

Considering Judicial Behaviour and Language in Sexual Assault Trials

David Ireland

Introduction

This chapter explores ways that judicial rationales have transgressed emerging moralities about sexual assault by reviewing the infamous cases in which judges have engaged in victim-blaming behaviour, stereotyping, and the perpetuation of myths based in sexist and misogynistic norms. It examines the role of the judicial discipline apparatus in dealing with judges who fall short of the high standards of acceptable language and behaviour in conducting sexual assault trials. Finally, this chapter looks at the recent recommendation for removal of Justice Camp by the Canadian Judicial Council (Camp subsequently resigned) for victim-blaming behaviour in the conduct of a sexual assault trial.

Before I begin to unpack the behaviour and language of judges in conducting these difficult and often emotive trials, a word of caution is warranted. We must remember that judges, like all of us, say things they wish they had not. It is doubtful that the notorious words spoken and written by Justices McClung, Dewar, or Camp (and others) are sources of pride for the authors. A person's life is not defined by a judgment they render or a mistake they once made. Some judges who have embodied stereotypes and damaged the vulnerable can, and do, go on to serve the public with wisdom. Human fallibility inculcates the language of judicial pronouncement as it does all endeavours. Yet the legal system strives to deliver wisdom and justice beyond reproach.

That caveat in place, we must consider the wider social implications of why a judge would tell a victim to "keep her knees together" or contextualize a horrific sexual assault by stating "sex was in the air." These examples come from real cases, and although they are outliers in some respects, they are also indicative of a pattern of ignorance and sexism belying a troubling public perception of sexual assault, sexual assault trials, and the victims and accused in those proceedings. Judges are nothing more than lawyers who through a combination of privilege, luck, excellence, and political or personal connection (in varying measure) graduate to the bench. To expect a judge not to carry certain biases, perceptions, and learned social behaviours to their job is as unrealistic as it is undesirable (Evans). In other words, judges are people too: "Some judges are extremely courteous, pleasant people: some are natural bullies. Some are patient and painstaking, balanced and judicious by nature: some are crude, tetchy and impatient, given to jumping to conclusions. Some are extraordinarily intelligent and some are almost incredibly obtuse. We advocates have to learn to cope with all of them" (Evans 74). This does not mean, however, that we should not expect the highest standards of education and social intelligence from our judiciary. Quite the opposite, in fact. To sit in judgment of others is a privilege. Those granted this privilege must serve the public with dedication and compassion. Most important of all though, judges must apply the law in word and spirit. When their own biases preclude their ability to do this, society suffers. Many of the examples below speak to an inability to correctly apply the law of sexual assault because of an adherence to sexist myths and stereotypes about victims. When an incorrect application of the law is fueled by stereotypes and myths, the justice system fails us all.

Before I examine the case law, a note on the importance of terminology in sexual assault cases is warranted. Academics, lawyers, judges, and community advocates have discussed the terms "victim" and "complainant" at length. Neither term is ideal in a legal context. The conative meanings of both are troubling. I have practiced criminal law as both Crown and defence counsel, and I have used both terms in court, often interchangeably. Some have argued a "complainant" only becomes a "victim" if and when the accused is convicted. I do not subscribe to this view. It ignores the reality of our justice system: factually guilty people are acquitted and, hopefully significantly less so, innocent people are convicted. Adhering to normative ideals in an attempt to dehumanize horrific interpersonal behaviour does little to advance our society. Although the lack of agency inherent in the word "victim" still causes me concern, it is the word I have used throughout this chapter. It in no way signifies my belief that every witness in every trial tells the truth about everything. In my experience, "truth" in court is a precarious and highly personal mixture of fallible memory and emotion. Nor does the use of the term "victim" signify a lack of respect for the foundational principles of criminal law represented by proof beyond a reasonable doubt and the presumption of innocence. Put another way, I assert that one may support victims while upholding the principles of fundamental justice as they relate to the rights of an accused. I believe that our criminal justice system can be rigorous, fair, and empathetic. One can embrace both due process and the enhancement of victim's rights.

Yet there remains a strong literature that demonstrates that survivors of sexual assault operate in a context of distrust with the criminal justice system, and indeed, the vast majority of sexual assault cases remain unreported (Craig, "Trials"). The trial process may create traumatic experiences for victims and reconstitute harms for victims through the process itself (Craig, "Trials"). The process at its worst is mired by systemic racism and sexism while the courtroom iterates a physical and relational manifestation of patriarchal symbols, attitudes, and practices that may leave the predominately women victims feeling objectified, humiliated, and discriminated against (Craig, "Trials"). If these claims are true, the prose of the judicial decisions discussed below may further exacerbate these harms. At the very least, they represent sombre and overt reflections of the tacit subjugations of the criminal trial process when it comes to victims of sexual assault.

The Law of Sexual Assault—A Brief Overview

In 1982, Parliament abolished the crime of rape and replaced it with the offence of sexual assault (along with the more serious offences of sexual assault with a weapon and aggravated sexual assault) (Roach, "Criminal Law"). The prior offence of rape did not include both genders, nor, in law, could a man be held accountable for the rape of his wife. When sexual assault was introduced as an offence, these abhorrent anomalies died. In 1993, Parliament codified the meaning of consent and set specific circumstances where consent could not be given (e.g., where the complainant is incapable of consenting) by enacting section 273.1 of the *Criminal Code* (Roach, "Criminal Law").

A simple assault is the intentional application of force on another without their consent. In order to be a sexual assault, the application of force (touching) must, of course, be of a sexual nature. Courts will view the conduct objectively to determine if the circumstances of the assault are sexual. Courts must look at "the part of the body touched, the nature of the conduct, the words and gestures accompanying the act and all other circumstances surrounding the conduct" (*R v Chase*).

A conviction for a criminal offence requires proof beyond reasonable doubt of two basic elements—that the accused committed the *actus reus* (the physical act of the crime) and that they had the necessary *mens rea* (mental intention to commit the crime). The *actus reus* of sexual assault is unwanted sexual touching and can be broken down as follows: (i) touching, (ii) the sexual nature of the contact, and (iii) the absence of consent. The *mens rea* of sexual assault is explained in the seminal *R v Ewanchuk* decision: "The *mens rea* of sexual assault is the intention to touch, knowing of, or being reckless of or wilfully blind to, a lack of consent, either by words or actions, from the person being touched" (*Chase* para 23). Consent cannot be obtained when the victim is unconscious (*Criminal Code* section 273.1(2) (a.1)) or otherwise unable to consent.

Sexual assault cases often revolve around one of two defences. Either the accused claims the victim consented or the accused claims he had a mistaken belief in the victim's consent. Which defence is presented will, in large part, be determined by the position of the accused and the evidence that unfolds at trial. A honest but mistaken belief in communicated consent must be reasonable (*Criminal Code* section 265.4; *R v Barton*), and there must be some plausible evidence to support such a claim before a jury will be left with the defence of mistaken belief in communicated consent (Roach "Criminal Law"; *Barton*). There are restrictions to the defence, such as the accused cannot be intoxicated, reckless, or wilfully blind (*Criminal Code* section 273.2). Also, to advance a defence of honest but mistaken belief in communicated consent, there must be some evidence that "the complainant voluntarily and affirmatively expressed consent by words or actively expressed consent by conduct" (*Criminal Code* section 273.2(c)).

Sections 276(1)-(4) of the *Criminal Code* outline the circumstances under which the accused in a sexual assault trial can ask questions about the victim's sexual activity (including prior sexual history). These sections of the *Code* are often referred to as the "rape shield" provisions. This is a complex and ever evolving area of the law born of dialogue between the courts and Parliament. As sexual assault trials are often centred on the credibility of the parties, these sections can take on great importance. In December 2018, legislative changes made it clear that sexual activity evidence would include communications of a sexual nature. The changes also provided a right for victims to make submissions in section 276 applications (*Criminal Code* section 278.94(2)), and be represented by counsel (*Criminal Code* section 278.94(3)). The intent of Parliament was to provide further protection against the use of myth and stereotype in sexual assault prosecutions. As will be seen below, commentators have questioned the role of defence, prosecution, and, indeed, courts themselves in perpetuating myths such as that promiscuous women are more likely to consent to sexual activity and are less worthy of belief.

In 2019, section 276 was considered in the case of *R v Goldfinch*. The case considered whether the accused sexually assaulted a woman he had dated and lived with—a relationship, the Supreme Court of Canada (SCC) referred to as "friends with benefits" (*para* 3). The court had to consider whether the context of the relationship should be put to a jury because the accused did not want the impression left that the relationship was platonic. The trial judge allowed the information in, and the accused was found not guilty, but the Alberta Court of Appeal thought this was reversible error and ordered a retrial. The majority of the SCC dismissed the accused's appeal and, at paragraph four, noted the following:

Introducing evidence of the sexual nature of the relationship served no purpose other than to support the inference that because the complainant had consented in the past, she was more likely to have consented on the night in question... While the sexual aspect of the relationship was evidence of "specific instances of sexual activity," it was not "relevant to an issue at trial."

The decision echoed another decision in 2019, *R v Barton*. The accused in *Barton* was charged with first degree murder in the death of an Indigenous woman who was also a sex worker; she had died in the bathroom of the accused's hotel room due to a severe vaginal wound. At trial, the Crown referred to the victim as a prostitute, and the accused referenced the previous sexual activity of the victim. The accused was found not guilty by a jury, but the case was appealed, and the Alberta Court of Appeal ordered a new trial. The SCC noted that the trial judge erred by not instructing the jury of the mandatory requirements of section 276 of the *Criminal Code* (paras 70-85). The majority of the court also made it clear that for the accused to rely on honest but mistaken belief in consent, the consent has to be communicated consent—affirmative consent by words or conduct about agreement to engage in sexual activity with the accused (para 90). At paragraph 9, the majority noted the following:

> The central error committed by the trial judge was his failure to comply with the mandatory requirements set out under the s. 276 regime. That error had ripple effects, most acutely in the instructions on the defence of honest but mistaken belief in communicated consent... In particular, non-compliance with the s. 276 regime, which serves a crucial screening function where an accused relies on the complainant's prior sexual activities in support of his defence, translated into a failure to expose and properly address misleading evidence and mistakes of law arising from Mr. Barton's defence. This in turn resulted in reversible error warranting a new trial.

Later, drawing on this reasoning, the majority also noted the following: "The accused cannot rest his defence on the false logic that the complainant's prior sexual activities, by reason of their sexual nature, made her more likely to have consented to the sexual activity in question, and on this basis he believed she consented. This is ... prohibited under s. 276(1)(a) of the *Code*" (para 94). The majority argued that the concepts of implied consent, broad advance consent, and propensity to consent are irrelevant to mistake of consent defences (*para* 99). Furthermore, an honest mistake as to consent requires reasonable steps:

> The accused must take steps that are objectively reasonable, and the reasonableness of those steps must be assessed in light of the circumstances known to the accused at the time (*para* 104) ... it is possible to identify certain things that clearly are *not* reasonable steps. For example, steps based on rape myths or stereotypical assumptions about women and consent cannot constitute reasonable steps. As such, an accused cannot point to his reliance on the complainant's silence, passivity, or ambiguous conduct as a reasonable step to ascertain consent... Accordingly, an accused's attempt to "test the waters" by recklessly or knowingly engaging in non-consensual sexual touching cannot be considered a reasonable step. This is a particularly acute issue in the context of unconscious or semi-conscious complainants... It is also possible to identify circumstances in which the threshold for satisfying the reasonable steps requirement will be elevated. For example, the more invasive the sexual activity in question and/or the greater the risk posed to the health and safety of those involved, common sense suggests a reasonable person would take greater care in ascertaining consent. The same holds true where the accused and the complainant are unfamiliar with one another, thereby raising the risk of miscommunications, misunderstandings, and mistakes. At the end of the day, the reasonable steps inquiry is highly contextual, and what is required will vary from case to case. (*paras* 107-108)

These recent interventions from the SCC provide welcome clarification that was, regrettably, still required in 2019. As will be seen below, there have been a number of court cases that necessitated this intervention to protect the rights of victims and remind judges of the damage caused by the application of myth and stereotype. Time will tell whether these recent interventions from Parliament and Canada's top court cure the defects evidenced in the complaint processes reviewed in this chapter.

The Legacy of *R v Ewanchuk*

Students of law will find few legal ratios as easy to distill as Justice L'Heureux-Dubé's unequivocal enshrinement of the doctrine of "no means no" in *Ewanchuk*. There is no defence of implied consent in Canadian law. Either you consent or you do not. Consent to sexual acts must be affirmative, unequivocal, and ongoing. The SCC reversed the decisions of the trial as well as the appeal courts in Alberta who had acquitted Mr. Ewanchuk. The facts of the case are simply stated. The victim, having arranged a job interview with the accused, Ewanchuk, sat in his vehicle for the interview with the van doors left open. After the interview, Ewanchuk asked the young woman to visit his trailer to view samples of his work. She reluctantly agreed. As he followed her into the trailer, he shut the door and immediately the woman felt something was wrong, and she became afraid. After closing the door, Ewanchuk made progressive sexual advances by touching the victim. At each advance the victim said no—a total of three times. Ewanchuk did not listen.

Mr. Ewanchuk was acquitted at the trial level, and the Crown appealed to the Alberta Court of Appeal. Justice John McClung upheld the acquittal. He stated in his decision that the victim did not present herself "in a bonnet and crinolines" (*R v Ewanchuk* ABCA para 88); Justice McClung also commented that she was a mother of a six-month-old and shared an apartment with her boyfriend and another friend. The behaviour of the accused was seen as "far less criminal than hormonal," and the victim's dress and conduct raised a reasonable doubt about a lack of consent (*R v Ewanchuk* ABCA para 92). Justice McClung went on to say, "in a less litigious age, going too far in the boyfriend's car was better dealt with on site—a well-chosen expletive, a slap in the face, or, if necessary, a well-directed knee" (*R v Ewanchuk* ABCA para 93).

McClung concurred with the trial judge that there was consent to sexual activity and that the Crown had failed to prove the criminal intent of the accused (*R v Ewanchuk* ABCA; Benedet). Criminal intent could not be proved when the victim, by conduct, implied consent and the accused was not aware of her true state of mind. McClung's comments included that the complainant's fear of force was misplaced in light of Ewanchuk's "clumsy passes" (*R v Ewanchuk* ABCA para 91; Benedet). As Professor Janine Benedet notes, comments by McClung "clearly echo the conclusions in earlier cases ... as to victims' so-called contributory behaviour, the relevance of their past sexual experience, and the idea that acquaintance rape is not real rape" (139).

Justice McClung's decision in the court of appeal was, to put it mildly, a study in the myths and stereotypes that surround victim behaviour. On February 25, 1999, the SCC overturned Ewanchuk's acquittal, entering a conviction, sent it back to the Alberta courts for sentencing, and declared that implied consent did not exist in law (*R v Ewanchuk* SCC).

Justice McClung was unhappy that his decision was overturned by the SCC. He was so unhappy that he took the unusual step of penning an open letter which was published by the *National Post*. In fact, as noted by Margaret Denike, the case achieved far more of its notoriety from the open letter Justice McClung wrote attacking Justice L'Heureux-Dubé than the originating case. McClung states of L'Heureux-Dubé in the letter: "[her] personal conviction...could be a plausible explanation for the disparate (and growing) number of male suicides being reported in the province of Quebec" (Denike 82).

McClung followed this letter with comments to the press that L'Heureux-Dubé harboured "consistently anti-male attitudes" (Denike 82). In relation to the decisions, Denike further comments as follows: "The provincial court decisions in Ewanchuk make apparent the extent to which members of some judicial circles have aggressively resisted the objectives of Parliament to enact reforms to judicial procedure, and the extent to which notions about women's sexual proclivity continued to be cultivated within the judiciary" (Denike 82). Although Justice McClung apologized to Justice L'Heureux-Dubé for his comments concerning suicide (Justice L'Heureux-Dubé's husband had committed suicide, which Justice McClung claimed not to have known), McClung maintained that the SCC was wrong to overturn his decision. In a subsequent interview with the *National Post*, Justice McClung courted further controversy by stating the victim in *Ewanchuk* was hardly "lost on her way home from the nunnery" (CBC News, "Alberta").

Many legal commentators and experts were, perhaps predictably, outraged by Justice McClung's behaviour. There was, however, almost no articulated outrage from the legal community over the ruling itself. McClung had gone too far in personally attacking another member of the judiciary, but members of the legal community were apparently not appalled at the derogatory and myth-filled ruling itself (Mitchell et al.).

Perhaps this response is not entirely surprising when other rulings that came before *Ewanchuk* are considered. As Benedet notes, during the 1970s and 1980s, similarly flawed reasoning appeared in the Alberta Court of Appeal. Benedet posits that many decisions during this period included myths such as that rape by a stranger should be considered more serious in law than rape by an acquaintance or date and that the seriousness of the rape was heightened when weapons or additional force were used or if the victim was attacked in her own home (131). It was not uncommon to read decisions reaffirming the notion that the actions by the complainant contributed to her predicament or explaining steps she may have taken to avoid being assaulted (131-32). Sometimes victim behaviour (e.g., failure to object or flee) was used to attack the victim's credibility or mitigate the sentence in a conviction. Benedet also describes cases in which contributory behaviour was used to reduce the offender's sentence on appeal (132). Interestingly, such victim blaming did not preclude a conviction in all cases. Nevertheless, it is not shocking that victim-blaming prose resurfaced in the Alberta Court of Appeal decision in *Ewanchuk*. More recent cases in Alberta have continued in the tradition of poorly educated judicial opinion on the law and dynamics of sexual violence (for example see *R v Adepoju*).

The Canadian Judicial Council (CJC), the body charged with disciplining judges at the federal appointment level, met as a three-member panel to decide Justice McClung's fate in the wake of the *Ewanchuk* decision and his open letter to the *National Post*. In a decision released on May 21, 1999, the panel expressed strong disapproval for McClung's comments about Supreme Court Justice L'Heureux-Dubé. Although the panel was clearly also unhappy with the language used in the judgment, they were most critical of Justice McClung's letter to the *National Post*. The panel ultimately concluded that the file should be closed and not subject to a full CJC review where McClung could have, ultimately, been removed. Even though the panel found that McClung's comments were "flippant, unnecessary and unfortunate," but the comments "did not reflect an underlying bias against women" and "would not preclude Mr. Justice McClung from treating all litigants fairly and impartially in future" (Canadian Judicial Council, "Panel" 205). In this decision, the CJC set the tone for acceptable judicial behaviour and language in relation to sexual assault cases.

Although some academics have opined that McClung's judgment may have been legally defensible, the inflammatory language used in the judgment may have sealed its demise (Henderson). Professor Greig Henderson wonders, with some justification, whether or not the SCC would have considered the case if the language used by Justice McClung was less extreme (although there was a right of appeal to the SCC given there was a dissenting judicial opinion in the court of appeal).

Linda Coates et al. have considered the importance of judicial language, more generally, in sexual assault prosecutions. They suggest that judges use vocabulary to describe sexual assault that draws on erotic or affectionate terminology, which is more suited to describe consensual acts of sex. Examples include when assaults are described as sexual events in sexual terms, such as when the term intercourse is used or when the details of the assaults are overtly sexualized (Coates et al. 191-92). In judicial prose, the act of assault is sometimes attributed to the defendant's desire, sexual appetite, or sexual difficulty rather than violence. Coates et al. have pointed out that grammatical choices can obviate the offender's agency, absolving them of the violent aspects of the offence through the use of passive or indirect phrasing and ascribing the complainant co-agency for the assault (Coates et al. 202). All of the tendencies in judicial language described above are problematic.

Commentary after *Ewanchuk*

Commentators have contextualized the perpetuation of myths and stereotyping in sexual assault prosecutions since *Ewanchuk*. Susan Ehrlich touches on the difference in how judges talk about sexual assaults committed by strangers versus acquaintances; she notes that judges are much more likely to invoke their own, potentially problematic, stereotypes about male and female sexuality when there is an acquaintance or date rape at issue (Ehrlich 392). Ehrlich also highlights the racialized aspects of language in sexual assault trials and shows how in one instance, police, prosecutors and judges regarded a sexual assault against an unconscious Inuit women as less severe in criminality (487). American studies have noted similar problems with racism in sexual assault trials during the last two decades, as evidenced in African American sexual violence victimization studies (Foley et al.; Willis).

The concept of the ideal victim is a myth that still functions to disqualify many victims' accounts of assault experiences. This myth undermines the credibility of those women who are seen to deviate too far from the stereotypical notions of authentic victims or reasonable victim responses (Randall "Sexual"). This myth is crucial when considering the centrality of the credibility contest that is often at the heart of many sexual assault cases (Randall, "Sexual" 398). The so-called good and bad victim are normative constructs, conjured up by popular culture and rooted in our history of suppressing women in Western society (Randall, "Sexual" 406-7). Following the shift to an affirmative consent standard, Lise Gotell has effectively exposed the ways in which judicial discourse in sexual assault cases have tended to regard credible victims as those who were seen to be both responsible and risk averse, protecting their own sexual safety (Gotell, "Canadian"; Gotell, "Rethinking"; Gotell, "The Discursive"). Gotell argues the following:

> Canadian judicial discourses consolidating an affirmative consent standard reinforce a decontexualized construction of sexual assault. Emphasis is placed on discrete sexual transactions, consent-seeking actions and the quality of agreement. And while valuable in focusing attention on the demonstration of positive consent, sexual violence is atomized; its manifestations and consequences are never collected, never considered in a context where sexual assault is a mechanism for sustaining gendered power relations. ("Canadian" 14)

Kent Roach has argued persuasively that reforms in sexual assault law were somewhat convenient for the government, as they advanced the politics of law and order—a matter that was met with a degree of popular support—while simultaneously placating the concerns of feminist activism groups such as the Women's Legal Education and Action Fund (LEAF) (Roach, *Due*).

Richard Jochelson and Kirsten Kramar describe the developments in the *Ewanchuk* era in the following terms:

> In these diverse feminist (and in some cases non feminist) interpretations of the development of the law of sexual assault one sees apposite but simultaneously contradictory summations of the law. These accounts see the legislative changes in the 1990s as generally beneficial to the feminist interventions, seeing useful

understandings of sexuality as the Court began to become aware of the gendered nature of sexual violence in Canada...[others see] a shift in the latter half of that decade to legal approaches to sexual violence that delegate the responsibility of sexual assault to victims themselves, that devolve the management of victimization to front line social service work, and which disciplines complainants' sexual conduct through, in part, the discourse of the Court... The implications for feminist inter-pretations of the law of sexual assault seem confounding. (91)

The response to *Ewanchuk* did not do much to stem the tide of troubling judicial discourse in sexual assault cases. In the coming pages, I review several recent examples of judicial prose that invoke rape myths despite the law reforms of earlier decades.

The Persistence of Myth and Stereotype in Sexual Assault Cases

R v Rhodes—Sex in the Air

In *R v Rhodes*, a judge of the Manitoba Court of Queen's Bench arguably reached a new low in misunderstanding the dynamics of sexual violence in the context of a sentencing decision. The victim was sexually assaulted in the middle of the night on the side of a dark highway in an isolated part of Northern Manitoba. It was, by any measure, a horrific event for the victim. Justice Dewar began his sentencing by stating the following: "after a night of drinking when four people decide to climb into a car around 2:30 am to continue to party rather than head home to their own beds, something bad is bound to happen" (*R v Rhodes* Sentencing transcript). Dewar explained that the case involved "misunderstood signals and inconsiderate behaviour" (*R v Rhodes* Sentencing transcript). Though the accused was convicted on the evidence, in the sentencing decision, Justice Dewar referred to the offender as no more than a "clumsy Don Juan" (*R v Rhodes* Sentencing transcript). Dewar continued his steady descent into myth and stereotype by commenting on the victim's attire (a tube top) and her ample make-up (*R v Rhodes* Sentencing transcript). As if this were not insult enough, Justice Dewar infamously claimed that "sex was in the air" on the night in question (*R v Rhodes* Sentencing transcript).

It is difficult to conceive of a less appropriate use of language and framing of facts. The sexual assault, like all assaults, is an act of violence against the victim. This assault was particularly brutal based on the findings at trial. To add insult to injury, Justice Dewar imposed a conditional sentence of house arrest for a period of two years. The Manitoba Court of Appeal ordered a new trial because of the legal errors made by the trial judge in assigning the burden of proof (*R v Rhodes* MBCA). The accused was convicted at his new trial in 2013 (*R v Rhodes* 2013 MBQB 166) and given a sentence of three years (*R v Rhodes* 2013 MBQB 251).

Rhodes and the CJC

Justice Dewar's matter went to the CJC, albeit not for a full review. The CJC announced on February 25 2011, that the CJC would be reviewing complaints made against Justice Dewar (Canadian Judicial Council, "CJC to Review"). While the review was ongoing, Justice Dewar was allowed to sit on the bench with a reduced caseload and not on cases involving sexual assaults (McIntyre). Justice Dewar acknowledged his use of stereotypical language and expressed regret during the CJC proceedings.

In Winnipeg, Dewar's comments sparked angry protests with demonstrators calling on the judge to resign (CBC News, "Manitoba"). Although Justice Dewar issued an apology to the victim, academics were also quick to pour scorn on Justice Dewar. Law Professor Karen Busby has pointed out that the case would have escaped scrutiny had a Winnipeg Free Press reporter not heard about it and that complaints made to CJC about Dewar's comments included those by the Manitoba minister responsible for the status of women (Busby).

The CJC decision was rendered on November 9, 2011. The head of the CJC expressed concern over Justice Dewar's sentencing but said no further action was required from Justice Dewar. Dewar was deemed to have shown a lack of sensitivity. Regarding complaints about the sentence itself, Chief Justice Wittmann for the CJC noted that the proper recourse was through the appeal mechanisms in the courts. Chief Justice Wittmann also considered Dewar's full apology to the victim, and active steps taken by Dewar to continue his educational efforts (Canadian Judicial Council, "CJC Completes").[1] Justice Dewar met with an expert on gender equality and agreed to continue pursuing professional development in the area (Santin).

R v Wagar—*The Perfect Storm*

R v Wagar is perhaps the most infamous recent example of judicial reliance on, and iteration of, myths in the adjudication of a sexual assault trial. In the case, Judge Robin Camp of the Alberta Provincial Court[2] acquitted the accused of sexual assault. During the trial, Justice Camp frequently referred to the victim as the accused. Additionally, Justice Camp said the following to the accused:

> I want you to tell your friends, your male friends, that they have to be far more gentle with women. They have to be far more patient. And they have to be very careful. To protect themselves, they have to be very careful .... You've got to be very sure that the girl wants you to do it. Please tell your friends so that they don't upset women and so that they don't get into trouble. We're far more protective of women—young women and older women—than we used to be, and that's the way it should be. (Camp qtd. in Koshan)

The acquittal was overturned by the Alberta Court of Appeal on Oct 15, 2015 (*Wagar* 2015) and a new trial ordered. The court stated the following:

> We are satisfied that the trial judge's comments throughout the proceedings and in his reasons gave rise to doubts about the trial judge's understanding of the law governing sexual assaults and in particular, the meaning of consent and restrictions on evidence of the complainant's sexual activity imposed by section 276 of the *Criminal Code*. We are also persuaded that sexual stereotypes and stereotypical myths, which have long since been discredited, may have found their way into the trial judge's judgment. There were also instances where the trial judge misapprehended the evidence. (para 4)

The accused was acquitted again on January 31, 2017, after his second trial (*Wagar* 2017).[3]

Wagar and the CJC

The *Wagar* case and the conduct of Justice Camp were brought to the CJC's attention by law professors, including Alice Woolley and Elaine Craig (Power). Their complaint submission to the CJC highlights a number of diverse and distinct problems with Justice Camp's behaviour, including that Justice Camp was dismissive of, and contemptuous towards, the substantive law of sexual assault and the rules of evidence (Woolley et al.). In the complaint, counsel contends that "he [Justice Camp] showed disregard, if not disdain, for the rape shield provisions under the *Criminal Code,* the legal definition of consent to sexual touching, and the *Criminal Code* provision and case law regarding the doctrine of recent complaint" (4). It also notes that Camp made negative comments about rape shield provisions and allowed cross-examination in this regard without complying with requirements of the *Criminal Code* (5).

The complaint from Woolley et al. also argues that Justice Camp in both his (comments throughout the proceeding, and his reasons for decision ... demonstrated absolute disregard and disdain for the affirmative definition of consent to sexual touching established by Supreme Court of Canada" (Woolley et al. 5). Furthermore, Woolley et al. posit that Justice Camp responded with what appeared to be sarcastic and disrespectful comments to Crown council in her attempt to explain the reasonable steps requirement at the sentencing hearing (5).

In the sentencing, Justice Camp had also criticized the Canadian legal system precedent that a judge ought not to draw an adverse inference as to credibility based on victim's failure to report assault immediately. Justice Camp commented that the victim had "abused the first opportunity to report" the incident before conceding that this was "no longer contemporarily relevant." At trial, during the Crown's final submissions, Justice Camp commented that the recent complaint doctrine was "followed by every civilized legal system in the world for thousands of years" and "had its reasons," although "at the moment it's not the law" (Woolley et al. 6).

Justice Camp was alleged to have perpetuated rape myths and stereotypes while trivializing the harm of sexual violence (Woolley et al. 8-9). Woolley et al. quote Justice Camp as saying, "men do react to challenges and women give challenges...there's nothing necessarily malign in that.... Sex is very often a challenge"; for Woolley et al., this quote indicates his "tendency to conceptualize issues of sexuality and gender based or stereotypical generalizations that should not inform any judicial process, let alone a sexual assault trial" (10).

This time, the CJC decided to hold a full hearing, and for the first time, a federally appointed judge had his career on the line over his conduct in a sexual assault trial (Markusoff et al.). Even in his submissions before the CJC, Justice Camp continued to refer to the victim as the accused, just as he had done in the trial. Justice Camp pleaded a lack of education (Markusoff et al.). Camp had only presided over one sexual assault trial prior to *Wagar*, a couple of preliminary inquiries, and some sentencing hearings (Markusoff).

The CJC committee unanimously accepted the call for removal, with twenty-four voting in favour and three against. Removal was recommended by the CJC on March 8, 2017. Rather than facing the prospect of a removal, Justice Camp retired effective March 10, 2017, prior to action by the Minister of Justice. Woolley notes that Justice Camp was only the third federal judge to ever be (effectively) removed from office (Woolley, "The Resignation").

During the course of the CJC proceedings, Christin Scmitz penned a piece in the *Lawyers Daily*, expressing hopefulness that the potential removal of Justice Camp represented a sea change in judicial discipline. In that piece, Lorne Sossin, former Dean of Law at Osgoode Hall, quoted in Scmitz's piece, opines as follows: "the express inclusion of [sexual assault] survivor perspectives in the context of 'public confidence' is an important step in refining the open-ended test for when public confidence in a judge is so compromised that removal is justified."

The CJC report recommending the removal of Camp states the following:

> Canadians expect their judges to know the law but also to possess empathy and to recognize and question any past personal attitudes and sympathies that might prevent them from acting fairly. Those qualities sustain public confidence in the judiciary. For the reasons that follow, we find that Justice Robin Camp failed to meet those high standards and acted in a manner that seriously undermined public confidence in the judiciary. Accordingly, we recommend that Justice Camp be removed from office (Canadian Judicial Council, "Inquiry" paras 2-3).

The CJC also found that the judge relied on "discredited myths and stereotypes about women and victim-blaming during the trial and in his Reasons for Judgment" (Canadian Judicial Council, "Inquiry" para 10). The committee concluded as follows: "the Judge's conduct in the trial was so manifestly and profoundly destructive of the concept of impartiality, integrity and independence of the judicial role that public confidence is sufficiently undermined to render the Judge incapable of executing the judicial office" (Canadian Judicial Council, "Inquiry" para 13).

Despite the ordeal, and his effective removal from the bench, Justice Camp was readmitted to his provincial law society and is now a practicing member of the Alberta Bar.

R v Al-Rawi—A Drunk Can Consent

R v Al-Rawi (unreported) was a recent case from the Nova Scotia Provincial Court. The case has since been overturned on appeal (*Al-Rawi* 2018). Nevertheless, it demonstrates how trial court judges continue to implicate rape myths in their judgements, especially the trope of the ideal victim.

The victim was severely intoxicated and in an emotional state when she entered a cab driven by the accused. Eleven minutes later, the victim was found in the rear seat, naked from waist down, her breasts exposed, and her legs propped over the front seats. She was unconscious. When she was roused, the victim did not have a memory of the entry into the taxi and what happened subsequently. The taxi was nowhere near the victim's home. Judge Lenehan presided over the trial and concluded that there was no evidence that the acts were non-consensual and that there was insufficient evidence to conclude that the complainant lacked the capacity to consent as a result of her intoxication.

Professor Elaine Craig undertook an in-depth treatment of this case and its myriad issues, citing the case as an example of the failure of the legal system to adequately address allegations of sexual assault (Craig, "Judging"). She argues that several legal errors were made in the decision, which were later corrected by the court of appeal. These errors included failing to apply the proper legal standard for capacity to consent; confusing the *actus reus* and *mens rea* elements for the offence of sexual assault; failing to consider circumstantial evidence of nonconsent; failing to uphold section 276 of the *Code*; and relying on stereotypical assumptions about women and sex to understand the complaint's behaviour. The judge also failed in "his legal approach to the evidence as a whole" (Craig, "Judging" 182-83).

Indeed, the overall tone of the judgment was based on speculation. Professor Craig notes the following:

> Judge Lenehan had substantial circumstantial evidence to support the inference that the sexual touching was non-consensual. He had no evidence before him to support the inference that the Complainant consented to sexual contact with the accused. While a lack of evidence of consent is certainly not fatal to the accused (who is entitled to a presumption of innocence) a reasonable doubt cannot arise from speculation or conjecture drawn from hypothetical scenarios. (Craig, "Judging" 195)

Craig also comments on the role of defence counsel in implanting stereotypes into the proceeding by suggesting the victim was not the same kind of person when she was drunk. This strategy invokes the "promiscuous party girl" stereotype: "the logic of this stereotype turns on the assumption that drunk women will have sex with anyone, anywhere, anytime-that the consumption of alcohol does not simply lower the party girl's inhibitions, it removes them entirely" (Craig, "Judging" 206).

Furthermore, the judgment was also devoid of case precedent and was not written but rather given orally from the bench, which Professor Craig also finds problematic:

> While Judge Lenehan's decision is filled with errors and it should be overturned, his conduct of the case in *Al-Rawi* does not appear to amount to judicial misconduct. What it does amount to, however, is further evidence of the need for both a legal rule requiring judges in sexual assault trials to provide written decisions, and much more rigorous sexual assault training for judges. (Craig, "Judging" 209)

On January 31, 2018, the Nova Scotia Court of Appeal overturned the trial decision and ordered a new trial (*R v Al-Rawi* NSCA). Beveridge J.A. found there were legal errors made because the lower court found no evidence concerning a lack of consent. According to the court of appeal, the trial judge had ignored and discredited an entire body of evidence that would permit an inference to be drawn that either the complainant did not voluntarily agree to engage in sexual activity with the respondent or lacked the capacity to do so (*R v Al-Rawi* NSCA). The court of appeal did not find that the language that the trial judge used—"a drunk can consent"—constituted an error in law. The adjudication of that matter would have to wait for another day.

LEAF intervened in the case at the court of appeal and advanced arguments that highlighted the discriminatory myths and stereotypes about women present in the trial decision, including those of intoxicated women: "LEAF is disappointed that the Court of Appeal did not take the opportunity presented by this appeal to address the discredited myths and stereotypes about sexual assault complaints that, in LEAF's view, played a role in the trial judge's reasoning in this case" (Karen Segal qtd. in LEAF, "LEAF and Avalon").

Al-Rawi and the Nova Scotia Judicial Council

Judge Lenehan's conduct was reviewed by the Nova Scotia Judicial Council Review Committee, but no order of misconduct was found (Nova Scotia Judicial Council, "Decision"). The committee found that the comment "clearly a drunk can consent" was not an incorrect statement of law and that the statement was reasonable in the circumstances of an oral decision delivered from the bench (Nova Scotia Judicial Council, "Decision" 130). It further opined that the place to deal with legal errors was through the appeal process in the court, not through judicial discipline (Nova Scotia Judicial Council, "Decision"). However, the committee somewhat missed the point. It is not simply that the judge misapplied the law but that he misapplied the law because he was unable to see past his own views surrounding victims of sexual assault.

The committee received 121 complaints related to the decision and Justice Lenehan, mostly related to the "clearly, a drunk can consent" comment (Nova Scotia Judicial Council, "Decision"). Other complaints referenced the track record of the judge, arguing that his past conduct in other proceedings indicated a gender bias.[4] The committee stated that the goal of the judicial review process is to ensure public confidence in the judiciary. The test to determine if public confidence can be maintained is to be determined through the eyes of a reasonable member of the public (para 3). This reasonable person is to be properly informed, dispassionate, and familiar with the basics of the rule of law in Canada and with the fundamental values of criminal law (para 10). The question the committee sought to answer was the following:

> From the point of view of a reasonable, dispassionate, and informed public could it be found to be so seriously contrary to the impartiality, integrity and independence of the judiciary that it has undermined the public's confidence in the ability of the judge to perform the duties of office, or in the administration of justice generally, and that it warrants a disposition other than dismissal of the complaints in order to restore that confidence? (Nova Scotia Judicial Council, "Decision" para 13)

The committee was not convinced Judge Lenehan had crossed the line of public confidence:

> While Judge Lenehan's choice of certain phrases....may have benefitted from more careful and contextual reflection, from the view of a reasonably informed person the conduct and comments that formed the subject of the various complaints could not be found to meet the test for judicial misconduct. (Nova Scotia Judicial Council, "Decision" para 4)

The committee determined that the everyday life of a provincial court judge does not permit the amount of analysis that the committee had the luxury of undertaking. It noted that complicated legal issues arose in the trial and that Justice Lenehan did not know what legal issues would arise until they unfolded in front of him. No pre-trial conferences or briefs were filed, nor were references to case authorities given by counsel throughout the trial (Nova Scotia Judicial Council, "Decision" 154-56). In short, the case was particularly complex because it involved an "unclear issue of capacity to consent by an intoxicated complainant," it implicated no direct evidence and provided only circumstantial evidence, the accused had a limited understanding of English, and the trial judge's oral decision was delivered from notes and not a script. It was, in the words of the committee, "the perfect storm" (Nova Scotia Judicial Council, "Decision" para 157): "Amidst this storm, Judge Lenehan wrestled with the issue of capacity to consent and concluded there was no direct evidence on consent. He was left to determine what all the circumstantial evidence meant" (Nova Scotia Judicial Council, "Decision" para 158).

Finally, deciding that there was no bias on the part of the judge, the Committee noted the following:

> Based on a holistic reading of the transcript of both the trial and the decision, and based on the interview with Judge Lenehan, that he was focused on the presumption of innocence and the requisite standard of proof. While he committed errors of law as found by the Court of Appeal, and could have more carefully reflected his reasons, the Committee could not find evidence to attribute the Judge's approach to bias. (Nova Scotia Judicial Council, "Decision" para 160)

It was recommended that Judge Lenehan write out his decisions in full in the future.

Is There a Path Forwards?

Although a great many judges across Canada perform their duties with diligence and wisdom, there have been a number who have behaved in a manner that falls short of an acceptable standard during sexual assault cases. Rarely has the CJC, or the provincial equivalents, acted to discipline judges when they have perpetuated the myths or stereotypes around sexual assault that still, regrettably, persist. Perhaps the review bodies deferred to judicial independence. Perhaps the reviewing bodies did not want to conflate the assessment of facts with social justice rationales, preferring to give credence to the discretion of judges in such cases. The tide of inaction seems to have turned. Social justice rationales cannot be dismissed as mere activism when the claims belie conceptions of fundamental equality in Canada and when they ignore decades of ameliorative law reform in the sexual assault context. In the notable case that did draw scorn from the CJC, that of Justice Robin Camp, the conduct of the sexual assault trial and the language used by the judge fell far short of the expectations of a reasonable person. The case is illustrative of how far a judge must stray beyond the line of reasonableness to suffer any real consequences.

Judges are not required to uphold a standard of perfection. They are, however, expected to apply the law and play their part in correcting outmoded societal attitudes about sexual violence. In the twenty years since Justice L'Heureux-Dubé reminded us that "no means no" in

Ewanchuk, the myths and stereotypes surrounding victim behaviour persist. Perhaps law reform cannot change the social world, or the initial law reforms did not go far enough. Regardless, it has taken over two decades to achieve compliance with SCC holdings in the area of sexual assault law. Appeal courts are required to correct judges who seem unable to understand basic concepts of consent, as judicial review bodies seem only willing to take action in the most egregious cases. We must work towards a judicial landscape that eradicates the language of myth and effectively disciplines those judges who continue to harbour and express these views. Most importantly of all, the unequivocal law of consent must be applied correctly and in the absence of personal biases. As Woolley suggests, judgments go from wrong to wrongful when they demonstrate disrespect for the law and a failure to empathize with those appearing before court ("When Judicial").

Some judges, including Justice Camp, have claimed that a lack of education was responsible for their transgressions. Melanie Randall has written about the need for continuing legal education in this area:

> This rehabilitative approach must also apply to those holding judicial office whose transgressions and misconduct are remediable. Most likely the overwhelming majority of judges appointed are ill equipped to preside over the complexities of a sexual assault trial. Given the rigours of the judicial role and the expansiveness and depth of legal knowledge required of judges, the brief training newly appointed judges receive on sexual assault law is hardly sufficient preparation. And the absence of regular mandatory training on this specialized and complicated area of law for those who must decide sexual assault cases, is clearly a systemic failure. (Randall "Judges")

Brenda Cossman, who worked with Justice Camp in advance of the CJC hearing, has also spoken out in favour of education over punishment in this arena: "Feminist lawyers and advocates recognize the pervasive nature of sexism in the judiciary. Are we going to fire each and every judge who has uttered sexist comments in the course of a trial? Or, are we going to try to educate them? Preferably before the sexual assault trials, but what about after?" (Cossman). Cossman does not want to see an encouragement of "postempathy," where the disaffected double down on their prejudicial views and harden their positions (Cossman; see also Woolley, "The Resignation").

Although judicial education is clearly important, the language and general behaviour that judges such as Justices McClung, Dewar and Camp display are emblematic of a far more insidious problem—embedded sexist biases that objectify woman and reify patriarchal sexual exploitation of women must be eliminated from the sexual assault trial. It is unlikely that education on the law of consent would have changed Justice Dewar's mind that "sex was in the air" the night of the sexual assault in question, nor would it necessarily alter Justice Camp's query of why the victim did not "keep her knees together" to avoid being sexually assaulted. These are emotive phrases. They are feelings that emanate from judges, perhaps unconsciously, as they listen to the evidence being presented at trial. They arise apart from the logical mind. Judicial education alone may not be able to intervene in the complex and dynamic process that manifests such impulses. Law reform alone, such as the recent *Criminal Code* changes codifying the SCC definition of consent and amending the rape shield provisions, may only categorize such logics as legal error. Although such actions may be better than nothing, the judicial mind must be equipped to understand and empathize with the lived experiences of women, especially in the context of the sexual assault matrix. Ensuring this will require more rigorous appointments, processes and radical overhaul of criminal law training processes.

In February 2017, Bill C-337, *Judicial Accountability through Sexual Assault Law Training Act*, was introduced into the House of Commons. This private member's bill proposes three significant changes to address the issue of judicial conduct in sexual assault trials. First, the bill amends the *Judges Act* to require comprehensive education in matters related to sexual assault law before appointment to the bench. Second, the bill requires the CJC to report on continuing education seminars offered on matters of sexual assault. Finally, the bill amends the *Criminal Code* to require that judges provide reasons in writing or in the record in sexual assault cases. As of spring 2019, the bill had been passed by the House of Commons and was in second reading in the Senate. By June 5, the Standing Committee on Legal and Constitutional Affairs had submitted its report to the Senate, which called for very modest and mainly technical changes. The bill's passage seems likely.

By examining the judgments of Justice McClung in *Ewanchuk*, Justice Dewar in *Rhodes* and Justice Camp in *Wagar*, we are able to see a lack of progress in eliminating sexual assault myths and stereotypes in sexual assault cases. Perhaps, the effective dismissal of Justice Camp and Bill C-337 will go some way to righting the ship. Perhaps the recent *Goldfinch* and *Barton* cases, and the December 2018 amendments to the *Criminal Code*, will help cure some of these same deficiencies. However, other judges who have demonstrated a similar lack of understanding of sexual violence have carried on with their careers on the bench. What can be said for sure is that there has been an inconsistent approach to judicial discipline. A more consistent approach is needed if we want to eradicate myth and bias from these trials once and for all. It is not encouraging that the SCC still has to remind judges that myths and stereotypes have no place in sexual assault trials in Canada (see for example: *R v ARJD* SCC; *R v W.L.S.*)—just as Justice L'Heureux-Dubé reminded judges in 1999.

Endnotes

1. The transcript of proceedings in *Rhodes* makes it clear that Justice Dewar was relying heavily on his own stereotypical views of the victim in *Rhodes*. For example:
   - Justice Dewar: "this looks like a one off. It doesn't look like it'll happen again as he has a difficulty in this activity" (p. 21, line 32).
   - Justice Dewar: "What about the signals that were given by the complainant ... and I know what her purpose was, but the fact is they were given, as they walked up the road to the highway... are those mitigating factors?" (p. 30, line 28-32).
   - Justice Dewar: "This is a case of misread signals and inconsiderate behaviour [and therefore is not able to be classified as a serious sexual assault]" (p. 76, lines 30-32).
   - Justice Dewar: "There were signals given by the circumstances and indeed by the complainant, albeit the latter based upon self preservation, which ought not to be overlooked. This is not a case in which Mr. Rhodes' anticipation was groundless.

However, its consummation without reasonable inquiry was not justified" (p.77, lines 1-5) "this type of assault is different than when there is no perceived invitation or where the complainant is sleeping" (p. 77, lines 6-10).

- Justice Dewar: "I'm faced with a man with no criminal record whatsoever, who appears to be industrious in his work and able to relate to others. But for this one instance, he does not live up to the designation as a criminal" (p. 77, lines 11-14).
- Justice Dewar: "Here there were no threats knowingly given, there was no violence knowingly imposed. Mr. Rhodes, in his testimony, had said that he wasn't out there to hurt anyone. Even his sexual activity, bizarre as it was and as hurtful as it was to the complainant, cannot be said to be only self-gratification. It had the characteristics of a clumsy Don Juan" [in reference to digital penetration of woman] (p. 77, lines 24-30).
- Justice Dewar: "Unlike the sleeping women cases, there was no insert woman giving no signals at all. There was some invitation however involuntary" (p. 78, lines 1-3).
- Justice Dewar: "I don't criticize the complainant. She was a frightened young woman all alone in the presence of a large, perhaps loud, overbearing older man. But she did give signals that he read the wrong way and was not considerate enough to make sure of what they were saying" (p. 78, lines 4-8).
- Justice Dewar: "I'm sure that whatever signals there were that sex was in the air were unintentional. But that does not change the fact that they were there [provocation/enticement on part of victim], more than just a manner of dress, more than the fact that she was a woman. And they are a relevant, mitigating factor" (p. 79, para 4-10).
- Justice Dewar: "The signals given here, in this case, are at least relevant to the degree of moral blameworthiness of Mr. Rhodes" (p. 80, lines 1-3).

2. Justice Camp was later appointed to the Federal Court, which provided jurisdiction to the CJC to discipline him.
3. Other Alberta examples were found in our research. For example, relatively recent cases from the Alberta Provincial Court also exemplify the reliance by trial courts on myths and stereotypes:

In *R v JR* (unreported), Judge Savaryn acquitted a youth offender of grabbing a youth's breasts and buttocks in a school hallway. The attack was caught on camera. The victim tried to defend herself with a water bottle. Judge Savaryn noted that the victim did not call for help from the janitor; she did not appear upset as she was smiling; and she did not clearly communicate any serious objection. What is more, the judge noted the victim later texted a friend a smiley face with tears and acronym 'lmao' (standing for "laughing my ass off"). The Alberta Court of Queen's Bench overturned the decision (*R v JR* 2016 ABQB 414), in part based on the trial judge's use of sexual stereotyping. The court entered a conviction and directed a different judge to handle sentencing (*R v JR* 2016 ABQB 414).

In *R v CMG* (unreported), a sixteen-year-old boy sexually assaulted the female victim in a park. Judge Pat McIlhargey acquitted the accused. The girl did not scream or run for help and did not confide in her aunt, with whom she was residing, about what had happened. The judge also noted that the girl did not appear to be affected by incident. Justice Martin (before her elevation to the Supreme Court of Canada in 2017) for the Alberta Court of Queen's Bench Ordered a new trial (*R v CMG* 2016 ABQB 368). Justice Martin stated that the trial judge had used a discredited line of reasoning and relied on myths and stereotypes in coming to his conclusions.

R v Adepoju (unreported) involved the acquittal of the accused after he was told numerous times by the victim she did not want to have sex. The accused resisted until she realized doing so was futile. Text messages were entered as evidence at the trial including, "I had to force you; you didn't want it" sent by the accused. Judge Sisson of the Alberta Court of Queen's Bench ruled that the victim consented after tiring. The Court of Appeal in March 2014 substituted the acquittal with a conviction (*R v Adepoju* 2014 ABCA 100). The trial judge had erred by inferring consent from submission (para 8) There was no disciplinary action taken against Judge Sisson though he did take early retirement in January 2017 (Graveland).

In the unreported decision of the Alberta Queen's Bench decision in *R v A.R.D.*, the accused was acquitted at trial of three sexual offences alleged to have been committed against his stepdaughter when she was between ages of eleven and sixteen. Judge Terry Clackson presided at the trial. Again, the behaviour of the victim was highlighted in the acquittal. In July 2016, the Alberta Court of Appeal overturned the acquittal, stating trial judge resorted to stereotypical reasoning (*R v A.R.D.* 2017 ABCA 237). A new trial was ordered, and the accused appealed to the SCC (*R v A.R.J.D.* 2018 SCC 6). On February 13, 2018, the SCC dismissed the appeal.

Justices Michael Savaryn and Patrick McIlhargery, discussed above were subject to internal reviews within their province's judicial review systems (Fine). Despite no further disciplinary action being taken by the Alberta courts,

Judge Savaryn was not permitted to sentence the accused after the decision came back from the Court of Queen's Bench (Fine). The Queen's Bench justice wrote that Savaryn's consideration of the victim's behaviour after the incident was reliant on victim myths. Despite this, no sanctioning action was taken.

4. Such past incidences include the Justice asking a breastfeeding woman to leave his courtroom and handing out light sentences on other sexual offences.

Works Cited
Secondary Sources

Benedet, Janine. "Sexual Assault Cases at the Alberta Court of Appeal: The Roots of *Ewanchuk* and the Unfinished Revolution." *Alberta Law Review*, vol. 52, no. 1, 2014, pp. 127-44.

Blatchford, Christie. "Manitoba Judge Is Dead Wrong in Rape Case." *The Globe and Mail*, 24 Feb. 2011, www.theglobeandmail.com/news/national/manitoba-judge-is-dead-wrong-in-rape-case/article 622513/. Accessed 13 Sept. 2018.

Blatchford, Christie. "In Manitoba, Sexual Assault Means Having to Say You're 'Sorry'" *The Globe and Mail*, 10 Mar. 2011, www.theglobe-andmail.com/news/national/in-manitoba-sexual-assault-means-having-to-say-youre-sorry/article623026/. Accessed 13 Sept. 2018.

Bundale, Brett. "Judicial Review Dismisses Complaints against NS Judge Who Said 'Clearly, a Drunk Can Consent." *National Post*, 4 April 2018, nationalpost.com/news/canada/complaints-dismissed-against-n-s-judge-who-said-clearly-a-drunk-can-consent. Accessed 13 Sept. 2018.

Busby, Karen. "The Rhodes Case: Thirty year of Law reform ignored." *The Forum Blog*, 22 Nov. 2011, feministlegalforum.wordpress.com/tag/justice-dewar/. Accessed 13 Sept. 2018.

Camp, Justice Robin. "Opening Submissions of Justice Camp, in the Matter of the Canadian Judicial Council's Review of Justice Camp." *Scribd*, www.scribd.com/document/323198240/Robin-Camp-opening docuemnts#fullscreen&from_embed. Accessed 13 Sept. 2018.

Canadian Judicial Council. "Canadian Judicial Council completes its review of complaints made against justice Robert Dewar." *News Release, Canadian Judicial Council*, 9 Nov. 2011, www.cjc-ccm.gc.ca/english/news_en.asp?selMenu=news_2011_1109_en.asp. Accessed 13 Sept. 2018.

Canadian Judicial Council. "Canadian Judicial Council to Review Complaints against Justice Robert Dewar." *News Release, Canadian Judicial Council*, 25 Feb. 2011, www.cjc-ccm.gc.ca/english/news_en.asp?selMenu=news_2011_0225_en.asp. Accessed 13 Sept. 2018.

Canadian Judicial Council. "Inquiry into the Conduct of the Honourable Robin Camp: Report to the Minister of Justice." *Canadian Judicial Council*, 8 March 2017, https://www.cjc-ccm.gc.ca/cmslib/general/Camp_Docs/2017-03-08%20Report%20to%20Minister.pdf. Accessed 13 Sept. 2018.

Canadian Judicial Council. "Panel Expresses Strong Disapproval of McClung Conduct." *News Release, Canadian Judicial Council*, 21 May 1999.

CBC News. "Alberta Judge Apologizes for Part of His Letter." *CBC News*, 27 Feb. 1999, www.cbc.ca/news/canada/alberta-judge-apologizes-for-part-of-his-letter-1.170036. Accessed 13 Sept. 2018.

CBC News. "Manitoba Judge Rebuked for Sex Assault Remarks." *CBC News*, 9 Nov. 2011, www.cbc.ca/news/canada/manitoba/manitoba-judge-rebuked-for-sex-assault-remarks-1.1099355. Accessed 13 Sept. 2018.

Coates, Linda et al. "Anomalous Language in Sexual Assault Trial Judgments." *Discourse & Society*, vol. 5, no. 2, 1994, pp. 189-206.

Cossman, Brenda. "For Judge 'Knees Together' Camp: Education Is Power." *The Globe and Mail*, 1 Dec. 2016, www.theglobeandmail.com/opinion/for-judge-knees-together-camp-education-is-power/article33121316/. Accessed 13 Sept. 2018.

Craig, Elaine. "Judging Sexual Assault Trials: Systemic Failure in the Case of *Regina v Bassam Al-Rawi*." *Can B Rev*, vol. 95, 2017, pp. 179-211.

Craig, Elaine. *Putting Trials on Trial: Sexual Assault and the Failure of the Legal Profession*. McGill-Queens University Press, 2018.

Denike, Margaret. "Dignifying Equality: The Challenge of Reform in Sexual Assault Proceedings." *Canadian Woman Studies*, vol. 19, no. 1-2, 1999, pp. 81-85.

Ehrlich, Susan. "Perpetuating-and Resisting- Rape Myths in Trial Discourse." *Sexual Assault in Canada: Law, Legal Practice and Women's Activism*, edited by Elizabeth Sheehy, University of Ottawa Press, 2012, pp. 389-408.

Evans, Keith. *The Language of Advocacy*. Oxford, 1998.

Fine, Sean. "Public Won't See Results of Review of Alberta Judges' Sex Assault Case Conduct." *The Globe and Mail*, 11 Jan. 2017, www.theglobeandmail.com/news/national/public-kept-in-the-dark-on-review-of-alberta-judges-over-sex-assault-case-conduct/article 3359 0247/. Accessed 13 Sept. 2018.

Foley, Linda A. et al. "Date Rape: Effects of Race of Assailant and Victims and Gender of Subjects on Perceptions." *Journal of Black Psychology*, vol. 21, 1995, pp. 6-18.

Gotell, Lise. "Canadian Sexual Assault Law: Neoliberalism and the Erosion of Feminist Inspired Law Reform." *Rethinking Rape Law*, edited by Clare McGlynn and Vanessa Munro, Routledge, 2010, pp. 209-23.

Morton F.L. "The McClung Affair." *Law, Politics and the Judicial Process in Canada*, 3rd ed, edited by F.L Morton and Dave Snow, University of Calgary Press, 2002, pp. 201-5.

Gotell, Lise. "The Discursive Disappearance of Sexualized Violence: Feminist Law Reform, Judicial Resistance and Neoliberal Sexual Citizenship." *Feminism, Law and Social Change: (Re)action and Resistance*, edited by Dorothy E. Chunn et al., University of British Columbia Press, 2007, pp. 127-163.

Gotell, Lise. "Rethinking Affirmative Consent in Canadian Sexual Assault Law: Neoliberal Sexual Subjects and Risky Women." *Akron L Rev*, vol. 41, 2008, pp. 865-98.

Graveland, Bill, "Alberta judge Criticized in Sexual Assault Case Takes Early Retirement." The Canadian Press, Dec. 20, 2016, www.cbc.ca/news/canada/calgary/alberta-judge-kirk-sisson-sexual-assault-criticism-retires-1.3905890. Accessed 13 Sept. 2013.

Henderson, Greig. "The Cost of Persuasion: Figure, Story, and Eloquence in the Rhetoic of Judicial Discourse." *University of Toronto Quarterly*, vol. 75, no. 4, 2006, pp. 905-24.

Jochelson, Richard, and Kirsten Kramar. "Essentialism Makes for Strange Bedmates: The Supreme Court Case of J.A. and the Intervention of LEAF." *Windsor Yearbook Access to Justice*, vol. 30, no. 1, 2012, pp. 77-100.

Koshan, Jennifer. "Judging Sexual Assault Cases Free of Myths and Stereotypes. Case Commented On: R v Wagar, 2015 ABCA 327 (CanLII)." *ABlawg.ca*, 2 Nov. 2015, ablawg.ca/wp-content/uploads/2015/11/Blog_JK_Wagar_Oct_31_2015.pdf. Accessed 10 Sept. 2018.

Markusoff, Jason et al. "The Robin Camp Case: Who Judges Judges?" *Macleans*, 14 Sept. 2016, www.macleans.ca/news/robin-camp-case-who-judges-the-judges/. Accessed 13 Sept. 2018.

Markusoff, Jason. "Robin Camp Testimony: Eight Things We Learned about the Judge." *Macleans*, 10 September 2016, www.macleans.ca/news/canada/robin-camp-testimony-eight-things-learned/. Accessed 13 Sept. 2018.

McIntyre, Mike. "Justice Dewar Removed from Cases of 'Sexual Nature.'" *Winnipeg Free Press*, 1 Mar. 2011, www.winnipegfreepress.com/breakingnews/Justice-Dewar-removed-from-cases-of-sexual-nature-117193448.html. Accessed 13 Sept. 2018.

Mitchell, Alanna et al. "Legal Experts Outraged by Personal Attack on Supreme Court Judge." *The Globe and Mail*, 27 Feb. 1999, www.fact.on.ca/newpaper/gm990227.htm. Accessed 13 Sept. 2018.

Moore, Oliver. "Supreme Court Rejects *Ewanchuk* Appeal." *The Globe and Mail*, 6 Mar. 2003, www.theglobeandmail.com/news/national/supreme-court-rejects-ewanchuk-appeal/article25685500/. Accessed 13 Sept. 2018.

Nova Scotia Judicial Council. "Judicial Conduct and Accountability." *The Courts of Nova Scotia, Nova Scotia Judicial Council*, www.courts.ns.ca/About_Judges/conduct_judges_fed.htm. Accessed 13 Sept. 2018.

Nova Scotia Judicial Council. "Decision of the Review Committee in the Matter of Complaints aagainst Judge Gregory Lenehan." *The Courts of Nova Scotia, Nova Scotia Judicial Council Review Committee*, 29 Mar. 2018, www.courts.ns.ca/documents/ReviewCommittee_FinalDecision.pdf. Accessed 13 Sept. 2018.

Power, Samantha. "How Women are Pushing Back on Sexual Assault Rulings in Alberta." *The Tyree*, 27 September 2016, thetyee.ca/News/2016/09/27/Alberta-Sexual-Assault-Rulings/. Accessed 13 Sept. 2018.

Randall, Melanie. "Randall: Judges Need More Education about Sexual Assault." *Ottawa Citizen*, 22 Mar. 2017, ottawacitizen.com/opinion/columnists/randall-judges-need-more-education-about-sexual-assault. Accessed 13 Sept. 2018.

Randall, Melanie. "Sexual Assault Law, Credibility, and Ideal Victims: Consent, Resistance, and Victim Blaming." *Can J Women & L*, vol. 22, 2010, pp. 397-433.

Roach, Kent. *Criminal Law*. Irwin, 2015.

Roach, Kent. *Due Process and Victims' Rights: The New Law and Politics of Criminal Justice*. University of Toronto Press, 1999.

Santin, Aldo. "Man Deemed a 'Clumsy Don Juan' by Judge Convicted in Second Trial." *Winnipeg Free Press*, 3 July 2013, www.winnipegfreepress.com/local/214208201.html. Accessed 13 Sept. 2018.

Scmitz, Cristin. "'Sea Change' wave crashing on Robin Camp." *The Lawyers Daily*, 15 December 2016, www.thelawyersdaily.ca/articles/3557. Accessed 13 Sept. 2018.

Willis, Cynthia E. "The Effect of Sex Role Stereotype, Victim and Defendant Race, and Prior Relationship on Rape Culpability Attribution." *Sex Roles*, vol. 26, 1992, pp. 213-26.

Woolley, Alice. "When Judicial Decisions Go from Wrong to Wrongful-How Should the Legal System Respond?" *ABlawg.ca*, 3 Nov. 2015, ablawg.ca/2015/11/03/when-judicial-decisions-go-from-wrong-to-wrongful-how-should-the-legal-system-respond/. Accessed 13 Sept. 2018.

Woolley, Alice. "The resignation of Robin Camp: background and reflections from Canada." *Legal Ethics*, vol. 20, no. 1, 2017, pp. 134-37.

Woolley, Alice et al. "Complaint submission to the Canadian Judicial council on Robert Camp." 9 November 2015, https://www.leaf.ca/wp-content/uploads/2016/05/2015-11-cjc-complaint-r-camp.pdf. Accessed 12 May 2019.

Women's Legal Education and Action Fund (LEAF) and Avalon Sexual Assault Centre Society. "Factum of the Intervenors: Nova Scotia Court of Appeal." *LEAF,* www.leaf.ca/wp-content/uploads/2017/11/LEAF -Al-Rawi -20171002-factum-of-the-intervenor.pdf. Accessed 13 Sept. 2018.

Women's Legal Education and Action Fund (LEAF). "Leaf and Avalon offer a feminist analysis of the Court of Appeal's decision in *R v Al-Rawi.*" *News Release, LEAF,* 21 Jan. 2018, www.leaf.ca/leaf-and-avalon-offer-a-feminist-analysis-of-the-court-of-appeals-decision-in-r-v-al-rawi/. Accessed 13 Sept. 2018.

Women's Legal Education and Action Fund (LEAF). "The Women's Legal Education and Action Fund (LEAF) and Avalon Sexual Assault Centre (Avalon) intervene at the Nova Scotia Court of Appeal (NSCA) in *R v Al-Rawi.*" *News Release, LEAF,* www.leaf.ca/the-womens-legal-education-and-action-fund-leaf-and-avalon-sexual-assault-centre-avalon-intervene-at-the-nova-scotia-court-of-appeal-nsca-in-r-v-al-rawi/. Accessed 13 Sept. 2018.

Jurisprudence

R v Adepoju, 2014 ABCA 100.

R *v Al – Rawi,* 2018 NSCA 10.

R v A.R.D., 2017 ABCA 237.

R v A.R.J.D., 2018 SCC 6.

R v Barton, 2019 SCC 33.

R v Chase, [1987] 2 SCR 293.

R v CMG, 2016 ABQB 368.

R v Ewanchuk, (7 Nov. 1995) Alberta Court of Queen's Bench, Edmonton, Alberta (Unreported).

R v Ewanchuk, 1998 ABCA 52, 57 Alta. LR (3d) 235, 13 CR (5th) 324.

R v Ewanchuk, [1999] 1 SCR 330.

R v Goldfinch, 2019 SCC 38.

R v JR, 2016 ABQB 414.

R v Rhodes, Trial transcript, J Dewar (MBQB) 12 Oct. 2010, feminist-legalforum.files.wordpress.com/2011/11/rhodes-transcript-conviction.pdf. Accessed 13 Sept. 2018.

R v Rhodes, Transcript of Proceedings of Sentencing Hearing, J Dewar (MBQB), 18 February 2011, Thompson, MB, www.scribd.com/document/50396234/Kenneth-Rhodes-Sentencing-Transcript. Accessed Sept. 13, 2018).

R v Rhodes, 2013 MBQB 166.

R v Rhodes, 2013 MBQB 251.

R v Rhodes, 2011 MBCA 98.

R v JR, 2016 ABQB 414.

R v Wager, Trial Transcripts (ABQB) June 5, 6, 10, August 1, 6 and September 9 2014, www.cjc-ccm.gc.ca/cmslib/general/Camp_Docs/ 2016-09-08%20Exhibts%20-%20Agreed%20Statement%20of%20Facts.pdf. Accessed 13 Sept. 2018.

R v Wagar, 2015, ABCA 327.

R v Wager, (31 Jan. 2017) Alberta Provincial Court (Unreported).

R v W.L.S., 2019 SCC 27.

Legislation

Bill C-337, *An Act to Amend the Judges Act and the Criminal Code (Sexual Assault)*, 1st Session, 42nd Parliament, 2015-2016-2017 (First reading 23 Feb 2017; bill is as of July 2019 nearing third reading at the Senate).

Criminal Code, RSC (1985) c C-4.

Conclusion

Reflections on Making the "Strange" Familiar and Future Directions

James Gacek and Richard Jochelson

This volume has worked towards a diverse and in-depth engagement with sexual regulation and the law. The aim of this book was to explore the many facets of sexual governance by bringing together a wide and diverse range of case studies and perspectives on versatile and still evolving phenomena. We have approached highly regarded academics and researchers in their field to contribute to this volume. We believe that the blend of contributions and the depth of critical analysis, as well as the range of topics, will make this a much-cited source as the debate over Canadian sexual governance develops in the future. Indeed, the individual contributions have provided engaging, innovative, and sometimes deeply unsettling explorations of sexual(ized) topics, all of which extend the field of sexual governance conceptually, empirically, and methodologically. Pursuing our aim—to absorb the absurd and make "strange" topics familiar to readers by probing the boundaries of sexual governance in Canada—was an exciting and challenging process. We fostered an in-depth dialogue across disciplines and fields, such as criminal law, socio-legal studies, sociology, criminology, and gender studies (to name a few). This pushed us to think deeply about the current state of sexual governance in Canada's legal system and where our volume fills the gaps and deficiencies in the extant and existing literature. The chapters in this collection signal the significance of extending the examination of sexual governance beyond what we have previously understood about sex and sexuality in Canada and towards a variety of timely concepts, practices, and spaces of discussion.

In the following, we bring together the key themes from the preceding chapters of this collection before highlighting future directions and further opportunities for research as well as for practical and activist dialogues across fields and disciplines.

Seeing the Socio-Legal in Canadian Sexual Governance

Might the law sometimes direct us towards new socialities? This is a question we asked our readers to reflect upon in the introductory chapter. We too have asked ourselves this very same question in the course of compiling this volume, as we have done in our earlier research efforts. In its own way, each chapter has galvanized attention towards a broader idea of how the work of the judiciary is exercised within and through the law. Such a creative exposition of judicial rhetoric and reasoning, we suggest, is not bound merely to precedent and constitutionalism as a doctrinal analysis of law would have you believe. There is more to explore within the inherent social ligatures of the law; we are called to make more visible, advocate, debate, and subject to further scrutiny the sexual identities and controversial sexual topics found within judicial rhetoric and reasoning. These chapters are proof of the ample opportunity for analyses outside of the distinct prize of doctrinal pursuits, and as much as judicial legal decisions direct and impact legal interpretation—binding the actions of Canadians in particular ways—the study of law as a type of media emanates the socio-legal. Social strictures that reflect, refract, or sublimate the social can have similar effects upon how Canadians see and understand sex and sexuality in contemporary society. As each chapter demonstrates, there is significant purchase in making these social strictures visible, scrutinizing the sexual governance at play, and querying the direction such governance is taking us, academics and laypeople alike.

Chapter 1 succinctly sets out the particular challenges in the areas of indecency and obscenity law, showing the incremental changes and inconsistencies in the law. Noting the judicial shifts from moral corruptibility concerns, to community standards of tolerance, and finally to a harm-based neoliberal approach, Jochelson and Gacek make the case that much of the legal system's treatment of the issues is premised on an implicit, and perhaps flawed, assumption of broad moral consensus and normativity. This, we believe, is a very apt point, which touches on broader concerns about boundaries of public and criminal law as well as the justiciability of issues in a pluralistic liberal democracy. On the basis of the judiciary's perception of "risk of harm" and the imagined negative effects of sexual conduct and materials, there has been a disconcerting expansion of criminalization. Making visible the inconsistencies in the application of the current harm-based neoliberal approach draws attention to how sexual conduct and materials are governed either haphazardly or overzealously and how the new test of culpability must be remedied and informed by objectively ascertainable harm rather than subjective approval and judicial tastes.

Merging sex work with a labour studies framework, Chapter 2 produces a thoughtful cross-disciplinary analysis. Gacek and Jochelson effectively make the link between the past and present. They note that the buying and selling of sexual services has been an issue for 250 years, from the Nova Scotia Act of 1759 to more recent times, including the *Prostitution Reference*. In this respect, the authors set out and describe an array of approaches to the question of the regulation of sexual services, including an analysis of the *Bedford* decision and the Nordic model, which was putatively the basis for legal changes in Canada post-*Bedford*. However, they also make a persuasive case that the interpretations of existing law have broadened the scope of criminality in this area and that the law remains the subject of considerable contestation. Making visible the sexual governance of sex work jurisprudence, the authors make clear that sex workers remain victims of abuse and dangerous conditions created and sustained by the current legislative framework. Only by critically examining the issue as a facet of a federal policy debate, will we begin to recognize the socio-legal and public discourse consequences for those who engage in sex work in their daily lives.

Chapter 3 by Jochelson, Dueck-Read, Gacek, and MacDonald addresses questions related to new technologies, social media, and the non-consensual distribution of intimate images (NCDII). The issue is framed by investigating the nature of "harm," which the writers persuasively deconstruct as a complicated issue; they illustrate this by introducing two recent and high-profile cases involving online bullying and cyber-sex crimes, which provoked public legal responses. Yet the writers also cogently point out and discuss that the rationale and intent behind these laws are often ambiguous and/or confused. Indeed, the discussion at the end of this chapter is a particularly insightful identification of several interrelated issues, including the challenges of framing the issue, the conflation of terminology, and the construction of victim-blaming narratives. Con-cluding the chapter, the authors offer useful suggestions for improving the existing law by providing a nuanced NCDII socio-legal analytic; this perspective is provided through a feminist lens looking at NCDII as a gendered phenomenon that perpetuates violence primarily against women and girls.

Chapter 4 by Menzie and Hepburn follows the discussions in the previous chapters to address the issue of technology and sexual offences against youth. The development of legislation and case law related to child luring is comprehensively detailed. The writers identify challenges in proactive investigations and survey legislative assumptions—entrapment, harm, constitutional issues, and "policing kink"—to propose that current laws and practices offer insufficient protections for youth. Here again, aspects of these challenges remain live issues before the courts. Child pornography is the focus of the second half of the chapter, outlining legislative developments and case law following the SCC decision in *Sharpe*. The chapter highlights this issue and extends the discussion of the nature of "harm" as explored elsewhere in the text. The authors examine offences in this area where no actual children are involved. The discussion about criminalizing depictions of crimes rather than actual criminal acts is both thought provoking and novel, as it makes visible how conceptions of morality and harm are bound up with (ill-perceived) anxieties underlying youth sexuality and vulnerability, touching upon broader concerns and conceptions of law and regulating expression.

Chapter 5 by Jochelson, Dueck-Read, and Gacek deals effectively with bestiality, its origins, and historical and current treatment in law. Exposing sexual governance in this light demonstrates the continued diminishment of animals in the eyes of the law. The interconnections between bestiality, interpersonal violence, and family law are clearly drawn out. Furthermore, the conceptual connection between bestiality and laws against such things as sodomy—which were often labelled "unnatural" and contrary to notions of human exceptionalism—are explored; the origins of this connection between bestiality and unnatural acts, as well as its association with same-sex sexuality, procreation, and the phallus, is summarized. This discussion informs the analysis of recent developments in law, including the Supreme Court of Canada ruling in *R v DLW*, which held that the offence of bestiality requires penetration. Furthermore, this chapter colourfully illustrates the historical and originalist approach to bestiality law and its subsequent social analysis, explaining how bestiality law inculcates other laws regulating sex, such as those identified in earlier chapters. The chapter also looks at provincial legislation and recent attempts at legislative reform; it ends with an incisive critical perspective dealing with the possible application of a harm test in this area. The authors problematize the treatment of animals in law as property and exemptions to bestial criminal provisions based on agricultural practices.

Chapter 6 by Laidlaw presents an interesting extension of the overall topic of sexual regulation and the law by addressing the current social and legal issues of pronoun use, using the controversial remarks of academic Jordan Peterson as a departure point. The main subject of the chapter effectively describes the fraught relations between the transgender community and authorities over the years, and the limits of legal gender-based protections for transgender sex workers and prisoners. By exposing sexual governance in this way, the chapter supports and supplements an important clarion call, raising the issue of the limits of free speech as well as freedom of gender and sexual identity in Canada. The lived experience of transgender people regarding oppression and the necessity for gender-based protections in the law is paramount to fostering and securing respect and inclusivity in Canadian society.

Finally, Chapter 7 by Ireland provides an interesting capstone to the collection, as it highlights, from a lawyer's perspective, the judicial treatment of sexual assault as well as emphasizes how the justice system sometimes responds poorly to the issues identified in sexual assault law and the precedents of foundational cases. This is particularly evident in recent decades when increasing public attention has been directed towards judges who have made inappropriate comments in sexual assault cases, seemingly based on longstanding myths and misconceptions. The major cases in this area are identified and the facts and issues are adeptly described. By making these issues of judicial behaviour and treatment visible through the lens of the legal practitioner, this chapter undertakes an insightful endeavour in understanding and effectively analyzing Canadian Judicial Council proceedings involving judicial discipline.

The Sexual Assemblage

As we have witnessed above, in various and diverse ways, law provides a medium in which the citizen is constructed in sociality; law is also the means through which the subject is incentivized, punished, or left alone. In our further investigation of the law-society relation, each chapter examines an array of judiciomentalities and, in doing so, provides more questions about our lives and the social world we live in. Efforts to understand or make sense of the law and its location in society can lead to the surfacing of many answers—and just as many, if not more, questions. It can make visible social constructions embedded within legal expressions and scripts, calling into consideration the logics underpinning legal texts and case adjudications. In their own way, each chapter draws upon the law-society relation to expose the regulatory cloud—the loosely affiliated assemblage of sexual regulation we discussed in the introductory chapter—looming overhead.

To query the sexual assemblage is to regard the law-society relationship not as a static but as a continuing, dynamic enterprise in which new questions emerge, novel answers to old questions are provided, and taken-for-granted assumptions are reformulated. Social situations may appear complex, and progress for ameliorating such social situations may seem all for naught, yet the potential for reforms is not a pipe dream. Engaging in the "strange" and taboo topics and making them familiar to the reader, as our collection has attempted to do, not only allows us to try to understand the routine nature of this strangeness, but also reveals a rich mosaic of socio-legal knowledge that has the potential to liberate the sexual subject. The content of Canadian sexual governance may appear absurd, disgusting, or difficult to grasp, but it is exactly this challenge that we find elucidating. To absorb the absurd is to face the socio-sexual realities that inure within our social worlds and to formulate strategies for substantive changes to the law. Making the strange familiar, as we have accomplished here, has the power to animate social action, if one is so inclined.

By comparison of the various threads it covers, our collection embraces and lays bare multivalent perspectives that inform the historical and ongoing practices of sexual regulation. Indeed, rooted in legal and social theory, each set of contributors navigates concerns regarding sex, sexuality, and the law. Presenting an energetic focus upon Canadian sexual governance is not a simple task, yet each chapter comprehensively and critically demonstrates a central need for warranted reforms in the Canadian legal system. As we demonstrate below, we view implications within multiple domains, such as progressive changes in legislative and sentencing patterns to judicial and civil liberty activism.

Future Directions and Policy Implications

By revisiting key ideas betwixt and between the chapters of this collection, we recognize the promises of, and threats to, sexualized groups and populations in Canada should the law refract the social and lead to regressive legal and legislative reforms. Whether such changes mark a decisive turning point, or in the fullness of time represent just another twist in the long and messy narrative of sexual governance in Canada, remains an open question. Nonetheless, we conclude with practical steps that promote progressive ends for the sexual, liberal subject of society and their social treatment.

With a keen eye towards sexual governance and the many facets it comprises, this book reflects a growing scholarly focus on the direction of socio-legal trends and their consequences for justice—and the provision of public goods more generally—and whether these competing paradigms and goals can be reconciled. Reconsidering the social conditions of our times is essential to how citizens shift their thinking towards progressive legal reforms that invoke prosocial change and safeguard the rights and freedoms of Canada's sexual subjects. Indeed, progressive shifts towards social and sexual justice—whether they be social, economic, legal, or legislative goals—involves the transformation of public goods, from education or health to welfare. It becomes clear that only a massive reinvestment in social welfare, public education, healthcare, affordable housing, and a guaranteed basic income—that is, a renewed struggle for a livable, social wage—can begin to address the structural violence produced by a system of sexual governance which is rooted in the normalization and suppression of sexual difference, diversity, identity and expression.

In varying degrees, current Canadian sexual governance contributes to the creation of policies that speak more to public moral panic and the need to cut the economic costs of welfare than to the outright amelioration of marginalized, oppressed, and sexual(ized) populations in Canada. Such policy problems are complex, not fully understood by policymakers, highly resistant to change, and seemingly immune to any evidence that is likely to bring about change for the better. We have seen instances in federal politics and public discourse where conversations about progressing policy in sexual governance are not necessarily driven by what works or what is evidenced-based. Instead, policy discussions are increasingly positioned by political expediency and the political rhetoric of "tough on crime." This needs to change. For the sake of the already marginalized groups in Canada, we can no longer afford to promote ill-conceived or illusory social ills that have no cause for concern or are not grounded in the empirical. Keeping in mind the interconnections between race, class, gender, and sexuality relations in society, we can do more to move along a path that leads to the repositioning of sexual regulation and law that begins, or continues, to favour the Canadian sexual subject.

Concluding Remarks

Sexual Regulation and the Law: A Canadian Perspective was a challenging and rewarding project. Although our work is not a definitive treatise, in the main it is a collection of thought-provoking chapters considering interesting developments of sexual regulation in Canada. We see significant purchase in an opportunity to provide an in-depth exploration of controversial yet insightful socio-legal topics.

This book is a deliberate mixture of taxonomical and critical analysis. Because this book is a socio-legal work, we endeavoured to parse out a rich engagement of both law and society, in part by asking the reader to follow us in reflecting upon the law, absorbing the absurd, and begin to level socio-legal critiques at the social conditions and legal responses in relation to the law. Having said this, we must stress that the doctrinal descriptions in this book are a necessary precursor to the socio-legal critiques we develop throughout this collection. When authors in this collection do engage in doctrinal explication, it is because the law in that area is particularly detailed and must be unpacked. In effect, without this detail, the socio-legal observations we have made would be far less grounded and would require further efforts on the part of the reader to discern the sociality that is significant to the law.

The inclusion of case law, legislation, and social science research make this text highly accessible to multiple audiences in a range of settings. Its identification of current legislative initiatives and ongoing developments in this area is particularly inviting as a departure point for student and researcher engagement alike to track ongoing changes and to envisage options for public policy responses.

This book serves an important purpose: bringing together the developments of a whole range of gender and sexuality-related aspects of law. Looking at the parallel evolution of the various doctrines provides insights unavailable through individual treatment. Furthermore, we have fewer than needed subject-matter treatises on topics in Canadian criminal law generally, which makes this project a useful contribution even from the educational standpoint. It is also a particularly timely moment in legal history to be taking this effort on in light of developments both north and south of the forty-ninth parallel. By outlining and addressing multiple facets of a dynamic and emerging subject area, our collection explores a particular socio-legal situation that has considerable currency within present and future Canadian legal culture.

Notes on Contributors

Alicia Dueck-Read is a law student at the University of Manitoba. Previously, she completed her bachelor of arts (honours) in History from the University of Winnipeg and her master of arts in peace, development, security, and international conflict transformation from the University of Innsbruck, Austria. Her master's thesis on lesbian, gay, and queer mennonites was published in 2012 and won the Recognition Award for Women's and Gender-Specific Research at the University of Innsbruck in 2011.

James Gacek James Gacek is an assistant professor in the Department of Justice Studies at the University of Regina. He completed his doctoral studies at Edinburgh Law School, University of Edinburgh. He has lectured in criminology and criminal justice at the University of Manitoba and the University of Winnipeg. He continues to publish in areas of incar-ceration, genocidal carcerality, critical issues in media, justice, and security studies, the exploitation of human-animal relations, and the broader politics of judicial reasoning. He is an American Sociological Association Paper Award winner (2014). He has recently co-authored *Criminal Law and Precrime: Legal Studies in Canadian Punishment and Surveillance in Anticipation of Criminal Guilt (2018, Routledge)*.

Taryn Hepburn is a PhD candidate at Carleton University in the Department of Law and Legal Studies. Her current research interests are youth criminal law and policing, theories of governance, carceral practices involving youth, intersectional concerns related to youth and criminality, and archival/genealogical methodologies. She is currently assisting on a Canada-wide inquiry of Indigenous adoption practices and on a study of the rural policing of youth.

David Ireland is an assistant professor at Robson Hall, Faculty of Law at the University of Manitoba. A graduate of both the LL.B. and LL.M. programs at Robson Hall, Professor Ireland practiced criminal law as both Crown and defence counsel before joining the faculty in 2016. His graduate thesis, "Bargaining for Expedience? The Overuse of Joint Recommendations on Sentence," supervised by Professor Debra Parkes, highlighted the prevalence of cultural joint recommendations in the plea-bargaining process in Manitoba. Professor Ireland is a frequent presenter in the criminal justice community, regularly speaking at conferences for judges, lawyers, and law enforcement officers.

Richard Jochelson is a full professor at the Faculty of Law at the University of Manitoba and holds his PhD in law from Osgoode Hall Law School at York University, a master's in Law from University of Toronto Law School, and a law degree from University of Calgary Law School (Gold Medal). He is a former law clerk who served his articling year at the Alberta Court of Appeal and Court of Queen's Bench, before working at one of Canada's largest law firms. He worked for ten years teaching criminal and constitutional law at another Canadian university prior to joining Robson Hall. He has published peer-reviewed articles dealing with obscenity, indecency, judicial activism, police powers, criminal justice pedagogy and curriculum development, empiricism in criminal law, and conceptions of judicial and jury reasoning. He is a member of the Bar of Manitoba and has co-authored and co-edited several books. He has recently co-authored *Criminal Law and Precrime: Legal Studies in Canadian Punishment and Surveillance in Anticipation of Criminal Guilt (2018, Routledge)*.

Leon Laidlaw is a PhD student in sociology at Carleton University, where he is conducting his dissertation research on the topic of transgender prisoners. His research interests fall within the scope of trans* studies, gender and trans theory, sex work, critical and feminist criminology, and intersectionality. Leon has headed several research projects, including his SSHRC-funded master's thesis, which revealed the experiences of trans women in the sex industry, and an independent project analyzing how trans students navigate through institutional cisgenderism within universities.

Brayden McDonald is a JD graduate from Robson Hall. He earned his Bachelor of Arts in Economics and Political Studies in 2016 from the University of Manitoba. In addition to his contributions to the present work, Brayden has done legal research in the field of international nuclear disarmament, and serves as a student editor of the law blog *Robson Crim*.

Lauren Menzie is a PhD candidate in the Department of Sociology at the University of Alberta. Her current research interests include the regulation and denunciation of marginalized sexual practices/interests, contemporary sexual citizenships, the evolution of Canadian criminal law surrounding sexual offending, and how virtual spaces influence judgments and accusations of sexual violence. She has published work in the areas of socio-legal theory and discourse surrounding consent and the legal regulation of marginalized sexual practices. She has most recently completed her MA thesis, *"ITT: Rape Analysts": Hosting Negotiations of Consent, Kink, and Violence in Virtual Space*. She also co-authored *Criminal Law and Precrime: Legal Studies in Canadian Punishment and Surveillance in Anticipation of Criminal Guilt (Routledge 2018)*.